Richard Clayton, Baron de St. Croix

A critical Inquiry into the Life of Alexander the Great

Richard Clayton, Baron de St. Croix

A critical Inquiry into the Life of Alexander the Great

ISBN/EAN: 9783337063993

Printed in Europe, USA, Canada, Australia, Japan

Cover: Foto ©ninafisch / pixelio.de

More available books at **www.hansebooks.com**

A

CRITICAL INQUIRY

INTO THE

LIFE

OF

ALEXANDER THE GREAT,

BY THE

ANCIENT HISTORIANS:

From the FRENCH of the BARON DE St. CROIX:

WITH

NOTES AND OBSERVATIONS,

By Sir *RICHARD CLAYTON*, Bart.

Illuſtrated with a Map of the Marches of ALEXANDER THE GREAT.

BATH:
PRINTED BY S. HAZARD:
For G. G. AND J. ROBINSON, PATER-NOSTER-ROW, LONDON.
M.DCC.XCIII.

TO THE

RIGHT HONOURABLE

The EARL of DERBY,

LORD LIEUTENANT and CUSTOS ROTULORUM

OF THE

COUNTY PALATINE OF LANCASTER.

MY LORD,

FROM the Friendſhip, with which you have long honoured me, I have no heſitation to whom I ſhould addreſs the following Work.——Permit me then to place your name at the head of it, and at the ſame time to offer it to your Lordſhip, as a trifling teſtimony of the attachment and regard of

YOUR FAITHFUL HUMBLE SERVANT,

RICHARD CLAYTON.

Sept. 12th 1793.

PREFACE.

THE Critical Examination of the Ancient Historians of ALEXANDER THE GREAT, which now appears in an English Dress, was first ushered into the World at the French Academy "des Inscriptions et Belles Lettres," where it obtained the Premium from that learned Society in the Year 1772. After an interval of three years the Author published it with additions and improvements; but the Impression was rapidly bought up, and there is not at present a single copy to be procured without difficulty upon the Continent. I have reason to believe that a knowledge of it has been hitherto confined within a narrow circle in GREAT BRITAIN, and that when it has crossed the Channel, it hath been to pass only into the hands of a few persons of Taste and Erudition.——Of the Original the French Academy

PREFACE.

demy hath expressed its unqualified approbation: of the Translation it becomes not me to speak. In justice however to the Baron de St. Croix, I ought to acknowledge that some alterations have been made, and for these I am responsible. Some redundancies I may have also pruned off, but I flatter myself the full vigour of the leading Shoot hath been preserved. If I have deviated from the Original, in the introduction of the quotations from the different Writers, that have been cited, I may not possibly have occasion for much apology. The learned Reader will readily forgive a number of his old Acquaintances being again brought immediately before his eye, and when Authors are referred to, they are undoubtedly the best Comment on themselves. On turning indeed to the Greek Writers, I was not particularly satisfied with the French Versions of the passages in question. Some of them were loose; in others the sense appeared to have been mistaken;

PREFACE.

mistaken; and, in these instances, I considered the production of the evidence, on which I formed my opinions, to be a duty, from which I could not honourably disengage myself. The references in many places have been by these means corrected; where they were wanting, they have been added; and from their number, the Work has taken insensibly a new shape. The Notes and Observations will be found in general connected with the Subject. Sometimes I may have wandered beyond the limits, that perhaps I should have prescribed to myself, yet I still trust the excursions are not of unpardonable extent.

ERRATA.

Page				for	read
55	Note	line	2	Kaſter	Kuſter
61	Text	line	12	Eldriſi	Eldriſi
	Note			Eldriſi	Eldriſi
76	Note t			Uſher.	Uſſerii
78	Note d	line	1	quinxe	quinze
80	Text	line	7	Phacelides	Phaſelides
82	Note	line	6	aucun	aucune
	Note	line	9	certain	certaine
115	Note l	line	5	Boyle	Bayle
122	Note h			Port	Poſt
136	Text	line	7	Tapſacus	Thapſacus
	Note	line	1	after Guides inſert are	
147	Note n			Uſherii	Uſſerii
156	Note i	line	1	ὅι	ὅι
216	Text	line	2	Le Brun	Le Bruyn
	Note d			de le Brun	de le Bruyn
217	Note m			de la Bruyn	de le Bruyn
261	Note a	line	1	Βαϐυλωνι	Βαϐυλωνι
301	Text	line	11	dele to	
310	Note b	line	1	Onne	Omne
383	Text	line	4	Atheneus	Athenæus
389	Text	line	3	Lahour	Lahore
400	Text	line	3	Cophina	Cophena
423	Text	line	17	miſtakes	miſtake

For Volga *read* Wolga *paſſim*

INTRODUCTION.

THE state of letters depends in every country upon its political constitution. Public liberty gives birth and animation to talents of every denomination: despotism strangles them at once.——Sparta, forgetful of the sage maxims of its legislator, and Athens, intoxicated with its successes, neglected their common safety, from principles of mutual distrust. The Peloponnesian war having wasted their forces, and the momentary glory of Thebes having expired with Epaminondas, Philip embraced the opportunity of the Grecian dissentions to dissolve their federal government, and to reduce the people that had so long resisted the arms of Asia. In vain was the eloquence of Demosthenes exerted to rouse his countrymen from their shameful lethargy. Their morals were corrupted, luxury had annihilated every manly sentiment, and the great exploits of so many heroes who had immortalized themselves in the fields of Marathon and Platæa, and in the naval victories near Salamis, instead of reviving in the breasts of the Athenians their antient enthusiasm for military virtue,

tue, ferved only by flattering their pride and vanity, to render them felf-fufficient and prefumptuous.——National effeminacy had gradually prepared the Perfian monarchy for its ruin, and on the death of Philip, Alexander mounted the throne and put a period to that empire. The death of this prince in its turn produced another revolution, which was attended with effects equally melancholy and fatal to the general repofe, and to the progrefs of fcience and of literature. At intervals the Greeks became the fport of ambition and of the caprices of Alexander's fucceffors, and thofe proud and fpirited republicans were rapidly metamorphofed into a degraded herd of flaves. Even the tribune where Demofthenes had thundered, foon only echoed with decrees dictated by adulation and fervility.——One little fpark of freedom was indeed ftill cherifhed in a part of the Peloponnefus, and the zeal of Aratus, the valour of Philopæmon, and the wifdom of Lycortas gave celebrity to the Achæan league, and fupported it in its delicate and diftreffing circumftances. The corruption however had extended too far to be checked, and the very vitals of the Grecian conftitution were infected with the general depravity. Callifthenes and his partifans made no fcruple of felling their country to the Romans, and this wary and crafty people, who had always the art of concealing the fervitude, to which they reduced the neighbouring nations, under the fpecious appearances of alliances and friendfhip, completed its fubjection. But Greece, by the deftruction of the Achæans, had indeed demolifhed the laft rampart of its liberty.

The

The arts and sciences did not long survive the loss, and despotism opened for them with the same hands one common tomb. Tragedy, whose peculiar province it was to call down the public detestation upon tyranny, and the ancient comedy, which had the happy privilege of holding up the abuse of power to contempt and irony, and of correcting by these means any excesses of the democratic spirit, lost at once their influence, and along with it their brilliancy. The Gymnastic games, so proper for the exercise of muscular strength, and to form soldiers in the times of peace, became but an useless spectacle, and the individuals who distinguished themselves on these occasions were principally remarkable for their scandalous deportment. That sublime art, which animated the statues of Harmodius and Aristogiton drooped and languished, when it was to figure but the images of slaves and parasites. Even the philosopher, who from having directed the instruction of the superior order of his fellow-citizens descended into their sycophant, was at last distinguished only by the habit of the ancient sects, which so many great names had dignified.——Here let us pause upon the fate of history in these disastrous days.

That enchanting harmony of style, with the art of giving energy to the most trifling details, which characterizes the works of Herodotus; the sublime and simple graces of Xenophon, uniting the most profound political knowledge with all the talents of an able general and of a philosopher worthy of the friendship of Socrates; the manly eloquence and stern virtue of Thucydides had

had disappeared, and we find but very few, if any, traces of their masterly productions in the writers who followed them in the historic line.—Yet Theopompus, Philistus, Ephorus and Timæus enjoyed a great share of popular applause, though their several works are deficient both in method and materials.—The civil revolutions undoubtedly occasioned this striking difference, and there are three remarkable eras, that should be particularly attended to.—The first is the precise period when Philip had rendered himself the master of Greece.

Tyranny naturally produces different effects on different dispositions and characters. Weak and pusillanimous some bend immediately beneath the blast, and losing on the first moment of attack every idea of resistance, they kiss with trembling adoration the hand which is lifted up for their oppression. With a superior force of mind, and indignant at the prospect of those evils, which arbitrary power hath always following at its heels, others endeavour to exasperate their country by virulent invectives against its new masters, and alternately exaggerate their vices, and diminish the little virtue, that they may accidentally possess. Such was the influence of the Macedonian power, and it is visible both in the conduct of those who were at the head of the Grecian states, and the writings of the times.

The reign of Alexander may be reckoned the second stage of the decline of history. Greece being accustomed to the Macedonian yoke, and dazzled by the victories of the conqueror of Asia,

Afia, in which it was in fome fort interefted from the glory reflected on it, the fermentation which Philip's enterprifes had excited in its republican breafts gradually cooled. Their hatred and animofity were at length fucceeded by enthufiafm, and the fplendid actions of the Macedonian warrior made an impreffion on the fpectators too forcible and powerful to be refifted. The later writers, who have taken up the fame fubject, have but too often imbibed their fentiments. They lived indeed under the Roman jurifdiction, but in the miferable times when the univerfe became a prey to the caprices of thofe fanguinary wretches, who filled fo difgracefully the throne of the Cæfars. This is the third epoch of the change in the hiftoric character, and it will be afterwards entered into at large.

The total extinction of the democratic form of government involved in it the fall of literature, and more particularly of hiftory, which admits of no cultivation with fuccefs under arbitrary power. Truth was then buried under a mafs of fabulous and contradictory traditions, and the penetrating fagacity of the philofopher can alone diftinguifh it from falfity, and reconcile the ftatements of various and jarring recitals.—It would be the height of folly to imagine, that in the following treatife the way hath been clearly feen amidft the darknefs in which ages are enveloped, or that facts have been at all times fufficiently difcriminated, which have been magnified beyond their juft proportion by adulation, and by that love of the marvellous, which was a prevailing paffion amongft the Greeks, and a foible from which

which even their best writers are not exempt. In the pursuit of the succeeding inquiries the truth hath not only been endeavoured to be discovered, but according to Aristotle's advice the probability. In some instances, it hath been necessary to substitute conjectures for proofs, and where the reality hath been totally concealed to be satisfied with reasonable suppositions.——Diodorus Siculus, Plutarch, Arrian, Q. Curtius and Justin are the principal historians, who have preserved at any length the actions in the reign of Alexander. A minute examination of each of these writers would be unavoidably embarrassed with their repetitions and obscurities. The route, that hath been chalked out, appears likely to secure it against these inconveniences, and to leave the full liberty of bestowing every degree of attention on the facts in chronological order. On this plan, the observations may be extended not only to the writers of the life of Alexander, but to every thing that antiquity hath transmitted to us relative to this celebrated conqueror.—In the first section, the sources, from which the several historians have drawn their information, and the degree of authority, that is their due, will be examined. The second will be confined to the military exploits of Alexander, and in the third, those actions will be treated of, that particularly delineate his character. The fourth will be set apart for some geographical details, which his different expeditions naturally furnish.

CRITICAL

CRITICAL INQUIRY

RELATING TO THE

ANCIENT HISTORIANS

WHO HAVE WRITTEN OF

ALEXANDER THE GREAT.

SECT. I.

AFTER the laſt ſigh of expiring Liberty in any State, patriotiſm in its language ceaſes to convey to us the ſame idea; and having loſt its influence, no longer warms the frozen breaſts of the inhabitants. Though united within the ſame walls, they concern themſelves no farther with public affairs than as their own private intereſts are immediately affected, and enjoying the preſent hour without any care of futurity, they are ever ready

to

to become the slaves of that master, who bids highest for their purchase. Self-interest dries up the source of every social virtue, and as the love of their country, which once inspired them with every great and noble sentiment for the public good, no longer actuates them, men of letters frequently employ their talents on subjects equally devoid of spirit and utility. Taken in this light the annals of a conqueror cannot agitate the reader, like those sublime and pathetic traits which are perpetually occurring in the history of a Free People. A single individual acts and triumphs, and a few divided rays of glory are faintly scattered on his troops. In a Republic, on the contrary, each member of the community hath a share more or less considerable in every event; and the happiness or misery of the public, from his relation to it, becomes that of his own family.——The actions of his fellow-citizens are hereditary distinctions transmitted to his children, and the national and private glory are the same.

In turning over the histories of the ancient Free states, notwithstanding the distance of time, and a revolution in the manners and forms of government, the events still fasten on the mind, and affect it with the liveliest emotions. Greece, however, when overpowered with the pressure of the Macedonian yoke, and afterwards with that of the Romans, paid little attention to public measures. The vigour of its historians was soon lost in the drudgery of their servile pens, and their genius vanished with the bright days of their country. Dionysius of Halicarnassus, after having mentioned that harmonious elocution which marked the

style

ſtyle of the ancient Grecian writers, adds "There is not one of the moderns that hath beſtowed the leaſt regard on it, or conſidered it as either neceſſary or adding elegance to their performances. The numerous writings therefore, which they have left us, are of ſuch a nature as few readers have the patience to go through them. In this claſs are to be included Phylarchus, Duris, Polybius, Saon, Demetrius Calantianus, Hieronymus, Antilochus, Heraclides, Hegeſias the Magneſian, and many others, whoſe names a whole day would not allow me to enumerate."*

In proportion as the weight of ſervitude was felt, the human mind ſhrunk within itſelf, and the ſtream of light, which letters had

---

* "Τοις δε μεταγενεστεροις ακετι, πλην ολιγων· χρονω δ'υστερον παντοπασιν ημελήθη· και ενεις αυτο δειν αναγκαιον αυτο ειναι, ουδε συμβαλλεσθαι τι τω καλλει των λογων. Τοιγαρτοι τοιαυτας συνταξεις κατελιπον, οιας ουδεις υπομενει μεχρι κορωνιδος διελθειν· Φυλαρχον λεγω, και Δεριν, και Πολυβιον, και Σαωνα, και τον Καλαντιανον Δημητριον. Ιερωνυμον τε και Αντιλοχον, και Ηρακλειδην, και Ἡγησιαν Μαγνητα, και αλλων μυρίων· ὧν ἁπαντων τα ονοματα εἰ βουλοιμην λεγειν, επιλειψει με ὁ της ημερας χρονος." Dion. Halicarn. de ſtructurâ orat. 39, 40. ed. Upton. 8vo 1728.

The following is the French Verſion of this Paſſage, "Elle fut dans les temps poſterieurs fort negligée. Perſonne n'a penſé ſans doute à faire ce parallele, (de cette nouvelle elocution avec l'ancienne) il ne ſoutiendroit pas juſque à la fin la lecture de tous les ouvrages que nous ont laiſſe *Plutarque,* Duris, Polybe, &c. &c." The miſtake of Plutarch for *Phylarchus* is alone ſufficient to prove the indiſpenſable neceſſity of the

"*Integros accedere fontes,*"

(Lucret. 1.–926.)

and of tracing authorities up to their ſource.——The Baron de St. Croix wiſhes to ſubſtitute the word Ψαμιο, for Ψαωνα, and to apply it to Duris, who he ſays, was always diſtinguiſhed by this addition, but for this reading a violent tranſpoſition will be requiſite, as well as a correction of the Text, and there is not certainly any occaſion for either, as Diodorus Siculus expreſsly mentions an Hiſtorian of this name. " Σαων δε ο Πλαταιευς τας περι τουτο διελεξατο δε πραξεις εγκα ει βιβλοις τριακοντα." Diod. Sicul. Eclogues Lib. 41.–490. Tom. 2. Ed. Weſſ. Arouſt. 1746.

had poured upon it, gradually receded, till it was totally extinguished in obscurity. That wretched species of adulation, which blasts every appearance of genius and cramps the intellectual faculties, was lavishly adopted under the Roman Emperors, and made a rapid progress towards general currency and usage. Actions almost below notice became the subjects of the declamations of the sophists, who described the most trifling circumstances in the most unnatural colours, and in a pomp of language wholly inconsistent with them. Lucian hath compared this phrensy to the epidemical fever of the Abderites,[b] who ran about the streets after

---

[b] The Αβδηρα καλη τηων απoικια was however proverbial. Vossius hath thus explained it. "Teii cognita ubertate et amœnitate soli Abderitici, hanc suam coloniam pulchram appellarunt, ideoque omnes illuc migrarunt. Sed postea cognoverunt eam soli aerisque in hoc tractu esse naturam, ut non tantum equi et jumenta in vicinis pascuis degentes, aut bibentes ex Cossineto flumine in rabiem agerentur, verum etiam ipsos homines sæpe corripi insaniâ, plurimosque ibi nasci deliros. Hinc ironice dictum Abdera, pulchra Teiorum colonia." I. Vossius ad P. Melam. Lib. 2. C. 2.

Lucian hath endeavoured to account for this general phrensy on more rational principles, by supposing the Andromeda to have been represented by Archelaus a very popular tragedian, in the midst of summer, and under the influence of burning weather, to such crouded audiences as occasioned a violent fever in most of the spectators, who had the image of the Andromeda so strongly impressed on the brain, that in their delirium they were perpetually repeating it, "Αιτιαν δε μοι δοκει τε τοιατε παρασχειν, Αρχιλαϙ ὁ τραγῳδος, ευδοκιμων τοτε, μεσεντϙ θερες εν πολλῳ τῳ φλογμῳ τραγῳδησας αυτοις την Ανδρομιδαν, ὡς πυριξαι τε απο τε θιατρε της πολλες, κỳ αναςαντας ὑςερον εκ την τραγῳδιαν παρηλιςαχσιν, επιπολυ εμφιλοχωρηστης της Ανδρομιδας τη μνημη αυτων, κỳ τε Περσεως ετι συν τη Μιδεση, την ικαρε γνωμην περιπατομενω." Quomod. Hist. Conscrib. sit. Tom. 2. 2.--3. 4to Amst. 1743.

Athenæus hath preserved the Fragment which was principally vociferated, and the curious reader may not be displeased to find it.

"Συ

after the reprefentation of the Andromeda of Euripides, repeating with violent agitations particular verfes of this poet. Some extraordinary fymptoms attended the complaint, but it was confined to the heats of fummer and ended with it.

On the flighteft fkirmifhes, details of them were given without end, teeming with incidents, that had no exiftence whatever, but in the difordered imaginations of their authors. Adding ignorance to effrontery, thefe chroniclers committed the moft egregious faults, and erred in the moft unguarded manner both againft the laws of geography and tactics. After a moft defperate battle, when victory had been long doubtful, the lofs of the enemy was reprefented as immenfe, whilft that of the Romans was barely perceptible; and in one of thefe fingular engagements, the former were ftated to have had feventy thoufand, and thirty-fix[c] men killed,

"Συ δ'ω Τυραννε θεων τε κ'Ανθρωπων, Ερως,
Η μη διδασκε τα καλα φαινεσθαι καλα,
Η τοις ερωσιν ων συ δημιουργος ει,
Μοχθουσι μοχθους ειτυχως συνεκπονει,
Και ταυτα μεν δρων τιμιος θνοις εσ7,
Μη δρων δ'ιπ'αυτου τε διδασκεσθαι φιλειν.
Αφαιρεθηση χαριτας αις τιμωσι σε."

Athenæus, Lib. 13. 561. Fol. Lugd. 1612.

[c] In the French Text the number ftands at, feven thoufand, two hundred and thirty-fix. Lucian's words are, "Των μεν πολεμιων, αποθανειν μυριαδας επτα, και τριακοντα, και εξ προς διακοσιοις, Ρωμαιων δε, μονυς δυο, και τραυματιας γενεσθαι εννεα." (Quomod. Hift. confcrib. fit. Tom. 2.--29.) but his Editors and Annotators have differed on the calculation. Reitzius hath tranflated the paffage, "Hoftium quidem cecidiffe *trecenties*, et feptuagies mille ducentos et fex: Romanorum vero

killed, and the latter, only two men killed and nine wounded. From an immoderate rage for defcription, we have a laboured difplay of arms and military weapons, of foffes, baftions and bridges; and the common accidents of war are worked up in fuch a ftyle, as to be more proper for the fock and bufkin. In fhort, the writers of thefe times disfigured their relations with fo many, and fuch extravagances, as often to have placed, to borrow one of Lucian's expreffions, the head of the Rhodian Coloffus[d] on the diminutive body of a dwarf.

This lively and judicious writer, that hath been juft cited, after expofing with his ufual poignancy the errors and defects of the hiftorians of his days, hath eftablifhed more folid rules, and pointed out a clearer method for fuch compofitions. With a view of oppofing a new and lafting barrier to the contagion of the times, and

---

vero folos duo, faucios autem factos novem." Gefner in his note upon the paffage hath with more modefty reduced the number to feventy thoufand, two hundred and thirty-fix, but he adds with fome pleafantry, " Qui mentiuntur, tales minutias non curant."

[d] " Τα 'Ροδιων Κολοσσου την κιφαλην γιγνωδει σωματι επιτιθεντας." (Quomod. Hift. confcrib. fit. Tom. 2.--32.) The Rhodian Coloffus, (for an account of which fee Plin. Hift. Nat. Lib. 34. Sect. 18.— Strabo, Lib. 14.— Philoftr. Vit. Apol. and alfo Scaliger, Animadverfiones in Eufebii Chronicon. No. 1794.–137.) was the work of Chares Lindius, the difciple of Lyfippus, on which he was employed twelve years. It was finifhed about 278 years before Chrift, and after ftanding fifty-fix years, was overturned by an earthquake. Its remains ftill exifted as late as the 672nd year of the Chriftian Era, when they were fold, on the capture of Rhodes by the Saracens. Notwithftanding the injuries this ftatue muft have fuffered, and the numerous depredations it muft have been expofed to, the brafs is faid to have then loaden no lefs than nine hundred camels. Allowing each camel a load of eight hundred pounds, (Monf. Volney reckons the ufual burthen about 750,) the whole muft have weighed above 700,000 pounds.

and wishing to strip the fashionable style of the ascendency, which it had usurped over the public opinions, his two books of real history were professedly undertaken. This work, which may be considered as an imaginary sketch, from its astonishing fecundity in those burlesque and gigantic ideas, which are scattered through it, with a prodigality almost without example, is in fact an ingenious fiction, intended to expose to general opprobrium those strange and monstrous productions, which were made up of history and romance, without being strictly either.

To fix perhaps the precise value of the works of every author, some knowledge of the age in which he lived is necessary, in order to appreciate the advantages that he was possessed of, what he owed merely to his own ingenuity and exertions, and to those of his cotemporaries. The observations on the fate of letters, as connected with the civil revolutions of states and governments that have been already made, appear to have partly answered the first of these ends, at least, as far as the historians of the life of Alexander are concerned; to the second, the result of a more particular examination of the historians themselves, will be more immediately applicable. But previous to any dissertation on these different historians, it may be requisite to estimate the degree of credit to which they are severally entitled, and to establish it with any certitude, the authorities from which they derived their informations must be resorted to. Where facts also rest upon traditions, whether oral or written, there will be an indispensable

pensable necessity of pursuing them back as far as possible, and of ascending to the first evidences which are accessible.

That enthusiasm, which is born in seasons of prosperity, and dies when they disappear, that enthusiasm, which, in moments of national intoxication, produces such rapid and astonishing successes, had undoubtedly fired the imaginations of the companions of Alexander's arms and their cotemporaries. Yet this factitious and temporary fervour was but in reality the phosphorus, which exhibits an apparent flame without its most essential qualities.—— It naturally occasioned a multitude of writings, where the marvellous rather seduced the understanding than affected it with any powerful emotions, and amazed it, without leaving on it any durable or lasting impressions.——Strabo informs us, that this love of the marvellous had so captivated almost all the historians of Alexander, that there were not any of them wholly free from this epidemic infection, or who made any hesitation at the sacrifice of truth to it, wherever they interfered [e] with each other.

Callisthenes, [f] Onesicritus, Hegesias and Clitarchus, seem to have

---

[e] " Cet amour du Merveilleux s'etoit emparé, selon Strabon, de la plume de presque tous les historiens du conquerant de l'Asie; aucun d'eux ne fut entierement exempt de ce defaut epidemique." Strabo's expression in the passage referred to, is, " Παντες μεν γαρ οι περι Αλεξανδρον, το θαυμαστον αντι ταληθους αποδεχονται." (Lib. 15.–1022.) A sentiment that I have added.

[f] Callisthenes succeeded Aristotle as preceptor to Alexander, and afterwards attended him in his oriental expedition. Cicero had but a mean opinion of his historical talents, as may be gathered

have been the authors of numerous miftakes, and we know by experience, that they are always propagated in proportion to their antiquity, and to the number and difpofition of the fucceeding writers who tranfcribe them or adopt them. At this diftance, we muft rely on the judgment which the ableft critics of the ancients have paffed on their refpective works, and the opinions which they entertained of them.——It was undoubtedly the intention of Callifthenes[g] to magnify the actions of Alexander, and to augment his glory by a ftyle as little adapted to hiftory as to real eloquence. " Some expreffions of Callifthenes," fays Longinus, " do not fhine like ftars, but glare like meteors."[h] The judicious criticifm of Polybius, on his defcription of the battle of Iffus, fhall be hereafter mentioned.—With equal ignorance in tactics, and fuperftition, which in a philofopher is extraordinary, Callifthenes relates, according to Strabo, that " Alexander having learnt that Perfeus and Hercules had vifited the Oracle of Jupiter Ammon, began his march with the fame emulation, from Parœtonium, and though ftrong foutherly

gathered from two of his expreffions. " Callifthenes comes Alexandri, fcripfit hiftoriam; et hic quidem rhetorico pene more." (De oratore, Lib. 11. Sec. 14.) "Itaque ad Callifthenem et Philiftum redeo: in quibus te video volutatum. Callifthenes quidem, vulgare et notum negotium." Epift. ad Q. Fratrem. Lib. 11. Epift. 13.

[g] " Οικουν αυτος αφιχθαι απ'Αλεξανδρου δοξαν κτησομενος, αλλα εκεινον ευκλεα ες ανθρωπους ποιητων. και ουν και του θειου την μετουσιαν Αλεξανδρω ουκ εξ ων Ολυμπιας υπερ της γενεσεως αυτου ψευδεται ανηρτησθαι, αλλ'εξ ων αν αυτος υπερ Αλεξανδρου συγγραψας εξενεγκη ες ανθρωπους." Arrian. de Exped. Alex. Lib. 4. Cap. 10. 283. 8vo Edit. Amft. 1757.

[h] Smith's Longinus. Sect. 3rd–10.——" Και τινα των Καλλιςθενες, οντα εχ υψηλα αλλα μετιωρα." Dion. Long. Sec. 3. 40. 4to Lond. 1724.

southerly winds opposed his progress, and he lost his way amidst clouds of sand, he was preserved by showers of rain and by two ravens, who served him for guides and pointed out to him the road.¹ These circumstances were dictated by flattery, and the following ones resemble them. The Monarch had alone the privilege allowed him, of entering the temple in his usual dress, the rest of his companions being ordered to change theirs, and to wait the answer of the Oracle at the doors.—Its responses instead of being delivered by the priest verbally, like those of Delphi and Branchus, were in a great measure communicated by signs and nods, in imitation of the Jupiter of Homer."

<blockquote>
Who spoke, and awful bent his sable brows,
Shook his ambrosial curls, and gave the nod,
The stamp of fate, and sanction of the God.
</blockquote>

POPE.

" The Monarch was however expressly told, that he was the son of Jupiter. In a more tragic and exaggerated style, Callisthenes

---

¹ A modern essayist might spin out a curious dissertation on the subject of these winged pioneers. I am in doubt whether crows (See Langhorn's Plutarch Vol. 4. 260.) or ravens are to be understood, but the latter being more respectable Gentlemen, I have made choice of them for the office. Plutarch, without specifying their number hath given us more at large the story of the crows or ravens, and their services, but he observes they were rather wonderful, an indirect method of attacking the credit of the whole. "Επειτα των ὀρων ὁ περ ν ναν τοις ὀδηγοις συγχιζοντων, κ) π) ε- νης α της κ) διασπασμη των βαδιζοντων δια την αγνοιαν, κοςακες εφανεντες επιλαμβανοι την ηγεμονικι της πορειας, επομενων μεν, εμπροσθεν πετομενοι κ) σπευδοντες, ετερυντας δε κ) βραδενοντας αναμενοντες· ὁ δε κ) θαυμασιωτατοι, ὡς Καλλισθενης φησιν. ταις φωναις, ανακαλουμενοι τους πλανωμενοις νυκτως, κ) αλαξοντες, ως ιχνοι καθιςασαι της πορειας." De vit. Alex. Tom. 1.–683. Ed. Francf. 1620.

Callisthenes adds, that Apollo had deserted the Oracle of Branchus since the temple had been pillaged by the followers of Xerxes, when its fountain failed; that it had again flowed, and that some Milesian envoys had brought to Memphis many of the Oracle's predictions, relative to Alexander the son of Jupiter, his future victory at Arbela, the death of Darius, and the Lacedæmonian political commotions. Athenais of Erythrea, another Erythrean Sibyl had before spoken of Alexander's illustrious origin.[k]

Was it by such a medley of fables and credulity, that Callisthenes flattered himself he should immortalize the Conqueror of Asia, and could such a ridiculous and turgid narrative bear any comparison whatever with that hero's actions? The philosopher indeed

---

[k] "Ὁ γοῦν Καλλισθένης φησι τον Αλέξανδρον φιλοδοξῆσαι μάλιστα, ανελθεῖν τι ἐπι το χρηστήριον, ἐπειδη κ̀ Περσία ηκουσε προτερον αναβηναι κ̀ 'Ηρακλέα· ὁρμησαντα δ'ἐκ Παραιτονιε κ̀ περ νοτων επιπεσοντων βιασασθαι· πλανωμενον δ'ὑπο τε κονιορτε σωθηναι γενομενων ομβρων, κ̀ δυσιν κορακων ηγησαμενων την ὁδον, ἠδε τετων κολακευτικως λεγομενων τοιαυτα δε κ̀ τα ἑξης· μενω γαρ δε τω βασιλει τον ἱερεα ἐπιτρεψαι παρελθειν τις τον νεων μετα της συνηθες στολης, τες δ'αλλες μεταδυναι την ἐσθητα, ἐξωθεν τε της θυμελης ακροασασθαι ταντας πλην Αλεξανδρε, τετον δ'ἐνδοθεν ειναι· εχ' ὡσπερ εν Διλφοις, κ̀ Βραγχιδαις τας αποθεσπισεις δια λογων, αλλα νευμασι κ̀ συμβολοις το πλεον· ὡς κ̀ παρ' 'Ομηρῳ,
Η, κ̀ κυανεησιν ἐπ' ὀφρυσι νευσι Κρονιων.

τε προφητε τον Δια ὑποκρινομενε· τετο μεντοι ρητως εἰπεν τον ανθρωπον προς τον βασιλεα, ὁτι εη Διὸς ὑιὸς. Προσραγωδει δε τετοις ὁ Καλλισθενης, ὁτι τε Απολλωνὸς το ἐν Βραγχιδαις μαντειον ἐκλελοιποτὸς, ἐξ ὁτε το ἱερον ὑπο των Βραγχιδων ἐσυληθη ἐπι Ξερξε περσισαντων, ἐκλελοιπυιας δε κ̀ της κρηνης, τοτε ἡ τε κρηνη ανασχοι, κ̀ μαντεια πολλα ὁι Μιλησιων πρεσβεις κομισθεντες εις Μεμφιν περι της ἐκ Διὸς γενεσεως τε Αλεξανδρε, κ̀ της ἐσομενης περι Αρβηλα νικης, κ̀ τε Δαρειε θανατε, κ̀ των ἐν Λακεδαιμονι νεωτερισμων· περι δε της ευγενειας, κ̀ την Ερυθραιαν Αθηναιδα φησιν ειπειν· κ̀ γαρ ταυτην ὁμοιαν γενεσθαι τῃ παλαιᾳ Σιβυλλῃ τῃ Ερυθραιᾳ." Strabo, Lib. 17.--1168, 1169.

indeed defigned to render the fame of Alexander dependent on his own abilities, and fubfervient to his interefts; but led aftray by his own vanity, he erred in the choice of his plan, and fell into difgrace. Yet we muft do him the juftice to acknowledge that he difcovered great firmnefs of mind, when Alexander infifted on exceffive and divine honours from his fubjects. Callifthenes then comes forward as the auguft protector of the injured religion of his country, and the laft and only champion of its liberty. But a moment's reflection on the precife period of this event, which was fo foon followed by his imprifonment, will convince us, that he had no more to hazard, when he fo courageoufly refifted the Macedonian monarch's inclinations, whofe indignation he had already roufed.——A ftriking and a memorable leffon for the writers of every age, who, forgetful of the duties, which they owe to their own times, to pofterity, and to themfelves, in vain endeavour to ally the low and little intrigues of the courtier with philofophical integrity and freedom!

Oneficritus of Ægina, a follower of Diogenes the Cynic, according to Diogenes Laertius, who feems to have been a mere compiler without tafte, and to have confounded the firft and fecond Cyrus, had written a hiftory of Alexander on the model of the Cyropædia, which he probably fuppofed to be fictitious; but his falfities and fables have not left us any poffibility of comparing him with the fage Xenophon. In imitation of the difciple of Socrates, who compofed the memoirs of the younger Cyrus,

Cyrus, the scholar of Diogenes entered on those of Alexander. Though he had an excellent original, it was miserably copied;[l] and Strabo hath admitted that, of all the historians of Alexander, this cynic philosopher had advanced with the most consummate assurance, tales and paradoxes the most singular and absurd.[m] But perhaps it was by these means, that he expected to continue in the favour of the Macedonian monarch, who entertained him at his court, and carried him along with him, for the declared purpose of writing his history.——From such venal hands, have we to expect any thing but distorted facts in the narrative of Alexander's expeditions! Truth cannot stoop to any bribes, and where rewards are begged with importunity, they are notoriously the wages of corruption.

Hegesias, the Magnesian, first introduced into Greece, as Strabo informs us,[n] the Asiatic style of eloquence, which wastes, like

---

[l] Diogenes Laertius hath passed a less severe judgment on this unfortunate historian, "Και τη ἑρμηνεια δε παραπλησιος πλην ὁτι ὡς απογραφος εξ αρχετυπου δευτερευει." (Lib. 6. Tom. 1.--354. 4⁰ Amst. 1709.) Little of the Archetype however seems to have been visible.

[m] Arrian hath recorded a very particular instance of the historical fidelity of Onesicritus, and in a fact, of which there could be no doubt. " Της δε αυτου νεως κυβερνητης Ονησικριτος, ὁς εν τη συγγραφη τη τινα ὑπερ Αλεξανδρου ξυνεγραψε, και τουτο εψευσατο, ναυαρχον ἑαυτον ειναι γραψας, κυβερνητη οντα." (De Exped. Alex. Lib. 6. C. 2.--409.) Strabo styles him, " Ουκ Αλεξανδρου μαλλον η των παραδοξων Αρχικυβερνητην." and adds, " Ὑπερβαλλεσθαι δε δοκει τοις τοιουτοις εκεινος τη τερατολογια." Strabo, Lib. 15.--1022.

[n] " Ἡγησιας τε ὁ ῥητωρ, ὁς ηρξε της Ασιανου λεγομενου ζηλου, παραφθειρας τι κατεστησκος εθος το Ατ-.. κον" Strabo, Lib. 14.--959.

like a courtezan, every artifice to enliven the passions that habitude hath palled. He was an orator and an historian, two professions which form at all times a dangerous combination, where a correct taste is not generally established, and its limits perfectly defined. His orations were equally faulty in sentiment and in expression; and when he exercised himself on history, his style was broken and unequal, and full of puerile embellishments. ⁰ Photius hath preserved some fragments of Agatharcides, in which he had keenly censured the works of Hegesias, and ridiculed both his description of the siege and capture of Thebes, and his method of deploring the misfortunes of its inhabitants. "Adversity rendered the place mute that was vociferous."—" Thou hast acted, Alexander, in destroying Thebes, as if Jupiter had torn the moon from one quarter of the heavens."——" The Macedonian phalanx having entered the walls of Thebes, sword in hand, deprived the city of existence: here was its grave, there was death." ᴾ

It

ᵒ This is nearly Cicero's opinion. " Et is quidem non minus sententiis peccat quam verbis." (De orat. 67. Tom. 1.–478.) " Charisii vult Hegesias similis esse. At quid est tam fractum, tam minutum, tam in ipsa, quam tamen consequitur, concinnitate puerile." (De claris oratoribus, 83. Tom. 1.–406.) Plutarch hath handed down to us one of these puerile conceits relative to the temple of Diana at Ephesus, which was burnt in the night that Alexander was born. "Εικοτως γαρ ιση καταφθιχθηναι τον νεων, της Αρτεμιδος αχολουμενης περι την Αλιξανδρου μαιωσιν." The observation that he makes is, "Επιφωνημα κατασβισαι την πυρκαιαν εκεινην ιπο ψυχριας δυναμενον." (De vit. Alex. Plut. opera, Tom. 1.–665.) I do not know whether the observation on the sentiment, or the sentiment itself, is most exceptionable.

ᴾ " Τον γαρ μεγιςα φωνησαντα τοπον, αφωνον η συμφορα πεποιηκε"——— "Ομοιον πεποιηκας, Αλικαιδρε, Θηβας κατασκαψας, ως αν τι ο Ζευς εκ της κατα Ουρανον μεριδος εκβαλοι την σεληνην"——— "Η

It is not without some reason, that Agatharcides hath observed, this miserable sophist appears to have mentioned this event rather to display his own wit, than to commiserate the lamentable fortune of the Thebans. ⁋

Longinus tells us, that Hegesias appeared in his own opinion to consider himself as inspired, but instead of being influenced by any divine impulse, he trifled like a child; ʳ and in short, Dionysius Halicarnassus pretends, that there is not a single well-turned period in all his works. ˢ A fragment is selected on the siege of Gaza and punishment of Betis, as an example of his poverty of style; and he compares his relation of the tragical end of Betis, with Homer's account of the ignominious treatment of Hector's dead

---

" Η δε φαλαγξ των Μακεδονων εισβιασαμενη τοις οπλοις εντος τειχους την πολιν απεκτεινεν· εκει μεν ταφη πολεως, ενταυθα δε θανατος."——— (Photii Bibliotheca, 1336. 1337. Fol. Rothomag. 1653.) The three passages are here given in the same order as the reader will find them on a reference to Photius. The Baron de St. Croix had transposed them. "Arracha la vie à cette ville," are the words of the French translation. The Greek original may bear the hyperbole, but I have softened the expression.

⁋ " Εμοι μεν ουν σκωπτειν και ο σοφιστης δοκει δια τουτων ουκ ολοφυρεσθαι των πολεων την τυχην." (Photii Bibliotheca, 1336.) Himerius seems to have copied Hegesias in his description of the capture of Thebes, (Photii Bibliotheca, 1080.) but the exploits of Alexander have been a fruitful subject for general declamation. The rhetorical flourishes of the elder Seneca, "Deliberat Alexander an oceanum naviget." (Suasor, Tom. 3. Amst. 8ᵛᵒ 1672.) "Deliberat Alexander an Babyloniam intret, cum denuntiatum esset illi responso auguris periculum." (Suasor, 4. Tom. 3.) are well known.

ʳ " Πολλαχα γαρ ενθυσιαν εαυτοις δοκουντες ȣ βακχευουσιν αλλα παιζȣσιν." Dion. Longinus, Sect. 3.

ˢ " Ευγουν ταις τοσαυταις γραφαις ως καταλελοιπεν ο ανηρ, μιαν ουκ αν ευροι τις σελιδα συγκειμενην ευτυχως." Dion. Halicarnass. de structura orationis. 144.

dead body by Achilles, in the Iliad, which the Magnesian sophist had ridiculously imitated.¹ Q. Curtius* seems not to have suffered this work of Hegesias to have escaped his attention: he hath, notwithstanding, touched on the event without entering into any of its disgusting circumstances. Clitarchus, the son of Dinon, acquired some reputation in his own times, by the publication of his work on Alexander's expeditions; but a bloated style produces regularly exaggerated facts. " Clitarchus comes under

---

¹ Dionysius Halicarnassus hath given us the passage at full length. "Ὁ δὲ βασιλεὺς ἔχων τὸ σύνταγμα πρόχειρον, ᾗ ὡς εἰσεδέχετο τῶν πολεμίων τοῖς κράτισι ἀπανταχόθεν ... [Greek text continues] ..." (De Structurâ orat. 146.) But I do not find the observation that "Il compare cette maniere de raconter les faits aux traitemens ignominieux qu'Achille fait essuyer au corps d'Hector," is well founded, and I have therefore adopted the sense of the Greek original. Dionysius Halicarnassus drew only a parallel between the two descriptions of the punishment of Betis, and the indignity offered to Hector's body; and had no intention whatever of comparing the sophist's manner of relating facts, to the disgraceful conduct of Achilles. He adds indeed and with strict justice, "Ὅτι δὲ ὁ Μάχης εἴρηκεν, ὡς ὑπὸ γυναικῶν ἢ κατεαγότων ἀνθρώπων λέγοιτ᾽ ἂν, καὶ οὐδὲ τούτων μετὰ σπουδῆς, ἀλλ᾽ ἐπὶ χλευασμῷ καὶ καταγέλωτι." De Structurâ orat. 153.

* Q. Curtius, Lib. 4. C. 6.

under this cenfure," fays Longinus, "ftill more, who blufters and blows, as Sophocles expreffes it,"

"Loud founding blafts, not fweeten'd by the ftop." [x]

The judicious author of the treatife, attributed to Demetrius Phalereus, hath confirmed with his authority the opinion of Longinus, and hath laughed at this writer's unnatural conceits and pomp. [y] Cicero exprefsly reproaches Sifenna [z] with his puerile manner, and declares that this Roman chronicler feemed, of all the Greek authors, to have been only acquainted with Clitarchus, whom he had imitated, and whofe defects included in all likelihood, that glare, which hath been improperly termed ingenuity, and which hath often corrupted talents of more than common expectation. The narrative of Clitarchus was moft probably full of this feductive glitter, fo fatal to the progrefs of letters, and

---

[x] Smith's Longinus, 10. "Και ετι μαλλον Κλειταρχου· φλοιωδης γαρ ο ανηρ, και φυσων κατα τον Σοφοκλεα,

Ου σμικροις μεν αυλισκοισι—
————φορβειας δ'ατερ." Longinus, Sect. 2.

Cicero in his epiftles to Atticus, (Lib. 2. Epift. 16.) hath cited the whole paffage.

"φυσα γαρ ω σμικροισιν αυλισκοις ετι,
Αλλ' αγριαις φυσαισι φορβειας δ'ατερ"

[y] A pompous defcription of the wafp or hornet is particularly cenfured. "Ο Κλειταρχος περι της τενθρηδονος λεγων, ζωα μελισση εοικοτος, κατασκευαζει, μεν φησι, την ορεινην εισιπταται δε εις τας κοιλας δρυς·— ωσπερ περι βοος αγριε η τε Ερυμανθιε καπρε λεγων, αλλ' εχι περι μελισσης τινος'" Demetrius Phalereus, Sect. 330. 331.

[z] "Is tamen neque orator in numero veftro unquam eft habitus, et in hiftoriâ puerile quiddam confectatur: ut unum Clitarchum, neque præterea quemquam, de Græcis legiffe videatur: eum tamen velle duntaxat imitari." Cicero, de legibus, Lib. 1. Sect. 2. Tom. 3.—117. Ed. Olivet. 4to 1740.

and always announcing their decline; and it is perhaps in this sense, that Quintilian is to be understood, when he informs us that this historian of Alexander was admired for his genius, though his veracity was universally decried.[a]——But the Rhetoricians arrogated to themselves, if we are to believe Cicero,[b] the privilege of lying with impunity, from the avowed motives of giving spirit to their works; and Clitarchus justifies the propriety of the observation, as may be proved from many instances, that Strabo, Pliny, and a crowd of the ancient authors have recorded of him. ——All these fabulous traditions, exaggerated facts, hyperbolical and improbable relations, with the imaginary descriptions of battles and of sieges, that Alexander's historians adopted, were in general borrowed from Callisthenes, Hegesias, Clitarchus, Onesicritus, Megasthenes and Daimachus, and they were more eagerly resorted to from the corruption of the public taste, and the numerous admirers of such extravagances, whose clamorous applauses overpowered any censures of their folly and absurdity. ——It is not undoubtedly from this tribe of writers that we are to be supplied with any faithful memoirs of the life and actions of Alexander.——They will form a separate and distinct class, which must be afterwards considered.——Let not however the most audacious Pyrrhonism pretend to confound the authentic monuments

---

[a] "Clitarchi probatur ingenium fides infamatur." Quintil. Inst. orat. Lib. 10. C. 1.--500. Ed. Gesner. 4¹⁰. 1738.

[b] "Concessum est rhetoribus ementiri in historiis, ut aliquid dicere possint argutius. ——Sic Clitarchus." Cicero, de claris oratoribus. Sect. 11. Tom. 1.--345.

monuments that have been left us, with those, which adulation and a love of the marvellous have alone erected. Without endeavouring to discriminate truth and falsehood, but willingly acquiescing in the malicious inclination of blending them both together, let us not suppose the exploits of the conqueror of Asia to have been as fabulous as the labours of Hercules; nor give credit to what has been asserted in a moment of paradoxical delirium, that the Macedonian hero never penetrated into India.

The memoirs of Ptolemy and of Aristobulus, deserve the first places amongst those works which have any pretensions to distinction: having been eye-witnesses of the facts, which they relate, these two generals of Alexander's army delayed their publications till this Prince's death, in order that flattery might not have any undue influence over them; and that truth might appear in their relations without either restriction or disguise. These prudential reasons, which we have on the faith of Arrian,[c] refute at once Lucian's story, that Alexander having listened to Aristobulus's account of his combat with Porus, enraged at such a mass of fables, ordered him to be thrown into the Hydaspes, crying out, "Thus ought you to have been served yourself, for pretending to describe my battles, and killing half a dozen elephants with

---

[c] "Εμοι Πτολεμαιος τε και Αριστοβουλος πιστοτεροι εδοξαν ες την αφηγησιν· ὁ μεν, ὁτι συνεστρατευσε τε βασιλει Αλεξανδρω, Αριστοβουλος, Πτολεμαιος δε, προς τω ξυςρατευσαι, ὁτι και αυτω βασιλει οτι αισχροτερον η τω αλλω ψευσασθαι ην, αμφω δε, ὁτι τετελευτηκοτος ήδη Αλεξανδρου ξυγγραφουσιν· ὁτι αυτοις ητε αναγκη και ὁ μισθος του αλλως τι, η ὡς συνηνεχθη, ξυγγραψαι κτλ." Arrian. Præfat. Exp. Alex. 2.

with a single dart."[d]——Lucian most probably intended to allude to Onesicritus, as he mentions a few pages afterwards, a conversation of the Macedonian Monarch's with this philosopher, in which he animadverted on the fulsome flattery of his biographers; and appeared anxious to know the sentiments that posterity would entertain of him, and of his actions. Alexander, it is well known, carried Onesicritus along with him as his historian, and the name of Aristobulus may have been inserted instead of that of the cynic philosopher, from some mistake of the author or his copyists.——This conjecture seems to be strengthened also by what Lucian says of the age of Aristobulus, who reached the extended period of ninety years, and with a wonderful strength of understanding, entered on the composition of his history at eighty-four.[e] Is it credible that Aristobulus at this advanced age, could have followed the Conqueror of Asia over such immense regions to the banks of the Hydaspes?

A journal of Alexander's exploits, had been reduced into form by Diodotus of Erythrya, and by Eumenes of Cardia, who shared with Hephæstion the favours of his master, and was one of the ablest

---

[d] Franklin's Lucian, Vol. 2.--277. 8vo Edit. "Και σε δε ὁτως εχειν, ω Αριστοβουλε, τοιαυτα ἱπερ ἡμων μονομαχοντα, και διαφανταs ἐν ακοντιω φονευοντα." Lucian. Quomodo. Hist. conscribenda sit. Sect. 12, Tom. 2.--17.

[e] Lucian. Quomodo. Hist. conscribenda sit. Sect. 40. Tom. 2.--54.

[f] Et composa son histoire à 80. "Την ἱστοριαν δε τιταρτον και ογδοηκοστον ετ[os] γεγονως ηρξατο συγγραφειν." (Lucian. Macrobii, Sect. 22. Tom. 3.--224.) which I have followed.

ableft and moft unfortunate generals of his age. If we are to judge of this work, by the numerous fragments of it in feveral authors of antiquity;[g] it was both a very accurate and circumftantial narrative of the public and private life of the Macedonian Prince.

The itinerary of Alexander's army, by Diognetus and Beton, employed by this Monarch in the meafurement of his marches, and the furvey of the countries, that he paffed through, would naturally have thrown a confiderable fhare of light on the expeditions of the Conqueror of Afia, and the geography of the Eaft. But this valuable work, which was not indeed neglected either by Ariftobulus or Ptolemy, hath not efcaped the ravages of time; and the defcriptions, which Alexander directed to be made of the different provinces of his empire by able and experienced perfons, have been equally unfortunate.—Patroclus affures us, that thefe memoirs had been communicated to him by Xenocles the King's treafurer;[h] and it is doubtlefs of thefe papers that the illuftrious Corfini thus expreffes himfelf, "The very exact defcriptions, which Alexander directed to be made of his conquefts, would have been of vaft fervice to geography, and rendered it much more perfect."[i]

It

---

[g] Arrian. Exped. Alex. Lib. 7. Chap. 25.—Plutarch. Vit. Alex. Tom. 1.-706.—Sympofiacon. Lib. 1. Tom. 2.-623.—Athenæus, Lib. 10.-434.—Ælian. Var. Hift. Lib. 3. C. 23.

[h] Strabo, Lib. 2. Tom. 1.-120.

[i] "Les defcriptions exactes qu'Alexandre eut foin de faire de fes conquêtes, donnerent une forme

It is even reasonable to imagine, that a collection of Alexander's letters remained long after his death; at least it must be allowed, that many of them had been made public, as they are cited by a number of the ancient authors.[k] If this correspondence had descended to us, it would certainly have placed in a still clearer point of view the military actions of this Prince, and unfolded to us more distinctly, the secret motives, that influenced his conduct, his manners and his character. Patroclus, Eratosthenes and Strabo, had severally made their observations on the historians of Alexander, but these treatises have also perished. Their labours would probably have rendered any other attempts of this kind useless; and the age, in which they lived, undoubtedly afforded them superior advantages for such discussions. The fabulous traditions, which descend from one generation to another, gradually obscure the light of truth; our efforts to discover it are enfeebled by our distance from the different events; the gloom augments; doubts accumulate; systems rise; our difficulties increase; and we lose even by the flux of time those succours, with which it is impossible to be again supplied.

Cephalon, a native of Gergetha[l] in the Troad, abridged universal

forme beaucoup plus parfaite à la geographie." De l'origin. et des progrès de l'Astronom. Acad. des Sciences Anc. Mem. Tom. 8.–13.

[k] Plutarch. Vit. Alex. Tom. 1.–688. 689. 691, 696. 697.
———— Vit. Phocion. Tom. 1.--749.
———— De sui laude. Tom. 2.--545.
Arrian. Exped. Alex. Lib. 7. Chap. 24.--534.

[l] Strabo, Lib. 13. Tom. 2.--882. Suidas hath confounded him with Cephalon the Rhetorician,

verfal hiftory; and the work was diftinguifhed by accuracy and by precifion. Every digreffion was ftudioufly avoided in it, and every recital that had not an immediate connection with the facts, that he had to explain or to defcribe. This hiftory written in the Ionic dialect, and after the manner of Herodotus divided into nine books, each of which bears the name of one of the Nine Mufes, was the fruit of unwearied application and immenfe refearches. The laft book, which had the title of Erato,[m] contained the exploits of the conqueror of Darius, and had been extracted with Herculean perfeverance from no lefs than thirty different authors. What a rich banquet might it not have furnifhed?

A comparifon of different and various evidence is the foul of rational inquiry.——Truth often rifes amidft the fhock of contending and contradictory opinions; whilft impofture acquires its only credit from the carelefs filence, or the accommodating concurrence of hiftorians. Sopater made great ufe of Cephalon's abridgment in his account of Alexander, but even his refearches have

---

cian, who lived under Adrian. Vide Suidas, Tom. 3.–305. Κεφαλιων. and alfo Voffius, de hift. Græcis. Lib. 11. Chap. 12.

[m] "Le dérnier livre intitulé Uranie." I have corrected this error, for on turning to the paffage in Photius, which was referred to, the Greek fentence appeared to me to be evidently miftaken; "Συμπεραινεται δε αυτη η ιστορια εν λογοις θ', κατ'επωνυμιαν των θ' Μεσων, Κλιως, Θαλιιας, Πολυμνιας, Μελπομενης, Τερψιχορης, Ευτερπης, Καλλιοπης, Ερατως, Ουρανιης, εν η (that is ιστορια) και τα κατα Αλεξανδρον τον Μακεδονα διεξεισιν." (Biblioth. 101.) I was happy afterwards to find I had the beft of all authorities, the authority of Photius himfelf, for this conftruction. Speaking of Sopater, he fays, "Ὁ δικατ⊙. δε συνθρεισθη εκ τε τα Κεφαλιων⊙. Ερατες, διαλαμβανεσης τα κατα Αλεξανδρον." Biblioth. 541.

have not reached us. Chares, Anticlides, Philo the Theban, Hecateus of Eretria, Duris of Samos, Nearchus and Timogenes have a juſt claim to the character of authentic writers, and their teſtimony is unexceptionable. If their ſucceſſors had formed themſelves after their example, and had employed the materials which they left them, we ſhould have had great reaſon to have applauded their diſcernment; but the farther they deviated from theſe indiſputable records, the more their authority becomes ſuſpected.——In taking a view of what is not to be doubted on the ſubject of Alexander's hiſtorians, it may be neceſſary to enter into ſome circumſtances relating to them.

Arrian of Nicomedia [n] lived under Adrian, Antoninus Pius, and Marcus Antoninus; [o] and from having frequented the ſchool of Epictetus he was a zealous advocate for its tenets. The ſame maſterly hand, which ſketched out the moral diſſertations of Epictetus, is eaſily perceptible in the hiſtory of the Macedonian Conqueror; and even the ſpeech, which Arrian puts into the mouth of Dandamis, [p] contains many of the ſentiments, which are to be

met

---

[n] See Tillemont. Hiſt. des Emp. Tom. 4.--453. Ed. 12ᵐᵒ and alſo Voſſius, de Hiſt. Græc. Lib. 2. Chap. 11.

[o] Photii Bibliotheca. 53.—Euſebius Chron. Canon. Suidas, Αρριαν. Tom. 1.--320.

[p] "Dans la bouche de Calanus." There is a fort of conſtitutional vivacity, which ſometimes hurries away men of real erudition, and occaſions them a multitude of inadvertencies. With the French, this lively volatility is remarkable, and enters largely into the mercurial character of the nation. It is into the mouth of Dandamis that Arrian hath put this ſpeech, and Calanus

is

met with in the collection of those of the Stoic Philosopher.[1] The most celebrated cities took an early opportunity of acknowledging his merit, and of enrolling him amongst their citizens.—Athens and Rome conferred this honour on him;[2] and the latter intrusted him with the command of a body of its forces. The government of Cappadocia was given to him: and his courage and capacity were equally conspicuous in the protection of the Province from the Alani,[3] who made an irruption into Asia Minor, in the 17th year of the reign of Adrian, and 134 years after Christ.——Arrian's services were afterwards rewarded with the Consular dignity.[4]

The

---

is only celebrated for the firm and undaunted manner, in which he voluntarily committed himself to the flames, on the approach of infirmity and sickness; "Πριν τινος ἰς πειραν ελθειν παθηματος, ὁ, τι περ εξαναγκαση αυτον μεταβαλλειν την προσθεν διαιταν." Arrian hath fairly stated, "Οι τινα μαλιστα δη αυτοι ακρατορα Μεγασθενης ανεγραψεν." but his method of winding up the affecting tragedy, "Οι τω δη επιβαντα τη πυρα, καταλιθηναι μεν εν κοσμω, ὁρασθαι δε προς της στρατιας συμπασης.—Ταυτα και τοιαυτα ἱπερ Καλανου του Ινδου ἱκανοι ανεγεγραφασιν, ουκ αχρεια παντα ες ανθρωπος, ὁτω γνωριι επιμελες, ὁτι ὡς καρτερον τε εστι και ανικητον γνωμη ανθρωπινον ὁ, τι περ ιθιλοι εξεργασασθαι." (Lib. 7. Chap. 3.---481, 482.) seems to intimate that he did not altogether agree in opinion with Megasthenes.

Strabo hath given a long account of these ancient Bramins, but Dandamis hath there the name of Mandanis. Lib. 15. Tom. 2.---1042, 1043. 1044.

[1] Epictetus, Tom. 1. Lib. 1. Chap. 25.

[2] Arrianus de venatione. C. 1.---190. Ed. 8vo Amst. 1683.—Lucian Pseudomant. Tom. 2.---209.

[3] Without any diminution of Arrian's merit, we are informed by Dion. Cassius, that the persuasive arguments of Volgæsius had also their influence: "Των Αλβανων τα μεν ΔΩΡΟΙΣ ὑπο του Ουολογαισου πεισθεντων, τα δε και Φλαβιον Αρριανον τον της Καππαδοκιας αρχοντα φοβηθεντων." (Lib. 69. 15. Tom. 2.---1163.) The Alani are here called "Των Αλβανων," and there is a very learned note upon the passage.

[4] Suidas. Αρριανος. Tom. 1.---320.—Photii Bibliotheca. 53.

The philosopher contemplates the conduct, the manners, and the genius of mankind, and takes into consideration the motives of human actions with the means, that are employed in their execution: his scrutinizing eye develops the rise, the progress and the fall of empires; but some military knowledge, joined to practical experience, seems necessary to describe the march of armies, and the operations of victorious generals. Few persons perhaps possessed these qualifications in a superior degree to Arrian; and his treatise upon tactics is an excellent abridgment of all that Greece knew upon the subject.* The details, on the regulation and evolutions of the phalanx, into which he enters, are justly the admiration of all military men* for their perspicuity and precision; and the fragment, which remains, relating to his march and the order of battle against the Alani, evidently proves that he had taken up his theory from real service. Knowledge and talents of such magnitude are not easily concealed, and they discover themselves in the whole history of Alexander. Yet it is extraordinary, that the luminous manner, in which Arrian hath explained the manœuvres of the Macedonian army, hath even called his veracity in question. An able professional writer hath had the boldness to advance, that Arrian endeavours to give lessons upon tactics at the expence of truth, in the description of the battle of Gaugamele that he hath left us. " If our account of this battle," says he, "was a real exercise on the art of war, the

application

---

* See the preface of Monf. Guifcard to his translation of Arrian's Tactics, 49.

* Memoires militaires des Grecs et Romains, par Monf. Guifcard. Disc. Prelim. 38.

application of all its grand principles could not be better brought before the eye."[y]——But becaufe an army, when oppofed to an undifciplined multitude upon equal ground, is faid to have made the moft judicious movements; are we to infer from this fimple circumftance, that the account, which hath been given us by a mafter in the art of war, is the fruit only of his imagination, and the mere refult of his own fyftems? Monf' Guifcard adds, "That he fhould never have attempted to doubt the authenticity of the circumftances of this battle, if Polybius had not treated the account of the battle of Iffus by Callifthenes in the fame manner."[z] ——If Polybius hath however detected the impofitions of Callifthenes, does the conclufion follow, that Arrian, who had the advantage of the memoirs of the generals of Alexander's army, hath forged what he related? With more juftice poffibly he may be open to fome cenfure on his exceffive vanity. It is indeed with fingular oftentation, that he tells us there was not any neceffity of his mentioning himfelf; that his birth, his country, and employments, were all well known; and in fhort, that he ftood as high amongft the Grecian writers of eminence, as Alexander

F did

[y] "Cette bataille," fays he, "fut-elle un vrai thême pour la theorie de l'art de la guerre? Tout cela ne prefenteroit pas mieux fous un feul coup d'œil; l'application de ces grands principes." Memoires milit. fur les Grecs et les Romains, Tom. 1.--181.

[z] "Qu'il ne fe feroit jamais avifé de répondre des doutes fur l'authenticité des circonftances de cette bataille, . . fi Polybe ne traitoit pas de même le récit que donne un certain Callifthene de la bataille d'Iffus," Mem. milit. &c. &c. Tom. 1,--280.

did in a military line.ᵃ But perhaps this open and undifguifed acknowledgment of his own confcioufnefs of his literary merit hath fome little claim to our indulgence.———It may be founded on fome plaufible pretenfions to general approbation, and is in fact a weaknefs, that increafes not unfrequently with the reputation, that a writer acquires in the public eftimation. Arrian concludes his work with the information, that he had not inconfiderately engaged in it, but had been animated by a divine impulfe to the enterprife.ᵇ In this fpecies of fuperftitious enthufiafm we difcover at once the prieft of Ceres, whofe functions Arrian had himfelf exercifed.ᶜ

Ptolemy, the chief of the Lagides,ᵈ and Ariftobulus were the principal guides, that Arrian followed; and Ptolemy feems to have had the preference,ᵉ though he has not copied either of them

---

ᵃ "Το μεν ουομα ουδεν δεομαι αναγραψαι, (ουδε γαρ ουδε αγνωςον ες Ανθρωπους ες ιν) ουδε πατριδα ητις μοι εςιν, ουδε το γενος το εμον, ουδε ει δη τινα Αρχην εν τη εμαυτου ηρξα.———και επι τωδε ουκ απαξιω των πρωτων ειν τη φωνη τη Ελλαδι, ειπερ ουν και Αλεκανδρος των εν τοις οπλοις. Arrian, Exped. Alex. Lib. 1. Chap. 12.--50.

ᵇ "Ουδε ανευ Θεου'" Arrian, Lib. 7. Chap. 30.--546.

See Dodwell, de ætate, Peripli maris Euxini. Sect. 8.

ᵈ " Ptolemy's mother was Arfinoe. Being with child by Philip of Macedon, fhe was married to Lagus, and Ptolemy was in confequence called the fon of Lagus. He had a principal command under Alexander, and afterwards obtained the kingdom of Egypt." Paufanias, Attica. 14. 15.

ᵉ "Ως λεγει Πτολεμαιος ὁ Λαγου, ὡ μαλιςα εγω επομαι·" Arrian, Exped, Alex. Lib. 6. Chap. 2.-409.

them fervilely, or without confideration. He hath extracted alfo from other hiftorians every thing relating to Alexander, that he thought worthy of prefervation, and not altogether deftitute of probability, though only founded on report. ——This may not be ftrictly juftifiable; but the proper moments for inveftigation are not thofe of enthufiafm, when the fever of imagination runs too high for calm and difpaffionate inquiry.

Arrian informs us there was not any perfon that had fo many hiftorians, or fo many contradictory ones as Alexander, and he finifhes his preface with the following fentence; " And if any now wonder why, after fo many writers of Alexander's acts, I alfo attempt the tafk, and endeavour to elucidate the fame, after he has perufed the reft, let him proceed to the reading of mine, and he will find lefs caufe of wonder than before." [g]——Drawing our obfervations

---

[f] "Lorfqu'ils ont rapporté des chofes dignes d'être confervées, et qui pouvoient paffer pour croyable, parce que felon lui, elles concernoient Alexandre, voila une logique pitoyable." I flatter myfelf I have correctly given Arrian's fentiments, and I confefs I fee nothing of that miferable logic, with which he is reproached. He does not mean to fay, that he believed the reports becaufe they related to Alexander, but that they did not appear to be entirely improbable, though founded only on common fame. "Ἔστι δὲ ᾅ ϗ̀ πρὸς ἄλλων ξυγγέγραμμένα, ὅτι ϗ̀ αὐτὰ ἀξιαφήγητά τι μοι ἔδοξαν, ϗ̀ ἀ ωκιτη ἀπιςα, ὡς λεγόμενα μόνον ὑπὲρ Ἀλεξάνδρου, ἀνέγραψα." (Exped. Alex. Lib. 2.) In the learned note on this paffage in the edition of Arrian's Expeditio Alexandri, 8vo Amft. 1757. the diftinction between the "Τα λεγόμενα μόνον" mere reports, and the "Τα οντα" real facts, is extremely well explained. Tacitus, as is judicioufly obferved, hath nearly the fame idea. "Ut conquirere fabulofa et fictis oblectare legentium animos, procul gravitate cæpti operis crediderim: ita vulgatis traditifque demere fidem non aufim." Tacit. 2. 50. 3.

[g] Rooke's Arrian. Preface. Vol. 1.--2. "Ὅςις δὲ θαυμάσεται ἀνθ' ὅτου ἐπὶ τοσοῖς δὲ συγγραφεῦσι, ϗ̀ ἐμοὶ ἐπὶ νοῦν ἠλθεν ἥδε ἡ συγγραφή, τα τε ἐκείνων πάντα τις ἀναλεξάμενος, ϗ̀ τοῖσδε τοῖς ἡμετέροις ἐντυχων, ὧω θαυμαξέτω."

observations from this passage along with that, which hath been already alluded to; the real motives, which engaged him to undertake the history of Alexander, may be guessed at.———The work itself is divided into seven books, but the last hath only come down to us in a crippled state. There is a deficiency, though not a very considerable one, which must have contained the flight of Harpalus, as appears from the abridgment, that Photius hath given us of this book, which in his time was still perfect and unimpaired.

This ingenious critic hath bestowed very liberal encomiums on Arrian's noble simplicity and clearness of style; and considering it as a very exact imitation of Zenophon, he will not allow of his being inferior to any of the great writers in history, that had previously distinguished themselves.—Photius commends also the narrative of Arrian for its precision without any tedious digressions; though perhaps that, which relates to the military bridges of the Romans, is not entirely clear of this objection. The parentheses, he adds, do not interrupt the narrative, which hath strong marks of eloquence; and indeed the harangue of Cœnus in the name of the Macedonian soldiers, satiated with conquests and with glory, is certainly both very affecting and pathetic. Photius after having given Arrian a decided preference to all the other historians of Alexander, finishes his account of his writings with the

τω." (Arrian. Exped. Alex. 2, 3.) The Baron de St. Croix would read 'Ουτι, but Arrian afterwards makes use of the same expression. " Οςις δε κακιζει Αλεξανδρον——ὁτω δη εκλογιζεσθω." Exped. Alex. Lib. 7. C. 30.--545.

the declaration, that on weighing his merits with those of the ancient historians in general, many of them will be found unequal to him [h].——Yet it would be uncandid to conceal, that Arrian's inclinations to exalt his Hero, to represent as favourably as possible those actions of the Macedonian Monarch, which may be justly censured, and to exaggerate his successes, are very evident.—Not satisfied with raising Alexander above all other conquerors, he assures us that he is no less illustrious than Minos, Eacus, and Rhadamanthus, the sons of Jupiter; and supposing even this comparison of his Hero with the venerable judges of the shades still gave too faint an idea of him, he extends it to Theseus the son of Neptune, and Ion, the son of Apollo.——Allowing for this momentary glow of enthusiasm, Arrian on the whole seems to have possessed a sound and discriminating understanding in the discussion of the several facts, which he hath related; to have adopted them only after a cautious examination of them; and even in some instances to have condemned Alexander with severity. On the subject of a letter, written by the Prince to Cleomenes, who then commanded in Egypt, in which, though he disapproved of his conduct, he assured him of a pardon not only for those crimes that he had already committed, but for any future

---

[h] "Photius apres avoir placé Arrian au-dessus meme de plusieurs anciens historiens finit par lui donner la preference sur tous ceux qui avoient ecrit l'histoire d'Alexandre." The fact is substantially exact, but is not correctly related. Photius first expresses himself of Arrian, "Ουτος δε συντάκτης παντων αμεινον ᾗ τα κατα Αλεξανδρον τον Μακεδονα." (Biblioth. 52.) And he finishes what he says of him with "Και απλως, ει τις κατ' αυτον επι τοις ιστορικοις αναχθειη λογοις, πολλους και των αρχαιων ιδοι της αυτη ταξεως ισαμενοις ταπεινοτερον." (Biblioth. 228.) which is the arrangement that I have observed.

ture ones, provided he found at his return temples and monuments erected to the memory and in honour of Hœpheſtion, Arrian riſes indignant at ſuch a ſhameful compromiſe, and declares with an honeſt zeal, that he cannot palliate a promiſe of this ſort to ſuch a culprit. But this is not the ſingle inſtance in which he hath reflected on the Conqueror of Aſia: he concludes in the following terms, "And though I take the freedom in this hiſtory of his actions, ſometimes to cenſure him, yet I cannot but own myſelf an admirer of them altogether: I have, however, fixed a mark of reproach upon ſome of them, as well for the ſake of truth, as the public benefit; upon which account, by the aſſiſtance of Providence, I undertook this work."[1]———A few geographical errors occur undoubtedly in Arrian, but if we compare them with the multitude, that all the other hiſtorians have fallen into, they will appear very trivial, and we ſhall be rather ſurpriſed they are ſo trifling and ſo few; conſidering the difficulties, that he had to ſtruggle with, and the intricacies in which his predeceſſors had involved him.—Without any heſitation we may therefore give him a decided preference, and after having diſtinguiſhed himſelf as a writer, a general, and a philoſopher, he may be juſtly reckoned the firſt hiſtorian of Alexander's actions, and the only one on whoſe authority any confidence is to be placed.

Without

Rooke's Arrian, Vol. 1.--200, 201. "Επει και αυτος εμεμψαμην εςιν α εν τη ξυγγραφη των Αλεξανδρου εργων, αλλ' αυτον γε Αλεξανδρον ουκ αισχυνομαι θαυμαζων· τα δε εργα εκεινα εκακιςα, αληθειας τε ἑνεκα της εμης, και ἁμα ωφελειας της επ' ανθρωπους· εφ' ὁτω ὡρμηθην, ουδε αυτος ανευ Θεου, ες τηνδε την ξυγγραφην." Arrian. Exped. Alex. Lib. 7. Chap. 30.--546.

Without entering into any argument, as to the precife time when Plutarch lived; it may be fufficient to obferve, that Eufebius mentions this philofopher in the 224th Olympiad, 120 years after Chrift; and that the particular circumftances relating to him, are too well known to be repeated.———His life of Alexander cannot be fuppofed by any means to be a regular and continued hiftory of this Prince's actions; thofe of great men being in general a fort of portraits, where the colouring is very high, and the likenefs hath frequently a brilliancy, which exceeds even that of the original.———The great hiftorian feems to collect facts for the fole purpofe of giving lectures on morality, and relates only that he may have an opportunity and a pretence for his reflections. A plan of this nature is inconfiftent with hiftorical accuracy, and it hath necefsarily confufed his different recitals. The principal public events are often abandoned, or barely touched upon, that more pains may be taken with the private life of the Hero; but it muft at the fame time be acknowledged, that the Monarch's inclinations and his character are diftinctly marked, notwithftanding the hiftorian's vifible partiality for him, and the many fables that efcape from him.———Aware of the probability of being accufed of an exceffive minutenefs in his details; he endeavours to explain away the objection in fome preliminary remarks, which may ferve as a preface to the lives of Alexander and of Cæfar. "We fhall only premife, that we hope for indulgence though we do not give the actions in full detail and with a fcrupulous exactnefs, but rather in a fhort fummary; fince we are not writing hiftories

but

but lives. Not is it always in the moſt diſtinguiſhed achievements that men's virtues or vices may be beſt diſcerned; but very often an action of ſmall note, a ſhort ſaying, or a jeſt, ſhall diſtinguiſh a perſon's real character more than the greateſt ſieges or the moſt important battles. Therefore, as painters in their portraits labour the likeneſs in the face, and particularly about the eyes, in which the peculiar turn of mind moſt appears, and run over the reſt with a more careleſs hand; ſo we muſt be permitted to ſtrike off the features of the ſoul, in order to give a real likeneſs of theſe great men, and leave to others the circumſtantial detail of their labours and achievements."[k]

Amongſt many other authors, Calliſthenes, Ariſtobulus, and Oneſicritus appear to have furniſhed Plutarch with his materials for the life of Alexander.——His parallel of this Prince with Cæſar hath unfortunately periſhed, but Appian, who in fact merely compiled his work from Plutarch's hiſtorical productions, hath in ſome meaſure ſupplied the loſs by the compariſon, that he

---

[k] Langhorn's Plutarch, Vol. 4.--223. "Ουδεν αλλο πρoηγουμεν, η παραιτησομεθα τους αναγινωσκοντας, ιν μη παντα, μηδε καθ'ἑκαϛον εξηργασμενως τι των περιβοητων απαγγελλομεν, αλλα επιτεμνοντες τα πλειϛα, μη σικοφαντειν· ουτι γαρ ἱϛοριας γραφομεν, αλλα βιους· ουτε ταις επιφανεϛαταις πραξεσι παντως ενεϛι δηλωσις αρετης η κακιας, αλλα πραγμα βραχυ πολλακις και ρημα, και παιδια τις εμφασιν ηθους εποιησεν μαλλον, η μαχαι μυριονεκροι, και παραταξεις αἱ μεγιϛαι, και πολιορκια πολεων· ὡς ουν οἱ ζωγραφοι τας ὁμοιοτητας απο τη προσωπου, και των περι την οψιν ειδων, ὁις εμφαινεται το ηθος, αναλαμβανουσιν, ελαχιϛα των λοιπων μερων φροντιζοντες· ουτως, ἡμιν δοτεον εις τα της ψυχης σημεια μαλλον ενδυεσθαι, και δια τουτων ειδοποιειν τον ἑκαϛου βιον, ιϛαντας ἑτεροις τα μεγεθη και τους αγωνας·" Plutarch. de Vit. Alex. Plut. Opera. Tom. 1.-664. 665.

he hath left us of the two Conquerors, which is apparently an extract.[1]

Two discourses concerning Alexander remain to be taken notice of, that have been attributed to this philosophical historian. In the first, the Macedonian Prince is supposed to answer the reproaches of fortune for the obligations, which she had conferred upon him, from whom he is unwilling to acknowledge that he had received any favours. The Monarch is afterwards compared to the most eminent philosophers: his words and actions are said to have been formed on the purest principles, and his practice to have been superior to the theory of their first and most celebrated schools.

The second contains only a flat and fulsome panegyric on nearly the same subject, in the form of a tedious and insipid dissertation. Its author is determined to prove his Hero superior to the fickle deity, who is represented as Alexander's implacable enemy; but some circumstances are introduced, that have no connection with the object immediately in view, and particularly those concerning Dionysius of Syracuse, and Clearchus the tyrant of Heraclea. The Macedonian Monarch is made to rival Agamemnon, and the issue of the contest may be easily divined.

With

---

[1] "Ἄμφω γὰρ γενέσθην φιλοτιμοτάτω τε πάντων καὶ πολεμικωτάτω, καὶ τὰ δόξαντα ἐπιλθεῖν ταχυτάτω, παρὸς τε κινδύνοις παραβολωτάτω, καὶ τοῦ σώματος ἀφειδεστάτω, καὶ οὐ στρατηγία πισποίδοτε μᾶλλον, ἢ τόλμῃ καὶ τύχῃ." Appian. Hist. Rom. de bellis civilibus. Lib. 2.--849. Ed. 8vo Amst. 1670. Where the parallel is continued to a great length.

With the ancients indeed, as well as the moderns, this rhetorical figure seems to have been adopted, as an easier method of adding to their Hero's reputation, or the indirect means of raising it at the prejudice of the character, which is brought into competition with it.—Whoever may have been the author of the latter treatise, it contradicts most certainly Plutarch in many instances; and from thence it may be inferred to have been rather some later sophist's, who wished to give it some little credit by passing it on the public for Plutarch's. The catalogue which Lamprias, the son of Plutarch, hath given us of all his father's works, in which only one of these discourses on the fortune of Alexander, is mentioned, probably a juvenile performance, seems to strengthen this supposition.——From the life of Alexander, Plutarch hath an undoubted right to a distinguished rank amongst this Prince's historians, and he may justly be considered as the second author on the subject. Many of the transactions, which he relates, may be very serviceable in determining our opinions of the character of the Conqueror of Asia; but still the writer's prepossessions must be guarded against, and what he advances must be received with caution, where the accuracy is of any moment.

Diodorus Siculus, a native of Agyria in Sicily, flourished under Julius Cæsar: any further inquiries concerning his person or his writings would be superfluous.[m] Pliny tells us, that he was the first Grecian author who turned his thoughts towards serious things,

---

[m] See Vossius, de Hist. Græcis. Lib. 11. C. 11.—Fabricii Biblioth. Græc. Lib. 3. C. 3.

things, and abandoned trifling ones;" but this judgment is certainly a strange one, as the first five books of this historian are full of fables. Being superstitiously devoted to the doctrines of Euemerus,° he ransacked the annals of various nations, and collected their religious traditions to strengthen only, by their authority, his own erroneous system. The first books of Diodorus Siculus, precious as they are from the facts which they have preserved, are still replete with a multitude of conjectures and contradictions, that greatly reduce their value; and in the description of the countries that he mentions, he appears in general both a credulous naturalist, and an ignorant philosopher. Sometimes he doubts apparently of the truth of what he relates, whilst he does not hesitate immediately afterwards to give credit to the most extravagant absurdities. Under this impression, it is not unfair to suspect his accuracy; and it may be reasonably supposed, that he hath misrepresented the several authors, to whom he was indebted for his information, from the manner that a passage of Herodotus relative to the Medes hath suffered in his hands, which

may

" "Que cet ecrivain est le premier parmi les Grecs, que se soit occupé de choses serieuses, et qui ait abandonne les bagatelles." I am in doubt whether the "Apud Græcos desiit ungui*h*Diodorus, et βιβλιοθηκης historiam suam inscripsit." (Plin. Nat. Hist. Lib. 1. Tom. 1.--10.) warrants this assertion in its extended sense.

° A philosopher of the Cyrenaic sect, for an account of whom, see Vossius, de Hist. Græcis, Chap. 11.—De Poetis Græcis, Chap. 8.—Fabricii Biblioth. Græc. Tom. 1. Lib. 3. Chap. 28.--694, 717.—Brucker: Hist. Crit. Philof. Tom. 1. P. 2. Lib. 2. Chap. 3. de secta Cyrenaicâ, 604, 606.—and also, Dr. Enfield's valuable history of Philosophy, Vol. 1. 189. with the authors referred to.

may be compared with the original.[p] We are at a loss for the motives on which the Roman naturalist founded his favourable sentiments of Diodorus, but perhaps he formed his opinion of the work from its preface. It offers to us, without a doubt, a correct plan of a great style of history; but unfortunately the interior parts of the edifice do not by any means correspond with its external magnificence and grandeur. In the other books, after a long excursion, he confines himself more closely to his subject, and there are fewer defects to be observed, or faults to censure. Yet the distance between this author and the ancient historians of Greece is still great, and the interval, that separates them, is immense.

The seventeenth book relates more particularly to Alexander, but the style is paltry, and the reflections, though few, are trivial. Diodorus Siculus never refers to any authority for the truth of what he advances; there are not any of the sources mentioned from whence he derived his intelligence; he is often inexact; and is not happy in the arrangement of his facts. In the first part of this book, which contains the events previous to the battle of Gaugamele, more pains have been bestowed, and more care hath certainly been taken: in the latter, an uncommon degree of negligence is very visible, and there is great difficulty in discovering any connection of the facts, and preserving the order of the marches

---

[p] Histoire de l'Acad. des Inscript. et des Belles Lettres. Tom. 23.--31.

marches and expeditions of the Macedonian army. Chronology is alfo totally overturned, and the chafm in it naturally augments the obfcurity, that arifes from this confufion. The Scythian war, the Sogdian revolt, the death of Clitus with that of Callifthenes, the marriage of Roxana, and the early part of the Indian expedition are wanting in the text of Diodorus Siculus, and there hath not been any manufcript yet difcovered, by which the deficiency hath been repaired.

Truths and falfehoods are generally told in the fame tone by Diodorus Siculus, who feems neither folicitous to dazzle, nor anxious to furprife. If he poffeffes the merit of being directed in fome moments by able and experienced conductors; at others, he hath wandered unconcernedly with Callifthenes, and hath faithfully copied his fabulous extravagances.[p] Notwithftanding thefe objections, this part of Diodorus Siculus may be ufeful in afcertaining many events of Alexander's life; and with a proper and continued attention, fome real advantages may be reaped from it. Taking the whole together, Diodorus Siculus appears to be entitled to the third place amongft the Conqueror's hiftorians.

The Latin authors, who undertook the hiftory of Alexander, had not the benefit of happier times than the Grecian writers,

who

---

[q] See Diodorus Siculus, Tom. 2.--218. and Wefeling's note on the "Ὁ καλειται μεν Ἀιθηδων." and alfo Tom. 2.--230. with Wefeling's notes on the "Ὀντας ἰκκαιδεκαπηκεις." and the "Των δε κυνηγων."

who preceded them in the fame career, and whofe materials they employed. That verbofe and tumid fpecies of eloquence, which paffed out of Afia to Athens, and like a malignant ftar had fpread its contagious influence[1] amidft all the young men of ingenuity and talents, made its way at laft to the Roman citizens, who were then governed with a rod of iron.——A rage for declamation ruined the public tafte, and added to it the laft corruption, that it could poffibly receive. Far from imitating the fchools, where only the figures of the firft and fineft forms, and thofe of the beft mufcular proportions, are introduced as models,[2] the Romans contemplated in preference the fervile attitude of fome effeminate and affected courtier, and eagerly adopted a correfponding frivolous and unmanly method of expreffion. To the fpecies of hiftory immediately before us, the prevailing fafhion was foon extended; and the Satirift Juvenal addreffed himfelf to its admirers in the following paffage.

"What luckier fate
Does on the works of grave hiftorians wait?
More time they fpend, in greater toils engage;
Their volumes fwell beyond the thoufandth page:

For

---

[1] Ventofa ifthæc et enormis loquacitas ex Afia commigravit, animofque juvenum ad magna furgentes, veluti peftilenti quodam fidere afflavit. Petron. Arbit. Chap. 2.--11.

[2] An vero ftatuarum artifices, pictorefque clariffimi cum corpora fpeciofiffima fingendo, pingendove ellicere cuperent, nunquam in hanc inciderunt errorem, ut Bagoam aut Megabyzum aliquem in exemplum operis funnerent fibi, fed Doriphoron illum aptum vel militiæ vel palæftræ, aliorumque juvenum bellicoforum et athletarum corpora, quæ effe decora vere exiftimarint." Quintilian, Inft. orat. L b. 5. Chap. 12.--245.

For thus the laws of history command,
And much good paper suffers in their hand."[1]

> DRYDEN's TRANSLATION.

It was perhaps by these historical amplifications that Q. Curtius was seduced.——The learned world hath been much divided as to the exact period, in which this historian lived; and it has been supposed, though the supposition can have only few advocates, that he wrote his history in the last years of Constantine the Great.[w] Vossius fixes it with more probability under the reign of Vespasian,[x] and the learned Tillemont,[y] in that of Claudius; but without any decision of this question, it is sufficient to observe, that the style leaves us not any room to doubt of its being written, when the public taste was on its decline.

Father Tellier, of some memory, accuses Q. Curtius of having frequently reversed the order of geography and history; of an ignorance of tactics; of indiscriminately subscribing to truth and falsehood without either the inclination or abilities to separate them;

---

[1] "Vester porro labor fœcundior, historiarum
Scriptores: petitur plus temporis atque olei plus:
Namque oblita modi millesima pagina surgit
Omnibus, et crescit multa damnosa papyro.
Sic ingens rerum numerus jubet, atque operum lex."
                                   Juvenalis. Sat. 7. Lib. 3.--98.

[w] L'Historico Ragionamento della gente Curzia et dell'eta di Q. Curzio, del Conte Bagnolo.

[x] G. Vossius de Hist. Lat. Lib. 1. Chap. 33.

[y] Hist. d. Emper. 370.

them; of attaching himself rather to probabilities than realities; of affecting little pointed witticisms, and ridiculous subtilties in his maxims; and in short, of lavishing a profusion of poetical flowers in his descriptions; and converting his harangues into declamations.¹ This is a judgment which carries no inconsiderable share of censure, but it is the judgment of a commentator, and we cannot reasonably tax it with extraordinary severity. Yet we must not refuse to Q. Curtius the merits of a brilliant and fruitful imagination; of a warm and picturesque mode of colouring; and of a grace and energy, which hardly any of the modern languages can make their own.——The speeches of the persons, that he brings forward on the stage, are not ever without interest, and they are sometimes moving and pathetic. These are beauties, which would certainly command our approbation in any other work, where the stern austerity of history did not consider them as inadmissible.

Q. Curtius ingenuously avows, that he hath transcribed more events than he believed, and that he meant not to be responsible for those of which he doubted, but was unwilling to suppress.²

After

---

¹ "Geographiæ nonnunquam et historiæ rationes turbasse; parum scienter in præliis describendis fuisse versatum; non satis accurato delectu vera discrevisse à falsis; speciosa magis, quam certiora, sectatum esse; sententiarum aculeos affectasse plusculum; descriptionibus quandoque poeticos flores; orationibus declamatorium colorem adspercisse!" Præf. in edit. Q. Curtii, ad usum Delphini.

² "Equidem plura transcribo quam credo: nam nec affirmare sustineo, de quibus dubito; nec subducere quæ accepi." Q. Curtius, Lib. 9. Chap. 1. Tom. 2.--676.

After such an acknowledged intimation, have we to expect any thing but a monstrous and mixed assemblage of truth and falsehood? Many learned men have imagined that he borrowed most of his relations from Diodorus Siculus, but it seems more probable, that Clitarchus, an author well known to the Romans, as appears from several passages in Cicero and Pliny, had been equally copied by these historians.——Q. Curtius however only cites him twice: in the first instance it is to refute Ptolemy. The valuable memoirs of this illustrious successor of Alexander were then, it seems, in being; but led astray by his love of the marvellous and a fondness for fables, Q. Curtius had given the preference to the recitals of Clitarchus, which agreed more with his own character and genius.

We are told that Nero gilt the statue of Alexander by Lysippus, imagining to en͡ ce   lue:[b] Q. Curtius acted on the same principle, when he su͡   ͡u that the flowers of his imagination would add a fresh wreath of glory to Alexander's laurels. But the Hero and the Artist lost by these foolish decorations.——The Roman historian gives way to an excessive passion for descriptions; and without considering whether they are connected with the incidents of which he treats, he frequently introduces them

---

[b] "Fecit et Alexandrum Magnum.—Quam statuam inaurari jussit Nero princeps, delectatus admodum illa. Dein cum pretio periisset gratia artis, detractum est aurum: pretiosiorque talis existimatur, etiam cicatricibus operis atque concisuris, in quibus aurum hæserat, remanentibus." Plin. Hist. Nat. Lib. 34. C. 19. Tom. 5.--117. 4to Par. 1685.

them abruptly. In endeavouring to make his pictures brilliant they are incorrect: in attempting to enrich them, they become confused. When Lucian, in his directions for historical composition, recommended a sober chastity of expression in the account of mountains and rivers,[c] the ingenious critic in all likelihood had Q. Curtius before his eye, and particularly the episodical details, into which he enters respecting the courses of the rivers Marsyas,[d] Pasitigris,[e] and Zioberis in Hyrcania,[f] which engrossed his attention in preference to events of real consequence. From an insatiable fondness for these descriptions many important circumstances are neglected; and the war between Alexander and the nephew of King Porus is scarcely noticed,[g] though both Arrian and Strabo have mentioned it.—In the last two books, he passes indeed with such rapidity from one transaction to another, that we have reason to apprehend many essential facts have been either totally forgotten, or very much neglected.——The seasons, in which the different events happened, are only

marked

---

[c] "Μαλιϛα δι σωφρονητιον εν ταις των ορων, η τειχων, η ποταμων ερμηνειας, ως μη δυναμιν λογων απειροκαλως παρεπιδεικνυσθαι δοκοιης, κ᾽ το σαυτα δραν, παρες την ισοριαν." Lucian. Quom. Hist. conscrip. C. 57. Tom. 2.--65.

[d] Q. Curtius. Lib. 3. C. 1. Tom. 1.--52.

[e] ———— Lib. 5. C. 3. Tom. 1.--328.

[f] ———— Lib. 6. C. 4. Tom. 1.--406.

[g] "Hinc Poro amnique superato." (Q. Curt. Lib. 9. C. 1. Tom. 2.--670.) See Friensheim's note upon the passage.

marked in a vague and obscure manner,[h] and of the several years we have not any indication whatever, but this disorder proceeds from his inaccuracy. Still is he less attentive to any geographical information,[i] and his authority in this respect may be with strict propriety rejected, whilst the explication, that he hath given of the eclipse of the moon, before the battle of Gaugamele, proves incontestably his ignorance of the common principles of astronomy.[k]—Adding to these observations the fables and exaggerations

so

---

[h] The Baron de St. Croix hath produced the expression of "Sub ipsum Vergiliarum sidus," (Lib. 5. Chap. 6. Tom. 1.--352.) as one instance of the uncertainty and obscurity of Q. Curtius. The Commentators have been much divided as to this expression, and have doubted, whether the rising or the setting of the Pleiades was to be understood. Their setting is now generally supposed to be intended, and indeed the passage of Plutarch in his life of Alexander, "Βουλομενος δε της ςρατιωτας αναλαβειν (και γαρ ην χειμων⊙ ωρα) τεσσαρις μηνας αυτοθι διηγαγεν" (Tom. 1. 686.) seems to elucidate it very plainly, as Pliny informs us the "Vergiliarum occasus hyemem inchoat, quod tempus in 3. Id. Novembris incidere consuevit." Hist. Nat. Lib. 2. Chap. 47. Tom. 1.--200.

[i] "De Curtio non laboramus, sæpe in geographicis aberrante." Cellar. Geograph. Antiq. Tom. 2.--3. Le Clerc with more severity says, "Immania etiam sunt peccata, quæ in eum admisit Curtius." Clerici Ind. de Curtio, Ars Critica. Tom. 2.--133.

[k] Monsf. Dupuy remarks that Q. Curtius, "Apres avoir decrit la consternation qui repandit dans l'armée d'Alexandre une eclipse de lune, observe que les divins Egyptiens, que ce prince fit consulter, savoient fort bien la raison de ce phenomene, mais qu'ils tenoient cachée au vulgaire." "At illi," "ce sont ses paroles," "qui satis scirent temporum orbes implere destinatas vices, lunamque deficere quam aut terra subiret, aut sole premeretur, rationem quidem ipsis perceptam non edocent vulgus." (Lib. 4. Chap. 10. Tom. 1.--241.) "L'Historien a-t-il eû une idée bien nette de la cause des eclipses lunaires? Il semble, à l'entendre, que la lune peut s'eclipser en deux cas; ou lorsque "terram subit," ou lorsque "premitur à sole." On peut donner un bon sens a la premiere expression, parce qu'effectivement la lune s'eclipse lorsqu'elle passe sous la terre, "terram subit," qui est entre elle et le soleil: mais qu'a-t-il pretendu, lorsqu'il a dit que la lune souffre eclipse "cum sole premitur." lorsqu'elle est pressée par le soleil. Hist. de l'Aca[d.] des Inscriptions. Tom. 29.--324.

so familiar to him, perhaps there is not a single author of antiquity, that should be read with more reserve, or with greater care against the seductions of his language. His evidence for these reasons is to be received with very limited credit, and cannot possibly be opposed to that of the other historians of Alexander, and of Arrian in particular.

Justin, who may be referred to the age of Antoninus Pius,[1] hath left us an abridgment of the more extensive compilation of Trogus Pompeius; but he signs his own sentence of condemnation, in his preservation of the order and method of the original. Confusion in the narrative, and inaccuracy in the facts are the common faults of this Latin writer, who hath devoted the eleventh and twelfth chapters of his work to the exploits of Alexander. Precision

---

The Jesuit Rader hath endeavoured to vindicate the historian, and to explain his meaning. "Curtius non rudis mathefeos, physicas rationes adfert defectionis lunæ, unam cum terram subit, alteram cum sole premitur. Una efficit eclipsem, altera silentium lunæ. Eclipsis fit in plenilunio, silentium in novilunio. Terram subit, cum in umbram terræ incurrit, non cum descendit ad inferius cælum, infra finitorem, quem Græci 'Ορίζοντα dicunt. Sole premeretur, sicut et ipsa vicissim solem premit, cum sol infra terram est, et luna supra recto libramento, cum in umbrâ terræ est, unde fortasse, est quod Lucretius dixit:

"——Et oppressum solem super ipsâ tenere."
(Lucret. Lib. 5.—762.)

Quamvis Lucretius de terrâ interjectâ loquatur." (Q. Curtius Raderi, 203.) But with all his subtilty, though we may allow of the poetic licence of the

"Defectus solis varios lunæque labores,"
(Virgil. Georg. Lib. 2.--478.)

in the cold and correct page of History, the expression is an awkward one.

[1] G. Vossius, de hist. Lat. Lib. 1. Chap. 31.

cifion ought indifpenfably to characterize an abridgment of every denomination, but when he fpeaks of Alexander's actions, he is extremely fuperficial. Exclufive of thefe defects, his authority is very queftionable, in comparifon with that of the other hiftorians of the Macedonian Monarch, that have been already mentioned, the text is very incorrect; and the names of the towns and people, that he hath introduced, are disfigured to a degree that renders them almoft unintelligible.

The Lower Empire memorable for its darknefs, its barbarity and fuperftition, hath notwithftanding produced fome authors, that have taken notice of Alexander. Exceptionable as their teftimony is, even when relating to the events, of which they were fpectators, undoubtedly it deferves lefs credit refpecting thofe, which paffed in more remote ages, and in times previous to their exiftence. There is not therefore any light to be procured from them, relative to any public tranfactions before the tranflation of the feat of Empire; and their performances are in general crude and ill-digefted compilations, fcraped together without learning, and collected without tafte.

George Syncellus makes Alexander to arrive in the middle of Affyria [m] immediately after the engagement at Iffus, and places Arbela and

---

[m] "Εν Ισσω της Κιλικιας αυτω πολιμει Δαρειω· και τελευταιον εισω χωρις της Ασσυριας·" G. Syncellus, 210. Folio. Venet, 1729.

and the field of battle known under its name in Media;" and assures us, that this Prince having reached Caucasus, reduced all the neighbouring barbarous nations under his subjection as far as the Palus Mæotis, ° and that after this expedition he extended his conquests over India, and came to the Ganges. ᵖ——Such is the accuracy of the writers of the Lower Empire!

From the multifarious additions, with which the Lexicon of Suidas hath been gradually loaden, many gross errors have been inserted in it; and as the article of Alexander ᵠ itself is not exempt

ⁿ "Η εν Αρβηλοις της Μηδικης ηχθη μαχη." G. Syncellus. 208.

° The French text stands as follows, "Et nous assure que ce prince partit des Palus Mæotis." but Syncellus says, "Γενομενος δε και εν Καυκασω κρατει των αυτοθι βαρβαρων μεχρι Μαιωτιδος λιμνης ελθων." (G. Syncellus. 210.) which has a very different import, and I have adopted it.

ᵖ "Κακειθεν μεταχωρησας, επι της Ινδους παντος τε κρατησας εθνες Ινδικα μεχρι ποταμου Γαγγη παλιν αναξευγνυσι δια τε Ινδα ποταμα μεχρι της Ινδικης θαλασσης." (G. Syncellus. 210.) Both these passages are to be found in the same words in Eusebius, Κρονικων. Lib. 1.--57.

ᵠ The account of Alexander hath most certainly increased in magnitude and length as it descended. The Baron de St. Croix considers the whole of it from the "'Οτι Αλεξανδρος ὁ Μακεδων," to the "Αυτος οκτασιοις ανδρασιν"' (Suidas, Tom. 1.--102.) as an interpolation, and it must be allowed, it bears strong symptoms of suspicion. Roxana, he judiciously observes, is there said to be the daughter of Darius, which is a direct contradiction of what Suidas had before advanced, where she is called the daughter of Oxyartes; that the adventure of Candace is evidently taken from the chronicle of Malala; that the anecdote concerning the music of Timotheus occurs in the same words under "Τιμοθεως," which is the proper place for it; and that the passage respecting the naval victory over the Lacedæmonians, the structure of the wall round the Piræus, and the festival given to the Athenians, as copied from Athenæus, and to be found again in the same words under "Αθηναι&.," (Suidas, Tom. 1.--71.) had been applied to Alexander by some

ignorant

empt from them, it can be of but little service to us in the history of this Prince.

Cedrenus hath entered into details of some length on the Macedonian Monarch's expedition. And he supposes him after the reduction of Judea and the capture of Cyrene, to have marched into Egypt, and from thence by a branch of the Nile to have advanced into Assyria, pressed on towards Paropamisus and the country watered by the Thermodon, and penetrated afterwards to Phasis,' the Straits of Gibraltar, and even into Britain. '——— The whole geography of the ancient world is by this means totally deranged, and there is not even the least historical resemblance attempted to be preserved. Amongst these events, he takes care however, to report Alexander's visit to Jerusalem, with the

---

ignorant transcriber, (the name of Conon having been accidentally effaced) and afterwards added to Suidas. Kaster, in his note on the word "Ἀλεξανδρος," (Suidas, Tom. 1.--103.) admits the falsity of these last assertions, but in that on the word "Ἀθηναιϲ," (Suidas, Tom. 1.--71.) he doubts whether Suidas or some of his copyists are responsible for it. "Quæ hic de Alexandro Magno referantur, Athenæus, unde locus Suidæ depromptus est, Cononi et quidem recte tribuit. Ratio diversitatis est, quod apud Suidam omissa sint verba quædam (ipsiusne Suidæ an vero aliorum culpa haud facile dixeris) quæ apud Athenæum leguntur." These interpolations the Baron de St. Croix hath laid to the charge of the writers of the middle age, who borrowed liberally from the oriental authors, and he adds that the contradictory statement of Roxana's birth was an Eastern tradition, arising from the Persian name of Rawshanè (the daughter of Darius, and married to Alexander, according to Abulpharagius) which had been confounded with that of Roxana, from some little similitude in the pronunciation.

' In Cedrenus, Phasis is called Aphasis. "Εκειθεν δε προς Αφασιν και Γαδειρα, και τα βρετταννησια ὁση γενομενος." G. Cedrenus, 321.

' G. Cedrenus, 151, 152. 153.

the principal circumstances imagined by the Jews, and with expressions,[1] that cannot reasonably be attributed to Dexippus,[w] devoted to Polytheism, of a sacerdotal family, and a priest himself singularly zealous and attached to his own creed.——Scaliger hath apparently deceived himself in the supposition that the author of these recitals was Dexippus; but this great scholar did not recollect that Cedrenus only cites[x] this celebrated writer on Alexander's

---

[1] "Επι την Ιουδαιαν ελθων, και ταυτην ελων, υπο του Αρχιερεως Αδδω τιμηθεις θυσας τω Θεω, ως περ αυτω την οικυμενην προστειληφως." G. Cedrenus, 121.

[w] Publius Herennius Dexippus lived in the 3rd age of the vulgar era, and was in rotation honoured with all the principal offices at Athens. He was celebrated also as a rhetorician and historian, and acquired a very extensive reputation from his literary labours. On the subject of universal history, his application was unwearied, and with a sort of intuitive sagacity he penetrated into the inmost and obscurest recesses of antiquity. His children were authorized, by a decree of the Areopagus and the council of 750, to erect a monument to his glory, and the inscription still subsists.

"Οικοθεν ιερα Παναγη"——
Και αγωνοθετησαντα των μεγαλων Παναθηναιων
Ανδρας αγακλειτυς τετροφε Κεκροπιη
Ην ενακας Δεξιππον, ος ιστοριαν εσαθρησας
Αιωνος δολιχην ατρεκεως εφασεν
Και τα μεν αυτος επειδε ταδ' εκ βιβλων αναλεξας
Ηυξατο παντοιην ιστοριης ατραπον
Η μεγακλεινος ανηρ ος να απο μυριον ομμα
Εκτεινας, χρονιυς πρηξιας εξεμαθεν."

Ed. Chandler, Inscript. Antiq. Pars 2.—56. Oxon. Folio, 1774.

[x] The Baron de St. Croix observes that on a comparison of St. Jerom's translation of the chronicle of Eusebius, with the pretended Greek text, which Scaliger ushered under his name into the world, the conviction will naturally follow, that many of its supplemental parts are flagrant contradictions of Eusebius. Cedrenus, according to his opinion only cites Dexippus concerning the education of Alexander. The learned reader will exercise his own judgment on the passage,

ander's education, and that the rest of what relates to this Prince cannot be considered as an extract, and much less as a fragment of

passage, with the introductory and following sentences. "Ἀρτι δε τα Φιλιππα τα παιδος Ἀλεξανδρα επι την ακμην της ἡλικιας προελθοντος, οἱ πρωτοι των Μακεδονων αυτον αιρουνται εις βασιλεια· επι δε εις την αρχην προηλθεν Ἀλεξανδρος, κατ' αμφοιν το γενος ἐσεμνυνεν· ουδε γαρ εςιν ἑυρειν εν παντι τω κοσμω ανδρα τοσετοις κατορθωμασι πλεονεκτουντα· ὡς γαρ Δεξιππος ἱςορει, πασαν ασκησιν ησκηθη σωματικην Ἀριςοτελες γνησιωτατος γεγονως φοιτητης, εις το λογες αριςος και εις εργα επαινεμενος ἑυρεθη· τα δε πολεμικα θαυμασως ἐπελθων πασας αξια διεπραξετο· Βασιλευσας γαρ χρονες οκτω, τες Μακεδονας και Ἰλλυριας, και Θρακας ἑπεταξε, την Ἑλλαδα κατεςρεψε· και τες τε πατρος φονεας τιμωρησαμενος, και τους Πέρσας ἀποταξας επι την Ασιαν διαπερα· και την Πριαμε πολιν, και τας εν Λυδια Σαρδεις ὑποταξας επι Κιλικιαν ἀφικνειται·" (Cedrenus. 121.) In Scaliger's edition of the chronicle of Eusebius, the account of Alexander's entry into Judea and his interview with the Jewish high priest, is there introduced with "Ἐκ τε Δεξιππε· Ἀλεξανδρος Ἰλλυριες και Θρακας ἑιλε· Θηβας κατεσκαψε τε Δαρειε ςρατηγες επι Γρανικω ποταμω Λυδων ενικησε, Σαρδεις ἑιλε· Τυρον επολιορκησεν· Ἰεδαιαν προσελαβετο, και τον ἀρχιερεα Ἰαδδεν ετιμησε θυσας τω Θεω ὡς παρ' αυτε οικεμενην ὁμολογων παρειληφεναι·" (Κρονικων. Lib. 1.–56, 57.) There is a detail afterwards of many circumstances concerning the Macedonian Monarch, which is also prefaced with the "Ἐκ τε Δεξιππε," and swells to some extent. I am ignorant of the precise authority on which Scaliger supposed them to be extracts from Dexippus, but being printed within inverted commas, they carry with them every typographical appearance of quotations. In support however of the Baron de St. Croix's opinion, it may be observed that the expression "Ὡς γαρ Δεξιππος ἱςορει," does not imply an exact quotation, but in a larger sense may signify that the relation corresponded with that of Dexippus. Syncellus also first speaks of Alexander's entry into Judea and his interview with the Jewish high priest, without saying any thing of Dexippus. To quote the passage would be to repeat that already cited from Eusebius, for it is literally the same, with the single exception of "Ἰαδδες" instead of "Ἰαδδεν." He then relates some farther particulars of Alexander, and gives a sort of history of the Heraclides, and of various other persons and events, and returning to the Macedonian Monarch, he tells us, "Ἀλεξανδρος ουν κ χγων ετος, κατα Δεξιππον, πασαν ασκησιν ησκημενος σωματικην. αιτε τε γνησιωτατης Ἀριστοτελες γνωνης του δαιμονωντος φοιτητης επι την πατρωαν παρηλθε βασιλειαν·" (Syncellus. 210.) It is remarkable that the same passage occurs in Eusebius, (Κρονικων. Lib. 1.–57.) and that the three accounts of Alexander's entry into Judea, and his interview with the Jewish high priest by the historians, that have been referred to, are delivered in nearly the same words, from which there arises a strong inference that they copied them from some other writer. The "Θυσας τω Θεω, ὡς παρ' αυτε οικεμενην, &c." is to be found in all of them, but Cedrenus makes the high priest "Ἀδδαν," instead of "Ἰαδδεν." Eusebius and Syncellus give us "Τον αρχιερεα ετιμησε," but Cedrenus, with a greater allowance for human fears and apprehensions, hath "Ὑπο τε Ἀρχιερεως τιμηθεις."

of Dexippus, whom Photius [7] hath not fcrupled to compare with Thucydides.

Paulus Orofius can only be reckoned the copyift of Juftin, and Zonares [z] in his turn feems to have derived his information from Diodorus Siculus. His abridgment however of Alexander's expeditions is not without merit, and is more correct, than might have been expected from a writer of the twelfth century, who quitted a court from fuperftitious motives, to bury himfelf within a cloifter. With the productions of thefe writers, the works of Eufebius of Cæfarea are not to be confounded, and important both to literature and to religion, they have undoubted pretenfions to particular diftinction. Yet it muft not be diffembled, that his difcernment was not always equal to his erudition.[a]——This laborious writer is not very exact in his chronicle concerning Alexander, and it was after the death of Darius, according to his ideas, that the Grecian Hero made himfelf the mafter of Babylon,[b] notwithftanding it was previous to the affaffination of the Perfian Monarch. Eufebius informs us alfo, that the Macedonian Prince having fubdued the Hyrcanians and the Medes, returned and founded

---

[7] "Εςι δε την φρασιν απεριίτος τι, και ογκω και αξιωματι χαιρων, και (ὡς αν τις ειποι) αλλ. μετα τινος ταχυτιας Θυκυδιδης." Photii Biblioth. 200.

[z] Zonares. Annales, 137, 148.

[a] "Πολεμαςὴς δε εςιν ὁ ανηρ, η κ την αχινοιαν κ το σαθηρον τε ηθες, ὡς παρα την ακριβειαν την εν τοις δογμασιν ενδετερος." Photii Biblioth. 12.

[b] "Obtinuit Babylonem interfecto Dario." Eufebius, 31.

founded Parætonium [c] in the country of Ammon; but this city was in being before Alexander, [d] and he never returned from the extremities of the East into Lybia.

Athenagoras, [e] and after him St. Augustin [f] and St. Cyprian, [g] relate that Alexander informed his mother by letter, that the priests of Heliopolis, of Memphis, and of Thebes, had confessed to him, that their gods were originally men, whom they had deified; [h] a sentiment disproved by the evidence of the priests themselves, [i] and which could not possibly be conciliated with the essence of Egyptianism.

---

[c] "Alexander Hyrcanos et Medos capit: revertens in Ammone condidit Parætonium." Eusebius, 34. See Scaliger's note on this passage. Scaligeri Animad. ad Eusebium. 126.

[d] Scylax. Peripl. 40. apud geograp. minores. Tom. 1.

[e] Legat. pro Christ. ad Cal. St. Justin. 325.

[f] De Civitate Dei. L. 8, 6, 27. L. 12, 6. 10.

[g] "Hoc ita esse Alexander Magnus infigni volumine ad matrem suam scribit. Metu suæ potestatis proditum sibi de Diis hominibus à sacerdotibus secretum: quod majorum et regum memoria servata sit, inde colendi et sacrificandi ritus insolverit." St. Cyprian, de Idd. Vauit. 9. Amst. Folio. 1700.

[h] This opinion however hath been formally attacked by one, who hath looked deep into antiquity. "On a pretendu qu'ils avoient etabli pour faire voir que les Dieux etoient tous des hommes, qui avoient eté deifiés a cause des services, qu'ils avoient rendus au genre humain. Mais il faudroit, pour que cela pût etre adopté, qu'on en trouvat de preuves dans l'antiquité, ce qui est impossible, l'antiquité n'ayant jamais deifié des hommes." Monde Primitif, par M. Court de Gebelin. 311.

[i] Herodotus. 120. to 132.

St. Clement [k] and St. Cyrill, [l] the patriarchs of Alexandria, accuse the Pagans with having acknowledged Alexander for their thirteenth deity; but such a rank had never been assigned him, and even the Athenians had the resolution to fine the orator Demades ten talents, for proposing to inscribe the Macedonian Monarch in the number of their divinities. [m] It is notwithstanding very certain, that Alexander's successors ordered divine honours to be paid to him, [n] and that the Romans erected temples [o] inscribed with his name; though there was not, as St. Chrysostom [p] hath

[k] "Οἱ δὲ γὰρ ἀνθρώποις ἀποθέσιν τετιλμήκασι, τρὶς καὶ δέκατον Ἀλέξανδρον τὸν Μακεδόνα ἀναγράφοντες Θεόν, ὃν Βαβυλὼν ἥλεγξε νεκρόν." Clement. Alex. Cohort. ad Gent. Tom. 1.--77. Oxon. 1715.

[l] "Ἀλέξανδρον δὲ τὸν Φιλίππου τρὶς καὶ δέκατον ἐδόκει Θεὸν ὀνομάζειν τοῖς κατ' ἐκεῖνο καιρῷ." Cyrill contra Julianum, Lib. 6. Juliani opera, Tom. 2.--205. Folio. Lipf. 1696.

[m] The Baron de St. Croix might have added the sentence of death against Evagoras, as related by Athenæus. "Δημάδης δὲ δέκα ταλάντοις ἐζημιώσαν, ὅτι Θεὸν εἰσηγήσατο Ἀλέξανδρον, καὶ Εὐαγόραν δὲ ἀπέκτειναν, ὅτι πρεσβεύων ὡς βασιλέα προσεκύνησεν αὐτόν" (Lib. 6. 251.) Plutarch hath preserved a Bon Mot on this occasion, "Πυθέας ἔτι μειράκιον ὤν, παρηλθεν ἀντερῶν τοῖς περὶ Ἀλέξανδρον γραφομένοις ψηφίσμασιν· εἰπόντος δὲ τινός, Σὺ νέος ὢν τολμᾷς λέγειν περὶ τηλικούτων; καὶ μὴν, Ἀλέξανδρος, εἶπεν, ὃν ψηφίζεσθε Θεόν, ἐμοῦ νεώτερος ἐστί." (Apothegm. Tom. 2.--187.) Such a sarcastic reply as the Baron de St. Croix hath observed, seems of itself sufficient to have rendered useless and ineffectual all the intrigues and eloquence of Demades. Yet he had made rather a serious appeal to the Athenians. "Videte," inquit, "ne dum cælum custoditis, terram amittatis." (Val. Max. Lib. 7. 62.--638. 4to Leid. 1726.) Lucian however, still seems to intimate it, "Ἐνίοι δὲ καὶ τοῖς δώδεκα Θεοῖς προσιθέντες, καὶ νεὼς οἰκοδομούμενοι καὶ θύοντες." Lucian. Dial. Mort. 13. Tom. 1.--391.

[n] La Dissertation de Monf. L'Abbé Belley. Memoires de l'Academie des Inscriptions et des Belles Lettres. Tom. 32.--685. See also Barthius ad Statium. Tom. 1.--403, 404.

[o] It was in one of these temples that Alexander Severus was born according to Lampridius. "Alexander nomen accepit, quod in templo, dicato apud Arcenem urbem Alexandro Magno, natus esset." Historiæ Angustæ Scriptores. Tom. 1.--889.

[p] Homil. 26. in Epist. ad Corinthios.

hath afferted, any obligation by a decree of the Senate, to offer him adoration as their thirteenth deity. The worfhip of the deities of other nations was in fact often prohibited at Rome, fometimes barely tolerated, and refpectful allowances are to be made for writings, in which fuch things are recorded, without either an outrage to veracity in a culpable filence, or inattention to them.

The memory of the exploits of the Macedonian Conqueror is ftill treafured up with veneration in the regions of the Eaft. Both the Perfian, and Arabian authors, often fpeak of him under the name of Efcander, and he figures as a principal Hero of their romance. Eldrifi[q] confounds him with Hercules, Abulpharagius and Ebnbatric[r] trace his defcent from one of the Kings of Egypt; and others affirm that the Empire of Iran, or of the Perfians, became his property by hereditary right, rather than by the force of arms.[s] Amidft all thefe fables, and a multitude of others, fome fhining traits are diftinctly vifible, which mark the Conqueror of Darius and of Afia; and many of his actions, though they may have fuffered alterations, clearly point out the fplendid Perfonage to whom they were applied.

[q] Eldrifi. Geograph. Nub. 148.

[r] Abulpharagius. Hift. Dynaft. ex Verf. Pocock. 57.

[s] Mirkhoud. Sect. 20.

SECT.

SECTION. II.

HAPPY are the People, in whose annals neither the enterprises of an ambitious Prince, nor the exploits of a Conqueror are to be traced, which seldom fail of being deplorable misfortunes for the subject. The history of Macedon affords us a striking instance of this truth, in the melancholy spectacle of the misery, that followed so immediately the moments of its glory.——Philip's power was the fatal source of repeated wars and numerous revolutions.——His Successor reaped the fruit of all his toils, and realized with ardour and activity those ideal conquests, with which the Macedonian Monarch was occupied, when he died suddenly, in the first year of the 111th Olympiad, during the chief magistracy of Pythodemus,* 418 years before the foundation of Rome, and

---

* We have this information from Arrian, (Exped. Alex. Lib. 1. Chap. 1.--5-6.) but he prefaces it with "Λεγεται δε." The Athenian Archon was the Chief of the nine magistrates, and the Athenian year was distinguished by his name like the Roman year by that of their consuls. "Γραφει δε τατε αλλα διοικησι τα σπυδες μαλιςα αξια, και παριχονται τον επωνυμον; καθα δη και Αθηναιοις των καθ' ἱκαςον ινιαυτον ιπωνυμος ιςιν ὁ αρχων." (Pausanius. Laconic. 231. 232.) These nine magistrates

and 336 before the vulgar era. The young Prince took the reins of government into his hands in the following year, according to Diodorus Siculus, when Evenætus was Archon,[b] but this historian contradicts himself afterwards, when he relates that Alexander reigned twelve years and seven months,[c] which carries back the time that Alexander became possessed of the throne of his ancestors to the fifth month of the chief magistracy of Pythodemus.

Dionysius of Halicarnassus, refers the commencement of Alexander's reign to the preceding year, when Phrynicus was Archon, in the fourth year of the 110th Olympiad, as he assures us that Demosthenes pronounced his oration on the crown under Aristophon, the third year of the 112th Olympiad, and six[d] years after Philip's

---

magistrates according to Julius Pollux bore the following names, "Αρχων, Βασιλευς, Πολεμαρχος, ἑξ Θεσμοθεται." (Lib. 8.) Julius Pollux hath also given the Archon the addition of "Του ενιαυτη επωνυμος," which Selden hath translated "Anni signator." (Marmon. Arund.) The English reader may learn many particulars of these offices from Potter's Grecian Antiquities, Vol. 1.-76. and the scholar may be gratified with more curious information by turning to Petit. Leges. Attic. 236. and Budæus, Comment. Græc. Linguæ. 172. &c. &c.

[b] "Επ'αρχοντος γαρ Αθηνησιν Γυαινετη———Αλεξανδρος διαδεξαμενος την βασιλειαν." Diod. Sicul. Lib. 17. Tom. 2.--161.

[c] "Τον προειρημενον τροπον ετελευσε; βασιλευσας ετη δωδεκα και μηνας επτα." Diod. Sicul. Lib. 17. Tom. 2.--253.

[d] "Huit ans apres la mort de Philip." Dionysius of Halicarnassus, in the passage referred to, speaking of the oration, "Περι τε στεφανε," says, "Ουτος γαρ μονος εις δικαστηριον εισεληλυθεν μετα τον πολεμον επ'Αριστοφωντος αρχοντος, ογδοω μεν ενιαυτω μετα την εν Χαιρωνεια μαχην, εκτω δε μετα την Φιλιππε τελευτην"' (Dionysius Halicarnassus. Epist. ad Ammæum. Tom. 6.--746.) I have corrected the error, but the Greek text is so very plain, and the eight years relate so very clearly to the battle of Chæronæa, that I must confess the mistake created in me some little indignation.

Philip's death. This calculation however does not appear to be correct, for Philip died during the magiſtracy of Pythodemus, in the Macedonian month Dius, which was the firſt month of their Solar year, and anſwered to that of Puanepſion in the Attic year. The certainty of this date is aſcertained by the twelve years and eight months, which Arrian allots to Alexander's reign, who died, as we ſhall find afterwards, at the end of the month Thargalion. Eratoſthenes hath alſo ſettled the period of this reign, who reckons thirty-five [e] years between Philip's death and the battle of Leuctra, which happened according to the chronicle of Paros [f] in the chief magiſtracy of Phraſiclides, the ſecond year of the 102nd Olympiad, and this evidently fixes Philip's death in the Archonſhip of Pythodemus.

The defeat of the Triballians, the Thracians, the Getæ, the Autoriates, the Tralentians, and of the Agrionians, and the reduction of the different people, who made on the death of Philip an effort to recover their liberty, with ſome flattering expectations from the youth of his Son, were Alexander's firſt exploits. [g]

Both

---

[e] Ap. Clement. Alex. Strom. Lib. 1. Tom. 1,--402. Apud Morell.

[f] Epoch. 73.

[g] Plutarch hath very briefly given us an account of the difficulties, with which Alexander was embarraſſed on the death of Philip. "Παρελαβε μεν ουν ετη γεγονως εικοσι την βασιλειαν, φθονους μεγαλους κ; δεινα μιση κ; κινδυνους πανταχοθεν εχουσαν· ουτε γαρ τα βαρβαρα κ; προσοικα γενη την δουλω συν εφεριν, ποθουντα τας πατριους βασιλειας· ουτε την Ελλαδα κρατησας τοις οπλοις ο Φιλιππος, όσον καταζευ-ξαι κ; τιθασευσαι χρονον ιχεν, αλλα μονον μεταβαλων κ; ταραξας τα πραγματα, πολυν σαλον εχοντα κ; κινησιν υπο απηθειας, απελιπεν." Vit. Alex. Plut. Opera. Tom. 1.--670.

Both Diodorus and Plutarch pafs haftily over thefe expeditions, in which the young Monarch's military talents were firft unfolded: Arrian is the only writer, that hath extended an account of them to any fatisfactory length,[h] and it even ftill includes fome difficulties. Thrace was the theatre of war, and it is fcarcely to be conceived, that the Taulentians, the inhabitants of a little tract of country northward of Epirus, fhould have been expofed to any mifunderftanding with Alexander, and fhould have come from fuch a diftance to have joined his enemies. Perhaps by the Taulentians, the Illyrians are to be underftood, over whom Glaucias the King of the Taulentians had ftretched his Empire, and who were afterwards confidered as the fame people with their conquerors, and diftinguifhed by one common name. This conjecture appears to be authorized by the text of Arrian,[i] and hath been adopted by the learned Palmer in his obfervations upon ancient Greece.[k]

The Celtes, whofe country bordered on the Ionic gulph, now the Adriatic fea, difpatched ambaffadors to Alexander, and in a converfation with them he inquired what was the greateft object of

[h] Arrian, Exped. Alex. Lib. 1. Chap. 1, 2, 3, 4, 6. -- 7, 30.

[i] And it feems to be confirmed by what Arrian fays of the Athenian embaffy, to congratulate Alexander on his profperous return from his expedition againft the Illyrians and Triballians. "Ὅτι τε σωος εξ Ιλλυριων ϰ̓ Τριβαλλων επανηλθε" (Exped. Alex. Lib. 1. Chap. 10.--43.) Thucydides hath alfo called the Taulentians "Ιλλυρικον εθν⸳." Thucydides, Lib. 1.--20.

[k] Palmer Græciæ Antiq. Defcriptio. Lib. 1. Chap. 18.

of their fears, imagining that the terror of his exploits had already reached them.' Of the fall of the fky, was fuppofed to have been their fpirited reply. This ftory which Arrian hath extracted from Ptolemy's memoirs, as appears by Strabo, ᵐ was in all likelihood an epifode invented as an ornament to the hiftory of Alexander. It is not probable that thefe Celtes, who were the ancient Boians or Senones, in poffeffion of a country inacceffible in point of fituation, and at a diftance from the contending nations, fhould without any motive have fent ambaffadors to court the friendfhipⁿ of a Prince, with whom they had not either any connection or concern.

Juftin ° relates, that Alexander felected the different tributary Kings, whofe abilities and talents were likely to be formidable to him,

---

¹ "Τοις Κελτικους δε κ̣ ηρετο, ὁ, τι μαλιϛα δεδιττεται αυτους των ανθρωπινων, ελπισας οτι μεγα ονομα το αυτου κ̣ ες Κελτικους κ̣ ετι προσωτερω ήκει·" Arrian. Exped. Alex. Lib. 1. Chap. 4.--20.

ᵐ "Φησι δε Πτολεμαιος ο Λαγου, κατα ταυτην την ϛρατειαν συμμιξαι τω Αλεξανδρω Κελτυς τυς περι τεν Αδριαν, φιλιας κ̣ ξενιας χαριν· δεξαμενον δε αυτυς φιλοφρονως τον βασιλεα, ερεϛαι παρ τον ποτον, τι μαλιϛα ειη ο φοβοιντο, νομιζοντα αυτον ερειν· αυτους δε αποκρινεϛαι, ουδενα, ει μη αρα ο ουρανος αυτοις επιπεσοι·" Strabo. Lib. 7.--462.

ⁿ The Baron de St. Croix's expreffion is "Seroient ils venus fans aucun motif proftituer leur hommage." Arrian does not warrant this idea, by the "Φιλιας δε παντες της Αλεκανδρου εφιεμενοι·" (Exped. Alex. Lib. 1. Chap. 4.--20.) There is a wide difference between the defire of a friendfhip and alliance with a Monarch, and the flavifh offer of paffive and unlimited obedience to him. The latter did not form any part of the Celtic character, and was utterly inconfiftent with the genius of that bold and warlike nation.

° "Reges ftipendiarios confpectioris ingenii ad commilitium fecum trahit: fegnioris ad tutelam regni reliquit." (Juftin. Lib. 11. Chap. 5.--265.) If we are to credit Juftin, Alexander acted

on

him, and carried them away with him. Frontinus[p] tells us, that the vanquished princes and even the principal persons of the conquered countries were taken, on the same refined plan of policy, into Asia, as honourable attendants upon Alexander; but the rest of the historians, without any observation on the subject, pass it over in profound silence.—Policy made it necessary for Alexander to assure himself of the fidelity of Greece by some great stroke before he quitted it, and the revolt of Thebes, afforded him an ample opportunity, in every respect favourable to his wishes. The city

---

on a still more barbarous principle, and to ensure the safety of his government, cut off without exception all his own family relations, who from a proximity of blood, or their high rank, might have taken the advantage of his absence and endeavoured to have seated themselves upon his throne. "Proficiscens ad Persicum bellum, omnes novercæ suæ cognatos, quos Philippus in excelsiorem dignitatis locum provehens, imperiis præfecerat, interfecit. Sed nec suis, qui apti regno videbantur, pepercit; ne qua materia seditionis, procul se agente, in Macedoniâ remaneret." (Lib. 11. Chap. 5.--265.) In the crooked and corrupted school of politics, such unhappy victims of imperial policy have frequently been slaughtered, but reason and humanity have always raised their voices against this dreadful waste of human blood. In proportion as the mild spirit of Christianity hath been attended to, these scenes have disappeared, and it is some consolation to reflect, that the historians of a future century will have fewer extravagant instances of tyranny and cruelty either to record, or to lament.

[p] "Frontine ne fait point cette distinction : il pretend que tous les princes vaincus subirent un pareil sort." I have been under the indispensable necessity of varying this sentence. Frontinus on the contrary, proves as far as his evidence hath any weight, that Alexander pursued the same system of retaining his sovereignty over the conquests, that he had made, by the removal of every individual, capable of creating either danger or disturbance. "Alexander, devictâ perdomitâque Thraciâ, petens Asiam, veritus, ne post ipsius decessus fumerent arma, reges eorum, præfectosque, et omnes, quibus videbantur inesse cura detractæ libertatis, secum, velut honoris causâ, traxit, ignobilibus autem relictis plebeios præfecit; consecutus, ubi principes beneficiis ejus obstricti, nihil novare vellent; plebs vero ne posset quidem, spo'iata principibus." 1. Frontinus. Strategemat. Lib. 2. Chap. 11.--298, 299. 8vo L. B. 1731

city was besieged and totally destroyed. Every germ of a war, which might have retarded, and perhaps have put a stop to the vast projects of this Prince, was thus blasted to its root, and Thebes in its ruins exhibited an awful and tremendous spectacle, which spread an impressive consternation over all Greece.

Thebes was taken by stratagem according to Polyænus,[q] but Ptolemy,[r] who was present at the siege, informs us that the besieged had rashly advanced too far in a sally, and on being repulsed by the Macedonian phalanx, the besiegers entered the town with them in their confusion. Diodorus Siculus[s] hath confirmed Ptolemy's

---

[q] "Ἀλέξανδρος ἔλαβε Θήβας τῆς δυνάμεως ἱκανὴν ἀποκρύψας, καὶ τάξας αὐτῆς Ἀντίπατρον. τὴν δὲ φανερὰν αὐτῆς ἦγεν ἐπὶ τοὺς ἰσχυροὺς τῶν τόπων· Θηβαῖοι δὲ ἐπεξῆλθον, καὶ πρὸς τὴν ὁρωμένην δύναμιν οὐκ ἀγεννῶς ἀντιπαρετάσσοντο· Ἀντίπατρος ἐν τῷ καιρῷ τῆς μάχης τὴν κεκρυμμένην δύναμιν ἀναστήσας, κύκλῳ περιηλθων ἢ σαθρὸν καὶ ἀφύλακτον ἦν τὸ τεῖχος, ταύτῃ κατελαβεῖτο τὴν πόλιν." Polyænus. Strat. Lib. 4. --333.

[r] "Λέγει Πτολεμαῖος ὁ Λάγου ὅτι——— Ἀλέξανδρος τοὺς μὲν αὐτοῦ φεύγοντας κατιδὼν, τοὺς Θηβαίους δὲ λελυκότας ἐν τῇ διώξει τὴν τάξιν, ἐμβάλλει ἐς αὐτοὺς συντεταγμένῃ τῇ φάλαγγι· Οἱ δὲ ὤθουσιν τοὺς Θηβαίους εἴσω τῶν πυλῶν· καὶ τοῖς Θηβαίοις ἐς τοσόνδε ἡ φυγὴ φοβερὰ ἐγίγνετο, ὥστε διὰ τῶν πυλῶν ὠθούμενοι ἐς τὴν πόλιν, οὐκ ἔφθησαν συγκλεῖσαι τὰς πύλας· ἀλλὰ συνεσπίπτουσί γὰρ αὐτοῖς εἴσω τοῦ τείχους, ὅσοι τῶν Μακεδόνων ἐγγὺς φευγόντων εἴχοντο." Arrian. Exped. Alex. Lib. 1. Chap. 8.--34, 35, 36.

[s] "Ἀνυπερβλήτου δὲ τῆς φιλοτιμίας γινομένης, ὁ βασιλεὺς, κατανοήσας τινὰ πυλίδα καταλελειμμένην ἀπὸ τῶν φυλάκων, ἐξαπέστειλε Περδίκκαν μετὰ στρατιωτῶν ἱκανῶν καταλαβέσθαι ταύτην, καὶ παρεισπεσεῖν εἰς τὴν πόλιν· τούτου δὲ ταχὺ τὸ προσταχθὲν ποιήσαντος, οἱ μὲν Μακεδόνες διὰ τῆς πυλίδος παρεισέπεσον εἰς τὴν πόλιν ——— τῆς δὲ πόλεως τὸν τρόπον καταλαμβανομένης, πολλαὶ καὶ ποικίλαι περιστάσεις ἐντὸς τῶν τειχῶν ἐγίνοντο." The terrible catastrophe is then pathetically described. "Οἱ μὲν γὰρ Μακεδόνες, διὰ τὴν ὑπερηφανίαν τοῦ κηρύγματος, πικρότερον, ἢ πολεμικώτερον προσεφέροντο τοῖς Θηβαίοις, καὶ μετὰ πολλῆς ἀπειλῆς ἐπιφερόμενοι τοῖς ἠτυχηκόσιν, ἀφειδῶς ἀνῄρουν πάντας τοὺς περιτυγχάνοντας· Οἱ δὲ Θηβαῖοι, τὸ φίλον τοῦ ζῆν τῆς ψυχῆς διαφυλάττοντες, τοσοῦτον ἀπεῖχον τοῦ φιλοζωεῖν, ὥς ἐν ταῖς ἀπαντήσεσι συμπλέκεσθαι,

Ptolemy's account with a few flight shades of difference. The historians reckon six thousand of the besieged to have been killed, and thirty thousand of them to have been made prisoners:' others have pretended that the Thebans lost ten thousand men in the siege. Agatharcides very reasonably suspects this calculation to be an exaggerated one, and improbable.ʷ On the supposition that

κ̓ τας παρα των πολεμιων επισπασθαι πληγας· εαλωκυιας γαρ της πολεως, ουδεις Θηβαιων εωραθη δεηθεις των Μακεδονων ζωγρασθαι τη ζην, ουδε προσεπιπτον τοις των κρατουντων γονασιν αγεννως·————των δε υπο-λελειμμενων Θηβαιων οἱ μεν κατατετρωμενοι τα σωματα, κ̓ λειποψυχουντες συνεπλεκοντο τοις πολεμιοις, συναποθνησκοντες τη των εχθρων απωλεια." (Diod. Sicul. Lib. 17. Tom. 2.--169, 170.) The generous mind will pause with admiration at this wonderful display of undaunted valour, and a sigh will naturally arise on the recollection that such exertions in the cause of freedom were unsuccessful.

ᵗ "Των δε Θηβαιων ανηρεθησαν μεν υπερ τους ἑξακισχιλιους, αιχμαλωτα δε σωματα συνηχθη πλειω των τρισμυριων." Diod. Sicul. Lib. 17. Tom. 2.--170.

"Εφονευσε δε των Θηβαιων εις ἑξακισχιλιους, αιχμαλωτους δε ελαφθησαν τρισμυριοι." (Ælian. Var. Hist. Lib. 13. C. 7. Tom. 2.-861. 4ᵗᵒ 1731.) We learn from the same authority that the descendants of the poet Pindar had a singular respect paid to them amidst the universal devastation, and that his house was the only one exempted from the general destruction. "Ετιμησε δε κ̓ τους εγγονους τους του Πινδαρου κ̓ την οικιαν αυτου μονην εασαν ἑσταναι." (Ælian. Var. Hist. Lib. 13. Chap. 7. Tom. 2.-860.) Plutarch hath confirmed Ælian's account of the respect shewn to Pindar's family, and agrees with him on the Theban Loss. "Υπεξελομενος δε τους ιερεις, κ̓ τους ξενους Μακεδονων απαντας, κ̓ τους απο Πινδαρου γεγονοτας, κ̓ τους εναντιωθεντας τοις ψηφισαμενοις την αποστασιν· απεδοτο τους αλλους; ωςει τρισμυριους γενομενους· οἱ δε αποθανοντες ὑπερ ἑξακισχιλιους ησαν." Plutarch. Vit. Alex. Plutarchi Opera. Tom. 1.--670.)

ʷ I am not happy enough to have found the passage, which the Baron de St. Croix hath referred to in Photius, for this opinion of Agatharcides. The only one that I have met with, which mentions the loss of the Thebans, is the following one. "Πλην προστιθησι κ̓ ἑτερα των ειρημενων ὁμοια, ὑπο την αυτην κ̓ ταυτα φερων διαβολην· οιον, Θηβαιοι εν τη μαχη τη προς Μακεδονας ὑπερ τους μυριους αναιτραπησαν." (Photii Biblioth. 1337.) where the expression was more an object of criticism, than the number of the slain. Simpson also thinks the number to have been magnified. Chronic. ad Ann. Mundi, 3670.

that this ſtatement was correct, the population of Thebes might be eſtimated at fifty thouſand ſouls, a number that bears no ſort of proportion to the crippled ſtate of this city, which had previouſly loſt much of its ancient ſplendour, had been enfeebled by many bloody battles, and whoſe power had been nearly annihilated in the ſacred war.ˣ Clitarchus only valued the whole riches of Thebes, when they became a prey to the Macedonians, at four hundred and forty talents,ʸ which directly contradicts the pompous account that Diodorus Siculus hath given of the pretended treaſure, found by the Conqueror on his capture of this place. But the authority of Diodorus Siculus, who is often very inexact, can here indeed have little influence, as we find in general the ſame calculations with thoſe of Clitarchus. Some arguments may alſo be drawn from the circumſtances, which Athenæus hath preſerved, reſpecting the manners and mode of life amongſt the Thebans, which denounce their poverty,ᶻ and appear inconſiſtent with a numerous population, which is generally the attendant of advantageous manufactures and extenſive commerce.

Alarmed

ˣ Pauſanias informs us that this ſacred war laſted ten years. "Τον Φωκικον πολεμον, ονομαζομενον δε ὑπο Ελληνων ἱερον, συνεχως δεκα ετεσιν επολεμησαν." (Pauſanias. Lib. 9. Chap. 6.—724.) A length of time that muſt neceſſarily have drained them both of men and money.

ʸ "Κλητἀρχ. εν πρωτη των περι Αλεξανδρον ἱστοριων διηγειτ., κ) ὁτι πας αυτων πλουτος ηὑρεθε μετα την ὑπ' Αλεξανδρου της πολεως καταςκαφην εν ταλαντοις τετρακοσιοις τεσσαρακοντα φησιν, ὁτι τε μικροψυχοι ησαν, κ) τα περι την τροφην λιχνοι." Athenæus. Lib. 4.—148.

ᶻ "Παρασκευαζοντες εν τοις δειπνοις θρια, κ) ἰψητας: κ) αφυας, κ) εκαρσιλυχνες, κ) αλλαντας, κ) σχελιδας, κ) ετνος." Athenæus. Lib. 4.—148.

Alarmed at the capture of Thebes, Athens by the perfuafion of Demades fent an embaffy to Alexander, to congratulate him on his fafe return from Illyria and the country of the Triballians, and to teftify their joy to him on his fuccefs at Thebes, and the chaftifement, with which he had punifhed its revolt. The Prince received it very gracioufly, but he wrote to the Athenians and demanded Demofthenes, Lycurgus, Hyperides, Polyeuctes, Chares, Charidemus, Ephialtes, Diotimus and Mærocles to be given up to him, whom he believed to have been the authors of the difturbances after Philip's death, and the caufe of the battle of Chæronea. A fecond embaffy was fent by the Athenians with the hope of foftening the Prince's refolution, and the bufinefs was at laft compromifed, on Alexander's infifting only on the exile of Charidemus.[a] Such is Arrian's account, but it neither agrees with that of his cotemporary authors, nor even with that of Diodorus Siculus, Plutarch, or Juftin. Thebes was not in fact deftroyed, and the young Conqueror was abfolutely engaged in the fiege, when the embaffy was fent, as appears by the oration of Æfchines againft Ctefiphon, in which he reproaches Demofthenes, one of the deputies, with his return from mount Cithæron, and having wanted the courage to execute his commiffion.[b] Plutarch confirms the charge of Æfchines, and adds that a meffage was fent by Alexander

---

[a] "Χαριδημον μεν τοι, μονον των εξαιτηθεντων τε κ, ου δοθεντων, φευγειν εκελευσε· κ, φευγει Χαριδημος
 εις την Ασιαν παρα βασιλεα Δαρειον." Arrian. Exped. Alex. Lib. 10. Chap. 10.--44.

[b] "Πρεσβευτης υφ'υμων χειροτονηθεις, αποδρας εκ μισε τε Κιθαιρων⊙ ήκιν υποστρεψας·" Æfchinis oratio contra Ctefiphont. 120.

ander himself to demand ten of the factious demagogues[c] according to Duris and Idomeneus, and eight according to more credible historians. Demades having joined the party of Demosthenes,[d] was named by the people of Athens, ambassador on this occasion to Alexander, and he had the address to procure the pardon of their orators.——Diodorus Siculus[e] hath not taken any notice of the first deputations of the Athenians, though he agrees in other particulars with Plutarch. Justin speaks of this deputation even before the siege of Thebes, and if we are to believe him, its object was to obtain a peace from the young Monarch, which he granted.

[c] "Αιρεθεὶς δὲ μεθ' ἑτέραν πρεσβευτὴς πρὸς Ἀλέξανδρον, δείσας δὲ τὴν ὀργήν, ἐκ τοῦ Κιθαιρῶνος ἀνεχώρησε ὀπίσω, καὶ τὴν πρεσβείαν ἀφῆκεν· εὐθὺς δὲ ὁ Ἀλέξανδρος ἐζήτει πέμπων τῶν δημαγωγῶν δέκα μὲν ὡς Ἰδομενεὺς καὶ Δοῦρις εἰρήκασιν· ὀκτὼ δὲ, ὡς οἱ πλεῖστοι καὶ δοκιμώτατοι τῶν συγγραφέων, τοὺς δὲ, Δημοσθένη, Πολύευκτον, Ἐφιάλτην, Λυκοῦργον, Μοιροκλέα, Δάμωνα, Καλλισθένη, Χαρίδημον·" Plutarch. Vit. Demosth. Plutarchi Opera. Tom. 1.--856.

[d] Diodorus Siculus informs us that Demades was supposed to have received five talents for this political manœuvre. "Δημάδης, πεπεισμένος ὑπὸ τῶν περὶ Δημοσθένην, ὥς φασι, πέντε ταλάντοις ἀργυρίοις, συνέβαλεν μὲν σώζειν τοὺς κινδυνεύοντας·" (Diod. Sicul. Lib. 17. Tom. 2.--171.) The Athenian senate it seems was as corrupt as a modern House of Commons.

[e] Diodorus Siculus agrees with Plutarch and Æschines as to the return of Demosthenes from mount Cithæron, but he doubts whether it was from fear, or other motives. "Ἐν δὲ τοῖς πρέσβεσι καὶ Δημοσθένης ἐκπεμφθείς, οὐ συνῆλθε μετὰ τῶν ἄλλων πρὸς τὸν Ἀλέξανδρον, ἀλλ' ἐκ τοῦ Κιθαιρῶνος ἀνεκαμψεν εἰς τὰς Ἀθήνας· εἴτε διὰ τὰ πεπολιτευμένα κατὰ Μακεδόνων φοβηθείς, εἴτε βουλόμενος τῷ βασιλεῖ τῶν Περσῶν ἀμέμπτον αὑτὸν διαφυλάττειν· πολλὰ γὰρ χρήματά φασιν αὐτὸν εἰληφέναι παρὰ Περσῶν, ἵνα πολιτεύηται κατὰ Μακεδόνων· περὶ ὧν καὶ τὸν Αἰσχίνην φασιν, ὀνειδίζοντα τῷ Δημοσθένει κατά τινα λόγον τὴν δωροδοκίαν, εἰπεῖν, "Νῦν μέντοι τὴν δαπάνην ἐπικεκλυκεν αὐτῷ τὸ βασιλικὸν χρυσίον· ἔσται δὲ οὐδὲ τοῦτο ἱκανὸν· οὐδεὶς γὰρ πώποτε πλοῦτος τρόπου πονηροῦ περιεγένετο·" (Diod. Sicul. Lib. 17. Tom. 2.--162, 163.) A variety of these pointed charges are made by Æschines in his oration against Ctesiphon, and as they are so feebly repelled by Demosthenes, in all probability, they were but too well founded.

granted.' This historian informs us likewise that Alexander pardoned the orators, but that the Athenian generals were under the necessity of retiring into exile; and, entering into the Persian service, were of infinite advantage to it.^g But this latter circumstance stands unsupported by any writer of antiquity. Justin possibly meant to speak of Charidemus, who distinguished himself very eminently in the Olynthian war, but it appears, by some expressions of Dinarchus,^h that this able general had voluntarily expatriated, for the purpose of rendering his country more important advantages with the King of Persia.ⁱ——Ephialtes soon followed the example, and retired from Athens.^k But it is not probable as Arrian hath asserted,^l that the Athenians could have

L applauded

---

f "Missis itaque legatis, bellum deprecantur: quibus auditis et graviter increpatis, Alexander bellum remisit, Inde Thebas exercitum convertit." Justin. Lib. 11. Chap. 3.--262.

g "Secundâ legatione denuo bellum deprecantibus, ita demum remiserit, ut oratores et duces, quorum fiducia toties rebellent, sibi dedantur: paratisque Athenienfibus ne cogantur subire bellum, eo res deducta est, ut retentis oratoribus, duces in exilium agerentur, qui ex continenti ad Darium profecti, non mediocre Persarum viribus accessere." Justin. Lib. 11. Chap. 4.--265.

h Dinarchi oratio contra Demosthenem. Ed. Steph. 99.

i From a jealousy of the Persian generals, he was afterwards ungratefully put to death by the orders of Darius. Q. Curtius (Lib. 3. Chap. 2. Tom. 1.--69.--70.) hath given us some of the leading circumstances. Diodorus Siculus (Lib. 17. Tom. 2.--181, 182.) hath entered into them more minutely.

k Dinarchi oratio contra Demosthenem. Ed. Steph. 94.

l "Αθηναιοι δε, μυςηριων των μεγαλων αγομενων, ως ηκον τινες των Θηβαιων εξ αυτου τυ εργου, τα μεν μυστηρια εκπλαγεντες εξελιπον, εκ δε των αγρων εσκευαγωγουν ες την πολιν." (Arrian. Exped. Alex. Lib 1. Chap. 10.-43.) This festival distinguished by the name of the greater mysteries was celebrated in

the

applauded Alexander on his cruel treatment of the Thebans, when they publicly deplored their lamentable fate, immediately put a stop to the celebration of their myſteries, and received within their walls ſuch of the wretched ſufferers as had eſcaped from the ſword or fetters of the Conqueror."

Having ſecured the tranquillity of Greece, Alexander prepared for his attack of the Perſian empire. The weakneſs of a neighbouring nation, ſtrong political probabilities of ſucceſs, and the deſtruction of an enemy, are often the real cauſes of wars, which are entered into with apparent principles of juſtice.—The Conqueror of Aſia had no other motives. Polybius,ª with his uſual acuteneſs, hath penetrated into them, and hath had the ſagacity to ſeparate them from thoſe pretended reaſons for hoſtilities, in which the Grecian vanity was too much intereſted, to allow of their ſuſpecting their propriety.

The

---

the month Boedromion with extraordinary and rigid ſolemnity. It laſted nine days, and was introduced at Rome under Adrian, when it bore the name of the Eleuſinian myſteries from the town of Eleuſis in Attica, where it had been celebrated with more than common ſuperſtition. Themiſtius, Proclus, Stobæus and Dion Chryſoſtom, have given us ſome intereſting circumſtances relating to theſe myſteries: Meurſius hath entered into them at large in his treatiſe on this feſtival, and Warburton (Divine Legation, Vol. 1.--239, 248. 8ᵛᵒ Edit. 1765.) hath extracted the eſſence, and ingeniouſly adapted it to his own ſyſtem.

ᵐ The flying Thebans according to Æſchines were received within the walls of Athens: "Τες ταλαιπωρες Θηβαιως φυγοντας ὑποδιδεχϑε τη πολει" (Æſchines contra Cteſiph. 116.) but Juſtin goes ſtill further and ſays, that they opened the city-gates to them, in defiance of Alexander's expreſs prohibition. "Miſeranda res Athenienſibus viſa. Itaque portus refugiis profugorum contra interdictum regis aperuere." Juſtin. Lib. 11. Chap. 4.--264.

ª Polyb. Hiſt. Lib. 3. Tom. 1.--398, 399, 400. Edit. Schweighæuſer. 8ᵛᵒ Lipſ. 1789.

The era of this expedition into Afia became a celebrated one in the Grecian calendars, and was marked in all their annals. Duris reckoned 1000 years from the deftruction of Troy to this epoch: Ephorus from the return of the Heraclides to the fame period 735: Timœus and Clitarchus 820: Eratofthenes 773, and laftly Phanius affures us that 715 had elapfed between that event and the Archonfhip of Evænetus, when Alexander entered Afia.[o] Diodorus, after the information that Alexander mounted the throne, during the magiftracy of this Archon, is reduced to the neceffity of fixing this expedition under that of Cteficles,[p] circumftances rendering an interval of a year[q] neceffary between Philip's death and the war, which his Son undertook againft Perfia. This opinion, however, is by no means preferable to that of St. Clement of Alexandria, who refers it to the Archonfhip of Evænetus his predeceffor.[r] It is at leaft certain, that Alexander's expedition into Afia was immediately fubfequent to the fall of

Thebes,

---

[o] "Επι Ευαινετον αρχοντα φ' ὑ φασιν Αλεξανδρον εις την Ασιαν διαβηναι, ὡς μεν Φανιας, ετη επτακοσια δεκαπεντε· ὡς μεν Εφορος επτακοσια τριακοντα πεντε· ὡς δε Τιμαι<del>ο</del>ς και Κλειταρχος οκτακοσια εικοσι· ὡς δε Ερατοσθενης επτακοσια ἱβδομηκοντα τεσσερα· ὡς δε Δυρις, απο Τροιας ἁλωσεως επι την τυ Αλεξανδρη εις την Ασιαν διαβασιν ετη χιλια." Clement. Alex. Stromat. Lib. 1.--337. Fol. apud Morell. 1629.

[p] "Επ'αρχοντος δ'Αθηνησι Κτησικλεως'------Αλεξανδρον δε μετα της δυναμεως πορευθεις επι τον Ἑλλησποντον διεβιβασε την δυναμιν εκ της Ευρωπης εις την Ασιαν." Diod. Sicul. Lib. 17. Tom. 2. --172.

[q] Zozimus hath boldly poftponed this Afiatic expedition to the third year of Alexander's reign. "Αλεξανδρος δε παραλαβων την βασιλειαν, ϗ παρεχχρημα τα κατα της Ελληνας διαθεις, τριτω της βασιλειας ετει μετα δυναμεως αρκεσης επι την Ασιαν εξηλθετο." Zozimus. Lib. 1.--7, 8. 8vo Lipf. 1784.

[r] Stromat. Lib. 1.--337.

Thebes, 335 years before Chrift.—We learn from Arrian, that Alexander began his march early in the spring, and reached Seftus in twenty days,' which proves as the learned Ufher' hath obferved, that the paffage of the Hellefpont ought to be fixed about three months before Ctefcles entered into office. The operations of the army in Afia Minor, and the battle of Iffus eftablifh this calculation, which Corfini' hath adopted in his Attic annals, though the Jefuit Petau^w from a devotion to Diodorus, rather more than warrantable, hath related thefe events and the remarkable paffage of the Grecians under the magiftracy of Ctefcles, notwithftanding they really happened under that of Evænetus.

The judicious counfels of the fage Memnon[x] were either not attended to, or not followed; and the Perfians having determined

to

---

* "Ἅμα δε τω ηρι αρχομενω εξελαυνει αφ'Ελλησποντε' ———————ες Σηςον αφικνειται εν εικοσι ταις πασαις ημεραις απο της οικοθεν εξορμησεως." (Arrian; Exped. Alex. Lib. 1. Chap. 11.-44, 45.) Diodorus Siculus hath recorded Antipater's and Parmenio's very curious advice to Alexander, previous to the commencement of his Afiatic expedition. "Των δε περι Αντιπατρον, κ Παρμενιωνα συμβαλινοντων, προτερον ΠΑΙΔΟΠΟΙΗΣΑΣΘΑΙ, κ τοτε τοις τηλικουτοις εγχειρειν εργοις'' (Diod. Sicul. Lib. 17. Tom. 2.--171.) The recommendation of fuch a fyftem of Royal Amufement might have warped a lefs vigorous and ambitious mind from its intended projects, and put a final ftop to the Perfian war.

' Ufher, Annal. 151.

' Corfini Faft. Attic. Tom. 4.--41, 42.

^w D. Petavius Doctrin. Temp. Lib. 13.

^x "Μεμνων ὁ Ῥοδιος παρηνει μη δια κινδυνου ιεναι προς τους Μακεδονας, τω τε πεζω πολυ περιοντα σφων, κ κατα Αλεξανδρε παροντες, αυτοις δε αποντος Δαρειε' Προιοντας δε, τον τε χιλον αφανιζειν καταπατουντας

τη

to defend the paſſage of the Granicus, their army agreeable to Arrian's computation, confiſted of twenty thouſand cavalry and an equal number of infantry,[y] of which the mercenaries formed the greateſt part. Diodorus Siculus magnifies the number into ten thouſand cavalry and one hundred thouſand infantry,[z] whilſt Juſtin taking the horſe and foot together, extends it to ſix hundred thouſand,[a] which ſhocks every idea of probability.

Arrian hath entered into a minute deſcription of this celebrated battle, in which the Perſian valour made victory for a long time doubtful, and which Alexander at laſt decided in his favour by plunging at the head of the Theſſalian horſe into the middle of the enemy. The defeated army loſt, according to this writer's calculation,

---

τη ίππω, κ᾽ τον εν τη γη καρπον εμπιπρᾶναι, μηδε των πολεων αυτων φειδομενους· ου γαρ μενειν εν τη χωρα Αλεξανδρον απορια των επιτηδειων· (Arrian. Exped. Alex. Lib. 1. Chap. 12.--53.) Diodorus Siculus confirms the circumſtance of Memnon's opinion with the addition of his wiſhing to carry the war into Europe, and make an attack on Macedonia. "Μεμνον μεν εν ὁ Ῥοδιος, διαβεβοημενος επι συνεσει ϛρατηγικη, συνεβυλευσε κατα ϛομα μεν μη διακινδυνευειν, την δε χωραν φθειρειν, κ᾽ τη σπανει των αναγκαιων ειργειν τυς Μακεδονας της εις τυμπροσθεν πορειας· διαβιβαζειν δε κ᾽ δυναμεις εις την Μακεδονιαν ναυτικας τε κ᾽ πεζικας, κ᾽ τον ολον πολεμον εις την Ευρωπην μεταγαγειν·" Diod. Sicul. Lib. 17. Tom. 2.--173.

[y] "Περσων δε ἱππεις μεν ησαν ες δισμυριους, ξενοι δε πεζοι μισθοφοροι ολιγον αποδεοντες διςμυριων·" Arrian. Exped. Alex. Lib. 1. Chap. 14.--57.

[z] "Οἱ δε παντες ἱππεις ὑπηρχον πλειους των μυριων· οἱ δε πεζοι των Περσων ησαν μεν ουκ ελαττους των δεκα μυριαδων·" Diod. Sicul. Lib. 17. Tom. 2.--174.

[a] "In Acie Perſarum ſexcenta millia militum fuere." (Juſtin. Lib. 11. Chap. 6.--270.) The commentators have unanimouſly given up this paſſage as indefenſible, but they have not agreed in what manner its extravagance is to be corrected.

calculation,[b] a thousand horse upon this fatal day, and the whole of their infantry, two thousand of the mercenaries excepted, who were made prisoners, but Diodorus[c] reduces their loss to somewhat above ten thousand infantry and two thousand of their cavalry.

Reflecting on the determined resolution, with which the Persians resisted the efforts of the Macedonian army, and the obstacles, that a river, defended by a numerous body of troops, under the command of an able and experienced general, naturally presents, it is impossible to believe[d] that the Conqueror suffered only the trifling

---

[b] "Τῶν δη μὲν ἱππέων τῶν Περσῶν ἀπέθανον εἰς χιλίους· Οὐ γὰρ πολλή, ἡ διωξις ἐγένετο, ὅτι ἐξετράπη Ἀλέξανδρος· ἐπι. τὲς ξένους τὲς μισθοφόρους·—Καὶ τούτες την τε φαλαγγα ἐπαγαγὼν, καὶ τὲς ἱππέας πάντη πρὸς πίεσιν κελεύσας, ἐν μέσῳ δε ὀλίγου κατακόπτει αυτους· ὥστε διεφυγε μὲν οὐδεις, ὅτι μη διελαθε τις ἐν τοις νεκροις." Arrian. Exped. Alex. Lib. 1. Chap. 16.--63.

[c] "Diodore reduit toute la perte de l'armée Perse à dix mille soldats." But the Baron de St. Croix hath mistaken Diodorus Siculus, and forgotten the two thousand horse. "Ἀπηρίθησαν δε τῶν Περσῶν οἱ πεζοι μὲν πλείους τῶν μυρίων, ἱππεις δ'οὐκ ἐλαττους δισχιλιων." (Sicul. Lib. 17. Tom. 2.--17, 176.) It is a gross error, and I have rectified it. Plutarch computes the Persians to have lost twenty thousand of their foot, and two thousand and five hundred of their horse, but he takes it on tradition: "Λεγονται δε, πεζοι μὲν, δισμυριοι τῶν βαρβάρων, ἱππεις δε δισχιλιοι πεντακοσιοι πεσειν." (Plut. de Vit. Alex. Plutarchi Opera. Tom. 1.--673.) There is perhaps no possibility of ascertaining the precise number, but truth, in all likelihood, may lie between the two extremes.

[d] "On ne sauroit croire que les vainqueurs n'aient perdu que soixante et quinze cavaliers et trente fantassins." From these repeated mistakes, it is to be apprehended that the Baron de St. Croix trusted for the fidelity of his references to some careless transcriber. Arrian to whom the appeal is made, states the loss as it now stands. "Μακεδόνων δε τῶν μὲν ἑταιρων ἀμφι τους εἰκοσι και πεντε τη πρωτη προσβολη ἀπεθανον·—Τῶν δε ἀλλων ἱππεων ὑπερ τους ἐξήκοντα, πεζοι δε ἐς τους τριακοντα." (Exped. Alex. Lib. 1. Chap. 16.--63.) Justin reckons it at nine of the foot and one

trifling lofs of eighty-five of his cavalry and thirty of his infantry. Yet this is the account of it, which the hiftorians of the life of Alexander have left us, who take a pleafure in diminifhing the loffes of their youthful Hero, and exaggerating the misfortunes of his enemies.

Arrian's account of the fiege of Halicarnaffus, which was defended with infinite courage and capacity by Memnon, hath been juftly admired by military men, and the reafon which he fuppofes to have had an influence upon Alexander's fuccefsful paffage to mount Climax, on the borders of the fea of Pamphilus, will equally extort the cooler approbation of the philofopher. The Macedonian Monarch with a part of his army effected this dangerous march with as much happinefs as temerity, a violent North-wind keeping back the waves, and preventing the fea from covering the fand with its ufual depth of water.[e]

Strabo,

one hundred and twenty horfe. "De exercitu Alexandri novem pedites, centum viginti equites cecidere." (Lib. 11. Chap. 6.--271.) But Ariftobulus, as we learn from Plutarch, is more abfurd, and imagines only thirty-four men to have fallen, of whom nine were foot foldiers. "Των δε περι τον Αλεξανδρον, Αριςοβαλθ· φησιν τεσσερα ϗ τριακοντα νεκρες γενεσθαι τους παντας, ων ενεα πεζους ειναι·" (De Vit. Alex. Plut. Opera. Tom. 1.--673.) Orofius (Lib. 3. Chap. 16.) agrees with Juftin, but as Orofius is only Juftin at fecond hand, I do not know that he adds any thing to his authority.

[e] "Αυτος δε παρα την θαλασσαν δια του αγιαλου ηγε τους αμφ'αυτον· ες δε ταυτη η οδος ουκ αλλως, οτι μη των επ'αρκτου ανεμων πνεοντων· ει δε νοτοι κατεχοιεν, απορως εχει δια τε αγιαλε οδοιπορειν· τοτε δ'εκ νοτων σκληρων, βορεαι επιπνευσαντες, ουκ ανευ του θευ (ως αυτ[ος] τε ϗ οι αμφ'αυτον εξηγουντο) ευμαρη ϗ ταχειαν την παροδον παρειχον·" Arrian. Exped. Alex. Lib. 1. Chap. 26.--92.

Strabo, who suppresses all the miraculous incidents of the march,[f] informs us, that the Macedonian soldiers passed through the sea with the water up to their waists, and Plutarch[g] hath cited some verses of Menander, in which the comic poet hath ridiculed the wonderful account, which several writers had given of this passage. Alexander in one of his letters [h] barely mentions it, and says, that after his departure from Phacelides he had advanced to mount Climax.

Josephus

[f] "Περι Φασηλιδα ὁ'ιςι τα κατα θαλατταν στιχ, δι ὡν Αλεξανδρος παρηϊαἰε την ςρατιαν· ιςι δε ορος Κλιμαξ καλουμενον· επικειται δε τω παμφυλιω πελαγει, ςενην απολειπων παροδον επι τω αιγιαλω, ταις μεν νηςεμιαις γυμνουμενην, ὡςε ειναι βασιμον τοις οδευεσι· πλημμυρουντος δε τα πελαγους, ὑπο των κυματων καλυπτομενην επιπολυ· ἡ μεν εν δια τα ορους ὑπερβασις, περιοδον εχει κ, προςαντης εςι, τω δ'αιςιαλω χρωνται κατα τας ευδιας· Ὁ δε Αλεξανδρος εις χειμεριον εμπεσων και ρον, κ, το πλειον επιτρεπων τη τυχη, πριν ανιεναι τα κυματα ὡρμησε, κ, ὁλην την ἡμεραν εν ὑδασι γινεσθαι την πορειαν συνεβη, μεχρι ομφαλα βαπτιζομενων." Strabo, Lib. 14. Tom. 2.--982.

[g] "Η δε της Παμφυλιης παραδρομη, πολλοις γεγονε των ἱςορικων ὑποθεσις γραφικη προς εκπληξιν κ, ογκον, ὡς θεια τινι τυχη παραχωρησασαν Αλεξανδρῳ την θαλασσαν, αλλως αει ταχειαν εκ πελαγους προςφερομενην, σπανιως δε λιπτους κ, προςηχεις ὑπο τα κρημνωδη κ, παρερρωγοτα της ορεινης παγους διακαλυπτουσαν δηλοι δε κ, Μενανδρος, εν κωμωδια παιζων προς το παραδοξον· 'Ως Αλεξανδρωδες ηδη τατο, ἢ ζητω τινα, αυτοματ<ο>ς οντ<ο>ς παρεςαι· καν διελθειν δηλαδη δια θαλασσης δει τοπον τιν, οντ<ο>ς εςαι μοι βαθος·" Plutarch. de Vit. Alex. Plut. Opera. Tom. 1.--674.

[h] "Αυτ<ο>ς δε Αλεξανδρος εν ταις επιςολαις, ουδεν τοιυτον τερατευσαμεν<ο>ς, ὁδοποιησαι φησιν, την λεγομενην Κλιμακα, κ, διελθειν ὁρμησας εκ Φασηλιδ<ο>ς·" (Plut. de Vit. Alex. Plut. Opera. Tom. 1.--674.) Yet Appian, in his parallel of Julius Cæsar with Alexander, by his expressions of "Δαιμονιως" and "Λυτε τα Δαιμον<ο>ς," appears to intimate a received opinion of a supernatural impulse on the sea. "Και τον Παμφυλιον κολπον της θαλασσης ανακοπεισης διετρεχε δαιμονιως, κ, το πελαγ<ο>ς αυτε του Δαιμον<ο>ς κατεχοντ<ο>ς·" (De bell. civil. Lib. 2. Tom. 2.--849. 8v°·Amst. 1670.) The latter part of this sentence is ridiculously rendered in this edition, "Fortuna marina undas cohibente." Appian here certainly meant more than is usually understood by the Greek word Τυχη, which is properly translated, Fortune: the idea of both the heroes of his comparison being, in a very particular manner, under the special protection of Providence, exalts their characters and fell exactly within his plan.

Josephus was not proof against these fabulous relations, and having occasion to take notice of the passage of the Red sea, he expresses himself in the following terms, "Nor let any one wonder at the strangeness of the narration; if a way were discovered to those men of old time, who were free from the wickedness of modern ages, whether it happened by the will of God, or whether it happened of its own accord. While for the sake of those that accompanied Alexander, King of Macedonia, who yet lived, comparatively but a little while ago, the Pamphylian sea retired and afforded them a passage through itself, when they had no other way to go: I mean when it was the will of God to destroy the Monarchy of the Persians. And this is confessed to be true by all that have written about the actions of Alexander. But as to these events let every one determine as he pleases."[i] Josephus in this indiscreet reference to the passage of the Red sea, seems to admit that there were doubts[k] of the reality of that miracle, though

---

[i] Whiston's Josephus. Book 2. Chap. 16. Vol. 2.—63. "Θαυμαζετω δε μηδεις τε λογε το παραδοξον, ει αρχαιοις ανθρωποις καὶ πονηριας απειροις ευρεθη σωτηριας ὁδος καὶ δια θαλασσης, ειτε κατα βουλησιν Θεε, ειτε αυτοματον· ὁποτε καὶ τοις περι τον Αλεξανδρον τον βασιλεα της Μακεδονιας χθες καὶ πρωην γενομενοις επεχωρησε το Παμφυλιον πελαγ⸫, καὶ ὁδον αλλην ουκ εχεσι παρεσχε την δ'αυτη, καταλυσαι την Περσων ἡγεμονιαν τε Θεε θελησαντ⸫· καὶ τετο παντες ὁμολογεσιν οἱ τας Αλεξανδρε πραξεις συγγραψαμενοι· περι μεν εν τετων ως ἑκαστω δοκει διαλαμβανετω·" Josephus. Lib. 2. Chap. 16. Tom. 1.—115.

* "La mer de Pamphile se retira pendant deux jours," is the French version. We learn from the Greek original that the sea "Ὑπεχωρησε" retired, withdrew itself, but there is not a syllable that specifies the duration of the recess.

[k] Reland hath very ably vindicated the Jewish historian, respecting the last sentence of the Greek quotation from the imputation of incredulity, and he hath proved by repeated instances that

though there were not any of the supernatural circumstances respecting the march under mount Climax, and he violates by the indecency¹ of the parallel both the sacred evidence of history and the religious creed of his ancestors.

After that Josephus made use of similar expressions, when not an atom of a doubt could have remained upon his mind. Whiston hath translated the whole of the remarks, (Josephus, Vol. 2. Dissertation. 1st. Sec. 82.) but I was sorry to observe that the "ετι αυτοματον" hath been left by them both to shift for itself.——The learned Michaelis, in his notes on the 14th Chapter of Exodus, considers the event as a natural effect of a very violent wind, which blew in a direct opposition to the tide, but he afterwards allows, "Moïse ne put par aucun raison humaine prevoir le dessechement de la mer qui sauva et lui et le peuple, il agit par inspiration divine. Ce dessechement fut une œuvre de la Providence, qui avoit resolu de delivrer son peuple. La prevision certain de cet evenement etoit surnaturelle au supreme degré, puisqu'il n'est jamais arrivé que cette seule fois, et sa connoissance prouvoit la mission divine de Moïse autant qu'aucun miracle eut pu le faire. Moïse qui contre le bout de sa marche et sans necessité se tourna vers le coté d'Afrique de la mer-rouge qui lui coupoit le chemin de l'Asie, qui le vit environné d'Egyptiens et qui auroit du perir, s'il n'etoit arrivé un fait inoüi et unique ; ce Moïse qui au lieu d'exhorter son peuple resserré entre la mer et l'ennemi à une vigoureuse defense, lui promet, que Dieu le delivrera sans armes, lui ordonne de marcher vers la mer, sur laquelle il etend sa verge, et lui commande d'ouvrir un chemin a ce peuple, et qui agit comme s'il prevoyoit d'une maniere sure cette ebe extraordinaire arrivée cette seule fois dans notre monde, cet homme doit tenir sa mission du maitre de la nature, qui seul pouvoit reveler ce qu'il avoit arrangé dans celle-ci pour le salut des Israelites."——Monsieur Niebuhr hath cited in his description of Arabia this passage from Michaelis, and he very sensibly observes, "J'avoue, que le decouvrement du fonds de la mer qui même selon Monsr Michaelis etoit surnaturel au supreme degré, l'operation de la Providence, la tempête supposée qui dans l'espace de 24 heures souffloit de deux plages contraires, pendant que le vent y est constamment six mois Nord et six mois Sud, l'obeissance de la mer qui offrit au peuple d'Israel un chemin des que Moïse avoit etendu sa main sur elle, j'avoue, dis-je, que toutes ces circonstances me paroissent autant de miracles. Si tout cela s'est passé tres naturellement, je ne sais pas encore ce que les savans entendent par le mot de miracle." (Description de l'Arabie, 359, 360.) I refer the curious reader to this authentic traveller for some elucidations on this subject, and he may be farther gratified on consulting, the Essai Physique sur l'heure des marées dans la mer rouge of Monsr Michaelis, and Le Clerc Dissert. de Traject. Mar. Idum.

¹ Josephus hath been supposed by some persons, to have endeavoured to prove the possibility of

OF ALEXANDER THE GREAT. 83

After the battle of Granicus, Alexander paſſed victoriouſly through Ionia, Caria, Lydia, and Pamphylia, when he quitted the borders of the Ægean ſea to penetrate into the interior part of the country, by Piſidia and the greater Phrygia to Gordium,[m]

---

of the paſſage of the Iſraelites from Alexander's march; but whatever may have been his doubts and intentions, the miraculous paſſage of the Iſraelites is recorded on evidence that is indiſputable. The veracity of the event is confirmed by various alluſions to it in the ſacred writings, and it is referred to by the prophets, (Iſaiah 63. V. 12, 13. Habakkuk 3. 10.) who lived comparatively ſpeaking, at no great diſtance from the time of this ſignal interpoſition of the Divinity in favour of his choſen people, and muſt have received the tradition, whilſt all its wonderful circumſtances were freſh upon the memory; who were above impoſition; and who were immediately inſpired by Omnipotence. As to the parallel itſelf, there is certainly an indecency in it, and what is more extraordinary, there is not the leaſt reſemblance.——In the paſſage of the Iſraelites, Moſes ſtretches out his rod, and the ſea in obedience opens and divides; the wind blows with violence from a new and unuſual point of the compaſs; the waters become a wall on the right hand and on the left, and the Children of Iſrael continue their route on the dry ſand.——Alexander on the contrary, with a part of his army made his way through the ſea with the water up to the waiſt, as Strabo (Lib. 14. Tom. 2.—982.) expreſsly tells us, and owed in all likelihood the ſafety of the paſſage to the fortunate circumſtance of a ſtrong wind, ſetting off the ſhore and againſt the tide, which he had the good ſenſe to take advantage of.

[m] It was at Gordium that Alexander cut the celebrated knot, on which the future deſtiny of Aſia depended. Q. Curtius hath given the following account of it. "Notabile erat jugum adſtrictum compluribus nodis in ſemetipſos implicatis, et celantibus nexus. Incolis deinde adfirmantibus, editam eſſe oraculo ſortem, Aſiæ potiturum, qui inexplicabile vinculum ſolviſſet: cupido inceſſit animo fortis ejus implendæ. Circa regem erat et Phrygum turba, et Macedonum: illa expectatione fuſpenſa, hæc ſollicita ex temeraria regis fiducia. Quippe ſeries vinculorum ita adſtricta, ut unde nexus inciperet, quove ſe conderet, nec ratione, nec viſu percipi poſſet, ſolvere adgreſſo injeceret curam, ne in omen verteretur inritum inceptum. Ille nequaquam diu luctatus cum latentibus nodis; nihil, inquit, intereſt quonodo ſolvantur: gladioque ruptis omnibus loris, oraculi ſortem vel eluſit, vel implevit." (Q. Curt. Lib. 3. C. 1. Tom.1---57, 58.) This was an expeditious method of ſolving the difficulty, but Ariſtobulus, according to Arrian, hath related the anecdote very differently. " Αριϛοβυλος δε λεγει, εξελοντα τον εϛηρα τυ ρυμυ, ὁς ην τυλος διαβεβλημενος δια του ρυμυ διαμπαξ, ξενιχον τον δεσμον, εξελκυσαι εξω του ρυμου τον ζυγον." He adds however afterward

the ancient capital of the province. From Gordium he directed his march towards the East and arrived at Ancyra,ⁿ where he received the Paphlagonian deputies. They were charged with a commission to offer him the homage of their nation, and to request that he would not order any of his forces into their territories. The negotiation was successful, and their petition was agreed to, on a promise of their obedience to Calas, the Satrap of Phrygia. The story then of Q. Curtius, who tells us, that the Macedonian army entered into Paphlagonia,° hath no truth in it; and it is indeed contradicted by the historian himself, who makes

Alexander

---

afterwards, that he was doubtful how the knot was absolutely loosened, though he considered the intention of the Oracle to have been fulfilled, from the subsequent appearances in the heavens. "Ὅπως μὲν δὴ ἐπράχθη τὰ ἀμφὶ τῷ δεσμῷ τούτῳ Ἀλεξάνδρῳ, οὐκ ἔχω ἰσχυρίσασθαι· Ἀπηλλάγη δ'οὖν ἀπὸ τῆς ἁμάξης αὐτός τε καὶ οἱ ἀμφ'αὐτόν, ὡς τοῦ λογίου τοῦ ἐπὶ τῇ λύσει τοῦ δεσμοῦ ξυμβεβηκότος. Καὶ γὰρ καὶ τῆς νυκτὸς ἐκείνης βροντάς τε καὶ σέλας ἐξ οὐρανοῦ ἐπισημῆναι κἂν ἐπὶ τούτοις ἔθυε τῇ ὑστεραίᾳ Ἀλέξανδρος τοῖς φήνασι θεοῖς τά τε σημεῖα, καὶ τοῦ δεσμοῦ τὴν λύσιν." Arrian. Exped. Alex. Lib. 2. Chap. 3.--110, 111.

ⁿ "Ἐπ'Ἀγκύρας τῆς Γαλατικῆς ἐστέλλετο, κἀκεῖ αὐτῷ πρεσβεία ἀφικνεῖται Παφλαγόνων τό τε ἔθνος ἐνδιδόντων, ᾗ ἐς ὁμολογίαν ξυμβαίνοντων· ἐς δὲ τὴν χώραν ξὺν τῇ δυνάμει μὴ ἐσβάλλειν ἐδέοντο· Τούτοις μὲν δὴ προσάσσει Ἀλέξανδρος ὑπακούειν κάλα τῷ σατράπῃ τῆς Φρυγίας." Arrian. Exped. Alex. Lib. 2. Chap. 4.--111.

° "Jamque ad urbem Ancyram ventum erat; ubi numero copiarum inito, Paphlagoniam intrat. ——Omnisque hæc regio: paruit regi datisque obsidibus, tributum quod ne Persis quidam tulissent, pendere ne cogerentur impetraverunt. Calas huic regioni præpositus est." (Q. Curtius, Lib. 3. C. 1.Tom. 1.—59.) It appears from this passage of Q. Curtius, that Alexander marched after his arrival at Ancyra into Paphlagonia, which was then much nearer him, and consequently the Baron de St. Croix's reasoning is not applicable. The error may have arisen from the city Ancyra in Phrygia having been mistaken for the Ancyra in Galatia, where the Paphlagonian deputies met Alexander, and which Arrian hath ascertained by the "Τῆς Γαλατικῆς." If Alexander was satisfied with the offers of the deputies, he certainly did not march into Paphlagonia against their explicit stipulation. The two historians are at issue on the point: I do not mean to decide the difference, but to state it fairly.

Alexander to march from Gordium to Ancyra, by which he muſt have paſſed Paphlagonia, at ſome diſtance on the left.

Cappadocia was involved in the fate of the neighbouring nations, and ſubmitted to the Macedonian Conqueror, who poſted a part of his troops on the ſame ground that the Younger Cyrus had halted upon, in his march to Cunaxa. Q. Curtius pretends that this poſt was the preciſe place, where Cyrus the Great had ſtopped in his expedition againſt Lydia.[p] Notwithſtanding a miſtake of this kind is of little conſequence, yet in one ſenſe it is material, and it may not be improper to refute it, in order to ſhew that he is very inaccurate in the moſt trifling details. We are told by Xenophon, who had a command under the Younger Cyrus, and was undoubtedly preſent, that he arrived at Dana[q] a great and
flouriſhing

---

[p] "Ciliciam petens cum omnibus copiis, regionem quæ caſtra Cyri appellatur, pervenerat. Stativa ibi habuerat Cyrus, quum adverſum Cræſum in Lydiam duceret." Q. Curtius, Lib. 3. C. 4. Tom. 1.—82, 83.

[q] "Κῦρος δὲ μετὰ τῶν ἄλλων ἐξελαύνει διὰ Καππαδοκίας, σταθμοὺς τέσσαρας, παρασάγγας εἴκοσι καὶ πέντε, πρὸς Δαναν, πόλιν οἰκουμένην, μεγάλην κỳ εὐδαίμονα· Ἐνταῦθα ἔμεινεν ἡμέρας τρεῖς.——Ἐντεῦθεν ἐπειρῶντο ἐσβάλλειν εἰς τὴν Κιλικίαν ἡ δὲ εἰσβολὴ ἦν ὁδὸς ἁμαξιτός, ὀρθία ἰσχυρῶς, κỳ ἀμήχανος εἰσελθεῖν ςρατεύματι εἰ τις ἐκώλυεν." (Xenophon de Cyri Exped. 17, 18. 4to Oxon. 1735.) Monſieur d'Anville thinks the text to have been corrupted, and that " Τυανα " is the true reading, but if he founds his opinion on Strabo, " Κύρου ςρατόπεδον διὰ Τυανων," (Lib. 12. Tom. 2.—813.) it is ſuſpicious authority, and even Strabo wants a correction before the " Κυρου " can be transformed into " Κυρυ."
——Hutchinſon ſeems to be of an opinion that " Αδανα " was the proper name of the city in queſtion, and in ſupport of it, he cites the following authors.---Ptolem. Lib. 5. Chap. 8.---Seylac Perip.--40.---Plin. Hiſt. Nat. Lib. 5. Chap. 27.---Steph. Byzant. Appian de Bello Mith.---Procop. Lib. 5. Ædific. 65.---Anton. Itin. 580.---See the diſſertation prefixed to his edition of the Anabaſis.

flourishing city, and after staying there three days traversed the boundaries of Cilicia.—Alexander's route agrees with that of the Younger Cyrus, and Arrian, who traces it with his usual accuracy, hath also informed us, that the Grecian Hero occupied the same ground before he passed the Gorges of Cilicia, that the Persian Prince had previously encamped on, with the ten thousand Greeks.'—As the Macedonian army descended into the plains of Cilicia, Arsames evacuated the province, which according to Q. Curtius, Darius had entrusted to him, and retreating with the forces under his command, set the city of Tarsus on fire,' and laid

---

' "Arrian nous dit que le Conquerant Macedonien campa," (a repetition in substance of the "Qui campa avec son armée") but the text of Arrian will hardly reach these expressions, as Alexander marched immediately to carry this dangerous pass by surprise, and left Parmenio with only the heavy armed infantry on this celebrated ground, who joined him early the next day. I have used a term that appears to me more analogous to the Greek.—" Προηγεν επι τας πυλας της Κιλικιας. Και αφικμενος επι το Κυρω του ξυν Ξενοφωντι ςρατοπεδον, ως κατεχομενας τας πυλας φυλακαις ισχυραις ιδε, Παρμενιωνα μεν αυτου καταλειπει συν ταις ταξεσι των πεζων, οσοι βαρυτερον ωπλισμενοι ησαν· ——Τη δ'υςεραια αμα τη εω ξυν τη δυναμει παση υπερβαλων τας πυλας, κατεβαινεν ες την Κιλικιαν·" (Arrian. Exped. Alex. Lib. 2. Chap. 4.-111,112.) The description which Q. Curtius hath left us of this passage, corresponds so perfectly with that of Xenophon, that there can be little doubt but they meant it for the same. "Angustias aditus, qui Ciliciam aperit, hostem jugumque imminens unde inultus subeuntem aut prohibere aut opprimere, potuisset.——Alexander fauces jugi, quæ Pylæ appellantur, intravit. Contemplatus locorum situs, non alias magis dicitur admiratus esse felicitatem suam; obrui potuisse vel saxis confitebatur, si fuissent, qui in subeuntes propellerent." (Q. Curtius, Lib. 3. Chap. 4. Tom. 1.--84, 87.) The only hesitation that can remain will be, whether greater credit is due to Arrian and Xenophon, or Q. Curtius.

' "Brula la ville de Tarse." I do not find that the city of Tarsus is said to have been actually burnt by Arsames, though it was set on fire if we are to believe Q. Curtius, and saved from destruction by the fortunate arrival of Parmenio. "Pervenit ad urbem Tarson, cui tum maxima Persæ subjiciebant ignem; ne opulentum oppidum hostis invaderet. At ille Parmenione ad inhi-

tendum

laid the whole country waste. Arrian on the contrary, assures us that Alexander overreached Arsames, and that the Persian general abandoned Tarsus and Cilicia without such devastation,ᵗ or doing them any damage.——Information was given Alexander at Mallos, that Darius was encamped at Sochus in the Commagene, and on the receipt of the intelligence, he began his march, passed the mountains of Cilicia, and pitched upon a camp near the Myriander. Understanding that the Persian army had changed its position, and quitted the advantageous post that it had occupied, he repassed the mountains in the night ʷ by the Gorges of Syria, at the very hour that the Persian troops were defiling by those of Amanica, two passes which serve for a communication between Cilicia and the regions on this side of the Euphrates.ˣ Q. Curtius hath given a very confused account of these important marches, and hath left the different movements of the armies in great obscurity.ʸ Diodorusᶻ is still less exact.

bendum incendium cum expeditâ manu premisso, postquam barbaros adventû suorum fugatos esse cognovit, urbem â se conservatam intrat." Q. Curtius, Lib. 3. Chap. 4. Tom. 1.--88.

ᵗ " Ὡς τε ὁ Ἀρσαμης μαθων αυτου την ὁρμην σπουδη φευγει εκ της Ταρσε παρα βασιλεα Δαρειον, ουδε ελαψας την πολιν·" Arrian. Exped. Alex. Lib. 2. Chap. 4.--112.

ʷ "Forte eâdem nocte et Alexander ad fauces, quibus Syria aditur, et Darius ad eum locum quem Amanicas Pylas vocant, pervenit." (Q. Curtius, Lib. 3. Chap. 8. Tom. 1.—107, 108.) Arrian hath described these manœuvres more at large. Exped. Alex. Lib. 2. Chap. 7, 8.--119, 124.

ˣ See Cellarii Geograph. Ant. Lib. 3. Chap. 6.

ʸ " Q. Curce pour n'etre pas entre dans aucun detail." Instead of it, he enters into an account of these movements to some extent, (Lib. 3. Chap. 8, 9, 10.) but he certainly entangles himself in a labyrinth of confusion.

ᶻ Diodorus Siculus. Lib. 17. Tom. 2.—183. Scarce worth a reference.

At the break of day the Macedonians defcended from the mountains, and difcovered with aftonifhment the Perfian line extended to a great length upon the plain. Alexander loft no time in forming his army, the right being protected by the mountains and the left by the fea,[a] a pofition which ought to have pointed out to Quintus Curtius the folly of advancing that the right was furrounded by the enemy.[b] This memorable battle was fought near Iffus, and the Perfian cavalry performed prodigies of valour, though fortune again followed the Macedonian ftandard. Many of the nobility of the Perfian court fell in this engagement, and after a gallant and generous defence of their unfortunate Monarch, were flain immediately before his eyes.[c]——The Greeks in the Perfian pay overturned every thing that was oppofed to them, and the Macedonian phalanx manœuvring on unequal ground was under the neceffity of breaking, and only repulfed at laft with the utmoft difficulty the repeated attacks that were made upon it by the enemy. Alexander was wounded in the action, but not by Darius, as Chares hath related, which was a circumftance that he certainly

---

[a] "Ως δε διαχωρει ες πλατος, ανεπτυσσεν ατι το κερας, ις φαλαγγα, αλλην και αλλην των οπλιτων ταξιν παραγων. Τη μεν, ως επι το ορος, εν αριτερα δε, ως επι την θαλασσαν." Arrian. Exped. Alex. Lib. 2. Chap. 8.--124; 125.

[b] "Dextrum Alexandri cornu circumibatur." Q. Curtius. Lib. 3. Chap. 11. Tom.—124.

[c] "Circa currum Darii jacebant nobiliffimi duces, ante oculos regis egregiâ morte defuncti, omnes in orâ proni, ficut dimicantes procubuerant, adverfo corpore vulneribus acceptis." (Q. Curtius, Lib. 3. Chap. 1. Tom. 1.--127.) Diodorus Siculus adds his teftimony to the flaughter round Darius. "Περι μεν το τν Δαρειο τιθριππον ταχυ νεκρων εσωρευδη πληθος." Sicul. Lib. 17. Tom. 2.--185.

certainly would not have omitted in his letter to Antipater, where he simply mentions his being wounded in the thigh.[d] Q. Curtius[e] reduces the loss of the conquerors to thirty-two of their infantry, and one hundred and fifty of their cavalry. Justin[f] makes it amount to one hundred and fifty of the former, and his number of the latter agrees with that of Q. Curtius and also Diodorus Siculus,[g] though the Grecian writer differs widely from them as to the infantry, and calculates the killed alone at three hundred. Arrian[h] only mentions the death of Ptolemy the son of Seleucus, and of one hundred and twenty Macedonians of rank and dignity, who fell in the attack of the phalanx.[i] If however such a considerable

---

[d] "Τρωθηναι ξιφει τον μηρον, ὡς μεν Χαρης φησιν, απο Δαρειου (συμπεσειν γαρ αυτους εις χειρας) Αλεξανδρῳ· δε περι της μαχης επιστελλων τοις περι τον Αντιπατρον, ουκ ειρηκεν, ὁτις ην ὁ τρωσας, ὁτι δε τρωθειη τον μηρον εγχειριδιω, δυσχερες δ'ουδεν απο του τραυματος συμβαιη, γεγραφεν." (Plut. de Vit. Alex. Plut. Opera. Tom. 1.--675.) Diodorus Siculus seems also to prove that the Macedonian Hero was wounded in the heat of the conflict, by some unknown hand. "Συνεβη και αυτον τον Αλεξανδρον τρωθηναι τον μηρον, περιχυθεντων των πολεμιων." (Diod. Sicul. Lib. 17. Tom. 2.--185.) and Q. Curtius only mentions the accident in general terms.---"Inter quos Alexandri dextrum femur leviter mucrone perstrictum est." Q. Curtius. Lib. 3. Chap. 11. Tom. 1.--128.

[e] "Ex parte Alexandri quatuor et quingenti saucii fuere : triginta omnino et duo ex peditibus desiderati sunt : equitum centum quinquaginta interfecti." Q. Curtius. Lib. 3. Chap. 11.---135.

[f] "Ex Macedonibus cecidere pedestres centum triginta, equites centum quinquaginta." Justin. Lib. 11. Chap. 9.--279.

[g] "Των δε Μακεδονων πεζοι μεν εις τριακοσιους, ἱππεις δε περι ἑκατον κ᾽ πεντηκοντα·" Diod. Sicul. Lib. 17. Tom. 2.--187.

[h] "Ενταυθα πιπτει Πτολεμαιος τε ὁ Σελευκε, ανηρ αγαθος γενομενος, κ᾽ αλλοι ες εικοσι μαλιστα κ᾽ ἑκατον, των ουκ ημελημενων Μακεδονων·" (Arrian. Exped. Alex. Lib. 2. Chap. 11.---134.) Arrian hath left us in the dark as to the whole of Alexander's loss, but the silence is suspicious.

[i] "Dans un seul choc." I do not find that this expression is correct. Arrian in the passage just

derable number of persons of distinction fell in the attack of the phalanx only, our ideas of the number of the slain on the whole field of battle during this action, which was as long as it was bloody, must be very different from the accounts of the historians, that have been referred to. And though the historians agree in the loss of the defeated army, no substantial reason is to be deduced from it, that adds any further credit to their calculations. One hundred thousand of the Persian infantry, and ten thousand of their cavalry perished in this fatal day, according to the general account,[k] which was more than a sixth of their whole forces, which they reckoned at six hundred thousand men. Justin hath not adopted a much more moderate opinion, though he only reckons sixty-one thousand of their infantry[l] to have been killed, as he reduces the Persian army to four hundred thousand infantry, and one hundred thousand cavalry.[m] Perhaps the text of this writer may have been corrupted, and we ought to read three hundred

---

just cited makes use of the term "Ενταυθα πιπτει," but it has not by any means that limited signification. I have left it more at large, and the Baron de St. Croix had before termed the attacks of the phalanx "Vives et reiterées."

[k] "Πληθ⊕ εις δεκα μαλιϛα μυριαδας κ̣ εν τουτοις, ἱππεις ὑπερ τες μυριες" (Arrian. Exped. Alex. Lib. 2. Chap. 11.) "In acie autem cæsa sunt Persarum peditum centum millia, decem vero millia interfecta equitum." (Q. Curtius. Lib. 3. Chap. 11.--134, 135.) "Κατα δε την μαχην ετελευ-τησαν των βαρβαρων πεζοι μεν πλειες των δεκα μυριαδων, ἱππεις δε ὐκ ελαττες των μυριων." Diod. Sicul. Lib. 17. Tom. 2.--187.

[l] "Cæsa sunt peditum unum et sexaginta millia, equitum decem millia." Justin. Lib. 11. Chap. 9.---279.

[m] "Darius cum quadringentis millibus peditum et centum millibus equitum in aciem procedit." Justin. Lib. 11. Chap. 9.---277.

OF ALEXANDER THE GREAT. 91

hundred thousand men instead of four hundred thousand, as the corresponding passage of Paulus Orosiusⁿ his copyist gives us room to imagine. The manœuvres of the two armies on this celebrated day are described with great perspicuity by Arrian, and he seems to be entirely free from the gross errors, with which Polybius hath reproached Callisthenes. The fragment of this author which contains this piece of military criticism, is entitled to a quotation at its full length.°——" In the account then which Callisthenes has given of this battle, he relates; that Alexander had already led his army through the passes which are called the Pylæ of Cilicia, when Darius, having advanced along the passes of the mountain Amanus, and being informed by the people of the country, that his enemy still continued his march forwards into Syria, resolved to follow him. That when he arrived near the passes of Cilicia, he encamped along the river Pyramus: that the ground which he occupied contained a space of only fourteen stadia from the sea to the foot of the mountain: and that the river, falling down the craggy sides of the mountain, ran obliquely through this ground, and passing over the plain, between

some

ⁿ "Darius cum trecentis millibus peditum et centum millibus equitum in aciem procedit."
P. Orosius. Lib. 3. Chap. 16.---182.

° "φησι μεν, Αλεξανδρον ηδη διαπεπορευσθαι τα στενα. κ̓ τας λεγομενας εν τη Κιλικια Πυλας· Δαρειον δε, χρησαμενον τη δια των Αμανιδων λεγομενων Πυλων πορεια, καταραι μετα της δυναμεως εις Κιλικιαν, πυθομενον δε παρα των εγχωριων, ωρμησεν τον Αλεξανδρον ως επι Συριαν, ακολουθειν· κ̓ συνεγγισαντα τοις στενοις, στρατοπεδευσαι παρα τον Πιναρον ποταμον· ειναι δε το μεν τοπο το διαστημα ου πλειω των τεσσαρων κ̓ δεκα σταδιων απο θαλαττης εως προς την παρωρειαν, δια δε τουτο φερεσθαι τον προειρημενον ποταμον επικαρσιον, απο μεν των ορων ευθεως εκρηγματα (πολλα ποιουντα) των πλειων, δια δε των επιπεδων εως εις θαλατταν

some hills that were rough and difficult of approach, discharged itself into the sea. After this description, he says; that, when Alexander returned back again with a design to engage, Darius and his officers drew up the whole phalanx in order of battle upon the very ground upon which they had encamped; and that they were covered in front by the river, which ran close to the camp: that they posted the cavalry near to the sea: next to these, in the same line, the mercenaries, along the bank of the river, and lastly the Peltastæ, adjoining to the foot of the mountain.

But it is not possible to conceive, that these troops could have been thus drawn up in order of battle between the phalanx and the river, if the river ran close to the camp: especially if we consider the numbers of which the several bodies were composed. For the cavalry, as Callisthenes himself affirms, amounted to thirty thousand; and the mercenaries to as great a number. Now it is easy to determine, what extent of ground this number of troops would require. The usual method of drawing up cavalry

in

λασσαν αποτομας εχοντα κỳ δυσβατυς λοφυς. Ταυτα δ'ὑποσιμιν⊙, επει συνεγγιζοιεν οἱ περι τον Αλεξανδρον, εξ ὑποστροφης επ'αυτοις αναχωρησντες· κριναι, φησι, Δαρειον κỳ τυς ἡγεμονας, την μεν φαλυγ'α ταξαι πασαν εν αυτη τη ϛρατοπεδεια, καθαπερ εξ αρχης ηχι, χρησεσθαι δε τω ποταμω προβλημχτι, δια το παρ'αυτην ϛειν την ϛρατοπεδειαν. Μετα δε ταυτα, φησι, τυς μεν ἱππεις ταξαι παρα θαλατ]αν, τυς δε μισθοφορυς ἑξης τυτοις παρ'αυτον τον ποταμον εχομενυς τουτων, τους δε πελταϛας συναπτοντας τοις ϛεισι.

Πως δε προεταξε τουτους προ της φαλαγ⊙, τε ποταμυ ϛιοντ⊙ παρ'αυτην την ϛρατοπεδειαν, δυσχιρες κατανοησαι· κỳ ταυτα τω πληθει τοσυτων ὑπαρχοντων. τρισμυριοι μεν γαρ ἱππεις ὑπηρχον, ὡς αυτος ὁ
Καλλισθενης

in the time of action is to range them eight in depth. It is necessary also to leave a certain space between each of the troops in front, that they may be able to perform their several motions. A single stadium then will contain eight hundred horse; ten stadia, eight thousand; and four stadia, three thousand and two hundred. According to this computation, a body of eleven thousand and two hundred horse would have filled the whole extent of fourteen stadia. And if the whole thirty thousand were formed in order of battle, there must have been three such bodies, within a very small number at least, drawn up each behind the other. In what place then were the mercenaries ranged? Was it behind the cavalry? But Callisthenes says no such thing. On the contrary he affirms, that the mercenaries were engaged against the Macedonians in the very beginning of the action. It is manifest therefore, that one half of the ground that has been mentioned, the part that was on the side of the sea, was occupied by the cavalry; and the other half, which was next to the mountain, by the mercenaries. And from hence we may clearly judge, what must have been the depth of the cavalry; and, by consequence, how very distant the river must have been from the camp.

Afterwards

Καλλισθενης φησι, τρισμυριοι δε μισθοφοροι. ποσου δ'ειχον ετοι τοπου χρειαν, ευχερες καταμαθειν. Πλειστον μεν γαρ ιππεων ταττεται βαθ©. επ'οκτω προς αληθινην χρειαν ᾗ μεταξυ των ιλων εκαστης συμπαρχειν δει διαςημα τοις μετωποις, προς το ταις επιςροφαις δυνασθαι ᾗ τοις περισπασμοις ευχρηςειν. εξ ων το ςαδιον οκτακοσιες λαμβανει, τα δε δεκα τες οκτακισχιλιες, τα δε τετταρα τρισχιλιες διακοσιες· ωςʹαπο των μυριων χιλιων διακοσιων πεπληρεισθαι τον των τεσσαρεισκαιδεκα ςαδιων τοπον. εαν δε παντας εκταθη τες τρισμυριες, βραχυ λειπει το τριφαλαγγιαν επαλληλον ειναι των ιππεων αυτων. Εις ποιον ουν τοπον εταττετο

Afterwards he relates, that, when the enemy approached, Darius, who was in the centre of the line, called the mercenaries to him from one of the wings. But how was this possible? The very part in which the mercenaries were joined to the cavalry was itself the centre. If Darius then was among the mercenaries, how, or from whence, or to what place did he call them? He then adds also, that the cavalry upon the right wing advanced, and vigorously charged the Macedonians: that the latter received them with equal courage; and that the fight on both sides was maintained with the greatest bravery. But he forgets that there was a river between this cavalry and the Macedonians; and such a river too, as he had just before described.

Nor is this writer more exact in his account with respect to Alexander. He says, that this Prince first carried with him into Asia forty thousand foot, and four thousand five hundred horse: and that, when he was ready to enter Cilicia, a new supply arrived from Macedon, of five thousand foot, and eight hundred horse.

τετο το των μισθοφορων πληθ۰; εἰ μη νη Δια κατοπιν των ἱππεων, αλλ᾽ ἐ φησιν, αλλα συμπεπτωκεναι τετες τοις Μακεδοσι κατα την επαγωγην. εξ ὡν αναγκη, ποιεισθαι τας εκδοχην, διοτι το μεν ἡμισυ τε τοπε, το παρα θαλατταν, ἡ των ἱππεων επηχε ταξις, το δ᾽ ἡμισυ, το προς τοις ορεσιν, ἡ των μισθοφορων. εκ δε τετων ευσυλλογιστον, ποσον ὑπηρχε το βαθ۰ των ἱππεων, κ᾽ ποιον ἐδει τουτων απεχειν τον ποταμον απο της ϛρατοπεδειας. Μετα δε ταυτα συναγιζοντων των πολεμιων, φησι, τον Δαρειον αυτον, κατα μεσην ὑπαρχοντα την ταξιν, καλειν της μισθοφορες απο τε κερατ۰ προς αυτον. πως δε λεγεται τετο, διαπορην ες͵ τῶν γαρ μισθοφορων αναγκη κ᾽ των ἱππεων την συναφην κατα μεσον ὑπαρχειν τον τοπον. ὡς᾽ εν αυτοις ἀν τοις μισθοφορεης ὁ Δαρει۰, πως, κ᾽ προς τι, κ᾽ πως εκαλει τες μισθοφορες; Το δε τελευταιον φησι, τας απο τε δεξιε κερατ۰ ἱππεας επαγχοντας εμβαλειν τοις περι τον Αλεξανδρον· τες δε γενναιως δεξαμενες αντεπαγχειν, κ᾽ ποιειν μαχην ισχυραν. ὁτι δε ποταμ۰ ην εν μεσω, κ᾽ ποταμ۰, ὁιον αρτιως ειπεν, επιλαθετο.

horse. If we take then from these three thousand foot, and three hundred horse; which is the greatest number that can be allowed for occasional and absent services; there will remain forty-two thousand foot, and five thousand horse. With this army Alexander, as the historian writes, being informed, after he had advanced beyond the Pylæ, that Darius had entered Cilicia, and was at the distance of only a hundred stadia behind him, immediately returned, and directed his march back again through the passes: having the infantry in his van; behind these, the cavalry; and the baggage in the rear. As soon as he came into the open plain, he separated the army from the baggage, and formed the troops into a phalanx, by thirty-two in depth. At some distance afterwards, he ranged them by sixteen in depth: and at last, when he was come near to the enemy, by eight.

Now these absurdities are even greater than those that were before remarked. For when a body of troops marches by sixteen in depth, if we allow the usual intervals of six feet between every rank,

rank, a stadium will contain only sixteen hundred men; ten stadia, sixteen thousand; and twenty stadia, thirty-two thousand. If Alexander therefore formed his phalanx by sixteen in depth, he must have filled a space of twenty stadia, and would still have wanted room for all his cavalry, and for ten thousand of his foot. Callisthenes then adds, that when this Prince was at the distance of forty stadia from the enemy, he ordered the phalanx to advance in an extended front towards them. A greater absurdity than this is scarcely to be conceived. For where is the ground, especially in Cilicia, that will admit such a phalanx as is here described to advance in an extended front against an enemy: a ground, containing twenty stadia in depth, and forty in length? The impediments also, which would inevitably break the order of such a disposition, are too many to be recounted. Callisthenes himself has mentioned one, which is alone sufficient. For he says, that the torrents, which descended from the hills, had formed so many pits in the plain, that the greatest part of the Persians were lost in those cavities as they fled.

But

τοις πολεμιοις, εις οκτω. Ταυτα δ'εςι μειζω των προειρημενων αλοημματα. τε γαρ ςαδια λαμβανοντ۵ ανδρας εν τοις πρευτικοις διαςημασιν, οταν εις εκκαιδεκα το βαθ۵ ωσι, χιλιες εξακοσιες, εκαςε των ςαδιων εξ ποδας απεχοντ۵· φανερον, οτι τα δεκα ςαδια ληψεται μυριες εξακισχιλιες, τα δε εικοσι της διπλασιες. εκ δε τετων ευθεωρητον, οτι, καθ'ον καιρον εποιησε την δυναμιν Αλεξανδρ۵ εκκαιδεκα το βαθ۵. αναγκαιον ην, εικοσι ςαδιων επεχειν το τε τοπα διαςημα, ᾗ περιπλεειν ετι της μεν ιππεις παντας, των δε πεζων μυριες.

Μετα δε ταυτα φησι, μετωπηδον αγειν την δυναμιν, απεχοντα των πολεμιων περι τετραρκοντα ςαδιες. Τετο δε μειζον αλογημα δυσχερες επινοησαι. που γαρ αν ευροι τις τοιετες τοπες, αλλως τε ᾗ κατα Κιλικιαν, ωςε επι ςαδιες εικοσι μεν το πλατ۵, τετραρκοντα δε το μηκ۵, μεταπηδον αγειν φαλαγγα σαριςοφορον;

But Alexander, perhaps this writer might fay, was willing to be ready to receive the enemy, in what part foever they fhould come to attack him. But nothing is more unfit for this purpofe than the phalanx formed in an extended front, if this front be broken and difunited. And would it not alfo have been much more eafy, to have ranged the feveral parts of this great body in the very order in which they followed each of them the other in the march: inftead of forming the whole army in a fingle line, in which there muft have been many vacancies, and leading it in an extended front to action, over a ground that was covered with bufhes and broken cavities. He ought rather then to have formed a double, or a quadruple phalanx. One part following behind another. For if the ground would have admitted this order in the march, there would have been time fufficient to draw up the troops in the fame order in battle: efpecially as he might have received notice from his fcouts of the approach of the enemy, even while they were at a confiderable diftance from him.

Another fault in this defcription is, that the hiftorian, while he reprefents the phalanx as advancing in an extended front over a plain,

φοςεν; τοσαυτα γαρ εςιν εμποδια πρὸς τὴν τοιαυτὴν ταξιν κ̣ χρηται, α τις εδ'εξαριθμησαιτο ραδιως. εκ δὲ των ὑπ'αυτε τε Καλλισθενες λεγομενων ἱκανον ὑπαρχει πρὸς πισιν. τες γαρ απο των ορων χειμαρρες καταφερομενες τοσαυτα φησι ποιειν εκρηγματα κατα το πεδιον, ὡςε κ̣ των Περσων κατα τὴν φυγὴν διαρθαρηναι λεγεσι τες πλεισες εν τοις τοιετοις κοιλωμασι. Νη Δι, αλλ'ετοιμ⍉ εβαλετ' ενα προς την των πολεμιων επιφανιαν. Τι δ'ανετοιμοτερον φαλαγγ⍉ εν μετωπω διαλελυμενης κ̣ διερχημμενης; ωστ γαρ εκ της εκτικης αγωγης αρμοζεσης παραταξαι ραδιον, η διαλελιμμενην εν μετωπω κ̣ διεσπασμενης δυναμιν επι την ακτιν εἰθιαν αναγκαιν, κ̣ συςησαι προς μαχην εν τοποις ιλωδεσι κ̣ περικεκλασμενοις. Διοπερ η'ὶ παρα μικρόν τι κρειτ᷄τω.

plain, forgets to make the cavalry march before; and places them upon the same line with the infantry. But the greatest of all his mistakes is this which follows. He says that Alexander, when he approached the enemy, drew up the phalanx eight in depth. The whole line therefore must have been equal in length to forty stadia. Or, let it be supposed, that the men stood so close together, as even to be wedged one within another. In that case, they must have covered at the least twenty stadia. And yet Callisthenes had before affirmed, that the whole length of the ground was less than fourteen stadia: that a part of it, which was nearest to the sea, was occupied by one half of the cavalry: that the other half was posted upon the right: and that between the whole line and the mountain there was left also a considerable distance; that the troops might not fall under a body of the enemy, which was posted upon the sides of the mountain. I know indeed, that, in order to oppose this body, he here forms a part of the line in the figure called the Forceps. Let us allow then ten thousand men; which is even a greater number than this purpose would require.

κριτ͞ον, αγειν διφαλαγ͞ιαν η τέτραφαλαγ͞ιαν αρμοζουσαν· ει κ͞ τοπον προς φοριαν ευρειν ουκ αδυνατον, κ͞ το παρταξαι ταχεως ραδιον γε, δυναμενον δια των προδρομων εκ πολλου γινωσκειν την των πολεμιων παρουσιαν. Ὁ δε, χωρις των αλλων, ουδε τας ιππεις προθετω, μετωπηδον αγων την δυναμιν εν τοποις επιπεδοις· αλλ᾽ εξ ισου ποιει τοις πεζοις.

Το δε δη παντων μεγιστον· ηδη γαρ συνιγυς οντα τοις πολεμιοις αυτον, εις οκτω ποιησαι φησι το βαθος. εξ ε δηλον, ὁτι κατ᾽ αναγκην επι τετλαρακοντα σταδιες εδει γινεσθαι το μηκ. της φαλαγ. ει δ᾽ ολως συμπιεσαι κατα τον ποιητην οὑτως, ὡςε συνεγγισαι προς αλληλες, ὁμως εικοσι σταδιων εδει τον τοπον υπαρχειν. αυτ. δε φησι, λειπειν των δεκατεσσαρων σταδιων, κ᾽ τουτο μερ. μεν τι προς θαλατ]η τας ἡμισιας επι τα δεξι-

require. In that cafe it is evident, that there would remain according to Callifthenes, eleven ftadia only at the moſt, for the length of the whole line: and that thirty-two thouſand men, contained in a ſpace of this extent, how cloſely foever they were crouded, muſt neceſſarily have been formed by thirty in depth. And yet Callifthenes affirms, that at the time of the action they were ranged by eight. Miſtakes like theſe cannot even be excuſed. For what credit is to be given to things that are impoſſible? When a writer lays down the exact meaſure of the ground, fixes the number of the men, aſcertains the diſtance of one man from another, and gives afterwards an account which is wholly incompatible with all theſe circumſtances; the falſehood is too glaring to be pardoned.

It would be tedious to examine all the errors into which this writer has fallen. One or two more however may juſt be mentioned. He ſays that Alexander took care to draw up his army in ſuch

δ' ετι δε την ολην ταξιν απο των οφων ικανον τοπον αφεςαναι, προς το μη τοις πολεμιοις επικαμπτεσθαι τους κατεχυσι τας παρυφεας. ισμεν γαρ ο ποιει προς τυτης επικαμπιον. υπολειπομεθα κ; νυν ημεις της μεςινς πιζες, παλαις οντας της εκεινυ προθεσεως ως εκ τουτων ενδεκα ςαδιους επι το πλεον απολειπεσθαι το τας φαλαγγ&. μηκ&, κατ'αυτον τον Καλλισθενη, εν οις αναγκη τους τρισμυριοις κ; διοχιλιους επι τριακοντα το βαθ&. υπαρχειν συνασπικοτας. ο δε φησιν, εις οκτω τεταγμενων γενεσθαι την μαχην. Τα δε τοιαυτα των αμαρτηματων ουδ' απολογιαν επιδεχεται· το γαρ αδυνατον εν πραγμασιν αυτοθεν εχει την πιςιν. διοπες ι· ταν κ; τα κατ'ανδρα διαςηματα. κ; το παν του τοπου μεγεθ&. ωρισμενον υποθωσι, κ; τον αριθμ:ν των αν· δρων, αναπολογητον γινεται το ψευδ&.

Τα μεν γαρ αμα τουτοις αλογηματα μακρον αν ειη λεγειν παντα, πλην τιθεως ολιγων. φησι γας. τον Αλεξανδρον σπουδαζειν κατα την ταξιν, ινα κατα τον Δαρειον αυτον ποιησηται την μαχην. ομοιως δε κατα

such a manner, that he might himself be engaged against Darius: and that Darius also had at first the same intention with respect to Alexander; but that he afterwards altered his design. But he neither mentions, how these princes knew, in what part of their respective armies they severally intended to engage; nor to what other part Darius retired, after he had changed his purpose. How again was it possible for the phalanx to advance, in order of battle, up the bank of a river, which was broken and uneven, and covered also with bushes in almost every part? Such an absurdity can never be ascribed to Alexander; who is acknowledged to have been trained both in the study and the exercise of war from his earliest age. It must therefore be imputed to the historian himself; who, from a want of skill in matters of this kind, was unable to distinguish what was possible to be done from that which was impracticable." [p]

If the spectators of these actions have published such faulty relations of them, and committed such considerable mistakes, the later writers who have too confidently followed them, must undoubtedly have been led into many errors by these dangerous guides.

The

μιν αρχας ᾗ του Δαρειου αιτον βουλεσθαι κατα του Αλεξανδρον, ὑστερον δι μετανοησαι, πως δ' επεγνωσαν αλληλους ὑτοι, που της ιδιας δυναμεως εχουσι την ταξιν, η που μετεβη παλιν ὁ Δαρεῖος, ἁπλως ουδεν λεγεται. πως δε προσανεβη προς την οφριν του ποταμου φαλαγγιτων ταξις, αποτομον ουσαν ᾗ βατωδη; ᾗ γαρ τουτο παρα λογον. Αλεξανδρω μεν ουν ουκ εποιστον την τοιαυτην ατοπιαν ὁμολογουμενον, παραλαμβανοντας περι αυτου την εν τοις πολεμικοις εμπειριαν ᾗ τριβην εκ παιδων· τω δε συγγραφει μαλλον, ὁς δια την απειριαν ουδε το δυνατον ᾗ το μη δυνατον εν τοις τοιουτοις δυνατως διεκρινεν." Polybius. Lib. 12. Chap. 17, 18. Tom. 3.--416----427.

[p] Hampton's Polybius. Vol. 4.--77----86. 8vo Edit. 1773.

The battle of Issus was fought in the month Mæmacterion, in the fourth year of the 111th Olympiad, when Nicocrates was Archon,[q] 333 years before Christ, and it decided the fate of Syria. Tyre had notwithstanding the courage to shut its gates against the Conqueror, and to punish a resistance as extraordinary as new to him in the regions of the East, it was immediately besieged. All the resources of art were employed in the defence of this unfortunate city, and they were seconded by the bravery of the inhabitants, who buried themselves under its ruins. An accuracy, which leaves the reader nothing to desire on the score of information, distinguishes the pen of Arrian[r] in his account of the labours of this memorable siege; whilst Q. Curtius,[s] from the luxuriance of his imagination, is rather the poet than historian. The construction of the mole, which Alexander made for the purpose of joining[t] Tyre to the continent, was too remarkable a piece of work to be passed over, without the embellishment of some fictitious decorations. An immense sea-monster agitated for some time the water, then forced itself upon the Grecian works, and after having been the astonishment of the besiegers and besieged, again plunged

---

[q] In Arrian, Nicostrates. "Τουτο τι..... τη μαχη εκεινη εγενετο, επι αρχοντ... Αθηναιοις Νικοςρατη. μεν... Μαιμακτηριων..." (Exped. Alex. Lib. 2. Chap. 11.--139.) But Diodorus Siculus hath "Νικοκρατης." Lib. 17. Tom. 2.--181.

[r] Arrian. Exped. Alex. Lib. 2. Chap. 18.--154——157.

[s] Q. Curtius. Lib. 4. Chap. 2, 3, 4. Tom. 1.--166——188.

[t] "Urbem à Continenti quatuor stadiorum fretum dividit." (Q. Curtius. Lib. 4. Chap. 2. Tom. 1.--167.) A distance of about eight hundred yards. According to Scylax, "Απικει καθ.. απο θαλαττης, γ." (Perip. 101.) which reduces it to six hundred.

plunged into the bosom of the deep. Sometimes the enormous beast was wholly visible; sometimes it was partly concealed by the waves, and it finally disappeared near the city walls.' Q. Curtius adds, that the assailants believed the monster to have pointed out to them the precise place, towards which they were to carry on their works. The Tyrians entertained a different opinion of the prodigy, and considering it as an indication of Neptune's resentment at the Macedonian encroachment on his empire of the sea, they flattered themselves with the expectation of seeing the whole speedily swept away.

T Alexander during the siege of Tyre, according to Arrian [w] and Q. Curtius,[x] made an excursion into Arabia. Plutarch[y] only tells us that he marched against the Arabs of Anti-Libanus, which Q. Curtius mistakes for Libanus itself. The first of these mountains,

---

[v] "Belua inusitatæ magnitudinis, super ipsos fluctus dorso emineus, ad molem, quam Macedones jecerant, ingens corpus adplicuit; diverberatifique fluctibus adlevans semet, utrinque conspecta est, deinde â capite molis rursus alto se immersit; ac modo super undas eminens magnâ sui parte, modo superfusis fluctibus, condita, haud procul munimenta urbis emersit. Utrisque lætus fuit beluæ adspectus: Macedones iter jaciendo operi monstrasse eam augurabantur; Tyrii Neptunum occupati maris vindicem adripuisse beluam, ac molem brevi profecto ruituram." Q. Curt. Lib. 4. Chap. 4. Tom. 1.--183, 184.

[w] "Ἐν τούτω δε ἀναλαβὼν τῶν δε ἱππέων ἴλας τινας, ᾗ τοὺς ὑπασπιστας, ᾗ τοὺς Ἀγριανας τε ᾗ τοὺς τοξότας, ἐπ' Ἀραβίας στέλλεται εἰς τὸν Ἀντιλίβανον καλούμενον τὸ ὄρος." Arrian. Exped. Alex. Lib. 2. Chap. 20.--160.

[x] "Cum expeditâ manu Arabiam petiit." Q. Curt. Lib. 4. Chap. 3. Tom. 1.--174.

[y] "Δια μέσης δε της πολιορκιας ἐπι τους Ἀραβας τους προσοικουντας τῳ Ἀντιλιβανῳ ςρατευσας." Plut. Vit. Alex. Plut. Opera. Tom. 1.--678.

tains, from the proximity of its situation, naturally furnished the Macedonian army with many of the materials, which they wanted for the siege; and as the Arabs had disturbed and plundered the workmen,[a] Alexander went with a detachment against them, to reprefs their depredations, and revenge the insult, which gave occasion to the supposed conquest of Arabia. Pliny[a] then advances without any foundation whatever, that the Conqueror, after having reduced the country, dispatched a vessel freighted with incense, for Leonidas his preceptor.

A civil war prevented Carthage from affording Tyre any succours in its distress;[b] but Q. Curtius is guilty of an Anachronism,

[a] "In Libano quoque Arabum agrestes incompositos Macedones adgressi triginta fere interficiunt, paucioribus captis." Q. Curtius. Lib. 4. Chap. 2. Tom. 1.--174.

[a] "Alexandro Magno in pueritiâ fine parfimoniâ thura ingerenti aris, pædagogus Leonides dixerat, ut illo modo, cum deviciffet thuriferas gentes, fupplicaret. At ille Arabiâ potitus, thure onuftam navem mifit ei, exhortatus ut large Deos adoraret. (Plin. Hift. Nat. Lib. 12. Chap. 32. Tom. 3.--26.) Pliny appears to have borrowed this anecdote from Plutarch, but it hath lost nothing by the repetition. "Επιθυμιωντι δε τοις Θεοις αφειδως αυτω, ϰ πολλακις επιδρατομενω τε λιβανιτω, ϖαρων Λεωνιδης ο παιδαγωγος, Ουτως, εφιεν, ω παι δαψιλως επιθυμιασεις, οταν της Λιβανοτοφορω κρατησης· ως αν εκρατησεν, επεμψε επιςολην ϖρος αυτον, Απεςαλκα σοι ταλαντα εκατον Λιβανωτε ϰ κασιας ινα μηκετι μικρολογη ϖρος τας Θεας, ειδως οτι ϰ της αρωματοφορω κρατωμεν." (Plutarch. Apothegm. Plut. Opera. Tom. 2.--179.) The "navem onuftam" I fuspected from the first.

[b] "Je ne vois dans l'histoire," says Monfr Bougainville, "aucun fait qu'on puisse appliquer ici, si ce n'est peut etre le complot tramé contre la liberté de Carthage, par un de ses premiers citoyens, que Justin nomme Hannon." (Juft. Lib. 21. Chap. 4.--471, 472.) "Cette conspiration n'eut pas de suites, quoique le chef de l'enterprise eut armé vingt mille esclaves, et soulevé quelques nations Africaines sujettes de la republique. Mais tant que la revolte dura, l'alarme dut etre vive à Carthage ; et comme l'auteur qui nous apprend le fait, n'en donne point la date, on peut, si je ne me trompe, presumer que ce fut cette guerre domestique qui reduisit les Carthaginois à n'etre que

nifm,' when he tells us that the Syracufians, who were then wafting Africa rendered it impracticable for the Carthaginians to fend the powerful reinforcement to their metropolis, that they intended. ——The fuccefsful defcent of Agathocles,ᵈ near Tunis, 310 years before Chrift, was the only inftance in which the Syracufian colours appeared floating in the plains of Africa, and this was twenty-two years after the capture of Tyre, which was taken in the month Hecatombœon, in the firft year of the 112th Olympiad, at the commencement of the magiftracy of Anicetus, called Nicetus

que fpectateurs oisifs du details de Tyr. Memoires fur le Voyage d'Hannon." (Mem. de l'Acad. des Infcriptions et des belles lettres. Tom. 28.--282.) Reineccius hath nearly the fame ideas,— Hift. Jul. 11.--455.

ᶜ " In iifdem diebus forte Carthaginienfium legati triginta fuperveniunt, majus obfeffis folatium quam auxilium: quippe domeftico bello Pænos impediri, nec de imperio fed pro falute dimicare nuntiabant. Syracufani tunc Africam urebant, et haud procul Carthaginis muris locarunt caftra." (Q. Curt. Lib. 4. C. 3. Tom. 1.--179.) The commentators have unanimoufly admitted the fallity of this hiftorical error, and the Jefuit Rader (ad Q. Curt. Lib. 4. Chap. 11.--144) hath fuppofed, that Timoleon had defeated about this time the Carthaginians, and ravaged all their territories in Sicily, and that they were apprehenfive of his landing with his troops and attacking Carthage. Cornelius Nepos and Plutarch, in their abftract of this great man's life, have given an account of his very formidable operations; but as we learn from Diodorus Siculus, (Lib. 16. Tom. 2.--145.) that a peace was agreed to by the Carthaginians and Timoleon, when Lyfimachides was Archon at Athens, in the fecond year of the 110th Olympiad, and Tyre was not befieged till the latter end of the fourth year of the 111th Olympiad, an interval of nearly fix years muft have effectually relieved them from any fears of fuch a ferious attack.----Timoleon alfo died in the fourth year of the 110th Olympiad, four years before the fiege of Tyre.

ᵈ " Agathocles, victis hoftibus, urbes caftellaque expugnat, prædas ingentes agit, hoftium millia trucidat. Caftra deinde in quinto lapide â Carthagine ftatuit, ut damna cariffimarum rerum, vaftitatemque agrorum, et incendia villarum, de muris fpecularentur." (Juftin. Lib. 22. Chap. 6.--488.) The Baron de St. Croix's expreffion is "Par fa defcente aux Lathomies pres de Tanete." Diodorus Siculus ftates it "Προς ταις καλυμεναις Λατομιας," and he adds afterwards "Τυντα κα-λεμενον αναζευξαι." (Lib. 20. Tom. 2.--410, 411.) Strabo fixes the fituation more precifely: " Εν αιτω δε τω κολπω εν ω περ η η Καρχηδων Τυνις ετι πολις, η Θερμα, η λατομιαι τινες." Lib. 17.--:191.

Nicetus[e] by Dionyſius of Halicarnaſſus, and Nicerates by Diodorus Siculus.[f]

Tyre, celebrated for its riches, and its numerous colonies, was taken by aſſault after a reſiſtance, that could not have been expected from a commercial people, who had long neglected their military eſtabliſhment. But the love of liberty will often animate the common boſom with ſuperior energy, and in a phrenſy for their Freedom, men of ordinary capacities are frequently expanded into heroes. The loſs of the beſieged is reckoned at ſeven thouſand by Diodorus Siculus,[g] and at ſix thouſand by Q. Curtius,[h] but the difference in the calculation of the number of the priſoners is more conſiderable. The latter writer ſtates thoſe only, who were ſaved by a pious fraud of the Sidonians in Alexander's camp, at fifteen thouſand:[i] Diodorus Siculus reckons them excluſive of thoſe

---

[e] Dion. Halicarnaſſ. de Dinarcho. Tom. 5.--649.

[f] Diod. Sicul. Lib. 17. Tom. 2.--189. Much information on this ſubject may be collected from Meurſius de Archon. Athen. Lib. 4. Chap. 13.

[g] "Οι δε Τυριοι προς αλκην τραπεντες, κ παρακαλεσαντες αλληλους, ανεῤῥαξαν τας ςευπας, κ μαχομενοι πλην ολιγων απαντες κατεκοπησαν, οντες πλειες των επτακισχιλιων" Diod. Sicul. Lib. 17. Tom. 2. --195.

[h] "Intra munimenta urbis ſex millia armatorum trucidata ſunt." (Q. Curt. Lib. 4. Chap. 4. Tom. 1.--187.) Arrian ſwells the account to eight thouſand: "Απεθανον δε των μεν Τυριων ες οκτακισχιλιυς" (Exped. Alex. Lib. 2. Chap. 24.--171.) but he certainly takes in the whole ſiege.

[i] "Le dernier ecrivain les fait monter à 15,000," but in the paſſage of Q. Curtius that is referred to, he hath only taken into his account the priſoners ſaved by the Sidonians, which is a circumſtance that the Baron de St. Croix hath not attended to. "Multis tamen ſaluti fuere Sidonii,

those that were transported to Carthage, to have been above thirteen thousand,[k] and Arrian takes the whole to have amounted to thirty thousand,[l] which hath the appearance of most probability, and is more consistent with the population of a city as flourishing as Tyre was then known to have been. Two thousand of these miserable captives were fastened upon crosses, and hung up by the order of the Conqueror, according to Q. Curtius[m] on the shore; and Diodorus Siculus[n] assures us that even all the Tyrian youth was comprised within this sanguinary sentence. It is however suppressed by Arrian,[o] and if we are to reason from the humanity

[j] Sidonii, qui intra Macedonum præsidia erant, hi urbem quidem inter victores intraverant, sed cognationis cum Tyriis memores (quippe utramque urbem Agenorem condidisse credebant) multos Tyriorum etiam protegentes, ad sua perduxere navigia: quibus occultatis, Sidona devecti sunt. Quindecim millia hoc furto subducta sævitiæ sunt." Q. Curt. Lib. 4. Chap. 4. Tom. 1.--186, 187.

[k] "Diodore à 13,000." The Greek text estimates them at somewhat above thirteen thousand. "Σωματα δ'αιχμαλωτα τοσαυτα το πληθ⊕. ευρεθη, ώςε των πλεις-ων εις Καρχηδονα κεκομισμενων, τα ὑπολειφθεντα γενεσθαι πλειω των μυριων κ͂ τρισχιλιων." Diod. Sicul. Lib. 17. Tom. 2.--196.

[l] "Και επραθησαν Τυριων τε κ͂ ξενων ὁτοι εγκατεληφθησαν, μαλιςα ες τρισμυριους" (Arrian. Exped. Alex. Lib. 2. Chap. 24.-171.) Though there must have been many foreigners in a commercial city like Tyre, yet in comparison with the rest of the inhabitants they could hardly form an item in the calculation.

[m] "Triste deinde spectaculum victoribus ira præbuit regis. Duo millia, in quibus occidendi desecerat rabies, crucibus adfixi per ingens litoris spatium pependerunt." Q. Curt. Lib. 4. Chap 4. Tom. 1.--187.

[n] "Τυς δε νεους παντας, οντας ουκ ελατ͂ες των δισχιλιων, εκρεμασε" Diod. Sicul. Lib. 17. Tom. 2.--195.

[o] This barbarous anecdote is recorded by Diodorus Siculus and Q. Curtius, and though Arrian hath omitted it, I fear, it was from that sort of discreet silence, which furnishes a strong presumptive

humanity, which had hitherto diftinguifhed Alexander's actions, whofe heart profperity had not yet hardened, a doubt, for his honour, may be ftill entertained of this fignal inftance of cruelty and vengeance.—Notwithftanding the precifion with which Juftin fpeaks of the fiege of Tyre,[p] he hath to anfwer for fome grofs errors. This city, he pretends, was foon treacheroufly delivered into Alexander's hands, but from its vigorous refiftance for feven months, it is evident that it was not fo very fpeedily captured; and as all the hiftorians agree in the account of its obftinate defence, the Tyrian glory is not to be fullied by the fuppofed infamy

---

fumptive evidence of the truth of the accufation. In the lax fyftem of ancient morality, the moft flagrant abufes of the right of conqueft were not uncommon; and we frequently read of whole nations being exterminated with a ftern indifference to their fufferings. Julius Cæfar in a later period put the whole Senate of Vannes to death, though they had furrendered and thrown themfelves upon his mercy, (Cæfar de Bello Gallico. Lib. 3. Chap. 16.--152. 4to 1737.) and the fame deftructive principles are often vifible in the future progrefs of the Gallic war. (Cæfar de Bello Gallico. Lib. 6. Chap. 43.--340. Lib. 7. Chap. 28.--372.) In juftice to Alexander's character, he certainly had fome provocations for his extraordinary irritation. Q. Curtius tells us, " Quum et claffem procul haberet, et longam obfidionem magno fibi ad cetera impedimento videret fore: caduceatores qui ad pacem eos compellerent, mifit; quos Tyrii contra jus gentium occifos præcipitaverunt in altum. Atque ille fuorum tam indigna nece commotus, urbem obfidere ftatuit." (Q. Curt. Lib. 4. Chap. 2. Tom. 1.--171.) And Arrian hath fubftantiated the fact, though it varies in a few particulars. "Οργη γαρ εχωρουν επιωων οι Μακεδονες, της τε πολιορκιας τε τριβη αχθομενοι, κ̀ οτι λαβοντες τινας αυτων οι Τυριοι πλεοντας εκ Σιδωνθ, επι το τειχθ αναβιβασαντες οπως αποπτον ειη απο τε ςρατοπεδυ, σφαξαντες ερρι̨ αν εις την θαλασσαν" (Exped. Alex. Lib. 2. Chap. 24.--170, 171.) Retaliation and revenge were cardinal virtues in many Pagan codes of Ethics, and it is no wonder, that fuch a fpectacle fhould have been followed by fevere and exemplary vengeance.

[p] "Non magno poft tempore per proditionem capiuntur." Juftin. Lib. 11. Chap. 10.--284.

108   CRITICAL INQUIRY INTO THE LIFE

infamy of a few traitors.——It is the wifh of Polyænus [q] to reduce almoſt all military manœuvres to ſtratagems, and we need not therefore be furpriſed to receive the information, that Alexander ſet out for Arabia, and the beſieged in his abſence made an advantageous and fuccefsful fally. On the intelligence of this accident, which Parmenio conveyed to him, he returned immediately, and whilſt one part of the army made a feint of retreating and raiſing the ſiege, he entered with another body of his troops into Tyre, which had been left open and unguarded. Such circumſtances are exactly confonant to the plan of Polyænus, but they do not in the leaſt coincide with the relations of the other hiſtorians.

Alexander marched from Tyre to Gaza, and from Gaza into Egypt. This was the Macedonian route, as related unanimouſly and without any difference, by all the hiſtorians of the Conqueror's exploits. Jofephus hath alone the confidence to contradict the united evidence of the companions of Alexander's arms, and he tells us that the Conqueror, being diſſatisfied with the Jews, advanced after the capture of Gaza towards Jeruſalem,[r] with the resolution

---

[q] "Αλεξανδρ©. Τυρɛ πολιορκιαν περιβαλων ɛπ' Αραβιας ɛƺɛλλɛτο· Τιƒιοι της απυσιας αυτɛ καταƺρονηϭαντɛς, των τɛιχων προɛλθοντɛς, τοις Μακɛδοσι προσπɛσοντɛς ɛκρατɛν πολλαχη· Παρμɛνιων Αλɛξανδρον ανακαλɛιται· 'Ο δɛ δια ταχɛς ɛπανɛλθων, Μακɛδονων τɛς ɛγκλινοντας ιδων, τοις ητ]ομɛνοις ɛκ ɛβοηθησɛν· ɛς δɛ την πολιν κɛνην ανδρων ορμησας, κατα κρατ©. αιρɛι την Τυρον." Polyænus. Lib. 4. Chap. 8.--327. 8vº 1691.

[r] "'Ο δɛ Αλɛξανδρ©. ɛξɛλων την Γαζαν, ɛπι την των Ιɛροσολυμιτων πολιν αναβαινɛιν ɛσπɛυδακɛι." Jofephus. Ant. Jud. 11. Chap. 8. Tom. 1.--580.

resolution of chastising¹ them for their attachment to Darius, and their refusal of military succours and provision for the Macedonian army. But a general of Alexander's talents could not have been so imprudent as to have left a city of this magnitude behind him, whose enmity to him was decided, and whose inhabitants might have cut off his supplies. Arrian, who hath minutely attended to every action of his hero, would undoubtedly have mentioned the reduction of a place of such importance, and in the very circumstantial journal of Alexander's marches which he hath preserved, that to Jerusalem would not have been omitted. The pacific disposition of the Jews, when the Conqueror approached, would as certainly have been spoken of, if this expedition from Gaza had not been an anachronism of Josephus, who seems to have varied the order of events, without breaking in upon their truth.'

Arrian

---

¹ "Qui avoient donné du secours aux Tyriens." There is not a single syllable expressive of any support having been given to the Tyrians. I have abandoned, therefore, the sense of the French sentence and substituted in some measure the original sentiment of Josephus. "Ἰξια τε, αποςηιλας γραμματα προς τον των Ιεδαιων αρχιερεα, συμμαχιαν τε αυτω πεμπειν, κ̓ αγοραν τω ςρατευματι παρασχειν, κ̓ οσα Δαρειω προτερον ετελει δωρα τετω διδοναι, την Μακεδονων φιλιαν ἑλομενον, ε γαρ μιτανοησειν επι τετοις· τε δε αρχιερεως αποκριναμενε τοις γραμματοφοροις, ὡς ὁρκες ειη Δαρειω δεδωκως, μη βαςαζειν ὁπλα κατ' αυτε, κ̓ τετες ἑως αν η Δαρειος εν τοις ζωσι μη παραβησεσθαι φησαντ۞· ακεσας Αλεξανδρ۞ παρωξυνθη, κ̓ την μεν Τυρον εκ εκρινε καταλιπειν, ὁσον ἐδειπω μελλασαν αἱρεσθαι· παρεςησαμεν۞ δε ταυτην, ηπειλησε ςρατευειν επι τον των Ιεδαιων αρχιερεα, κ̓ διδαξειν πάντας δι αυτε, προς τινας δη αυτοις φυλακτεον τας ὁρκες· ὁθεν πονικωτερον χρησαμεν۞ τη πολιορκια, λαμβανει την Τυρον· καταςησαμεν۞ δε τα εν αυτη, επι την Γαζαιων πολιν ηλθεν." Ant. Jud. Lib. 11. Chap. 8. Tom. 1--579, 580.

' I cannot subscribe without some limitations to the authority of as late a writer as Eusebius, but his residence in Palestine, as Bishop Newton observes (Dissertation on the Prophecies, 15.—

Arrian only tells us, that all Palestine had submitted, Gaza excepted, and consequently Alexander had no occasion to quit the line of his intended march, and enter Judæa, for the purpose of reducing it. An examination of the circumstances, related by the Jewish historian, may perhaps lead us to a definitive opinion on their authenticity.

The high priest Jaddua, in the habit of the priesthood, and its splendid ornaments, leaves Jerusalem to meet the Conqueror, and implore his clemency. Alexander struck with his majestic mien, and venerable appearance, prostrates himself before him, and adores the Deity, whose name was engraven in golden characters upon the tiara of the pontiff. Parmenio, continues Josephus,

---

Vol. 2.--41.) adds weight to his evidence, and he asserts that Alexander marched from Tyre into Judæa. "Αλεξανδρ⊙. Τυρον άμα Σιδωνι δηωσας επι την Ιυδαιαν ελθων, κὴ ταυτην παραλαβων, τον ιερεα Ιαδδυν ετιμησε, θυσας τε τω Θεω·" (Chron. Can. 177.) Usher agrees with him in opinion, (Annales, 160. Fol. 1722.) and also our Prideaux, who imagines Josephus to have been mistaken. Connect. of the history of the old and new Testament. Part. 1st. Book 7. Vol. 1.--386. Fol. 1728.

v "Και ην αυτω τα μεν αλλα της Παλαιςινης καλυμενης Συριας, προσκεχωρηκοτα ηδη· ευνεχ⊙. δε τις ω ονομα ην Βατις, κρατων της Γαζαιων πολεως, υ προσειχεν Αλεξανδρω·" Arrian. Exped. Alex. Lib. 2. Chap. 25.--173.

w "Γεροισι μετα των ιερεων κὴ τυ πολιτικυ πληθυς, ιεροπρεπη κὴ διαφερυσαν των αλλων εθνων ποιεμενω· την υπαντησιν εις τοπον τινα Σαφα λεγομενον,———'Ο Αλεξανδρ⊙, ετι πορρωθεν ιδων το μεν πληθ⊙. εν ταις λευκαις εσθησι, τυς δε ιερης προεςωτας εν ταις βυσσιναις αυτων, τον δε αρχιερεα εν τη ιακινθινη κὴ διαχρυσω ςολη, κὴ επι της κεφαλης εχοντα την κιδαριν, κὴ το χρυσεν επ'αυτης ελασμα, ω το τυ Θευ εγγεγραπτο ονομα, προσελθων μον⊙., προσεκυνησε το ονομα, κὴ τον αρχιερεα πρωτ⊙. ησπασατο." Joseph. Ant. Jud. Lib. 11. Chap. 8. Tom. 1.--581.

x "Ce prince avoit sans doute un interprete pour connoitre le sens de l'inscription." I do not think this sceptical sneer deserves a translation. It is in fact but the Crambe concocta of Vandale.

"Unde

sephus,[y] expressed his astonishment to Alexander, and asked his reasons for this extraordinary humiliation, and why he had fallen so inconsistently at the high priest's feet, when universal adoration had hitherto been paid to him. Alexander replied, that he did not worship the high priest, but the Deity, whose minister he was; and he then informed his general, that a person like Jaddua, and in his habit, had appeared to him in a dream before he left Macedonia, and had announced to him the support of heaven in the war that he then meditated against the Persian empire. The Prince added, that on his seeing the high priest, he instantly recollected the figure in stature and dress, which had appeared to him.

The observation of Parmenio is a suspicious circumstance,[z] as Alexander had not hitherto pretended to any divine honours, nor exacted

---

"Unde vero is quoque inscriptionem istam in laminâ Tiaræ legere, atque ita intelligere potuerit, quod illa veri Dei nomen esset, ut inde talis adoratio ipsius, ante alloquium pontificis secuta sit, non comprehendo." Differt. super Aristæam. 77.

[y] "Παρμενιων᷎ δε μονε προσελθοντ᷎ αυτω, κ᷎ επιθεμενε, τι δηποτε προσκυνετων αυτον απαντων αυτ᷎ προσκυνησε των Ιεδαιων αρχιερεα ε τετον, ειπε, προσκυνησα, τον δε Θεον, ε τη αρχιερωσυνη αυτ᷎ τιτιμη ται· τετον γαρ κ᷎ κατα τες ιπνες ειδον εν των νυν σχημαατι, εν Διω της Μακεδονιας τυγχανων· κ᷎ προς εμαυτον διασκεπτομενω μοι πως αν κρατησαιμι της Ασιας, παρεκελευτο μη μελλειν, αλλα θαρσεντα διαβαινειν· αυτ᷎ γαρ ηγησεσθαι μοι της στρατιας κ᷎ την Περσων παραδωσειν αρχην· οθεν αλλον μεν εδεικα θεασαμεν᷎ εν τοιαυτη στολη· τετον δε νυν ιδων κ᷎ της κατα τες ιπνες επιμνησθεις οψεως τε κ᷎ παρακελευσιως, νομιζω θεια πομπη την στρατειαν πεποιημεν᷎ Δαρειον νικησειν, κ᷎ την Περσων καταλυσειν δυναμιν, κ᷎ παιθ᷎οσα κατα νεν εστι μοι προχωρησειν·" Joseph. Ant. Jud. Lib. 11. Chap. 8. Tom. 1.--581.

[z] "La discours de Parmenion prouve la fausseté de tout ce recit." I differ in opinion, and have accordingly qualified the expression. The subject I shall soon have occasion to resume.

exacted any adoration before the death of Clitus, which happened long after this fuppofed interview, fo little appofite to the character and genius of the Grecian Hero. Befides, the high prieft Jaddua died, according to the chronicle of Alexandria, fome years before Darius mounted the Perfian throne.—The immortal Newton, who hath poured fuch an effufion of light on the fucceffion of the Jewifh high priefts after the return of that nation from captivity, makes alfo Jaddua to have lived under Artaxerxes Mnemon; and Simon the Juft, agreeable to his computation, was the high prieft at the time of the invafion of the Perfian empire by the Greeks, who had fucceeded to the exercife of this high function, on the death of his father Onias the fon of Jaddua.[a]

Alexander, on his entry into Jerufalem, went up to the temple, where they fhewed him the paffages in the prophecies of Daniel, which related to him, and he afterwards offered facrifices to the Deity on the Jewifh altars.[b] Jealous of this preference, the Samaritans requefted that he would alfo honour their city with his devotions.[c] But Jofephus here contradicts himfelf, and forgets his

---

[a] Sir Ifaac Newton's Chronology of ancient kingdoms. 363, 365. 4to 1728.

[b] " Εις την πολιν παραγινεται· και ανελθων επι το ιερον, θυει μεν τω Θεω κατα την του αρχιερεως ύφηγησιν, αιτει δε τον αρχιερεα και τους ιερεις αξιοπρεπως ετιμησε· δειχθεισης δε αυτω της Δανιηλε βιβλε, εν ή τινα των Ελληνων καταλυσειν την Περσων αρχην εδηλε, νομισας αυτον ειναι ο σημαινομενος, τοτε μεν ησθεις απελυσε το πληθος." Jofeph. Ant. Jud. Lib. 11. Chap. 8. Tom. 1.--582.

[c] " Και παρηλθεν, παραγενομενον προς την πολιν αιτων τιμησαι και το παρ' αυτοις ιερον" Jofeph. Ant. Jud. Lib. 11. Chap. 8. Tom. 1.--581, 582.

his having mentioned the permiſſion to build a temple, given by Alexander during the ſiege of Tyre to theſe enemies of the Hebrews,[d] which could not have been finiſhed in ſuch a ſhort ſpace of time.

The ſame hiſtorian informs us, that Alexander was attended in this expedition by Phœnicians and Chaldæans,[e] but was it poſſible for them to have accompanied him, when they were at that time his declared enemies, and had not then acknowledged him for their maſter?[f] The high prieſt, is ſaid likewiſe, to have applied to the Conqueror for a grant to the Jews, who were at Babylon,

Q and

[d] "Περι Αλεξανδρου ηκε· κ̣ καταλαβων αυτον τον Τυρα πολιορκιας ———— συγχωρησαντ۞ δε Αλεξανδρυ, πασαν επισπευκαμεν۞ σπουδη, ωκοδομησεν ὁ Σαναβαλλετης τον ναον." (Joſeph. Ant. Jud. Lib. 11. C. 8. Tom. 1.--580.) Prideaux admits the Samaritan temple, in which Alexander was requeſted to ſacrifice, muſt have been ſome other temple, or that Joſephus muſt have been miſtaken reſpecting it, as the foundations of that, which Alexander allowed them to build, could ſcarcely have been laid by this time. (Connect. of the Hiſtory of the old and new Teſtament. Part 1ſt. Book 7. Vol. 1.--386.) Joſephus however makes uſe of the words "Σπουδη ωκοδομησεν," and provided the materials were ready, and they had a ſufficient number of workmen, the building might have been ſoon run up. We are ſtrangers to the dimenſions of this edifice, but as Sanballat was the head only of a ſect, which had ſeparated from the mother church, in all likelihood it was not large. In the Jewiſh war, Joſephus hath likewiſe given as a wonderful example of the rapidity, with which a wall of very conſiderable extent was conſtructed, that ſurrounded Jeruſalem, "Το μεν εν τειχ۞ εν۞ δεοντ۞ τισσαρακοντα ςαδιων ην, εξωθεν δε αυτω προσωκοδομηθη τρισκαιδεκα φρυρια, κ̣ τυτων οι κυκλοι δεκα συνεξιθμηντο ςαδιων· τριςι δ'ωκοδομηθη το παν ἡμεραις." De Bello Judaico. Lib. 5. C. 12. Tom. 2.--358.

[e] "Των δε Φοινικων κ̣ των ακολυθεντων Χαλδαιων." Joſeph. Antiq. Jud. Lib. 11. C. 8. Tom. 1.--581.

[f] Phœnicia, muſt, I apprehend, have been then conquered: as to the Chaldæans, ſome individuals undoubtedly might have attended Alexander, and Joſephus does not intimate their number.

and in Media, of the free exercife of their religion. [g] Yet this requeft, as the learned Moyle [h] hath judicioufly obferved, fuppofes Alexander to have been already in poffeffion of that part of Afia beyond the Euphrates, which was evidently falfe, as it was reduced only under his fubjection in the following year.

After a confirmation of the privileges of the Jewifh nation, Alexander left Jerufalem, and marched with his army to the neighbouring cities. Jofephus thus finifhes his relation with an error. The Macedonian Conqueror neither retarded his march to attack places, which opened their gates to him, nor wafted his time in receiving their ufelefs homages, but pufhed forwards from Gaza directly to Pelufium.

To fum up the whole, the filence of Scripture weakens the credit of this narrative of Jofephus; [i] which hath been adopted and

[g] " Ἵνα κ̣ τȣς ιν Βαϐυλωνι κ̣ Μηδια Ιȣδαιȣς τοις ιδιοις επιτρεψη νομοις χρησασθαι." Jofeph. Ant. Jud. Lib. 11. C. 8. Tom. 1.--582.

[h] Moyle's Remarks upon Prideaux. Connect. Moyle's Works. Vol. 2.--32. I confefs I fee no abfurdity in this requeft. Alexander was then in a courfe of hoftilities, which muft directly have conducted him to Babylon and into Media, and the Jewifh high prieft might with ftrict propriety have petitioned for this liberty of confcience, forefeeing Alexander's future conquefts, which were announced in the paffages of the Prophet Daniel, that he had juft fhewn and explained to him.

[i] This hypothefis, though it may have a fpecious appearance of folidity, will not ftand the teft of fevere and rigid examination. Numerous events are recorded in the facred writings, but it cannot be from thence inferred, that they have recorded every event which happened. The Scriptural

and magnified by the writers of the middle age,[k] though its authenticity hath been disputed by several modern authors.[l]

Taking into cool and candid consideration the circumstances of the event, they may not altogether be as glorious for the cause of religion, as some persons, with more superstition than discernment, have piously believed. The true faith could not have received much honour from the casual adoration of the worshipper of other Deities, that it disclaimed; and its hallowed altars were but little dignified with any incense from the hand, which was ready to scatter it with the same profusion on those of Apis and of Belus.

In

---

tural prophecies extended only to the great revolutions, which were to pass in the world; and from the nature of them, it could not possibly be expected, that they should have included events of a subordinate and inferior class. They ceased previous to Alexander's existence, and the old Testament hath not transmitted to us any detail of the Jewish history later than that of Nehemiah, which ends at least a century before the birth of Alexander. From the days of Nehemiah, there is a chasm to the Apocryphal book of Maccabees, which commences with the last acts of Alexander's reign. The silence, therefore, of the scripture is not extraordinary, and weighs nothing in the scale of argument.

[k] Eusebius, Chronic. Num. 1685.—G. Syncellus. 260.—Cedrenus. 121.—Zonares. Lib. 4.--197, 198.

[l] This celebrated passage of Josephus hath opened a wide and extensive field of controversy. Collins (Scheme of Lit. Prophecy. 452.) rushed on to the attack with all the impetuosity of a Volunteer. Vandale (Dissert. super Aristeam. Chap. 10.) and Moyle (Moyle's Works. Vol. 2. --26.) advanced with more regular approaches, and endeavoured to overpower it by weight of metal. The sceptical Boyle (Dict. Article Macedo.) coldly admitted the possibility of its being supported, without throwing in a single succour for its relief; but the two Chandlers (Vindication of his defence. Chap. 2. Sect. 1.—And S. Chandler's vindication of Daniel. 76.) with Lloyd (Letter to Sherlock) and Prideaux (Connect. Part 1st. Book 7. Vol. 1.--384, 385.) have defended it with the ability of veteran Generals. Bishop Newton (Dissert. on the Prophecies. Vol. 2.) hath since thrown up a number of fresh Entrenchments.

In all likelihood the whole was a Jewish artifice, and a stratagem invented by that nation,[m] after the death of Alexander, to furnish it with pretensions to the favour and protection of his successors. In later ages a similar history prevailed in the East, and Ghengizkhan pretending to have seen in a dream a Christian bishop, sent on the part of heaven to assure him of its assistance, the vision of the Tartar prince was as advantageous to the Christians of the Mogul empire, as that of Alexander had been to the Jews.[n]

Gaza

[m] I persuade myself I am not capable of attempting to defend a passage if I believed it to be entirely untenable. I trust, however, I may be allowed to suggest, that admitting many of the circumstances related by Josephus to be improbable; and, giving the objections in their widest range every advantage, erroneous; it still does not follow that the whole is false. The dream and the interview may be substantially correct, the additional embellishments faulty and fictitious. The belief of the "Οναρ ικ Διος εςι (Hom. Iliad. Lib. 1.--63.) was very ancient, and with the Jews, when the prophetic spirit ceased with Malachi, particular dreams were considered as a secondary kind of inspiration, and the Almighty was supposed on extraordinary occasions to adopt this method of communication. "The same Providence," to borrow an expression of the late amiable and learned Dr. Jortin, "which conducted Cyrus and prevented the rash Macedonian from perishing till he had overthrown the Persian empire,"[*] might have taken this mode of rousing his ambition, and directing it to the great end which it had in view. Allowing the scriptural prophecies to allude to Alexander, which hath never been disputed, he then becomes confessedly an immediate instrument in the hands of Providence, and I see no violation of consistency in the supposition of his having been led by a preternatural impression on his mind to their completion.

[n] "Ce fut par le même motif, que dans les siecles fort posterieurs, les Chretiens de l'orient inventerent une histoire à peu pres semblable. Ghengizkhan y joue le même role qu'Alexandre; et la vision du prince Tartare est aussi avantageuse aux Chretiens, que celle du roi Macedonien l'avoit été aux Juifs." I owe the reader some explanation of my reasons for this violent deviation from the sense of the French sentence. The Christians are there expressly charged with a direct forgery, and the following evidence is referred to, in support of the accusation. "Apres avoir ainsi soumis toute la Tartarie, les Mogols marcherent vers Otrar, qui appartenoit au Sulthan de Kharisme.———Ghengizkhan qui n'etoit occupe que du projet de cette guerre, fit publier que

Dieu

[*] Remarks on Ecclesiastical History. Vol. 1.--36.

Gaza oppofed the rapid progrefs of the Macedonian arms as much by its advantageous pofition, as the generous defence of its governor and garrifon. Alexander received a contufion on the fhoulder by the difcharge of a catapulta,° and Q. Curtius hath defcribed a fingular conflict between an Arabian foldier and the Macedonian Monarch, in which he was again wounded.ᵖ This fact hath been difcreetly fuppreffed by the other hiftorians, and they have by this means avoided the abfurdity, that Q. Curtius hath been guilty of. After the reduction of Gaza, if we are to

believe

Dieu lui accordoit fa protection. Il prctendoit avoir vû en fonge un Eveque, qui etoit venu lui annoncer de la part de Dieu, ce perfonage, comme il depeignit à fon reveil, etoit Mardenha, Eveque du pays d'Igour. Ghengizkhan voulut le voir. On ajoute que c'eft depuis ce temps-la, qu'il a protege toujours les Chretiens." (Hift. Gen. des Huns par Degui nes. Tom. 3.--41, 42.) I am afraid fuch injufrious mifrepretentations could only arife from wilful inadvertency.

° " Αυτ᾽Θ. δε βαλλιται καταπελτη δια της ασπιδ'Θ. διαμπαξ, κ; τε ϑωρακ᾽Θ. εις τον ωμον." (Arrian. Exped. Alex. Lib. 2. C. 27.--177..) Ariftander the foothfayer, if we are to believe the hiftorians, had requefted Alexander to be careful of his perfon on this day, and Arrian adds "Ταυτα ακκσας Αλεξ-ανδρ᾽Θ., τεως μεν προς ταις μηχανεις εξω βελας αυτον ειχιν." (Exped. Alex. Lib. 2. C. 26.--175.) Q. Curtius varies the account: "Sed, ut opinor, inevitabile eft fatum. Quippe dum inter primores promptius dimicat, fagittâ ictus eft : quam per loricam adactam, flantem in humero medicus ejus Philippus evellit. (Lib. 4. C. 6. Tom. 1.--200.) Plutarch barely mentions the wound: "Ετρωϑη μεν γαρ Αλεξανδρ᾽Θ. εις τον ωμον." Vit. Alex. Plutarchi Opera. Tom. 1.--679.

ᵖ "Arabs quidam Darii miles, majus fortunâ fuâ facinus aufus, clypeo gladium tegens, quafi transfuga genibus regis advolvitur. Ille adfurgere fupplicem recipique inter fuos juffit. At gladio barbarus ftrenue in dextram tranflato, cervicem adpetit regis: qui exiguâ corporis declinatione evitato ictu, in vanum manum barbari lapfam amputat. (Q. Curt. Lib. 4. C. 6. Tom. 1.--200.) Hegefias ftates in fubftance the fame anecdote. "Αμα γαρ των πολεμιων εις γονατα συγ-καμϑεις εδοξε τετ᾽Αλεξανδρον της ικετηας ινεκα πραξας· προςιμεν᾽Θ. δ'εγγυς μικρον εκκενει το ξιφ᾽Θ. ινεγκαντ᾽Θ. υπο τα πτερυγια τε θωρακ᾽Θ. ωςε γενεσθαι κ; την πληγην ε καιρωτατην" αλλα τον μεν αιτον απωλισι, κατα κεφαλης τυπτων τη μαχαιρα." Dion. Hal. de ftruct. Orat. 146. 8ᵛᵒ 1728.

believe this writer,[q] Alexander fastened Betis to his chariot wheels, and with a barbarous indignity, in imitation of Achilles, dragged the dead body of the unfortunate governor round the walls. To magnify the defence of Betis, Q. Curtius falls into a palpable contradiction, and though he assures us he sustained the various assaults of the enemy with a very moderate [r] garrison, he makes no scruple a few lines afterwards of reckoning the loss at ten thousand Persians or Arabs.[s] Most of the inhabitants of Gaza, capable of bearing arms, had gallantly fallen in its defence; the rest were distributed in slavery,[t] and Alexander according to Arrian, converted

[q] "Q. Curtius hath heightened this affecting tragedy. "Betim, egregiâ editâ pugnâ, multifque vulneribus confectum deferuerant fui: nec tamen fegnius prælium capessebat, lubricis armis suo pariter atque hostium sanguine. Sed quumque undique adducto, infolenti gaudio juvenis elatus alias virtutes etiam in hoste miratur, non ut voluisti, inquit, morieris Betis; fed quidquid tormentorum in captivum invenire potest, passurum esse te cogita. Ille non interrito modo, sed contumaci quoque vultu intuens regem, nullam ad minas ejus reddit vocem. Tum Alexander, videtisne obstinatum ad tacendum? inquit. Num genu posuit? num supplicem vocem misit? vincam tamen filentium, et si nihil aliud, certe gemitu interpellato. Ira deinde vertit in rabiem: jam tum peregrinos ritus novâ subeunte fortunâ. Per talos enim spirantis lora trajecta sunt; religatumque ad currum traxere circa urbem equi: glorianterege, Achillem, a quo genus ipfe deduceret, imitatum [´] fe esse pænâ in hostem capiendâ. (Lib. 4. C. 6. Tom. 1.--202--204.) If the whole is not a fiction, it is to be hoped, there are at least some poetical embellishments.

[r] "Modicoque præsidio muros ingentis operis tuebatur." Q. Curtius. Lib. 4. C. 6. Tom. 1. --197. 198.

[s] "Cecidere Persarum Arabumque circa decem millia." Q. Curt. Lib. 4. C. 6. Tom. 1. --205.

[t] "Les habitans de Gaza furent reduits en esclavage." Arrian hath transmitted to us their resolution and despair. "Οἱ δὲ Γαζαιοι, κ) τῆς πολιως σφισιν ηδη εχομενης, ξινεςηκοτες ὁμως εμαχοντο, κ) απιθανον παντες αυτη μαχομενοι, ως εκαςοι εταχθησαν." (Exped. Alex. Lib. 2. C. 27.--177.) I have receded from the Baron de St. Croix and nearly adopted Arrian.

verted his new conquest into a place of arms, which he peopled by a colony drawn from the neighbouring country.[v] Strabo on the contrary pretends that this unfortunate city was destroyed,[w] and remained a desert. Gaza made however, a very considerable figure in the different wars of Alexander's successors, and the judicious geographer might probably have confounded its state under the two first ages of the Seleucides, with its melancholy fate, after its total destruction by Alexander Zebina, 96 years before Christ.[x] It then became a prey to the flames, as the prophet Amos[y] had denounced, and its inhabitants were carried into captivity from their attachment to the Ptolemies. The similitude of the name of the two princes, to whom it owed its misfortunes, easily led Strabo into the mistake.

Egypt submitted without a struggle, and Alexander determined to

[v] "Την πολιν δε ξυνοικισας εκ των περιοικων, εχρητο οσα φρυριω ες τον πολεμον." Arrian. Exped. Alex. Lib. 2. C. 27.--177.

[w] "Ειθ' ὁ των Γαζαιων λιμην πλησιον· ὑπερκειται δε κ̣ ἡ πολις εν ἑπτα σαδιοις, ενδοξῷ ποτε γενομενη, κτισπασμενη δ'ὑπο Αλεξανδρε κ̣ μενεσα ερημ⊕-." Strabo. Lib. 16.--1101, 1102.

[x] Josephus hath compressed into a short compass a history of this siege. Ant. Jud. Lib. 13. C. 13. Tom. 1.--670.

[y] "I will send a fire on the wall of Gaza, which shall devour the palaces thereof." (Amos. Chap. 1. Verse 7.) A new Gaza appears, however, to have risen, like a Phænix, out of its ashes, which is mentioned on several of the medals of Hadrian's days. Sozomen speaks of it, (Lib. 5. C. 5.) and a list of its Bishops may be still found in the dormant repository of Ecclesiastical Knowledge, the history of Councils and their Acts. A livelier reader may consult Reland. Palæst. Lib. 3.--787.

to signalize his new empire by the foundation of a city, which might one day be the staple of the commerce of the two seas, and unite by interest the inhabitants of the eastern and western world. The Conqueror consulted his true glory in the enterprise. Humanity recommended the design, and a work of this kind is entitled to a more distinguished column in the page of history, than those monstrous edifices which are at once the prodigies of human labour, and the lasting monuments of the tyranny of the princes, that erected them amidst the misery and unavailing agonies of their subjects.——The Macedonian Monarch in his foundation of Alexandria opened a new source of riches, and Egypt soon enjoyed the happiness of seeing its land cultivated by a multitude of industrious inhabitants, and the temples of its Deities filled with crowds of people enriched by its commerce.

Arrian[z] and Plutarch[a] tell us, that the plan of Alexandria was traced out under Alexander's inspection, and that the workmen were ordered to begin the buildings previous to his departure for

---

[z] "Και εδοξεν αυτω ὁ χωρῶ καλλισ῀ κτισαι εν αυτω πολιν, κ᾽ γενεσθαι αν ευδαιμονα την πολιν· Ποθῶ εν λαμβανει αυτον τε εργε, κ᾽ αυτῶ τα σημεια τη πολει εθηκεν, ἱνα τε αγοραν εν αυτη δειμασθαι εδει, κ᾽ ἱερα ὁσα, κ᾽ Θεων ὡν τινων, των μεν Ἑλληνικων, Ισιδης δ᾽ Αιγυπτιας, κ᾽ το τειχῶ η περιβεβλησθαι.——
——Επι τετοις δε πο9῀ λαμβανει αυτον ελθειν παρ Αμμωνα ες Λιβυην," Arrian. Exped. Alex. Lib. 3. C. 1.--3.--181, 183.

[a] "Εργω κελευσας, εσχεσθαι τες επιμιλητας, αυτῶ ὁρμησεν εις Αμμων῀ ὁδον." Plutarch. De Vit. Alex. Plut. Opera. Tom. 1.--680.

for Ammon;[b] Diodorus Siculus[c] and Juſtin[d] date its foundation after that expedition, but Q. Curtius[e] refers both the idea and the execution to his return. Theſe different hiſtorians, Q. Curtius excepted, may be correct in their information, and it is not improbable that Alexander directing his march along the ſeaſhore, might firſt have traced the outlines of this flouriſhing city,[f] and afterwards on his return augmented the number of the workmen, and puſhed on by his encouragement the numerous and ſtately edifices, that were then riſing up. This is notwithſtanding no excuſe for Diodorus Siculus, who fixes the foundation

---

[b] "L'epoque de la foundation d'Alexandrie eſt rapportée par Plutarque et Arrien avant celle du depart d'Alexandre pour Ammon." I have not ſcrupulouſly adhered to the French text, but by this means the diſcordant hiſtorians are more in uniſon, and to juſtify me I have the evidence of Plutarch and Arrian that I have juſt cited. Q. Curtius, ſtill remains at an irreconcilable diſtance.

[c] "Επανηλθεν εις Αιγυπτον· Κρινας δ'εν ταυτη πολιν μεγαλην κτισαι, προσεταξε τοις επι την επιμελειαν, ταυτην καταλειπομενοις, ανεμεσον της τε λιμνης κ̓ της θαλασσης οικισαι την πολιν." Diod. Sicul. Lib. 17. Tom. 2.--200.

[d] "Reverſus ab Hammone Alexandriam condidit." Juſtin. Lib. 11. Chap. 1:.--286.

[e] "Alexander ab Hammone rediens, ut a mari ad Mareotim paludem, haud procul inſulâ Pharo ſitam, venit; contemplatus loci naturam, primum in ipſâ inſulâ ſtatuerat urbem novam condere. Inde, ut adparuit, magnæ ſedis inſulam haud capacem; elegit urbi locum, ubi nunc eſt Alexandria." Q. Curt. Lib. 4. C. 8. Tom. 1.--220, 221.

[f] Plutarch hath preſerved a curious anecdote reſpecting Alexander's tracing out the plan of this city. "Και γη μεν ὁ παρην λευκη· των δε αλφιτων λαμβανοντες εν πεδιω μελαγειω κυκλοτερη κολπον ηγεν, ὁ την εντὸς περιφερειαν ευθειαι βασεις, ως περ απο κρασπιδων εις σχημα χλαμυδος ὑπελαμβανων, εξ ισου συναγουσαι το μεγεθος· ἡσθεντος δε τη διαθεσει τε βασιλεως, αιφνιδιον ορνιθες απο του ποταμου, κ̓ της λιμνης, πληθει τε απειροι, κ̓ κατα γενος παντοδαποι, κ̓ μεγαλοι, επι τον τοπον κατεροντες, νεφεσιν εοικοτες, ουδε μικρον ὑπελιποντο των αλφιτων· ὡς τε κ̓ τον Αλεξανδρον διαταραχθηναι προς τον οιωνον· ου μην γε των μαντεων θαρρειν παραινουντων πολυκρεσατην γαρ οικιζεσθαι πολιν ὑπ' αυτη, κ̓ παντοδαπων ανθρωπων ἑσομενην τροφον." (Plutarch, De Vit. Alex. Plut. Opera. Tom. 1.--680.) A leſs accommodating fortune-teller might have put a different conſtruction on the accident.

foundation of Alexandria under the Archon Ariftophanes, in the fecond year of the 112th Olympiad,[g] which was in fact the fixth year of Alexander's reign; though it only became the fifth according to this hiftorian, Alexander having begun his reign, by his computation under the magiftracy of Evænetus, as was before obferved. The miftake of Diodorus Siculus moft probably occafioned thofe of Eufebius[h] and St. Cyrill,[i] who have pretended to eftablifh the foundation of Alexandria in the feventh year of Alexander's reign. But the true period of its foundation was the fifth year of the Macedonian Monarch's reign, which was the firft year of the 112th Olympiad when Nicetas was Archon, as appears by the fubfequent military operations of this Prince.—The certainty of the date is alfo confirmed by the Canon of Theon, which allows only four years to the reign of Darius Codomanus, and begins to reckon that of his victorious rival in the 417th year of the era of Nabonaffar, the conqueft of Egypt and the foundation of Alexandria being included in the four firft years after Alexander's acceffion to the throne of Macedon.[k]

The

[g] Diod. Sicul. Lib. 17. Tom. 2.--200. T. Livy differs very confiderably, (Lib. 8. C. 24. Tom. 2,--760.) and alfo Julius Solinus (C. 32.--45.) from Diodorus Siculus, but Dodwell (Differt. de Cycl. 10. 73.) hath fully proved the former to have deceived himfelf, and Salmafius (Plin. Exer. 338.) allows the latter to have been miftaken.

[h] "Αλεξανδρεια η κατ'Αιγυπτον ιβδομω ετει Αλεξανδρυ εκτισθη." Eufebii Chronic. Port. 177.

[i] "Εκατοςη δωδεκατη ολυμπιαδι Αλεξανδρειαν την προς Αιγυπτον κτισθηναι φασιν, ετει ιβδομω της Αλεξανδρυ βασιλει@." (St. Cyrill. contra Julian. Lib. 1. Julian. Opera. Tom. 2,--13.) To give the Patriarch fair play, he only ftates it on tradition.

[k] This fubject hath been extremely well explained by Monf. de Freret. Hift. de l'Acad. des Infcript. Tom. 27,--149, 150.

The new city had at its foundation a form, nearly similar to that of the Macedonian' mantle, but as it increased, it naturally lost its shape and figure. Monsr d'Anville's plan of Alexandria, which he sketched out with such pains and accuracy, hath little resemblance with this part of the Macedonian dress as engraven by Cuper,[m] and he endeavours in vain to apply it to the ground between the Mareotic lake and the shore of the Egyptian sea. Its circuit, according to Pliny,[n] was about fifteen miles, which may amount to one hundred and twenty stadia, instead of eighty agreeable to the calculation of Q. Curtius.[o] But the sentiments of these two authors will not materially differ, if we suppose with Monsr d'Anville[p] Pliny's stadium to have been a third less than that of Q. Curtius. This measure will be found likewise to be nearly adequate to the thirty stadia by seven or eight, which Strabo[q] hath

---

[l] "Του δε τυπον αποτελων χλαμυδι παραπλησιον" (Diod. Sicul. Lib. 17. Tom. 2.--200.) Or as Pliny more diffusely expresses it, "Ad effigiem Macedonicæ Chlamydis orbe gyrato liniofam, dextrâ lævâque angulofo procurfu." (Nat. Hist. Lib. 5. 10. Tom. 1.--562.) Strabo hath described the figure with mathematical precision: "Το χλαμυδοειδες σχημα εγεγραπται ετως, ως τε τα μηκ⊕. τα μηκει ομολογεν, κ̀ οσον ειναι το μιγιςον, κ̀ το πλατ⊕. τω πλατει" Lib. 2. Tom. 1.--179.

[m] See the Homeri Apothesis. 158.

[n] "Metatus est eam Dinochares Artichectus, pluribus modis memorabili ingenio. xv. M. passuum laxitate infessa." Plin. Nat. Hist. Lib. 5. C. 10. Tom. 1.--561. 562.

[o] "Complexus quidquid est loci inter paludem et mare, octaginta stadiorum muris ambitum destinat." Q. Curtius. Lib. 4. C. 8. Tom. 1.--221.

[p] Memoire sur l'Egypt Anc. et Mod. 56. 57.

[q] "Εςι δε χλαμυδοειδες το σχημα τε ιδαφες της πολεως· η τα μεν επι μηκους πλευρα εςι τα αμφικλυστα, οσον τριακοντα ςαδιων εχοντα διαμετρον· τα δε επι πλατ⊕. οι ισθμοι επτα η οκτω ςαδιων εκατερ⊕." Strabo. Lib. 17.--1143.

hath given to this city. Josephus' reckons its length to have been thirty stadia and its breadth ten,[r] but Diodorus Siculus[s] with less probability relates that it reached four hundred stadia in length, and was a Plethrum broad.[t]

When Diodorus Siculus passed through Egypt, the number of Freemen in Alexandria were said by the Police officers to amount to three hundred thousand,[w] and if we adopt the calculation of Cteficles,[x] respecting the proportion between the Freemen and the slaves

[r] "Μηκ‍ος μεν γε αυτης τριακοντα ϛαδιων, ευρ‍ος δε ουκ ελαττ‍ον δεκα." Joseph. de Bello Judaico. Lib. 2. C. 16. Sect. 4. Tom. 2.--190.

[s] The Baron de St. Croix observes "Cette mesure est conforme à la longueur de trente stades sur dix de largeur, donneé par Strabon et Joseph a cette ville." I am not altogether satisfied that he perfectly understood the Greek geographer, but Father Harduin in his notes on Pliny (Hist. Vit. Tom. 1.--562.) appears to have looked through the same intellectual telescope, and in a generous court of criticism "De minimis non curat lex." The "sur dix" applied to both authors is inexcusable, and I have made each writer responsible for his own calculation.

[t] "Απο γαρ πυλης επι πυλην διηκουσα, τισσαραξοντα μεν ϛαδιων ιχ‍ει το μηκ‍ος, πλιθρου δε το πλατ‍ος." (Diod. Sicul. Lib. 17. Tom. 2.--200.) The Plethrum was originally reckoned to contain a hundred square feet, but "the practice of some Greeks," as the great historian of the decline of the Roman empire hath judiciously remarked, (16th Chap. Vol 1.) and the authority of Monf. de Valois would lead us to believe the "Πλιθρον," was used to express the Roman "jugerum," which consisted of twenty-eight thousand eight hundred square Roman feet.

[w] "Καθ'οι γαρ δη καιρον ημεις παριβαλομιν εις Αιγυπτον, εφασαν οι τας αναγραφας εχοντες των κατοικουντων, ειναι τες εν αυτη διατριβοντας ελευθερους, πλειυς των τριακοντα μυριαδων." Diod. Sicul. Lib. 17. Tom. 2.--201.

[x] "Κ‍τησικλης δε εν τριτη χρονικων φησιν επι τη δεκατη Ολυμπιαδι Αθηνησιν εξιλασμον γενεσθαι υπο Δημητρι‍η τε Φαληρεως των κατοικευτων την Ατ‍τικην‍ κ‍αι ευρεθηναι Αθηναιυς μεν δυσμυριυς προς τοις χιλιοις, μετοικυς δε μυριυς, οικιτων δε μυριαδας τισσαραξοντα." (Athenæus. Lib. 6. Tom. 1.--272.) This immense population

slaves at Athens, we cannot reckon the whole mass of inhabitants at less than fifteen hundred thousand, which is an astonishing degree of population considering the obstacles that checked it. Notwithstanding the precaution which the Royal Founder had taken in its construction, that the streets might be open to and refreshed by the Etesian winds,[y] the new capital of Egypt was very unhealthy, and the inhabitants had only dead and stagnant water for their common use. Their diet was also very ordinary, and consisted of bad vegetables of the worst qualities, paste, dry cheese, inferior kinds of fish, snails, snakes, the flesh of asses and of camels, and in general all sorts of salt provisions.[z] From such a regimen, as Galen hath observed, the leprosy and other inveterate

---

population did not still equal the Roman Capitation about this period. (See Just. Lips. Elect. Lib. 1.—-De Magnitudine Romæ. Lib. 1. 7.) In the quotation from Athenæus, I have adopted the ingenious emendation of the "Ἑπτα χ͝ δικατη," with which the Baron de St. Croix hath furnished me, on the very strong evidence of Demetrius having been the Athenian Archon in the fourth year of the 117th Olympiad, which he produces from Corsini. Fast. Attic. Tom. 4.--63, 64.

[y] "Ευτοχια δε της ευμοτομιας ποιησας διαπνεισθαι την πολιν τοις ετησιοις ανεμοις· χ͝ τυτων πνεοντων μεν δια τυ μεγιτε πελαγυς, καταψυχοντων δε τον κατα την πολιν αερα, πολλην τοις κατοικυσιν ευκρασιαν χ͝ υγιειαν κατισκευαστι" (Diod. Sicul. Lib. 17. Tom. 2.--200.) "Και οι ετησιαι πνευσιν εκ των βορεων, χ͝ τυ τοσυτυ πελαγυς· ωστε καλλιτα τυ θερες Αλεξανδρεις διαγυσιν." (Strabo. Lib. 17. --1143.) A warm and luxuriant description of Alexandria may be found in Achilles Tatius. (Lib. 5. C. 1. 397——400. 8vo Lips. 1776.) Monf. Savary (Letters on Ægypt, Vol. 1.--21——42.) hath amplified it, and introduced the revolutions that it hath experienced, but with both ingenuity and taste.

[z] Yet to this wretched bill of Fare, Diodorus Siculus gives a flat contradiction. "Και προσοδων πληθει χ͝ των προς τροφην ανηκοντων πολυ διαφερει των αλλων. Lib. 17. Tom. 2.--201.

inveterate fcorbutic complaints were very frequent. Cocchi, from whom the remark is borrowed, defcribes the foil of Alexandria as very hot and impregnated with falts, and he adds that from the expence of the inceffant watering which the vegetables wanted, they were not within the reach of general ufe, and the malady from this circumftance was both very common and very virulent.

The place on which Alexandria ftood, had been ufed to feed cattle[a] in, and ferved occafionally for the retreat of a few miferable fhepherds or fifhermen, who refided in the little village of Racotis. Alexander looked undoubtedly with a penetrating eye into futurity, and made choice of the fituation without any attention to the falubrity of the air, from the commercial advantages that it offered, and which foon rendered it one of the moft flourifhing cities of the ancient world.[b]

The

[a] "Οἱ μὲν ὂν προτεροι τῶν Αἰγυπτίων βασιλεῖς ἀγαπῶντες οἷς εἶχον, κ̓ ὒ πανυ ἐπεισακτῶν δεομενοι, διαβεβλημενοι προς ἅπαντας τȣς πλεοντας, κ̓ μαλιϛα τȣς Ἕλληνας (πορθηται γαρ ἠσαν κ̓ ἐπιθυμηται της ἀλλοτριας κατα σπανιν γης) ἐπεϛησαν φυλακην τῳ τοπῳ τȣτῳ, κελευσαντες ἀπειργειν τȣς προσιοντας· κατοικιαν δ' αυτοις ἐδοσαν την προσαγορευομενην Ρακωτιν, ἡ νυν μεν της Ἀλεξανδρεων πολεως εϛι μερ Θ. τὸ ὑπερκειμενον των νεωριων· τοτε δε κωμη ὑπηρχη· τα δε κυκλῳ της κωμης βȣκολοις παρεδοσαν, δυναμενοις κ̓ αυτοις κωλυειν τȣς εξωθεν ἐπιοντας." (Strabo. Lib. 17.--1142.) The "Βȣκολοις παρεδοσαν" leads me to believe with Diodorus Siculus that Alexandria was not confined to the flefh of camels and of affes.

[b] A modern traveller who vifited the Turkifh empire on a profeffional plan, hath paffed a high encomium on the Macedonian Monarch's difcernment in his choice of the fituation of Alexandria. " L'Egypte fituée pour affocier à fon commerce, l'Europe, l'Afrique et les Indes, avait befoin d'un port. Il devait être vafte, et d'un abord facile : les bouches du Nil n'offraient aucun de fes avantages : le feul port qui fût fur cette côte, placé à douze lieues du fleuve, dans un défert

The difficulties, which the Macedonian foldiers had to encounter in their march from the frontiers of Egypt to the temple of Jupiter Ammon, have been greatly exaggerated by all the hiftorians, and particularly Q. Curtius, whofe hyperbolical expreffions are alone fufficient to create a doubt of their veracity.

Diodorus Siculus refers the origin of the temple of Ammon to the time of Danaus;[c] and we are informed by Apollodorus[d] that Cepheus expofed his daughter Andromeda by the counfels of this oracle. But even the fables of Herodotus[e] on the foundation of the

défert, ne pouvait être apperçu que par un génie hardi. Il falloit y bâtir une ville ; ce fut lui qui en deffina le plan. A quel degré de fplendeur n'a-t-il pas porté Alexandrie dans fa naiffance ? il la joignit au Nil par un canal navigable, et utile à la culture ; elle devint la ville de toutes les nations, la Métropole du commerce ; il en honore les cendres que les fiecles de barbarie ont amoncelés, et qui n'attendent qu'une main bien faifante qui les délaie, pour cimenter la réconftruction du plus vafte edifice que l'efprit humain ait jamais conçu.

Ses ruines offrent à chaque pas le temoignage de fon ancienne fplendeur ; et le manteau Macédonien que fon enceinte repréfente, en repellant le fondateur, femble en avoir impofé aux Barbares dans les différentes faccagemens de cette ville. Les mêmes murailles qui garantiffaient fon induftrie et fes richeffes, défendent encore aujourd'hui fes ruines, et préfentent un chefd'œuvre de maconnerie." Mem. du Baron de Tott. Tom. 2.--179. 180. 12mo Paris, 1785.

c " Το μεν εν τιμενῶ φασιν ιδρυσασθαι Δαναον τον Αιγυπτιον·" Diod. Sicul. Lib. 17. Tom. 2.--198.

d " Ποσειδων——————πλημμυραν τι επι την χοραν επεμψε κ̃ κητ̃ Αμμων̃ δε χρησαντ̃ την απαλλαγην της συμφορας, εαν η Κασσιπιας θυγατηρ Ανδρομεδα προτιθη τω κητει βορα· τουτο αναγκασθεις ο Κηφευς ὑπο των Αιθιοπων επραξε, κ̃ προσεδησε την θυγατερα πετρα." Apollod. Lib. 2. C. 4.--98. Ed. Heyne. 12mo Gott. 1782.

e " Ταδε δε Δωδωναιων φασι αἱ προμαντεις, δυο πελειαδας μελαινας εκ Θηβεων την Αιγυπτιων αναπταμενας, την μεν αυτεων ες Λιβυης, την δε παρα σφεας απικεσθαι, ἱζομενην δε μιν επι φηγου, αυδαξασθαι φωνῃ ανθρωπηιῃ, ὡς χρεων ειη μαντηιον αυτοθι Διος γενεσθαι· κ̃ αυτους ὑπολαβειν θειον ειναι το επαγγελλομενον

the edifice, are favourable to its antiquity and carry back its existence to a very remote period. The Oracle of Jupiter Ammon was highly celebrated in the firſt ages of Greece. Crœſus [f] conſulted it on the probable ſucceſſes of the war, which he intended to undertake againſt the Perſians, and the Lacedæmonians [g] and Eleans afterwards frequently reſorted to it. Temples roſe in gratitude for the ſuppoſed munificence of the local Deity, and Pindar compoſed hymns in honour of the ſhrine, which were tranſmitted to the Ammonites in Lybia. One of theſe ſacred odes, which had been engraven on a triangular column near an altar erected to this Divinity by Ptolemy the ſon of Lagus, was legible in the days of Pauſanias, and is mentioned by him. [h]

The Oracles of Ammon, of Dodona and of Delphos, acquired a great influence in Greece, and poſſeſſed an unlimited confidence on the moſt important occaſions. Whenever there were any apprehenſions

μενον αυτοισι, κ̃ ϲφιας εκ τουτυ ποιησαι· την δε ες τους Λιβυας ειχ̃μενον πελεκυα, λεγυσι Αμμωνος χρηστηριον κελευσαι τυς Λιβυας ποιεειν· εϛι δε κ̃ τουτο Δι⊕." Herodotus. Lib. 2.--130.

[f] "Λιβυης δε παρα Αμμωνα απιϛιλι αλλυς χρησομενυς————τι επιχειρεοι επι Περσας ϛρατευεσθαι." Herod. Lib. 1.--21.

[g] "Εντευθεν, ιερον εϛιν Αμμων⊕· φαινεται δε απαρχης Λακεδαιμονιοι μαλιϛα Ελληνων χρωμενοι τω εν Λιβυη μαντειω." (Pauſanias. Lib. 3. C. 18.--253.) The courteous Deity ſeems to have felt the obligation, and to have patroniſed the Lacedæmonians in return. "Φησιν αν βελεϛθαι αυτω την Λακεδαιμονιων ευφημιαν ειναι μαλλον, η τα συμπαντα των Ελλήνων ιερα." Plato Alcibiad. 2.--135.

[h] "Οι πορρω δε ιϛι να⊕ Αμμωνος· κ̃ το αγαλμα ανεθηκε μεν Πινδαρος, Καλαμιδος δε εϛι εργον· απιτιμψι δε ο Πινδαρος κ̃ Λιβυης επ' Αμμωνα τω Αμμωνι υμνος· ουτος κ̃ ες εμε ην ὁ υμνος εν τριγωνω ϛηλη παρα τω βωμον, εν Πτολεμαιος ὁ Λαγυ τω Αμμωνι ανεθηκε." Pauſanias. Lib. 9. C. 16.--741.

prehenfions of a war, or a new colony was to be eftablifhed, one of the three fhrines was confulted, and its anfwer governed their future refolutions.¹ The credit of Jupiter Ammon, who delivered his refponfes under the figure of a ram,ᵏ continued to hold its empire over the mind, and declined only on the introduction of the Roman government, under which more religious veneration was beftowed on the Sibylline verfes and Etrufcan divinations.¹ Yet the temple of this Deity fubfifted with fome reputation, as low as the fifth age, as may be gathered from Synefiusᵐ the bifhop of Ptolemais a writer of that time.

From the credit of the Oracle and its antiquity, there can be little doubt that the country, where its refponfes were delivered, was frequented by crowds of vifitants. Strabo,ⁿ to avoid a con-

S   tradiction,

---

¹ "Quam vero Græcia coloniam mifit in Æoliam, Ioniam, Afiam, Siciliam, Italiam, fine Pythio aut Dodonæo, aut Hammonis Oraculo? aut quod bellum fufceptum ab eâ fine confilio Deorum eft." M. T. Cicero de Divinatione. Lib. 1. Tom. 3, 4. 4ᵗᵒ 1740.

ᵏ "Λιβυης προβατον, ὁ καλυσιν Αμμωνα, Θεον ιχυσι·" (Athanafius adverf. Gentes. 20. Ed. Comelin.) and the Scholiaft on Pindar hath preferved a verfe of Phæftus.

"Ζευ Λιβυης Αμμων κεραπεφηρε κικληθι μαντι·"
                                                                 Pyth. 4.

¹ "Πολλα δε ειρηκοτες περι τυ Αμμωνος, τοσυτον ειπειν βυλομεθα· Ὁτι τοις αρχαιοις μαλλον ην εν τιμη, κ᾽ ἡ μαντικη καθολυ, κ᾽ τα χρηστηρια· νυνι δε ολιγωρια κατεχει πολλη, των Ρωμαιων αρκυμενων τοις Σιβυλλης χρησμοις, κ᾽ τοις Τυρρηνικοις θεωπροσπιοις, δια τε σπλαγχνων, κ᾽ ορνιθειας, κ᾽ διοσημειων· Διοπερ κ᾽ το εν Αμμωνι σχεδον τι εκλελειπται χρηστεριον, προτερον δε εικμηντο." Strabo. Lib. 17.--1168.

ᵐ De Infomniis. 116.

ⁿ "Ταχα δη κ᾽ το τυ Αμμωνος ιερον περιερον επι της θαλατης ον· εκρυσιας ξενομενης ην εν τη μεση λα κισθαι· αλαζειν τι, κ᾽ το μαντειον ευλογως επι τοσυτον γινεσθαι επιφανες τι, κ᾽ γνωριμον επι θαλατ⸏ι ον· τον τε επιπο-

tradition, and get rid of the inconfiftency which appeared between its ancient celebrity and its difficult accefs, adopts the opinion of Eratofthenes, who affures us, on fome feeble conjectures, that the temple once ftood on the fhore, from which the fea had gradually retired. But this able geographer would not have confidered the approach to the temple as impracticable, if he had attended to Herodotus,° and the route that he hath traced acrofs Africa, which was in all probability travelled by the Greeks during the reign of Pfammaticus, when they had the liberty of carrying on their commerce and fettling in Ægypt.

There was a tradition, that one part of the army of Cambyfes had perifhed ᵖ in this country, but from this route it may be concluded

λυ ετως εκτοπισμον απο της Θαλατης, υκ ιυλογον ποιειν την νυν υσαν επιφανειαν κ͵ δοξαν." Strabo, Lib. 1.--86, 87.

° Herodotus, Lib. 4.--361, 362. Monsʳ Bougainville hath illuftrated with much ingenuity this route, and hath left nothing to be added on the fubject. Hift. de l'Academie des Infcriptions et Belles Lettres. Tom. 28.--302.

ᵖ Herodotus gives the melancholy hiftory of the lofs of this detachment between Oafes and Ammon. " Λεγεται δι ταδι υπ'Αμμωνιων· επιιδη εκ της Οασιος ταυτης ιιναι δια της ψαμμον επι σφεας, γινεσθαι τι αυτους μιταξυ κε μαλιςα αυτεων τε και της Οασιως αριςαν αιριομινοισι αυτιοισι ιπιπιευσαι νοτον μεγαν τε και εξαισιον, φοριοντα δε θινας της ψαμμυ, καταχωσαι σφεας κ͵ τροπω τοιυτω αφανισθαι·" (Herodotus. Lib. 3.--208.) and I cannot allow the Baron de St. Croix's evidence to be decifive, though he peremptorily ftyles the account a falfity. Seneca appears to have believed the accident, " Aliquando Cambyfes ad Ammoniam mifit exercitum: quem arena Auftro mota, et more nivis incidens, texit, deinde obruit," (Queft. Nat. 2. 30. Seneca. Opera. Tom. 2. 8ᵛᵒ 1672.) and the fublime and terrible defcription that a modern traveller hath given of thefe moving mountains, which he witneffed on his return from Abyffinia, leaves little doubt of the frequency of fimilar difafters. Monsʳ Savary is of opinion that the Perfians were purpofely led aftray and left by their Ægyptian guides to perifh in the deferts,

cluded to be a falsity. Alexander took the road to Parætonium, which though less frequented, was not less passable, and the ambassadors from Cyrene met him there.ᑫ The Prince according to Aristobulus returned with his army by the same route, but if the troops had been in such danger of perishing in their march to Ammon,

deserts, and he supports Herodotus with some strong probabilities.———Thompson hath beautifully described the accumulated horrors of these horrid regions.

"Commission'd Demons oft', Angels of wrath,
Let loose the raging elements. Breath'd hot
From all the boundless furnace of the sky,
And the wide-glittering waste of burning sand,
A suffocating wind the pilgrim smites
With instant death. Patient of thirst and toil,
Son of the desert! ev'n the camel feels
Shot thro' his wither'd heart, the fiery blast.
Or from the black-red ether, bursting broad,
Sallies the sudden whirlwind. Straight the sands,
Commov'd around, in gath'ring eddies play;
Nearer and nearer still they dark'ning come;
Till, with the gen'ral all-involving storm
Swept up, the whole continuous wilds arise;
And by their noon-day fount dejected thrown,
Or sunk at night in sad disastrous sleep,
Beneath descending hills, the caravan
Is buried deep. In Cairo's crowded streets
Th' impatient merchant, wondering, waits in vain,
And Mecca saddens at the long delay."

Thompson's Seasons. Summer. 960---979.

ᑫ "Κατα μεσην δε την οδον απηντησαν αυτω πρεσβεις παρα Κυρηναιων, στεφανον κομιζοντες, ϗ μεγαλοπρεπη δωρα" (Diod. Sicul. Lib. 17.---197.) Q. Curtius briefly tells us, "Descendit ad Mareotim paludem. Eo legati Cyrenensium dona adtulere; pacem et ut adiret urbes suas petentes." Lib. 4. C. 7. Tom. 1.---209.

Ammon, it is not to be imagined, that a general of Alexander's abilities would have exposed them a second time, without any necessity, to the same perils of being buried in the sands, or expiring by a more lingering death, from hunger[1] and thirst.

Ammon, in the bosom of Lybia, notwithstanding its distance from the borders of the sea, was resorted to by most of the European nations, and supplied them with several objects for exportation.[2] It had been peopled by a colony of Æthiopians and Ægyptians, as the language spoken by the Ammonites in the time of Herodotus, which was a mixture of the language of both these people, sufficiently demonstrates.[3] Is it likely, that men whose intention in their migrations was as much to procure the conveniences of life, as to enjoy its necessaries, should have voluntarily established

---

[1] "Ενταυθα Αλεξανδρ⊕.————ανεζευξεν επ'Αιγυπτου· ως μεν Αριςοβυλ⊕. λεγει, την αυτην οπισω ὁδον" but Arrian adds, "Ὡς δε Πτολιμαι⊕. ὁ Λαγυ, αλλην ευθειαν, ὡς επι Μεμφιν," (De Exped. Alex. Lib. 3. C. 4.--187.) which appears most likely, from the difficulties and dangers experienced in their route to Ammon.

[2] This commerce is supposed to have consisted of salt, gum and dates. Arrian mentions the first, and from this account, there must have been a considerable demand for it. "Γιγνονται δε κȷ αλες αυτοματοι εν τω χωριω τουτω ορυκτοι· κȷ τουτων εςιν ὡς ες Αιγυπτον φερουσι των ἱερων τινες του Αμμων⊕. επειδη γαρ επ'Αιγυπτε ςελλονται, ες κοιτιδας πλεκτας εκ φοινικ⊕. εςβαλοντες, δωρον τω βασιλει αποφερουσιν, η ει τω αλλω·———κȷ τουτο επι ταις θυσιαις χρωνται, ως καθαρωτερω των απο θαλασσης ἁλων Αιγυπτιοι τε κȷ ὁσοι αλλοι τε θειω εκ αμιλως ιχωσιν." (Exped. Alex. Lib. 3. C. 4.--187.) The Baron de St. Croix remarks likewise from Jablonski, (Panth. Ægypt. Tom. 3.--82.) that the Ægyptians owing to some religious scruples had a horror of sea-salt, which must have increased the consumption of the rock-salt of Ammon.

[3] "Απο δε Αιγυπτιων Αμμωνιοι, ιοντες Αιγυπτιων τε κȷ Αιθιοπων αποικοι, κȷ φωνην μεταξυ αμφοτερων νομιζοντες." Herodotus. Lib. 1.--123, 124.

established themselves in a situation, which could only have been fit for the lion and the tiger, if the difficulties of getting to it had been as insurmountable as they have been represented? Is it also probable that a colony should have planted itself by choice in a country so totally deprived of water, as the historians of Alexander have described it.[w]

We are told, as a fact universally acknowledged, by Synesius,[x] a native of Cyrene, whose authority hath naturally a claim to some influence, that the country of Ammon was remarkable for its fertility, and the abundance of provisions, that it afforded to the inhabitants and their cattle, which cannot possibly agree with the pretended barrenness of the soil. Diodorus Siculus admits it likewise to have been fruitful,[y] and Strabo compares a tract of country well watered

---

[w] The Baron de St. Croix adds "Arrien refute cette opinion absurd." I have omitted this sentence, and varied the preceding one, because I draw a very different conclusion from Arrian's expressions. "Εςι δε ερημη τε η οδος, κ ψαμμ⊙ η πολλη αυτης, κ ανυδρ⊙·——ο δε χωρος ιναπερ το Αμμων⊙ το ιερον εςι, τα μεν κυκλω παντα ερημα; κ ψαμμ⊙ το παν εχει, κ ανυδρ⊙." Exped. Alex. Lib. 3. C. 3, 4.--185, 186.

[x] "Τον Αμμωνα κ Αμμων⊙ γην ε μαλλον ειναι μηλοτροφορον, η κυροτροφον αγαθην·" Synesii Epist. 4.--43.

[y] I am apprehensive a more extensive signification hath been forced on Diodorus Siculus, than the passage of this author warrants, who speaks only of the fertility in the immediate vicinage of the temple, and confines it within the narrow bounds of fifty stadia. "Η δε περι το ιερον τουτο χωρα περιεχεται υπο ερημου κ ανυδρου της αμμου, πασης φιλανθρωπιας εςερημενη· αυτη δ' επι μηκ⊙ κ πλατ⊙ επι σταδιους πεντηκοντα παρηκυσα, πολλοις μεν κ καλοις υδασι ναματιαιοις διαρρειται, δενδρων δε παντοδαπων κ μαλιςα καρπιμων πληθεις· κ τον μεν αερα τη κρασει παραπλησιον εχει ταις εαριναις ωραις, τοποις δε καυματωδεσι περιεχομενη, μονη παρηλλαγμενην παρεχεται τοις ενδιατριβυσι την ευκρασιαν."

tered and beautified with palms, at the diſtance of four days' journey from the Syrtes, to the country of Ammon.ᶻ

The ſands which the Macedonian army traverſed, according to Q. Curtius, were heated in ſuch a manner as to ſcorchᵃ the feet, and

ιυκρασιαν'" (Diod. Sicul. Lib. 17. Tom. 2.--198.) Arrian confirms the reality of this local fertility, but he allows it to extend only to forty ſtadia. "Αυτϱ̅ δε εν μεσω ολιγϱ̅ ων (οσον γαρ πλησον αυτε ις πλατϱ̅ διηχει, ις τισσαρακοντα μαλιςα ςαδιες ερχεται) καταπλεως εςιν ημερων δενδρων, ελαιων, και φοινικων, κ̓ ευδρωσϱ̅ μονϱ̅ των περιξ· Και πηγη ιξ αυτε ανισχει'" (Exped. Alex. Lib. 3. C. 4.-186.) Q. Curtius is a little more luxuriant. "Tandem ad ſedem conſecratam Deo ventum eſt. Incredibile dictu, inter vaſtas ſolitudines ſita, undique ambientibus ramis, vix in denſam umbram cadente ſole contecta eſt: multiqae fontes dulcibus aquis paſſim manantibus alunt ſilvas. Cæli quoque mira temperies, verno tempori maxime ſimilis, omnes anni partes pari ſalubritate percurrit." (Lib. 4. C. 7. Tom. 1.--210, 211.) Le Clerc hath diſſected with critical acrimony this deſcription of a temperate climate under a blazing ſun, but Perizonius (Curt. Vind. 144.) defends both Diodorus Siculus and Q. Curtius, with great judgment and ability. Lucan infers the divinity of the place from its ſurrounding ſcenery.

"Eſſe locis ſuperos, teſtatur ſilva per omnem
Sola virens Libyen. Nam quidquid pulvere ſicco
Separat ardentem tepida Berenicide Lepti,
Ignorat fondes; ſolus nemus abſtulit Hammon
Silvarum fons cauſa loco."

Lib. 9.--522.

By a ſtrange revolution of events the neighbourhood of the temple of Jupiter Ammon became the reſidence of ſeveral Chriſtian prelates, during the Arian perſecution. Athanaſius mentions it. Apol. ad Conſt. 317. Hiſt. Arrian. 387.

ᶻ "Τιταρταιες μεν ουν φασιν απο τε μυχε της μεγαλης Συρτεως τες κατ' αυτο μαλακως βαδιζοντας, ως επι χειμερινας ανατολας αφικνεισθαι· Εςι δε ο τοπος ουτϱ̅ εμφερης τω Αμμωνι, φοινικοτροφϱ̅, τι κ̓ ευυδρϱ̅." Strabo. Lib. 17. Tom. 2.--1196.

ᵃ "Terra cæloque aquarum penuria eſt: ſteriles arenæ jacent; quas ubi vapor ſolis accendit, fervido ſolo exurente veſtigia, intolerabilis æſtus exſiſtit. Luctandumque eſt, non tantum cum ardore et ſiccitate regionis, ſed etiam cum tenaciſſimo ſabulo, quod præaltum, et veſtigio cedens,

ægre

and as they gave way as the troops paffed over them, the march became uncommonly painful and fatiguing. To augment their fufferings, neither the Heavens nor the Earth fupplied them with any [b] water. In a few lines afterwards we are told of a tremendous ftorm, [c] attended with very heavy rain, by which the army was greatly refrefhed; but the ftory that had juft been related to us, does not feem to be authenticated by fuch an anecdote. It may be afked how Alexander could penetrate into this vaft folitude, and direct his march through fuch a pathlefs defert. Q. Curtius hath given him a flight of crows [d] for guides, and Callifthenes, [e] to make the circumftance more extraordinary, informs us

the

ægre moliuntur pedes. (Q. Curtius. Lib. 4. C. 7. Tom. 1.--208.) I find no authority for the "ils ebouloient fous les pas des voyageurs et menacoient à chaque inftant de les engloutir," and I omit it.

[b] " Repente, five illud Deorum munus, five cafus fuit; obductæ cœlo nubes condidere folem: ingens æftu fatigatis, etiamfi aqua deficeret, auxilium. Enimvero, ut largum quoque imbrem excufferunt procellæ; pro fe quifque excipere eum, quidam ob fitim impotentes fui, ore quoque hianti captare cœperunt." Q. Curt. Lib. 4. C. 7. Tom. 1.--209, 210.

[c] " Quatriduum per vaftas folitudines abfumptum eft. Jamque haud procul oraculi fede aberant; quum complures corvi agmini occurrunt, modico volatu prima figna antecedentes: et modo humi refidebant, quum lentius agmen incederet; modo fe pennis levabant, antecedentium iterque monftrantium ritu." Q. Curt. Lib. 4. C. 7. Tom. 1.--210.

[d] " Aperuere fe campi alto obruti fabulo; haud fecus quam profundum æquor ingreffi, terram oculis requirebant. Nulla arbor, nullum culti foli occurrebat veftigium." Q. Curt. Lib. 4. C. 7. Tom. 1.--209.

[e] "Ὁ δε ην θαυμασιωτατον (ὡς Καλλισθενης φησιν) ταις φωναις ανακαλεμενοι τες πλανομενες νυκτωρ κ̓ κλαζοντες, ὡς ιχνος καθιϛασαν της παρειας." (Plutarch de Vit. Alex. Plut. Oper. Tom. 1. 680.) The flight of crows is reduced by many of the hiftorians to a pair, and by Ptolemy thefe two

black

the stragglers from the main body of the army were recalled into the road by their croaking.

Darius in the mean time was not inactive, but again collected an immense number of men, from every corner of his extensive empire, to oppose the farther progress of his formidable enemy, who advanced rapidly, on quitting Ægypt, towards the Euphrates, which he crossed at Tapsacus. Pliny [f] and Dion Cassius have entertained a different opinion, and imagine Alexander to have crossed the river near Zeugma on a bridge, suspended by chains of iron.[g] These writers were however undoubtedly led into an error by the etymology

---

black Guides metamorphosed into Dragons. Arrian naturally appears to have his doubts, but his understanding and his inclinations are at variance. "Πτολεμαιος μεν δη ο Λαγου λεγει δρακοντας δυο ιεναι προ του στρατευματος, φωνη ιεντας, ᾗ τουτοις Αλεξανδρον κελευσαι επεσθαι τους ηγεμονας, πιστευσαντας τω Θειω· τους δε ηγησασθαι την οδον την τε ες το μαντειον, ᾗ οπισω αυθις· Αριστοβουλος δε (ᾗ ο πλειων λογος ταυτη κατεχει) κορακας δυο προπετωμενους της στρατιας, τουτους γενεσθαι Αλεξανδρω τους ηγεμονας· Και οτι μεν θειον τι ξυνεπελαβεν αυτω, εχω ισχυρισασθαι, οτι ᾗ το εικος ταυτη εχει· τοδε ατρεκες τω λογω αφαιρουντο οι αλλη ᾗ αλλη αυτο εξηγησαμενοι." Arrian. Exped. Alex. Lib. 3. C. 3.--185, 186.

[f] "Et exstare ferream catenam apud Euphratem amnem in urbe quæ Zeugma appellatur, qua Alexander magnus ibi junxerat pontem. (Plin. Hist. Nat. Lib. 34. C. 43. Tom. 5.--150, 151.). "Κατα το Ζευγμα ουτω γαρ απο της του Αλεξανδρου στρατειας το χωριον εκεινο, οτι ταυτη επερχιωθη, κεκληται." (Dion. Cassius. Lib. 40. Tom. 1.--235.) Lucan hath a similar idea,

———————"Nunc Parthia ruptis
Excedat clauſtris vetitam per secula ripam
Zeugmaque Pellæum."

Lib. 8.--235.

[g] And of this opinion is Strabo. "Θαψακε, καθ'ο ην το Ζευγμα του Ευφρατου το παλαιον επι του Τιγρωδη διαβασιν, καθ'ην διεβη Αλεξανδρος αυτον." (Strabo. Lib. 17.--1082.) It is probable that the younger Cyrus crossed the Euphrates in nearly the same place. Xenoph. Expeditio Cyri. Lib. 1.--72.

etymology of the word, but the itinerary of the Macedonian army, from Tyre to Arbela, proves decidedly the impofition.

Mazæus had been ordered by Darius to defend the paffage of the Euphrates, but he abandoned the poft and retreated, having firft laid wafte the country to deprive the Macedonian army of forage and fubfiftence. Four days after Alexander had paffed the Euphrates and the Tigris without any oppofition, he difcovered a body of cavalry, which was immediately purfued. Many prifoners were taken, and they gave him the intelligence, that Darius was encamped on a wide plain upon the banks of the Bumado, not far from Gaugamele. The troops had a few days allowed them to recover their fatigues, and the Macedonian Monarch then moved forward again, and took poft at the diftance only of fixty ftadia from the Perfian camp. Arrian furnifhes us with thefe particulars,[h] which are very neceffary to correct the inaccuracy of Diodorus Siculus.

This latter hiftorian relates that Mazæus was detached to defend the river,[i] without fpecifying what river it was, that he was ordered to fecure. It muft, however, have been the Euphrates, though it is not named. The Macedonian army paffed the anonymous river, and Alexander ftretched on the following day

directly

[h] Arrian. Exped. Alex. Lib. 3. C. 7, 8, 9.--193——199.
[i] "Την διαβασιν τȣ ποταμȣ" Diod. Sicul. Lib. 17. Tom. 2.--203.

directly towards the enemy, and encamped in their presence. The remainder of the narrative seems to intimate, that the two armies came to blows two days after the passage of the Euphrates.[k]—— Diodorus Siculus may have mistaken the Euphrates for the Tigris, and his errors in consequence of this conjecture will become less palpable and of less importance, but their number will not be diminished.

The imagination is ever on the watch to escape from the fetters of historical restriction, and, regardless of contradictions and their consequences, is apt to wander through the flowery fields of fancy, as the inclination leads it. Q. Curtius proves the propriety of the observation in his account of the battle of Gaugamele. On the plain, as he tells us, where the two armies encountered, neither bush nor tree was to be seen, and the view was as boundless as the horizon.[l] Such a description does not correspond with Alexander's orders to level every obstacle, that interrupted the motions of his troops,[m] and the position which a detachment occupied a little

---

[k] " Τη δ'υςεραία συντεταγμενην εχων την ςρατιαν, προηγεν επι τες πολεμιες, κ̑ συνεγγυς γενομεν⊕ των Περσων, κατεςρατοπεδευσεν." Diod. Sicul. Lib. 17. Tom. 2.--203.

[l] "Opportuna explicandis copiis regio erat, equitabilis et vasta planities. Ne stirpes quidem et brevia virgulta operiant solum : liberque prospectus oculorum etiam quæ procul recessere, permittitur." Q. Curtius. Lib. 4. C. 9. Tom. 1.--233.

[m] "Itaque si qua campi eminebant, jussit æquari, totumque fastigium extendi." Q. Curtius. Lib. 4. C. 9. Tom. 1.--233, 234.

little before the action upon a height, that the Perſians had abandoned.ⁿ

Moſt of the hiſtorians reckon the Perſian army to have amounted to a million of men, and though the calculation may appear extravagant, it certainly does not exceed the bounds of probability. All the nations in fact from the Euxine ſea to the extremities of the Eaſt had made a common cauſe, and ſent Darius very numerous and powerful reinforcements. It was the cuſtom of the Aſiatics to carry their wives and children along with them in their military expeditions, and Perſian luxury could not diſpenſe with the want of a crowd of the uſeleſs followers of a camp ; two circumſtances which will conſiderably diminiſh the number of the real and effective troops. If we conſider likewiſe the living clouds of Barbarians, that have ſpread themſelves in different ages over the Weſtern world, and thoſe immenſe bodies of more regular troops, that under the conduct of many Tartarian princes, poſſeſſed themſelves of almoſt all the realms of Aſia, we may eaſily conceive that ſuch a multitude might have been collected to combat on the plains of Aſſyria for the ſafety of the Perſian empire.

ⁿ "Mazæus———cum delectis equitum in edito colle, ex quo Macedonum proſpiciebantur caſtra, conſederat. Macedones eam ipſum collem, quem deſeruerat, occupaverunt : nam et tutior planitie erat," (Q. Curtius. Lib. 4. C. 12. Tom. 1,--263.) But the woods and valleys which echoed with the ſhouts of the armies are ſtill more inconſiſtent and abſurd.——" Macedones, ingentem, pugnantium more, edidere clamorem. Redditus et a Perſis, nemora valleſque circumjectas terribili ſono implevere." Q. Curtius. Lib. 4. C. 12. Tom. 1,--264.

The Scythians and Bactrians diſtinguiſhed themſelves by their valour on this memorable day, and ruſhed with impetuoſity on the left wing of the Macedonian army, on which they made ſome impreſſion. A detachment alſo of the Perſians made its way to the baggage of their enemy, who loſt, notwithſtanding theſe vigorous attacks leſs than three hundred men according to Q. Curtius,[o] and five hundred agreeable to Diodorus Siculus,[p] excluſive of the wounded. One hundred men and a thouſand horſe are ſuppoſed by Arrian[q] to have been left on the field of battle, or to have fallen in the purſuit. The loſs of the Perſian army amounted by his account to three hundred thouſand men,[r] but it ſeems exaggerated. Dexippus[s] lowers it to one hundred and thirty thouſand, and Diodorus Siculus[t] to nearly ninety thouſand. Zozimus[w] hath boldly aſſerted that almoſt the whole of the Perſian

[o] "Macedonum minus quam trecenti deſiderati ſunt." Q. Curt. Lib. 4. C. 16. Tom. 1.--297.

[p] "Των δε Μακεδονων ανηρεθησαν μεν εις πεντακοσιυς, τραυματιαι δ'εγενοντο παμπληθεις." Diod. Sicul. Lib. 17. Tom. 2.--207.

[q] "Απεθανον δε των αμφ' Αλεξανδρον, ανδρες μεν ις εκατον μαλιςα· ιπποι δε εκ τε των τραυματων κ̀ της κακοπαθειας της εν τε διωξει, ὑπερ τους χιλιυς·" Arrian. Exped. Alex. Lib. 3. C. 15.--214.

[r] "Των βαρβαρων δε, νεκρων μεν ελεγοντο ες τριακοντα μυριαδας·" (Arrian. Exped. Alex. Lib. 3. C. 16.--215.) Arrian however qualifies it with the "Ελεγοντο."

[s] Apud. Cedrenum. 125.

[t] "Των βαρβαρων εν ταυτη τη μαχη κατεκοπησαν οι παντες ισπεις τε κ̀ πεζοι πλειυς των εννεα μυριαδων." Diod. Sicul. Lib. 17. Tom. 2.--207.

[w] "Και την μαχην εις Αρβηλαν προς αυτον (Δαρειον) ποιησαμενο-, τοσουτον εκρατησεν, ὡςε παντας μεν σχεδον ανελειν, Δαρειν δε ςυν ολιγοις φυγοντ-." Zozimus. Lib. 1. C. 4.--9. 8vo Lipſ. 1784.·

sian troops was destroyed, but Q. Curtius appears to have adopted the most probable calculation, and states their loss at forty thousand.* It is indeed the only circumstance in his relation of this action, that we can literally subscribe to; in every other, the qualifications of the historian are totally wanting, and we have the descriptions of a poet, or the declamations of an orator.

The following sentences convey to us some parts of the speech of Darius to his troops immediately before the engagement. "Dare ʸ to conquer and the work is done. Renown and fame are but weak arms against brave men, therefore do not regard them in the enemy. For it is rashness you have hitherto feared, and mistaken for courage; which when its first fury is spent, becomes languid and dull, like those animals that have lost their stings.— As for Alexander, how great soever he may appear to the cowardly and fearful, he is still but one individual creature; and, in

my

---

x "Cecidere Perfarum, quorum numerum victores finire potuerunt, millia quadringenta."
Q. Curt. Lib. 4. C. 16. Tom. 1,--297.

y " Audete modo vincere ; famamque, infirmissimum adversus fortes viros telum, contemnite ? Temeritas est, quam adhuc pro virtute timuistis : quæ ubi primum impetum effudet, velut quædam animalia amisso aculeo, torpet.————Alexander, quantuscunque ignavis et timidis videri potest; unum est animal : et, si quid mihi creditis, temerarium et vecors ; adhuc nostro pavore, quam sua virtute felicius! nihil autem potest esse diuturnum, cui non subest ratio, licet felicitas adspirare videatur; tamen ad ultimum temeritati non sufficit. Præterea breves et mutabiles vices rerum, et fortuna nunquam simpliciter indulget————nisi quod in vobis est, ipse ego majore parte captivus sum. Eripite viscera mea ex vinculis: restituite mihi pignora, pro quibus ipse mori non recuso; parentem, liberos, nam conjugem in illo carcere amisi." Q. Curt. Lib. 3. C. 14.--280, 282, 284.

my opinion, both rash and foolish. Now nothing can be lasting that is not supported by reason, and though he seems to be successful, yet at long run he'll pay for his temerity. Besides, the turns and revolutions of things are of short duration, there is no such thing as an unmixed felicity.——I myself am more than half a captive, unless you exert yourselves: free my bowels from their bondage, restore to me those dear pledges, (for which I am willing myself to die) my mother and children, for I have lost my wife in that prison."[a]

It is impossible perhaps to transfuse into any language the warm picturesque expressions of Q. Curtius, but whilst they display the brilliancy of his imagination, they condemn effectually his judgment. This harangue of the Persian Monarch is utterly inconsistent with the character of Darius, and he seems rather to be declaiming in a school of rhetoric, than to address his troops with the dignity of a Monarch and in a manner that his peculiar situation ought to have prescribed to him. The narrative of Q. Curtius is also full of ill-timed reflections, and his ignorance of military affairs is attempted to be concealed in impenetrable obscurity, and a labyrinth of words, that are accumulated without reason or necessity. These fastidious amplifications have sometimes rendered his descriptions almost incomprehensible, and the manner in which he speaks of the chariots armed with scythes is particularly confused.

[a] Digby's Q. Curtius, Vol, 1,--255, 256, 257.

fused.[a] Arrian[b] in every respect is entitled to a preference, and his account of the battle of Gaugamele, is the only source, from which we can derive any certain information of the manœuvres of either the Persian or Macedonian army.

The eclipse of the moon at the commencement of the Mysteries, on the fifteenth day of the month Boedromion, happened according to Plutarch,[c] twelve days before this celebrated battle, which is therefore irrevocably settled to have been fought on the twenty-seventh day of the month Boedromion, in the second year of the 112th Olympiad, and 331 years before Christ. Arrian's computation then, who fixes this action in the month Puanepsi-on,

---

[a] "Ex summo temone hastæ præfixæ ferro eminebant: utrimque a jugo ternos direxerant gladios: et inter radios rotarum plura spicula eminebant in adverfum: aliæ deinde falces summis rotarum orbibus hærebant; et aliæ in terram dimissæ quidquid obvium concitatis equis fuisset amputaturæ." (Q. Curt. Lib. 4. C. 9. Tom. 1.--228, 229.) After all the labours of the commentators this passage still retains its original perplexity. Drakenborch in his edition of Q. Curtius hath abridged most of their observations, and Scheffer (De Re Vehiculari. Lib. 2. C. 15.) hath launched into the subject at length.

[b] Arrian. Exped. Alex. Lib. 3. C. 12, 13, 14, 15.--205----215.

[c] "Την δε μεγαλην μαχην προς Δαρειον ουκ εν Αρβηλοις (ως περ οι αλλοι γραφουσιν) αλλα εν Παυσαμι-λοις γενεσθαι συνεστασιν·————η μεν ουν σεληνη τω Βοηδρομιωνος εξελιπεν, περι την των μυστηριων των Αθηνησιν αρχην ενδικατη δε απο της εκλειψεως νυκτι τον στρατοπεδων εν οψει γεγονατων· &c. &c. &c. (Plut. de Vit. Alex. Plut. Oper. Tom. 1.--683.) " Preceda de onze jours————la bataille de Gaugamele," is the Baron de St. Croix's expression, but he did not sufficiently attend to that of Plutarch, and Langhorn appears to have fallen into the same error. If Darius only ranged his troops in order of battle, and took a review of them by torch-light on the eleventh night, " Ενδικατη νυκτι." after this lunar eclipse, the action must have been fought on the succeeding day. By the Julian calendar this eclipse was supposed to have happened on the twentieth of September, and the calculation therefore of Sir Isaac Newton, who fixes the action on the second of October following is very accurate. See the Chronology of ancient Kingdoms. 355.

on,[d] is erroneous. Ariftophanes was the Athenian Archon at that time, and both Dionyfius of Halicarnaffus[e] and Theophraftus[f] relate this event under the magiftracy of Ariftophon, his fucceffor. But thefe two writers deceived themfelves, and concluded from the news of this decifive action having reached Athens after the expiration of the Archonfhip of Ariftophanes, that it was alfo fought under that of Ariftophon. Juftin hath mentioned the defeat of the united forces of the Perfian empire in the fifth year of the reign of Alexander, but the fixth was the true period of this engagement, which was attended with the total ruin of the Perfian monarchy.

The Conqueror of the Eaft, after he had poffeffed himfelf of Babylon[g] and Suza, then marched for Perfepolis. Q. Curtius

---

[d] "Τουτο τελος της μαχης εγενετο, επι αρχοντος Αθηνησιν Αριςοφανους, μηνὸς Πυανεψιωνὸς." Arrian. Exped. Alex. Lib. 3. C. 15.--215.

[e] "Επ Αριςοφωντὸς αρχοντος ———καθ' ον χρονον Αλεξανδρος την εν Αρβηλοις ενικεν μαχην." Dion. Halic. Epift. ad Ammæum. Tom. 6.--746.

[f] "Και την επ' Αριςοφωντὸς ποτε γενομενην τε ρητορὸς μαχην." (Theophrafti Charact. 7.--34. 8vo Cant. 1712.) Theophraftus does not here particularly fpecify the engagement, and I believe Caufabon is the only Editor who fuggefted that the fentence alludes to the battle near Gaugamele.—On this conftruction the Greek author muft undoubtedly have miftaken the year. As the celebrated battle, however in which Agis the fon of Archidamus fell at Megalopolis, and in which Greece had fuch an intereft, was really fought under the Archonfhip of Ariftophon. (Diod. Sicul. Lib. 17. Tom.--2. 208.) It is more natural to imagine that action was intended to be referred to.

[g] Q. Curtius hath given the following account of the furrender of Babylon.——"Babylonem procedenti Alexandro Mazæus, qui ex acie in urbem confugerat, cum adultis liberis fupplex occurrit, urbem fequededens." He adds, "Gratus adventus ejus fuit regi. Quippe magni operis futura

us [h] relates that four thousand Greeks, who had been barbarously mutilated in addition to the misfortune of captivity, here threw themselves in Alexander's way. This melancholy spectacle affected him exceedingly; and melting with compassion at the recital of their sufferings, he offered them the choice of a residence in the country which they then inhabited, or a return into Greece. —A quiet and undisturbed asylum, where they might wear out the remainder of their days, was all that in their situation could be wished; and they preferred a settlement at a distance, by which their fellow-citizens and friends might at least be spared the shock of seeing their deplorable condition. Q. Curtius, as usual, does not fail to furnish us with a speech [l] to these unfortunate captives, whose number as appears from Diodorus Siculus [k] and Justin, [l] did not exceed eight hundred. Arrian hath not mentioned them, and from his silence we may still doubt of this wanton excess of cruelty.

---

futura erat obsidio tam munitæ urbis." (Q. Curt. Lib. 5. C. 1. Tom. 1.--307.) But if we are to believe Herodotus, Darius had dismantled the city and ruined its fortifications after its revolt. "Βαβυλων νυν μεν ουτω τοδευτερον αιρεθη· Δαρειος δε επει τε εκρατησε των βαβυλωνιων, τουτο μεν, σφεων το τειχος περιειλε, ἢ τας πυλας πασας απεσπασε·" Herodotus. Lib. 3.--278.

[h] "Miserabile agmen, inter pauca Fortunæ exempla memorandum, regi occurrit. Captivi erant Græci ad quatuor millia fere, quos Persæ vario suppliciorum modo adfecerant, alios pedibus, quosdam manibus auribusque amputatis, inustisque barbararum literarum notis." Q. Curt. Lib. 5. C. 5. Tom. 1.--342.

[i] Q. Curt. Lib. 5. C. 5. Tom. 1.--341.

[k] "Απηντησαν γαρ αυτω μεθ'ικετηριων Ἑλληνες ὑπο των προτερον Βασιλεων αναςατοι γεγονοτες, οκτακοσιοι μεν σχεδον τον αριθμον οντες, ταις δ'ηλικιαις οἱ πλεισοι μεν γεγηρακοτες, ηκρωτηριασμενοι δε παντες· οἱ μεν χειρας, οἱ δε ποδας, οἱ δε ωτα ἢ ῥινας·" Diod. Sicul. Lib. 17. Tom. 2.--213.

[l] "Octingenti admodum Græci occurrunt Alexandro, qui pœnam captivitatis truncatâ corporis parte tulerunt." Justin. Lib. 11. C. 14.--295.

The Macedonian army paſſed the Caſpian defiles, and followed Darius in his retreat with aſtoniſhing celerity. Soon afterwards they received intelligence, that Beſſus and his accomplices, after loading Darius with chains, had added aſſaſſination to their crimes, and put their unfortunate Monarch to death. The hiſtorians of Alexander, and particularly Q. Curtius, have taken no little pains to heighten the death of Darius with every intereſting and pathetic circumſtance.——In his laſt moments he is repreſented addreſſing his prayers to Heaven for the proſperity of his victorious enemy, and diſcovers a grandeur of ſoul, that may not poſſibly have been his own.——They finiſh the affecting portrait by painting his amiable and humane qualities, and a ſtrong and ſtriking contraſt ariſes between his misfortunes and his virtues. But the Eaſtern traditions have handed down to us the character of this laſt King of the Kaianides in darker ſhades, and the cruelty of his temper in conjunction with his tyranny, is recorded to have drawn down upon him the general indignation of his ſubjects, and led him to his ruin. [m]

The

---

[m] Herbelot Bibl. Oriental. Dara. Dr. Gillies in his valuable Hiſtory of Greece, obſerves, if "the faſhionable ſcepticiſm of the times ſhould heſitate, the reader has only to aſk what Oriental hiſtorian has related the tranſactions of Darius with the fulneſs and accuracy ſo conſpicuous in Arrian?"——The ſeveral authors who have tranſmitted to us an account of the cruelty of the Perſian Monarch may be ſeen in Herbelot : I do not vouch for their authority, but in the aggregate, notwithſtanding they vary in a few circumſtances, they may have ſome weight. Q. Curtius hath left a memorable inſtance of his barbarity upon record. "Nam etiam ſaucii quidam et invalidi, qui agmen non poterant perſequi, excepti erant. Quos omnes, inſtinctu Purpuratorum, barbarâ feritate ſævientium, præciſis aduſtiſque manibus circumduci, ut copias ſuas noſcerent ; ſatiſque omnibus ſpectatis, nuntiare quæ vidiſſent regi ſuo, juſſit." (Lib. 3. C. 8. Tom. 1.--108.)

The Persian Monarch closed his unhappy reign in the month Hecatombæon, when Aristophon was Archon at Athens, as Arrian [n] tells us, in the third year of the 112th Olympiad, nine months after the fatal battle of Gaugamele, according to Usher,[o] instead of a year and some months, as Sir Isaac Newton hath conjectured.[p]

The Greeks in the Persian pay, continued to serve Darius with unshaken fidelity and fortitude to the last moment of his life. At the death of this Prince they amounted to fifteen hundred, and followed the standard of Artabases, but he was soon obliged to

V 2 accept

1.--108.) and where he mentions the original mildness and tractability of the Persian Monarch's disposition, it seems, in the latter part of life, these virtues had disappeared. "Erat Dario mite ac tractabile ingenium, nisi suam naturam plerumque fortuna corrumperet. Itaque, veritatis impatiens, hospitem ac supplicem, tunc maxime utilia suadentem, abstrahi jussit ad capitale supplicium." (Lib. 3. C. 3. Tom. 1.--69, 70.)——Arrian mentions the massacre of the sick and wounded Macedonians at Issus, by Darius, in severe terms, " Χαλιπως αικισαμενος απεκτεινεν" (Lib. 2. C. 7.--120.) and though he hath afterwards defended his character, it is in a manner perhaps that shews it was liable to objection. "Εις δε τα αλλα ουδεν ανεπιεικες εργον αποδειξαμενω, η ουδε εγγενομενον αυτω αποδειξασθαι· οτι ομου μεν εις την βασιλειαν παρελθειν, ομου δε προσπολεμεισθαι προς τε Μακεδονων και των Ελληνων ξυνεβη· ουκουν ουδε εθελοντι εξην ετι υβριζειν ες τους υπηκοους, εν μειζονι κινδυνω ηπερ εκεινοι καθεστηκοτι·" (Arrian. Exped. Alex. Lib. 3. C. 22.--233.) The "Ουκουν ουδε εθελοντι εξην ετι υβριζειν ες τους υπηκοους," is no very flattering compliment to his memory. When there is no power of being vicious, virtue becomes equivocal, and ceases almost to deserve the name.

[n] "Τουτο το τελ^Q Δαρειω εγενετο, επι αρχοντ^Q Αθηναιοις Αριστοφωντ^Q, μην^Q Ἑκατομβαιων^Q." Arrian. Exped. Alex. Lib. 3. C. 22.--233.

[o] See Usherii Annales. 324, 325. Folio. 1650.

[p] Chronology of ancient kingdoms. 355.

accept of the terms which the Macedonian Monarch offered him, and the Greeks were perſuaded to ſurrender. Diodorus Siculus ⁱ and Q. Curtius ʳ inform us, with ſome trifling variations, that they were diſtributed in the different diviſions of the Macedonian army, but Arrian ˢ aſſerts they formed a ſeparate and detached corps under the command of Andronicus, who had prevailed on them to rely on Alexander's clemency, and to offer him their future ſervices.

This little intrepid band of Warriors ſurvived the ruin of the
Perſian

ⁱ Diodorus Siculus ſeems to intimate that this Grecian corps, hearing of the favourable reception that many of the officers of Darius had met with, made a voluntary offer of its ſervices to Alexander. "Πολλοι των συμπεφευγοτων ηγεμονων τω Δαρειω παρεδωκαν αυτες· οις επιεικως προσενιχ-θεις, μεγαλην δοξαν επιεικειας απηνεγκατο· ευθυς γαρ οἱ Δαρειω συνεςρατευμενοι των Ἑλληνων, οντες περι χιλιως κ̀ πεντακοσιως, ανδρεια τε διαφεροντες, παρεδοσαν ἑαυτες Αλεξανδρω· κ̀ συγγνωμης αξιωθεντες, κατιταχθησαν εις τας ταξεις επι ταις αυταις μισθοφοραις." Lib. 17. Tom. 2.--219.

ʳ Q. Curtius hath preſerved this generous but ineffectual effort for the ſafety of the Spartans who had joined them. "Græcos, quos Artabazus adduxerat, convocari jubet : at illi, niſi Lacedæmoniis fides daretur, reſpondent, ſe quid agendum ipſis foret, deliberaturos. Legati erant Lacedæmoniorum miſſi ad Darium, quo victo adplicaverunt ſe Græcis mercede apud Perſas militantibus, Rex omiſſis ſponſionum fideique pignoribus, venire eos juſſit, fortunam quam ipſe dediſſet habituros. Diu cunctantes, pleriſque conſiliis variantibus, tandem venturos ſe pollicentur. At Democrates Athenienſis, qui maxime Macedonum opibus ſemper obſtiterat, veniâ deſperatâ, gladio ſe transfugit. Ceteri, ſicut conſtituerant, ditioni Alexandri ſe ipſos permittunt. Mille et quingenti milites erant. Præter hos legati ad Darium miſſi nonaginta. In ſupplementum diſtributus miles : ceteri remiſſi domum, præter Lacedæmonios, quos tradi in cuſtodiam juſſit. (Q. Curt. Lib. 6. C. 5. Tom. 1.--416, 417.) The negotiation may be ſeen in Arrian, (Exped. Alex. Lib. 3. C. 23, 24.--239.) who hath ably vindicated the Macedonian Monarch.

ˢ "Της δε αλλης ξυςρατευεσθαι οἱ επι μισθω τω αυτω εκελευσι· κ̀ επιταξεν αυτοις Ανδρονικον, ὁσπερ ηγαγε τε αυτως, κ̀ ευδηλ⊕ ε͗ξ ονος ὁ φαυλον ποιημεν⊕ ζωζαι τως ανδρας." Arrian. Exped. Alex. Lib. 3. C. 24.--239.

Persian Empire, after having defended it with uncommon bravery, at the battles of the Granicus, of Issus, and of Gaugamele. Their companions had either all fallen under the Macedonian arm, or had been made prisoners. Leosthenes seems therefore to have no pretensions to be ranked by Pausanias' amongst the benefactors of his country for his embarkation, in opposition to Alexander's inclinations, of fifty thousand Greeks, who had served in the Persian armies, and his restoration of them to their country. Greece itself was hardly capable of maintaining an army of fifty thousand men, and the circumstance is not confirmed by any work of the ancients, that hath descended to us.

Alexander's conduct and the resolution, that he took in the pursuit of Bessus, prove the strength of his understanding, if any credit is due to Q. Curtius. The Macedonian army having discovered some symptoms of dissatisfaction at the Prince's future projects, which opened to them only fresh scenes of difficulty and danger, he ordered both his own baggage, and that of the whole army to be burnt.ʷ Plutarch

---

t "Ειναι δε απαντων Ελληνων κỳ Λεωσθενην τιθιναι κỳ Αρατον εεγετας· ο μεν γε το Ελληνων μισθοφορικον, κỳ εν Περσαις περι πεντε τε μυριαδας επι θαλασσαν καταβαντας ναυσιν, ες την Ελλαδα ανεσωσε κỳ ακοντ@ Αλεξανδρε." Pausanias 706.

w "Quum grave spoliis, adparatuque luxuriæ agmen vix moveretur; suas primum, deinde totius exercitus sarcinas, exceptis admodum necessariis, conferri jussit in medium. Planities spatiosa erat, in quam vehicula onusta perduxerant. Expectantibus cunctis, quid deinde effet imperaturus, jumenta jussit abduci; suisque primum sarcinis face subditâ, ceteras incendi præcepit. Flagrabant exurentibus dominis, quæ ut intacta ex urbibus hostium raperent, sæpe flammas restinxerant; nul-
lo

tarch [x] relates the same fact, but he gives it a later date, and refers it to the commencement of the Indian expedition; though Ptolemy and Aristobulus appear not to have taken notice of it, as may be inferred from Arrian's silence, who made great use of their memoirs.

The Macedonian Monarch extended his conquests beyond the Iaxartes, and defeated the Scythians who sent an embassy to him previous to the engagement. Q. Curtius hath transmitted to us the substance of the speech, in which the deputies addressed Alexander, but its authenticity hath been disputed. "If [y] the gods had given you a body suitable to the insatiable greediness of your mind,

---

In sanguinis pretium audente deflere, quum regias opes idem ignis exureret." Q. Curt. Lib. 6. C. 6. Tom. 1.--429.

[x] " Μελλων δε ὑπερβαλλειν εις την Ινδικην, ὡς εωρα πληθει λαφυρων την ςρατιαν ηδη βαρειαν κ̀ δυσκινητον ετιν, ἁμ ἡμερα συνισκευασμενων των ἁμαξων, πρωτας μεν ὑπεπρεσεν τας αυτε κ̀ των ἑταιρων· μετα δε ταυτας εκελευσε κ̀ ταις των Μακεδονων ἑιναι πυρ." Plut. De Vit. Alex. Plut. Opera. Tom. 1.--696, 697.

[y] "Si Dii habitum corporis tui aviditati animi parem esse voluissent; orbis te non caperet: alterâ manu Orientem; alterâ Occidentem contingeres. Et hoc adsequutus scire velles, ubi tanti numinis fulgor conderetur. Sic quoque concupiscis, quæ non capis. Ab Europâ petis Asiam; ex Asiâ transis in Europam: deinde si humanum genus omne superaveris; cum silvis, et nivibus, et fluminibus, serisque bestiis gesturus es bellum. Quid tu, ignoras arbores magnos diu crescere, unâ horâ extirpari? Stultus est, qui fructus earum spectat, altitudinem non metitur. Vide, ne dum ad cacumen pervenire contendis; cum ipsis ramis, quos comprehenderis, decidas. Leo quoque aliquando minimarum avium pabulum fuit: et ferrum rubigo consumit. Nihil tam firmum est, cui periculum non sit etiam ab invalido. Quid nobis tecum est? nunquam terram tuam adtigimus. Qui sis, unde venias, licet ne ignorare in vastis silvis viventibus? nec servire ulli possumus, nec imperare desideramus." (Q. Curt. Lib. 7. C. 8. Tom. 2.--543, 544.) "Scythæ ipsi omnium literarum rudes rhetorico calamistro inusti in medium prodeunt," is a part of the severe judgment that Le Clerc (Jud. Cort. 326.) hath passed upon this harangue.

mind, the world would not be able to contain you; you would stretch one arm out to the farthest extremities of the East, and the other to the remotest bounds of the West; and not content therewith, would be for examining where the glorious body of the Sun hid itself; but even as you are, your ambition attempts what you are not capable of. You pass out of Europe into Asia, and from Asia you return again to Europe; and when you have overcome all mankind, rather than be quiet, you'll quarrel with the woods and the mountains, the rivers and wild beasts. Can you be ignorant, that large trees are a long time a growing, tho' an hour be sufficient to cut them down? he is a fool that coveteth their fruit, without duly considering their height. Take heed that while you strive to climb up to the top, you do not fall headlong with those branches you have grasped. A lion has been sometime the prey of the smallest birds; and iron itself is consumed by rust. In fine, there is nothing so firm and strong, but is in danger of perishing by what is weaker. What have you to do with us? we never so much as set foot in your country. Shall not we who pass our lives in the woods, be allowed to be ignorant who you are, and whence you come? know, that as we are not greedy of empire, so neither can we submit to be slaves." [t] Q. Curtius continues the harangue, and in some sentences perhaps expresses himself with a delicacy rather too refined, and a philosophy in some measure inconsistent with the speakers' characters.

"Our

[t] Digby's Q. Curtius, Vol. 2.--42, 43.

"Our poverty will still be too nimble for your army, that is laden with the spoils of so many nations. Again, when you think us the farthest from you, you shall find us within your camp. We are equally swift either to fly or pursue.———Hold therefore your fortune as close as you can, for she is slippery, and will not be held against her will. Wholesome advice is better discovered by the consequences, than the present. Put a curb therefore to your prosperity, and you will govern it the better. We have a saying amongst us, that fortune is without feet, and has only hands and wings, and that when she reaches out her hands, she will not suffer her wings to be touched."[b] This allegory on the vicissitudes of fortune, and the uncertainty of human greatness is possibly too ingenious for a people drawn from pastoral life, which hath little, if any, connection with literature and learning. If Q. Curtius had shortened this oration the sentiments would certainly have had more force, and the images more expression, but he could not deviate from himself. The matter however, it must be allowed, is very analogous to the genius of the persons, who are supposed to have pronounced the harangue, and the Costume, to speak metaphorically,

---

[a] "Paupertas nostra velocior erit, quum exercitus tuus, prædam tot nationum vehit. Rursus quum procul abesse nos credes, videbis in tuis castris, eadem velocitate et sequimur et fugimus.———Proinde fortunam tuam pressis manibus tene. Lubrica est, nec invita teneri potest. Salubre consilium sequens quum præsens, tempus ostendit melius, impone felicitati tuæ frenos, facilius illam reges. Nostri sine pedibus dicant esse fortunam, quæ manus et pennas tantum habet; quum manus porrigit, pennas quoque comprehendere non sinit. Q. Curtius. Lib. 7. C. 8. Tom. 2.--247, 248.

[b] Digby's Q. Curtius. Vol. 2.--44.

metaphorically, is well preserved. Under these circumstances, there may be therefore some injustice in suspecting its reality.ᶜ

The language of a rude and uncivilized people is generally a figurative language, and their metaphors, which are both bold and nervous, are as often introduced in their familiar conversation, as by our modern poets in an Epic poem. Their speeches and harangues are naturally replete with images, with energy, and passion, and the same allusions are resorted to by the Scythian and the Savage.ᵈ The imagination of a people, neither enslaved by artificial wants, nor corrupted by prejudices, must be strongly affected by the great objects of nature, and every thing, that interests their preservation and their liberty, must be one of the most powerful incentives that can actuate them.

Every sentiment in this Scythian speech is borrowed from the visible

---

ᶜ Mascardi. Tract. della Art. Hist. C. 2. Ep. 1.—Rooke's Translation of Arrian. Vol. 1. --220.—Voltaire Essai sur le Mœurs et l'Esprit des Nations. Tom. 14.--52. Ed. 8ᵛᵒ Geneve, 1775.

ᵈ "Figurative language," a great Writer hath observed, "owes its rise chiefly to two causes; to the want of proper names for objects, and to the influence of imagination and passion over the form of expression. Both these causes concur in the infancy of Society. Figures are commonly considered as artificial modes of speech, devised by orators and poets, after the world had advanced to a refined state. The contrary of this is the truth. Men never have used so many figures of style, as in those rude ages, when, besides the power of a warm imagination to suggest lively images, the want of proper and precise terms for the ideas they would express, obliged them to have recourse to circumlocution, metaphor, comparison, and all those substituted forms of expression, which give a poetical air to language. An American chief, at this day, harangues at the head of his tribe, in a more bold metaphorical style, than a modern European would adventure to use in an Epic poem." Blair's Dissert. Ossian. Vol. 2.--285, 286. 8ᵛᵒ 1785.

viſible world, and every compariſon drawn from fenſible and immediate objects, which are hourly preſented to the ſavage eye. One while, it is the ſetting ſun, the fall of an aged oak, the ruſt that devoureth the iron; at another it is a war declared againſt the woods and waters, and in a word the fear of groaning under a foreign yoke, and ſeeing an enemy penetrate into their foreſts, to trouble their repoſe and civilize them. Theſe are their firſt and principal apprehenſions, and they give both an impulſe to their eloquence, and rouſe every faculty of the ſoul, for the purpoſe of repelling to a diſtance the ſtorm, which menaces at once their liberty and manners.

The Latin hiſtorian was, notwithſtanding, aware that his fidelity was open to ſome difquiſition, and that his Scythian oration had no great pretenſions either to belief or popular applauſe. "It is ſaid," he tells us, "they addreſſed themſelves to the King in the following terms; which though perhaps different from our manners, who live in a politer age, and have our parts better improved, yet ſuch as it is, we ſhall faithfully relate, hoping that if their ſpeech be deſpiſed, our integrity will not be ſuſpected."*

Giving Q. Curtius credit for this proteſtation there are ſtill ſome apparent variations in the form of the harangue, and the colouring,

---

* "Abhorrent forſitan moribus noſtris et tempora et ingenia cultiora ſortitis; ſed ut poſſit oratio eorum ſperni, tamen fides noſtra non debet, quæ utcunque tradita ſunt, incorrupta perferemus." Q. Curt. Lib. 7. C. 8. Tom. 2.--542.

† Digby's Q. Curtius. Vol. 2.--42.

ing, that he hath given it, to render it more agreeable to the taste of his own times, as well as to shew a little of his own ingenuity, is easily discernible. The last reproach he seems to have particularly foreseen, as he assures us, the Scythians[g] were persons of superior talents, and more improved understandings, than the rest of the Barbarians; but his ideas on the difference of the taste of his own times and that of the Scythians weaken the force of the observation. The Latin historian does not appear also to have sufficiently considered the nature of the eloquence of a savage people, which equally originates from a poverty of language, and a simplicity of manners.[h] As nations become civilized, their ideas change, and the imagination is no longer affected, as in the ruder state of society, by the same objects. Their manner of viewing things, and their method of expression necessarily vary, and their language cannot at the same time bear the impression of the separate and distinct characters of a savage and a polished people. It is not in the power of Q. Curtius to reconcile the contradiction, but it is time to return to Alexander and his expeditions.

If the companions of the Macedonian Hero, who were best able to describe his exploits from having been personally concerned in them, do not always agree in their accounts of the same facts, some

---

[g] "Scythis autem non ut cæteris barbaris rudis et inconditus sensus est." Q. Curtius. Lib. 7. C. 8. Tom. 2,--542.

[h] The Abbé Arnaud hath made some sensible observations on this subject. Discours sur les Langues, Var. Lit. Tom. 1.

some indulgence is certainly due to writers, who have afterwards taken up the same subject, and described it differently. Arrian hath faithfully preserved the contradictory testimony of Ptolemy and Aristobulus¹ on the capture of Cyropolis. Ptolemy pretends that the city surrendered, and that its inhabitants were made prisoners: Aristobulus assures us that it was taken by assault, and that the garrison and citizens were indiscriminately put to the sword. It is extraordinary that there should have existed a city with the name of Cyropolis in these remote regions; but notwithstanding the Greeks sometimes translated into their own language the names of cities, they chose in preference to give them new ones founded on some tradition, which they adopted without discernment, and Cyropolis may have been amongst the number.

Q. Curtius hath committed an error, and been led into a mistake by the name of Hecatompylos, which Seleucus Nicanor bestowed on a city in Parthia.ᵏ Mentioning this city in the progress of Alexander's conquests, he infers that it was founded by the Greeks,¹ though they were utter strangers to Parthia, before it was reduced under this Prince's obedience.

These

---

¹ "Τὴν δὲ ἑβδόμην, πόλιν ἐξ ἐφόδου ἔλαβε. Πτολεμαῖος μὲν λέγει ὅτι αὐτὸς σφᾶς ἐνδόντας· Ἀριστόβουλος δὲ, ὅτι βίᾳ κỳ ταύτην ἐξεῖλε, κỳ ὅτι πάντας τοὺς καταληφθέντας ἐν αὐτῇ ἀπέκτεινε· Πτολεμαῖος δὲ κατανέμαι λέγει αὐτὸν τοὺς Ἀνθρώπους τῇ στρατιᾷ κỳ δεδέμενους κελεύσας φυλάττεσθαι." Arrian. Exped. Alex. Lib. 4. C. 3.--263.

ᵏ Appian. De Bello Syriac. Tom. 1.--201. Amst. 8ᵛᵒ 1670.

¹ "Urbs erat eâ tempestate clara Hecatompylos, condita a Græcis: ubi stativa rex habuit." Q. Curtius. Lib. 6. C. 2. Tom. 1.--398, 399.

Thefe Fables and Anachronifms are the refult of the changes in the names of places, and cities, and they occafion a multitude of miftakes and difficulties.

After many different expeditions, the Macedonian army went into winter-quarters at Mautaca; but early in the fpring it took again the field, and marched to attack the Rock, to which Oxyartes had retreated with the Sogdians. The Macedonian bravery and difcipline were again confpicuous, and the garrifon overawed and aftonifhed at the wonderful efforts of their enemy, laid down their arms.

The capture of Aornus which had fuccefsfully refifted Hercules,[m] and the fubmiffion of Nyfa, fuppofed to have been founded by Bacchus, were two events that naturally furnifhed Alexander's followers with the fubject of a parallel between the Grecian Hero and the two Pagan Deities. But it may be queftioned if Bacchus and Hercules were ever known in India or the Eaft. The adoration of thefe Divinities was equally repugnant to the religious principles and manners of the inhabitants, and Megafthenes, a profeffed partifan of the fuppofition, fpeaks of it only as traditionary,[n] and of Greek extraction. The arrival of Hercules in India,

---

[m] "Εφασαν τον Ἡρακλεα, τρις μεν προσβαλειν τη πιτρα ταύτη, τρις δ'αποκρουσθηναι." Strabo. Lib. 15.--1008.

[n] "Και προ Αλεξανδρου, Διονυσε περι πολλῶ λογῶ κατεχει, ὡς ϰ τουτου ϛρατευσαντῶ ις Ινδυς, ϰ κατας ρεψαμενο Ινδυς· Ἡρακλιυς δε περι, ο πολλῶ·" Arrian. Hift. Ind. C. 5.--559.

India, is confidered even by this writer as very problematical,° but the opinion hath neverthelefs been adopted by writers fince the reign of Alexander, and tranfmitted to pofterity on the apparent decifive evidence of public monuments.ᵖ Strabo gives us the fentiments of feveral writers who fuppofed the Oxydrachians to have been defcended from Bacchus, and the Sibians to have fprung from the companions�q of Hercules ; but he refutes very rationally thefe abfurd traditions, and introduces the opinions of the writers, that he mentions, with the following fentence. "Megafthenes and a few other authors believe the ftories which have been told of Hercules and Bacchus, but Eratofthenes and the greater number confider them as fables, and as little deferving of any credit, as many other relations of the Greeks."ʳ

Alexander traverfed the Paropamifus, entered into an alliance with Taxilus and Abifares, and afterwards advanced to give battle to Porus, who had the courage to oppofe the victorious army of the

---

° "Ἡρακλεης δε ὁ πολλα ὑπομνηματα·" Arrian. Hift. Ind. C. 5.--559.

ᵖ The Farnefian palace at Rome, contains an infcription, in which the arrival of Hercules on the banks of the Indus, and the foundation of a city with his name amongft the Sibians are mentioned. Corfini hath very amply commented upon it. Herculis Exped. Gefta et Labores. 37.

ᑫ The weak pretenfions to this confanguinity may be feen in Strabo, Lib. 15.--1008. and Arrian, Hift. Ind. C. 5.

ʳ "Και τα Ἡρακλεως δι, κỳ Διονυσυ, Μεγασθενης μεν μετ'ολιγων τισα ἡγειται· των δ'αλλων οἱ πλειες, ὡν ισι κỳ Ερατοσθενης, απιςα κỳ μυθωδη, καθαπερ κỳ τα παρα τοις Ἑλληςιν." (Strabo. Lib. 15.--1007.) The Baron de St. Croix fays "Il finit en ces termes." To have expreffed himfelf correctly he fhould have faid "Il commence en ces termes." The error is a ftrange one.

the Macedonian Monarch, and endeavoured to check the rapidity of his conquests. The Indian prince was advantageously posted on the banks of the Hydaspes,' in a situation that he had judiciously chosen to secure the passage of the river. A variety of manœuvres were made by the Macedonian army, which had been divided into different bodies, to deceive the enemy, and conceal the real place, in which the Hydaspes was intended to be crossed. Their first attempt was unsuccessful, and miscarried. During a very stormy night attended with very heavy rain, another effort was made, and the Macedonian Monarch eluded the vigilance of his antagonist and aided by the elements effected the passage of the river with safety. The Hydaspes, which was intersected by islands, and its steep and broken banks covered with wood, afforded him some local advantages, which he did not suffer to escape him. Arrian hath described the interesting movements[t] of both armies with great clearness and accuracy, but it is unnecessary to enter into them at length. Aristobulus[w] relates that the son of Porus, who at first appeared disposed to dispute the passage, afterwards retreated with sixty chariots, that he had with him; but other writers[x] assure us on the contrary, that the young prince

attacked

' The modern Behut or Chælum.

[t] Arrian. Exped. Alex. Lib. 5. C. 12, 13, 14.--363——368.

[w] " Αριστοβολ۞ δε τον Πορυ παιδα λεγει σφαζαι αφικομενον ξυν αρμασιν ως εξηκοντα, πρ.. το ἱερ᾽ε. την τοῦ της μοιρας περασαι Αλεξανδρον·" Arrian. Exped. Alex. Lib. 5. C. 14.--367.

[x] " Οι δε κ μαχην λεγυσιν εν τε εκβασει γενεσθαι των Ινδων των ξυν τω παιδι τω Πωρυ αφιγμένων. προς Αλεξανδρον·———— Και γαρ κ αφικισθαι ξυν μειζονι δυναμει τον Πωρυ παιδα, κ α. τον τε Αλεξ

attacked the Macedonian army with a superiority of forces, and wounded with his own hand both Alexander's horse Bucephalus, and Alexander. Arrian rejects these accounts, and bestows his principal attention upon Ptolemy who signalized himself very particularly in this memorable engagement. From this general's report,[y] the son of Porus was detached with a hundred and twenty chariots and two thousand horse, but he arrived too late to be of the intended service, as Alexander had already passed the last channel of the river. The Grecian Hero instantly attacked the Indian detachment, and the son of Porus was left dead upon the field, and a part of his troops and chariots taken. A general action soon followed, and Cænus with a detachment of the Macedonian troops appearing in the rear of the Indian army, it was under the necessity of changing its order of battle. In this distressing moment, Alexander made a successful attack with his cavalry on the division opposed to him, and it was pushed back upon the elephants, who became very unruly and increased the confusion. The whole of the Macedonian cavalry being afterwards

---

ανδρων τρωθηναι παρ'αυτα, κ᾽ τον ιππον αυτα αποθανειν τον Βυκιφαλαν, φιλτατον Αλεξανδρω οντα τον ιππον, κ᾽ τυτον τρωθεντα υπο τυ παιδος τυ Πωρυ." (Arrian. Exped. Alex. Lib. 5. C. 14.--367.) The Baron de St. Croix's expression is "Que Justin a pris pour guides," but I do not find it authorized by the text of Justin. "Nec Alexander pugnæ moram fecit: sed prima congressione vulnerato equo, cum præceps in terram decidisset, concursu Satellitum servatus. Porus multis vulneribus n̄ rutus capitur," (Justin. Lib. 12. C. 37.--322, 323.) is the brief description of this decisive action.

[y] "Πτολεμαιος ὁ Λαγυ, οτω κ᾽ ξυμφερομαι, αλλως λεγει· εκπεμφθηναι μεν γαρ κ᾽ τον παιδα υπο τυ Πωρυ, αλλ᾽ υκ εξηκοντα μονα ἁρματα αγοντα———αλλα δισχιλιυς γαρ λεγει ιππεας αγοντα αφικεσθαι τον Πωρυ παιδα, ἁρματα δε ἑκατον κ᾽ εικοσι· φθασαι δε περασαντα Αλεξανδρον κ᾽ τον εκ της νησυ τον τελευταιον πορον." Arrian. Exped. Alex. Lib. 5. C. 14.--367, 368.

wards thrown into a body, and hemming in the enemy, the phalanx was directed to form very closely and attack them, by which great numbers of them were slain. Craterus also, who had been left on the opposite banks of the Hydaspes to deceive Porus and divide his attention, crossed the river during the engagement, and completed the rout. The vanquished Monarch lost two of his sons in the action, near twenty thousand of his infantry, three thousand of his cavalry, and all his chariots and elephants. Arrian from whom these circumstances [z] are borrowed, reduces the Macedonian loss to two hundred and thirty of the cavalry, and eighty of the infantry, but Diodorus Siculus differs with him. The latter writer reckons the Indians to have left twelve thousand men on the field of battle, and to have had nine thousand made prisoners. The victory, however, according to his statement, cost Alexander two hundred and eighty of his cavalry and above seven hundred of his infantry, [a] which certainly appears more probable than

---

[z] On a review of these circumstances, which the Baron de St Croix had extracted from Arrian, I felt the obligation of new moulding the whole. They now stand nearly as Arrian relates them, but the first confusion was not the consequence of "Le desordre que les elephants causoient dans le rangs." "Οἱ περι Κοινον, ὡς παρηγγελτο, κατοπιν αυτοις επεφαινοντο· Ταυτα ξυνιδοντες οἱ Ινδοι, αμφιςομον ηναγκασθησαν ποιησαι την ταξην της ἱππυ——τυτο τε ει ευθις εταραξε τας ταξεις τε κ᾽ τας γνωμας των Ινδων." "Alexandre rassembla sa cavalerie" is directly contradicted by the "Και εν τυτω πασα ἡ ἱππ᾽ Αλεξανδρῳ ες μιαν ιλην ηδη ξυνηγμενη, ουκ εκ παραγγελματ᾽, αλλα εν τω αγωνι αυτω ες τηνδε την ταξιν κατεσαζα·" and the "Ce prince perdit dans cette bataille——deux mille hommes de pied," is an unpardonable translation of the "Απιθανον δε των Ινδων πεζοι μεν ολιγον αποδεοντες των δυσμυριων·" Arrian. Exped. Alex, Lib. 5. C. 17, 18.--372——375.

[a] "Επεσον δ᾽εν τη μαχη των Ινδων πλειες των μυριων κ᾽ δισχιλιων, εν οἱς ὑπηρχον κ᾽ δυο ἱιοι τυ Πωρυ, κ᾽ οἱ ςρατηγοι, κ᾽ οἱ επιφανεςατοι των ἡγεμονων· ζωντες δε ανδρες ἱαλωςαν ὑπερ εννακισχιλιυς·———Τω δε Μακεδονων επεςον μεν ἱππεις διακοσιοι κ᾽ ογδοηκοντα, πεζοι δε πλειες των ἑπτακοζιων·" Diod. Sicul. Lib. 17. Tom. 2,--229.

than Arrian's account, though his defcription of the engagement merits great encomiums. That of Diodorus Siculus is marked with ftrong features of uncommon negligence, and even the paffage of the Hydafpes, which was of fo much confequence, is totally omitted.

The confufion of Q. Curtius, with his contradictions and abfurdities, might afford materials for a long digreffion, but a few examples will be fufficient. " When you fee me, with Ptolemy, Perdiccas and Hephæftion, charge the enemy's left wing, and fhall obferve us to be in the heat of action, put the right wing in motion and charge the enemy,[b] &c. &c."—To attack the left wing of the enemy it was neceffary for Alexander to have been at the head of his right wing, and Cœnus then could not have poffibly commanded it. Yet a few lines afterwards, Q. Curtius tells us, that the Macedonian Prince having commenced the action agreeable to this difpofition, Cœnus attacked with impetuofity the enemy's left wing.[c]

The extraordinary ftature of King Porus, he tells us alfo, was apparently

---

[b] "Quum ego, inquit, Ptolemæo Perdiccâque et Hephæftione comitatus in lævum hoftium cornu impetum fecero, viderifque me in medio ardore certaminis; ipfe dextrum move et turbatis figna infer." (Q. Curtius. Lib. 8. C. 14. Tom. 2.--661, 662.) The commentators have laboured to rectify this paffage, but without effect.

[c] "Jamque; ut deftinatum erat, invaferat ordines hoftium; quum Cœnus ingenti vi in lævum cornu invehitur." Q. Curtius. Lib. 8. C. 14. Tom. 2.--663.

apparently augmented by the fize of his Elephant,[d] which is an offence againſt the common rules of Perſpective. Porus received nine wounds in the action, from which he loſt a vaſt quantity of blood, and was ſo much weakened, that he had not ſtrength to throw a dart, but it fell uſeleſs from his hands.[e] We are afterwards informed, that a brother of Taxiles was ſent by Alexander to prevail on the Indian Monarch to lay down his arms. At the voice of this temporizing Prince, in a paroxyſm of rage, he ſeized the only remaining arrow in his quiver, and diſcharged it with ſuch violence, that it ſtretched the indiſcreet negotiator on the ground.[f] It might have been reaſonably imagined that this exertion would have entirely exhauſted him, but notwithſtanding his extreme debility, he reſumes his flight with greater expedition, and was ſtopped only by the wounds of his elephant.[g]

Arrian's account is not filled with ſuch glaring contradictions, nor manifeſt abſurdities. Porus receives a wound in his right shoulder,

[d] "Magnitudine Pori adjicere videbatur belua, quâ vehebatur, tantum inter ceteras eminens, quanto aliis ipſe præſtabat." Q. Curtius. Lib. 8. C. 14. Tom. 2.--660, 661.

[e] "Novem jam vulnera hinc tergo, illinc pectore exceperat, multoque ſanguine profuſo languidis manibus magis elapſa, quum excuſſa tela mittebat." Q. Curtius. Lib. 8. C. 14. Tom. 2. --665.

[f] "At ille quamquam exhauſtæ erant vires, deficiebatque ſanguis; tamen ad notam vocem excitatus: agnoſco, inquit, Taxilis fratrem imperii regnique ſui proditoris: et telum, quod unum forte non effluxerat, contorſit in eum, quod per medium pectus penetravit ad tergum." Q. Curtius. Lib. 8. C. 14. Tom. 2,--665.

[g] "Hoc ultimo virtutis opere edito fugere acrius cæpit, ſed elephantus quoque, qui multa exceperat tela, deficiebat, itaque fiſtit fugam." Q. Curtius. Lib. 8. C. 14. Tom. 2,--665.

shoulder, the only vulnerable part of his body, which was every where else covered by his excellent armour, and unable to continue the engagement in person, he found it necessary to quit the field.——Taxiles is sent afterwards to him, and at the sight of his ancient enemy, Porus attacks him with a dart, from which he escapes only by flight. A second negotiation is then opened under the management of Meroes, and Porus is prevailed upon to accept the terms, which Meroes was authorized by the Macedonian Monarch to offer him.[h]

This celebrated action bears date, according to Arrian,[i] in the month Munychion, during the magistracy of Hegemon, who was the Athenian Archon, in the second year of the 118th Olympiad, 327 years before Christ. Diodorus Siculus[k] refers it to the magistracy of Chremes, the successor of Hegemon, but Arrian's computation is confirmed by the authority of Dionysius of Halicarnassus,[l] which is both preferable to that of Diodorus Siculus, and is also demonstrated to have been correct by Corsini in his Attic annals.[m]

Every

---

[h] Arrian. Lib. 5. C. 18.--377.

[i] "Τετο το τιλθ. τη μαχη τη προς τον Πωρον———επ'αρχοντθ. Αθηναιοις 'Ηγεμονθ., μηνθ. Μυνυχιωνθ." Arrian. Exped. Alex. Lib. 5. C. 19.--379.

[k] "Επ'αρχοντθ. δ'Αθηνησι Χρεμητθ.———Αλιξανδρθ. εν τη Ταξιλυ χωρα προςαναλαβων την δυναμιν, εςρατευζεν επι Πωρον." Diod. Sicul. Lib. 17. Tom. 2.--228.

[l] Dionysius of Halicarnassus adds nothing to Arrian's authority, for he barely mentions Hegemon amongst the other Athenian Archons. De Dinar. Judicium. Tom. 5.--649.

[m] Corsini. Att. Annal. Tom. 4.--47, 48.

Every thing ſtooped to Alexander after this victory, and he paſſed the Hyphaſis full of ardour and of expectation, with the reſolution of penetrating to the Ganges and of bounding his conqueſts only with the Univerſe. But the murmurs of his army ſtopped him in the midſt of his mighty projects, and ſhortened his vaſt career. Plutarch hath acknowledged to us the real cauſes of the diſſatisfaction of the Macedonian ſoldiers, [a] on whoſe ſpirits victory had only a momentary influence. The valour of Porus and the obſtinate reſiſtance of his troops were what they had neither foreſeen, nor been prepared for, and new difficulties and dangers threatened them at every ſtep that they advanced. On the banks of the Ganges they were aware of the formidable

---

[a] Both Philoſtratus (De Vit. Apoll. Lib. 2. C. 33.--86.) and Strabo (Lib. 15.--1025.) have ſuppoſed that ſome oracular denunciations ſtopped the Macedonian Monarch on the banks of the Hyphaſis, but mere political reaſons appear to have regulated his movements. "Τȣς μεν τοι Μακεδονας ὁ προς Πωρον αγων αμβλυτερȣς εποιησιν, ϗ το προσω της Ινδικης ετι προσελθειν επισχειν· μολις γαρ εκεινον ωσαμενοι, δισμυριοις πεζοις, ϗ δισχιλιοις ἱππευσι παραταξαμενον, αντεςησαν ισχυρως Αλεξανδρω βιαζομενω ϗ τον Γαγγην περαζαι ποταμον, ευρ@· μεν αυτε, δυο ϗ τριαχηντα ςαδιων ειναι πυνθανομενοι, ϗ βαθ@· εργιας ἱκαλον· αντιπερας δε τας οχθας αποκεκρυφθαι, πληθεςιν ὁπλων ϗ ἱππων ϗ ελεφαντων· ελεγοντο γαρ οκτω μεν μυριαδας ἱπποτων, εικοζι δε πεζων, ἁρμαλα δε οκλακισχιλια, ϗ μαχιμȣς ελεφαντας εξακισχιλιȣς εχοντες ὁι Γανδαριδων ϗ Πρεζιων βαζιλεις ἐπεμενειν· ϗ κομπ@· ȣκ ην περι ταυτα." (De Vit. Alex. Plut. Opera. Tom. 1.--699.) Diodorus Siculus differs as to the power of the Gandarides, but imputes Alexander's retreat to the ſame prudential motives. "Καταντησας γαρ επι τον Γαγγην πολαμον μετα πασης της δυναμεως, ϗ τȣς αλλȣς Ινδȣς καταπολεμησας, ὡς επυθετο τȣς Γανδαριδας εχειν τετραχισχιλιȣς ελεφαντας πολεμικως κεκοσμημενȣς, απεγνω την επ' αυτȣς ςρατειαν." (Lib. 2. Tom. 1.--150.) And he declares afterwards that "Των Μακεδονων ȣδαμως συγκαταθεμενων, απεςη της επιβολης." (Lib. 17. Tom. 2.--233.) Arrian alſo with great candour ſtates the mutiny. "Ὁι δε Μακεδονες εξεκαμνον ηδη ταις γνωμαις, πονȣς τε εκ πονων ϗ κινδυνȣς εκ κινδυνων επανιερȣμενον ὁρωντες τον βαζιλεα· ξυλλογοι τε εγιγνονlο κατα το ςρατοπεδον, των μεν τα σφετερα οδυρομενων, ὁσοι επιεικεςαλοι· των δε ȣκ ακολȣθησειν, ηδ' ην αγη Αλεξανδρ@·, επισχυριζομενων." Exped. Alex. Lib. 5. C. 25.--393.

formidable powers, the Gangarides and Prafians, and the profpect before their eyes was filled with numerous and repeated engagements, in which there was every probability that the Grecian bravery muſt at laſt fink, overpowered by continual exertions againſt ſuch hoſts of enemies.

The banks of the Hyphaſis were then the barrier, which Alexander could not paſs. The followers of the Macedonian Monarch have indeed extended his military operations, and Craterus informed his mother Ariſtopatra, by letter,[o] that the Conqueror of the Eaſt had made his way to the Ganges. This letter was publiſhed, and, in all likelihood, gave ſome foundation for the error,[p] but

---

[o] "Ἐκδεδολαι δε τις κ̣ Κραίερω προς την μητερα Αριστοπαίραν επιϛολη, πολλα τε αλλα παραδοξα φραξεσα, κ̣ ἐκ ὁμολογεῖσθαι εδενι· κ̣ δη κ̣ το μιχρι το Γαγε προιελθειν τον Αλεξανδρον." Strabo. Lib. 15.--1027.

[p] "Και Αλεξανδρος ὁρμηθεις απο των μερων τέτων αχρι τε Γαγγες διηλθε." Arrian. Perip. Maris Eryth. 169. 8vo Amſt. 1683.

"————Macetum fines, latebraſque ſuorum
Deſeruit, victaſque patri deſpexit Athenas.
Perque Aſiæ populos ſatis urgentibus actus,
Humanâ cum ſtrage ruit, gladiumque per omnes
Exegit gentes: ignotos miſcuit amnes,
Perſarum Euphraten, Indorum ſanguine Gangen."
Lucan. Phars. Lib. 10.--28————33.

See alſo Syncellus. 210.—Zonares. Lib. 4.--144. Philoſtratus pointedly denies the pretended fact : "Την δε χωραν ταυτην εδε επηλθεν ὁ Αλεξανδρος." (De Vit. Apoll. Lib. 2. C. 33.-- 86. Folio. Lips. 1709.) and though Diodorus Siculus ſtates in the 2nd Book (Tom. 1.--150.) that Alexander reached the Ganges, in the 17th Book, he ſtops at the Hyphanis, (or Hyphaſis, See Salmaſii. Plin. Exercit. 55.) "Επι τον Ὑπασιν ποταμον προηιν." (Diod. Sicul. Lib. 17. Tom. 2.--332.) Whether the Greek hiſtorian afterwards diſcovered his miſtake, or had forgotten the firſt part of his Work, I leave to be determined.

but the rest of the occurrences, that it mentioned, were equally fictitious.——Justin relates that Alexander reduced the Acesies, the Prasides and Gangarides, and that he carried his victorious arms into the country of the Cuphites. Many other people are also taken notice of, whose names are as little known as that of the Cuphites; but this may be perhaps attributed to the corruption of the text. Neither Paulus Orosius nor any of the manuscripts have hitherto afforded any satisfactory information respecting the names of various towns and nations, which are so generally and so much disfigured in Justin. Little suspicion is to be apprehended of any alteration in Plutarch's expressions, and if they carry the construction, that the kingdom of Porus was the last of Alexander's conquests, the obscurity may be naturally deduced from the confusion of this writer, who hath not been sufficiently attentive to the relation of events, and hath frequently inverted the order of the facts, that he mentions.[q]

The Itinerary of Bæton and of Diognetus,[r] and even the letters of Alexander, as well as all the historians of his life and actions, have

[q] Plutarch. De Vit. Alex. Plutarchi Opera. Tom. 1.--699.

[r] "Diognetus et Bæton itinerum ejus mensores scripsere————ad Hypasin,——qui fuit Alexandri itinerum terminus, exsuperato tamen amne, arisque in adversâ ripâ dicatis. Epistolæ quoque regis ipsius consentiunt his. (Plin. Hist. Nat. Lib. 6. Tom. 1.--683, 684.) Philostratus hath preserved the votive inscriptions. " ΠΑΤΡΙ ΑΜΜΩΝΙ, ΚΑΙ ʽΗΡΑΚΛΕΙ ΑΔΕΛΦΩΙ ΚΑΙ ΑΘΗΝΑΙ ΠΡΟΝΟΙΑΙ, ΚΑΙ ΔΙΙ ΟΛΥΜΠΙΩΙ, ΚΑΙ ΣΑΜΟΘΡΑΞΙ ΚΑΒΕΙΡΟΙΣ, ΚΑΙ ΙΝΔΩΙ ʽΗΛΙΩΙ, ΚΑΙ ΑΔΕΛΦΩΙ ΑΠΟΛΛΩΝΙ." (De Vit. Appol. Lib. 2. C. 43.--94.) A brazen column was said also to have been raised, on which " ΑΛΕΞΑΝΔΡΟΣ ΕΝΤΑΥΘΑ ΕΣΤΗ," was engraven.

have described the Altars erected by his order on the Eastern shore of the Hyphasis,[i] which were twelve in number and rivalled the loftiest towers in height and elevation. These immense masses of stone were intended to perpetuate to future ages the memory of his conquests, and were considered at the same time as a grateful and acceptable offering to the Gods. Yet monuments, erected by hands stained with the blood of every Asiatic nation, were certainly very questionable methods of imploring the favourable regard of Heaven, and from the insatiable vanity of the Conqueror of the East more probably the real though concealed motives of the structures are to be deduced.—The various towns and cities which Alexander founded in the different countries, that he passed through, are to be considered in the same point of view, and as trophies[t] of his victories. Plutarch[w] reckons them to have exceeded seventy,

---

[i] The modern Settledge or Suttaluz.

[t] Pausanias advances "Ου γαρ τι Μακιδοσιν ιςαναι τροπαια ην νινομισμενον·" and he produces Alexander as an instance: "Μαρτυρει δε τω λογω κỳ Αλεξανδρ⊖· εκ ανεσκζας ετι επι Δαρειω τροπαια, ἐδε επι ταις Ινδικαις νικαις." (Lib. 9. C. 40.--794, 795.) But Q. Curtius (Lib. 3. C 12. Tom. 1.--143.) mentions three altars erected by the Macedonian Monarch after the battle of Issus, of which there were some remains in Cicero's time; (Epist. Famil. Lib. 15. Tom. 7.--526.) and Herodian more decisively speaks of a city built by the Macedonian Monarch in memory of the battle of Issus: " Μενει δε ετι νυν τροπαιον, κỳ δειγμα της νικης εκεινης πολις επι τυ λοφυ· &c." (Lib. 3.--63. Ed. Steph. 4to 1584.) Pocock suspects a ruin that he saw to have been the foundation of the altars erected near Pinarus, and the remains of a thick wall on the southern hills to have been part of this city of Nicopolis, built in honour of Alexander's victory over Darius. Pocock's Travels. Vol. 2. --176, 177.

[w] "Αλεξανδρ⊖· δε υπερ εβδομηκοντα πολεις βαρβαροις εθνεσιν ετισας, κỳ κατασπειρας την Ασιαν Ελληνικοις τελεσι της ανημερυ κỳ θηριωδυς εκρατησε διαιτης·" (Plut. De Fort vel Virt. Alex. Plutarchi Opera. Tom. 2.--328.

ty, and he assures us that under Alexander's reign the wilds of Asia were peopled by Grecian colonies, who disseminated instruction amongst the natives, and reclaimed them from their rude and savage state of life. Diodorus Siculus even pretends that the Conqueror built, near Paropamisus, several towns which were only a single day's journey from each [x] other.

Bucephalia [y] owed its name to the Conqueror's celebrated horse Bucephalus, who died in its environs, and Sotion, according to Plutarch, relates his having heard from Potamon the Lesbian, that the Macedonian Monarch directed a town also to be built in honour of his favourite dog Perites. [z] Stephanus Byzantinus [a] speaks of eighteen different cities under the name of Alexandria, one of which was situated in the island of Cyprus, and the author of the chronicle [b] of Alexandria places another in the Pentapolis of Africa, which the Conqueror of the East had never visited.

This is apparently decisive evidence of the existence of these cities, but their foundation is not to be attributed to the Macedonian

---

[x] "Ὁ δὲ Ἀλέξανδρος κỳ ἄλλας πόλεις ἔκτισεν, ἡμέρας ὁδὸν ἀπεχούσας τῆς Ἀλεξανδρείας." Diod. Sicul. Lib. 17. Tom. 2.--224.

[y] Supposed to be the modern Lahore.

[z] "Καὶ πόλιν οἰκίσας ἐπ' αὐτῷ πέρα τοῦ Ὑδάσπην Βουκεφαλίαν προσηγόρευσεν· λέγει. δὲ κỳ κατὰ Περίταν ὄνομα τεθραμμένον ὑπ' αὐτῷ, κỳ στεργόμενον ἀποβαλὼν κτίσαι πόλιν ἐπώνυμον· τοῦτο δὲ Σωτίων φησὶν Ποταμωνξ ἀκοῦσαι τοῦ Λεσβίου." Plut. De Vit. Alex. Plutarchi Opera. Tom. 1.--699.

[a] Stephan. Byzantinus. Ἀλεξάνδρεια·

[b] Chronic. Alex. Ed. Raderi. 398.

nian Monarch without deliberate examination. Alexander's rapid march, or more correctly speaking, his military journey, would barely have allowed him time to think of such numerous establishments, and his army could not possibly have supplied him with a sufficiency of inhabitants for these infant colonies. The rooted attachment in the Grecian bosom for its native soil was likewise well known to have kept a long and lasting hold upon it, and the chosen band which had ranged itself under the banners of the Younger Cyrus preferred a return to their own country at the risk of a thousand perils, to all the advantages, that were offered them by a great and grateful Monarch. Xenophon, their leader, made every effort, but in vain, to induce them to settle in Asia, where an easy conquest would have fixed them in a situation, that must soon have rendered the establishment the most flourishing and richest on the Euxine sea. The soldiers of such a nation would not willingly have renounced the happiness of revisiting their country, where the united voices of their families recalled them, and have given up the consolation of expiring amidst the embraces of their relations and their friends, which formed in their opinions the last, though not least precious, of earthly blessings.ᶜ With these

---

ᶜ Death, in a strange country, and at a distance from every endearing connection, was reckoned by the ancients to be peculiarly distressing, and the thoughts of it sharpened the pangs of separation and of exile. The mournful office of closing the eyes of their expiring parents, or children, was a duty of religious importance, and wherever it could not be performed, it was feelingly lamented. Penelope offers up a prayer for it.

"Di precor hoc jubeant, ut euntibus ordine Fatis,
Ille meos oculos comprimat, ille tuos."

Ovid. Heroïd. Epist. 1,--101, Tom. 1,--13. 4ᵗᵒ Amst. 1727.

these sentiments a voluntary exile in the middle of Asia could not have been expected from them, which at the same time exposed them to inveterate enemies, who were jealous of their prosperity, and considered them both as usurpers of their territories, and their future Tyrants. The improvement of the colony in this precarious situation could have been little attended to, and in a state of continual apprehensions or hostilities, where the whole force was requisite for its defence, few hands could have been spared for the cultivation of the ground or the labours of Agriculture.

Commerce sometimes infuses a portion of life and vigour into new establishments, but it depends on the easy and secure conveyance of merchandise, and a proper medium of barter and exchange. Mutual wants will likewise often form an intercourse between distant nations, but if the inhabitants of the cities, ima-

Z 2 gined

And afterwards makes use of the argument to hasten the return of Ulysses to Ithaca.
"Respice Laerten: ut jam sua lumina condas."
Ovid. Heroïd. Epist. 1.--113.
Polyxena also offers the same soothing idea to Hecuba in an agony of grief.
"——Και θανεσης ομμα συγκλεισει το σον."
Euripidis Hecuba. 430. Tom. 1.--21. 4*to* Lips. 1778.
In their last moments therefore the "Συντροφον ομμα" (Sophoclis Philoctetes. 173. Tom. 2. --367. 4*to* Paris. 1781.) of their family and friends, an expression that sets translation at defiance, afforded them the most cheering satisfaction. Gray hath alluded to the wish for it in the Church-yard Elegy: Pope hath bewailed the want of it.
"No friend's complaint, no kind domestic tear,
Pleas'd thy pale ghost, or grac'd thy mournful bier.
By foreign hands thy dying eyes were clos'd,
By foreign hands thy decent limbs compos'd."
Elegy to an Unfortunate Lady. 49.

gined to have been founded by the Conqueror, were only furnished with the common productions of the country from their own settlements, they were not likely to be poffeffed of many articles of traffic, that could have been an object to their neighbours, and as to their own country, every hope of a fafe and regular communication between Greece and the Paropamifus or the banks of the Iaxartes was totally cut off. The number therefore of thofe towns in all probability ought to be reduced, and many of them, whofe foundation is not to be doubted, muft be looked on as Trophies, which were foon demolifhed by the neighbouring nations, or abandoned by their own inhabitants.[d] Some, from their advantageous pofition, were afterwards rebuilt, and their ancient names on their new creation were revived out of refpect for the memory of the Conqueror of Afia. Thofe, which Abulpharagius mentions, ought certainly to be ranked in this clafs, and the fuppofition is not perhaps an imaginary one, that the fucceffors of Alexander from vanity

[d] "Græci milites nuper in colonias a rege deducti Garabactrâ, orta inter ipfos feditione, defecerant; non tam Alexandro infenfi, quam metu fupplicii. Quippe occifis quibufdam popularium, qui validiores erant, arma fpectare cœperunt; et Bactrianâ arce, quæ quafi negligentius adfervata erat, occupata, barbaros quoque in focietatem defectionis impulerant. Athenodorus erat princeps eorum, qui regis quoque nomen adfumpferat; non tam imperii cupidine, quam in patriam revertendi cum iis, qui auctoritatem ipfius fequebantur." (Q. Curtius. Lib. 9. C. 7. Tom. 2.-714, 715.) Dr. Robertfon (Notes on the Hift. Difquifition concerning India, 193.) hath very ably combated this opinion of the Baron de St. Croix. Yet Cœnus in his fpeech, which may be found in Arrian at length, lets us without referve into the Grecian fentiments. "Των δε αλλων Ἑλληνων, οἱ μεν εν ταις πολισι ταις προς σε οικισθεισαις κατωκισμενοι, ουδ'ετοι παντη ἑκοντες μενουσιν——— κ̣ τουτοις ξυμπασι ποθ<σ>. μεν γονεων εςιν, ὁσοις ἑτι σωζονται, ποθ<σ>. δε γυναικων κ̣ παιδων, ποθ<σ>. δε δη της γης αυτοις της οικειας." (Arrian. Lib. 5. C. 27. 399, 400.) I fincerely refpect and admire Dr. Robertfon's great learning and uncommon talents, and I feel with reluctance the force of Arrian's expreffions.

vanity or gratitude diftinguifhed many of their own foundation with his name.ᵉ

Man generally communicates his partialities and prejudices to the fociety of which he is a member. The idea of an illuftrious origin hath flattered the ambition of individuals, cities, and nations, and they have repeatedly ranfacked the annals of the world to demonftrate their antiquity, and carry back their hiftory to a time, in which every thing was loft in one common and general obfcurity. Many towns from thefe motives have chofen Alexander for their founder, and Smyrna, having no pretenfions to that diftinction hath contented itfelf with the honour of being reftored by Alexander,ᶠ though its title to it, is not confirmed by any cotemporary writer.

But it may be proper to attend to the progrefs of the Macedonian army, which embarked on veffels conftructed or collected on the banks of the Hyphafis, and afterwards dropped down this river to the Indus.ᵍ Q. Curtius and Diodorus Siculus have equally deceived themfelves in fuppofing the Macedonian fleet to have been

---

ᵉ See Appian. De Bello Syriac. 201.

ᶠ Paufanias however ftyles Alexander "Της πολεως οικιςης" (Lib. 7.–533.) but Ariftides ridicules the fable. "Μη γαρ μοι Λυσιμαχον ετι, μηδε Αλεξανδρον αυτον, μηδε Θησια κ̣ μυθες· αλλ'ἡμεις ωκισαι της πολεως γενεσθε." Orat. Tom. 1.–513. 4ᵗᵒ Oxon. 1722.

ᵍ "Inde Alexander ad amnem Acefinem pergit; per hanc in oceanum devehitur." Juftin. Lib. 12. C. 9.–327.

been built on the shore of the Acesines,[h] and Alexander to have returned by a retrogade march, as useless, as contradictory to every other writer. A war followed between the Macedonians and the Malli, and in the attack of one of their towns the Grecian Hero was personally exposed to the fury of an enraged enemy, and the Conqueror of the East was in imminent danger of perishing like a common and ordinary adventurer.[k]

Alexander having reached the mouth of the Indus, directed his march towards Gedrosia, without leaving the sea at any great distance.

---

[h] "The modern Ienaub.

[i] "Μετα πασης της δυναμεως ταις αυταις οδοις πορευθεις ανεκαμψεν επι τον Ακεσινην ποταμον· καταλαβων δε τα σκαφη νεκυπηγημενα, κ; ταυτα καταρτισας, ετερα προσεναυπηγησατο." (Diod. Sicul. Lib. 17. Tom. 2.--234.) "Repetens quæ emensus erat, ad flumen Acesinem locat castra———jam in aquâ classis, quam ædificari jusserat, stabat." Q. Curtius. Lib. 9. C. 3. Tom. 2.--688, 689.

[k] Plutarch, (Tom. 1.--700.) Arrian, (Exped. Alex. Lib. 6. C. 9, 10.--423---428.) Diodorus Siculus, (Lib. 17. Tom. 2.--236, 237.) and Q. Curtius (Lib. 9. C. 4, 5. Tom. 2.--700———704.) have given a diffusive detail of this wonderful instance of Alexander's temerity, and still more wonderful escape. Justin (Lib. 12. C. 9.--328, 329.) hath compressed it into a narrower compass, but the two Latin historians have varied the scene of this singular mixture of rashness and courage. Q. Curtius relates it on the attack of the capital of the Oxydracians, and Lucian, (Dialog. Mort. 14. Sect. 5. Tom. 1.--397.) Appian, (De Bell. Civil. Lib. 2. Tom. 2.--852.) Stephanus Byzantinus, (Οξυδρακοι) and Pausanias (Lib. 1.--15.) agree with him. It is possible the Malli might inhabit a part of Oxydrachia, and the expression of "Τας σναμαζομενας Μαλλας" may perhaps give some little plausibility to the conjecture, which will then reconcile the different writers, Justin excepted. Alexander is supposed, by this Latin author, to have hurried himself into this dangerous combat at the city of the Ambri and Sugambri, but Orosius, who copied Justin, hath boldly transformed these people into the Malli and Oxydrachians. The Ambri and Sugambri have hitherto retained with inflexible obstinacy their station in the text of Justin, but the commentators have allowed the reading to be spurious.——Major Rennel hath marked, near the banks of the Hydraotes or Rauvee of our times, the probable situation of this city.

tance, and paſſed through a country of great extent, which was both barren, uncultivated, and deſtitute of water. Diodorus Siculus after this account of the deſerts, which the Macedonian army traverſed, adds, that Alexander ſeparated his army into three diviſions, and gave orders for the country to be ravaged, which was inſtantly executed, and the troops returned from the general pillage loaden with plunder and beſmeared with the blood of millions of the inhabitants, that they had maſſacred.[l] The reſt of the hiſtorians are ſilent on this ſhameful ſubject.

The Bacchanalian march, however, of the Macedonian army through Carmania hath been admitted without heſitation by many of them,[m] and Arrian hath alone rejected this ſcene of riot and intemperance,

[l] "Diodore apres avoir parlé de la pauvreté des Gedroſiens, et des deſerts que traverſerent les troupes Macedonienes, ne craint pas d'avancer qu'Alexandre ayant diviſée ſon armée en trois corps ordonna aux commandants de ces diviſions de ravager ce pays." I have deviated eſſentially from the French ſentence for the purpoſe of reſcuing Diodorus Siculus from at leaſt this charge of in-conſiſtency, with which he hath been reproached. It was after the Macedonian army had tra-verſed theſe extenſive deſerts that the pillage was made on the borders of the Oritæ, according to the Text of Diodorus Siculus, and the term "Ce pays" is not authorized. "Και τας Κεδρωσι-αν οικεντας χωρις κινδυνων προς ηγαγετο. Μετα δε ταυτα, πολλην μεν ανυδρον, εκ ολιγην δε ερημον διελ-θων, επι τα Ωριτιδ⊙ ορια κατηντησιν· εις τρια δε μερη την δυναμιν διελομεν⊙————εγεμι πας τοπ⊙ πυρ⊙ κ διαρπαγης κ πολλων φονων————οι μεν ςρατιωται πολλης λειας επιρηυσαν, των δε αναιρεθει-των σωματων αριθμ⊙ εγενετο πολλων μυριαδων." Lib. 17. Tom. 2.--242.

[m] "Αυτον μεν εν ιπποι σχεδην εκομιζον οκτω μετα των εταιρων υπερ θυμελης εν υψηλω κ περιφανει πλαισιω πεπηγυιας, εωχεμενον συνεχως ημερας κ νυκτ⊙· αμαξαι δε παμπληθεις, αι μεν αλυεργοις κ ποι-κιλοις περιβολαιοις, αι δε υλης αει προσφατυ κ χλωρας οκιαζομεναι κλαδοις, ειποντο, τυς αλλυς αγυσαι φιλυς κ ηγεμονας εςεφανωμενυς, κ πινοντας· ειδης δ' αν ε πελτην, ε κραν⊙, ε σαρισσαν, αλλα φιαλαις κ ρυτοις, κ θηρικλειοις παρα την οδον απασαν οι ςρατιωται βαπτιζοντες, εκ πιθων μεγαλων κ κρατηρων
αλληλοις

intemperance, as both improbable and abfurd. " Neither Ptolemy nor Ariftobulus nor any of the cotemporary writers have mentioned it, and there feem to have exifted fome phyfical and fubftantial reafons, which lead us to doubt of its reality.—It is not probable that the Macedonian forces, after the exceffive fatigues of their long and laborious march to Gedrofia, in which they had fuffered the extremities of hunger and thirft, and had been reduced fo very confiderably by ficknefs, ° fhould have plunged at once into

an

αλληλοις προπινον, οι μεν, εν τω προαγειν αμα κ̃ βαδιζειν, οι δε κατακειμενοι· πολλη δε Μεσα συριγ'ων κ̃ αυλων, ωδης τε κ̃ ψαλμε κ̃ βακχειας γυναικων, κατηχε παντα τοπον." (De Vit. Alex. Plutarchi Opera. Tom. 1.--702.) "Vicos, per quos iter erat, floribus coronifque flerni jubet: liminibus ædium crateras vino repletos, et alia eximiæ magnitudinis vafa difponi: vehicula deinde conftrata, ut plures capere milites poffent, in tabernaculorum modum ornari, alia candidis velis, alia vefte pretiofa. Primi ibunt amici et cohors regia, variis redimita floribus coronifque, alibi tibicinum cantus, alibi lyræ fonus audiebatur: item in vehiculis pro copiâ cujufque adornatis commeffabundus exercitus, armis quæ maxime decora erant circumpendentibus. Ipfum convivafque currus vehebat, crateris aureis ejufdemque materiæ ingentibus poculis prægravis. Hoc modo per dies feptem bacchabundum agmen inceffit; parta præda, fi quid victis faltem adverfus commeffantes animi fuiffet: mille hercule, viri modo et fobrii, feptem dierum crapula graves in fuo triumpho capere potuerunt." (Q. Curt. Lib. 9. C. 10. Tom. 2.--742, 743.) The reflection that follows is certainly an appofite one. "Et præfens Ætas et Pofteritas mirata eft, per gentes nondum fatis domitas inceffiffe temulentos, barbaris, quod temeritas erat, fiduciam effe credentibus." Whether it may not impeach the credit of the relation may be a queftion.

ⁿ "Ταυτα δε ετι Πτολεμαι©· ὁ Λαγε, ετι Αρι̣οβολ©· ὁ Αρι̣οβολε ανεγραψαν, εδε τις αλλ©· οντινα ικανον αν τις ποιησαιτο τεκμηρ εωσαι ὑπερ των τοιωνδε· κ̃ μοι ὡς ε πιςα αναγιγραφ Ͽαι εξηκισαν." Arrian. Exped. Alex. Lib. 6. C. 28.--467.

° "Dans la Gedrofie." Thefe exceffive fatigues, if we are to believe fome of the Greek and Latin authors, were experienced before the army reached Gedrofia, and on that account I have varied the expreffion. "Αυτ©· δε σιζη δι'Ωρειτων πορευομεν©·, εις ισχατην απορ ιαν προηχ Ͽη, κ̃ πληθ©· ανθρωπων απωλισεν, ωςι της μαχιμε δυναμιως μεδε το τελαρον εκ της Ινδικης απαλαfε ιν—αλλα κ̃ νοσοι χαλεπαι, κ̃ διαιλαι πονηραι, κ̃ καυμα ̀͡α ξηρα, κ̃ πλειςες ολυμ©· διεφθειρειν————μολις ην εν ἡμιςεκις

an excefs of debauchery, and that a general of Alexander's ability could have either authorized by his example a licentioufnefs deftructive of military difcipline, or even allowed of it, by a weak and impolitic connivance.ᵖ

Alexander returned with his army into Perfia, and there communicated to the troops his intention of difcharging the Invalids, which occafioned a dangerous infurrection in the Macedonian camp. A ftroke of authority ftopped its progrefs, and thirteen of the principal mutineers were inftantly feized and put to death. Alexander then fhut himfelf up within his tent, excluded the Macedonians, and admitted only the Perfians to his confidence. The experiment was a hazardous one, but it fucceeded. The Macedonians returned with tears to their duty and obedience; and the Monarch overpowered by the fenfibility that they difcovered on a fenfe of their mifconduct, both pardoned the ferment, and reftored them to his favour. Ten thoufand Veterans foon afterwards

---

ἐχις ἑξήκοντα ταυτην διελθων, κ̃ της Γεδρωσιας ἀψαμεν⊙, εὐθὺς εν ἀφθονοις ἦν πασιν." (Plut. De Vit. Alex. Plut. Opera. Tom. 1.—702.) Q. Curtius hath given a florid defcription of the diftrefs of the Macedonian army, which he winds up with "Itaque fame duntaxat vindicatus exercitus, tandem in Gedrofiæ fines perducitur. Omnium rerum fola fertilis regio eft, in quâ ftativa habuit, ut vexatos milites quiete firmaret." Lib. 9. C. 10. Tom. 2.—740.

ᵖ That Alexander might have inftituted fome feftival, and introduced fome fplendid and triumphal proceffions is very probable: that he fhould have marched in fuch diforder through an enemy's country is not to be credited. Arrian takes the ground, which Ariftobulus had occupied before him. " Εκεινα ηδη Αριστοβουλω ἱπομενΘ. ξυνγραφω, θυσιαι εν Καρμανια Αλεξανδρου χαριστηρια της κατ'Ινδων νικης, κ̃ ὑπερ της ςρατιας ὁτι απεσωθη εκ Γαδρωσιων, κ̃ αγωνα διαθειναι μετ... τε κ̃ γυμνικες." Exped. Alex. Lib. 6. C. 28.—463.

wards set out for Macedonia, having first received their arrears of pay, a sum to defray the expences of their route, and a talent as a voluntary present.[q] Diodorus Siculus relates, that the veterans were discharged, had their arrears of pay liquidated, and that the rest of the army then revolted.[r] But their arrears of pay were first discharged, the Monarch's generosity extended not only to that part of his troops but to the whole army, and the mutiny was both discovered and put a stop to, before the veterans began their march.[s]

Alexander's last military exploit was the reduction of the Cossæans.—Plutarch, in general so partial to this Prince, here adopts a recital as false, as injurious, to his memory. By way of consolation on the death of Hephæstion, he pretends, that the Macedonian Monarch employed himself in hunting the Cossæans like wild beasts,

[q] Plutarchi Opera. Tom. 1.--704.—Arrian. Exped. Alex. Lib. 7. C. 8, 9, 10, 11, 12.--491---499. Plutarch expresly states that there were also some jealousies of Alexander's indiscreet partiality for the foreigners and Persians in his service. "Παντας ων εκελευσι αφιεναι, κỳ ωαντας αχρηςυς νομιζειν Μακεδονας, εχοντα τυς νεας τυτυς ωυερριχισας, συν οις επιων κατακτησεται την οικυμενην." (Plut. Opera. Tom. 1.--704.) And Arrian mentions some other offensive circumstances. "Πολλοις κỳ αλλοις αχθεσθεντες, ότι πολλακις ηδη ελυπει αυτυς η, τι εσθης η Περσικη ες τυτο φερυσα κỳ των Επιγωνων των βαρβαρων τα Μακεδονικα ηθη· κοσμησις κỳ αναμαξις των αλλοφυλων ιππυων ες τας των ιταιρων ταξεις"· (Exped. Alex. Lib. 7. C. 8.--492.) Callines afterwards makes a formal complaint upon the subject. "Ω βασιλευ, τα λυπυντα εςι Μακεδονας, ότι συ Περσων μεν τινας ηδη ωεποιησαι σαυτω συγγενεις, κỳ καλυνται Περσαι συγγενεις Αλεξανδρυ, κỳ φιλεσι σε· Μακεδονων δε υπω τις γηευται ταυτης της τιμης"· Arrian. Exped. Alex. Lib. 7. C. 11.--501.

[r] Diodorus Siculus. Lib. 17. Tom. 2.--246.

[s] Arrian. Exped. Alex. Lib. 7. C. 5.--485, 486.

beasts, and in the total destruction of that nation, which was slaughtered indiscriminately, and without any distinction of age or sex. Arrian and Diodorus Siculus have suppressed this savage expedition, and for the honour of humanity, it is to be hoped, that it was never realized.

The scripture represents the Conqueror of Darius as coming from the West, and sweeping over the surface of the earth with a velocity, that excluded the possibility of touching [w] it. Nothing indeed is more astonishing than the rapid marches of the Macedonian Monarch, and, in the words of Montesquieu, [x] "the Empire of the world seemed to be rather the prize of an Olympian race, than the fruit of a great victory. [y] "

Yet it may be questioned, if Alexander's historians have not sometimes lengthened his marches, and if their accounts are to be received with implicit and unlimited authority. Some observations on the measures, which were employed, may close with propriety the present section; and a comparison of the marches of Alexander with those of the ten thousand Greeks may possibly elucidate

---

[1] "Τω δε πληθυς παρηγορια τω πολεμω χρωμεν‑, ως περ επι θηραν κ; κυνηγεσιαν ανθρωπων εξηλθε, κ; το Κοσσαιον εθν‑ κατεφθειρετο, παντας ηβηδον αποσφατίων." Plutarchi Opera. Tom. 1.--70;.

[w] "Και εκ ην απτομεν‑ της γης'" Daniel. C. 8. V. 5.

[x] "Vous croyez voir l'empire de l'univers le prix de la course comme dans les jeux de la Grèce, que le prix de la victoire." Montesquieu. De l'Esprit des Loix. Lib. 10. C. 14. Tom. 1. --197, 198.

[y] Nugent's Translation. Book 10. Chap. 14. Vol. 1.--212.

elucidate the subject. The ancients undoubtedly employed stadia of unequal distances, and many learned men[1] have laboured to ascertain their different extent. De l'Isle appears to have ascertained with the greatest success those referred to by the writers of the life of Alexander, and to have proved with accuracy their real length. The difference of longitude between Ecbatana and Aria, according to the Oriental astronomers, was eleven degrees and twenty minutes, which are equal to eight degrees and fifty-seven minutes of a great circle, allowing for the diminution of the degrees of longitude of the parallel of these two cities, and it varies materially from the measure of ten thousand two hundred and ninety stadia, which amount to fourteen degrees according to the calculation of Eratosthenes, and more than twenty on that of Ptolemy. This single difference leads us to conclude, that the stadia employed by Alexander's engineers were much shorter than those of the later geographers. Aristotle's computation of the measure of the earth furnishes a convincing proof of this circumstance, for he reckons the distance of ten thousand two hundred and ninety stadia between Ecbatana and Aria to be equal to nine degrees and sixteen minutes of a great circle, which only differ nineteen minutes, or three hundred and fifty stadia, from the calculation of the Oriental astronomers, and they may be easily allowed for the curvature of the roads.[2]

Monsieur

---

[1] See the Memoirs de Guill. de l'Isle. Academie des Sciences. 1714.—Essai sur les Mesures Itin. Acad. des Inscriptions. Tom. 19.—Observations sur les Mesures Itin. par Gibert. Acad. des Inscriptions. Tom. 19.—And Traité des Mesures Itin. par D'Anville.

[2] Recherch. Geograph. sur l'Etendue de l'Empire d'Alexandre. par Monf. Buache. Acad. des Sciences. 1731.--117——121.

Monsieur d'Anville hath illustrated the marches of the Macedonian army, and lopped off many difficulties, by fixing the stadium of Alexander's engineers at fifty toises, which has every appearance of probability. Five hundred of the Macedonian cavalry, carrying each a foot soldier, marched, according to Arrian, four hundred stadia in a night. Employing the Pythian stadium of one hundred and twenty-five toises, this detachment of cavalry must have marched twenty leagues, which could not have been possible. Alluding to the stadium of fifty toises, the march is reduced at once to eight leagues, and becomes in consequence, not only possible, but probable.

The Macedonians, in the pursuit of Satibarzanes, marched in two days six hundred stadia, amounting to thirty leagues, on the ordinary calculation. By that computation they must have marched each day fifteen leagues instead of six, which the lesser stadium only produces.

Alexander, in his march to Marcanda for the purpose of attacking Spitamenes, traversed one thousand five hundred stadia in three

---

[h] Traité sur les Mesures Itin. 84. The Fractions are omitted.

[c] The French expression is "Dans une partie d'un jour et nuit entiere." Arrian says that Alexander began his march in the evening, and surprised the enemy at the dawn of the next day, and I have not on that account adhered so closely to the French sentence. "Αυτῷ δὲ ἀμφὶ δείλην ἄγειν ἀρξαμένῳ, δρόμῳ ἡγεῖτο· διελθὼν δὲ τῆς νυκτὸς σταδίους, ἐς τετρακοσίους, ὑπὸ τὴν ἕω προσυγχάνει τοῖς βαρβάροις ἀτάκτως ἰοῦσι κ͂ ἀνόπλοις." Arrian. Exped. Alex. Lib. 3. C. 21.--232.

[d] Arrian. Exped. Alex. Lib. 3. C. 25.--242.

three [e] days. The Pythian stadium makes up a distance of seventy-five leagues, which are reduced to thirty by the stadium of fifty toises. The Macedonian soldiers being very robust and accustomed to laborious service, might in all likelihood by a forced march traverse ten leagues each day, since the Roman legions in their exercises marched often twenty-four miles or eight leagues in a day, as we learn from Vegetius, who wrote in the decline of the Roman discipline. [f]

A comparison also of the marches of the younger Cyrus and the ten thousand Greeks, so faithfully described by Xenophon, with those of the Macedonian Monarch, will again demonstrate the practibility of those immediately before us.

The troops of the younger Cyrus, in their route to Cunaxa, marched generally five parasengs [g] before they halted, and sometimes

[e] Arrian. Exped. Alex. Lib. 4. C. 6.--272.

[f] "Præterea et vetus consuetudo permansit, et divi Augusti atque Hadriani constitutionibus præcavetur, ut ter in mense, tam equites quam pedites, educantur ambulatum; hoc enim verbo, hoc exercitii genus nominant. Decem millia passuum armati instructique omnibus telis pedites, militari gradu ire, ac redire jubebantur in castra." Vegetius. Lib. 1. C. 27.--25. 8vo Vesal. 1670.

[g] I am under some embarrassment for a term that exactly corresponds with the Σταθμῷ, and I know of no single word in the English language, that fully meets the Greek idea. The Baron de St. Croix renders it by "Campement," because the troops, where they stopped, generally formed a species of temporary encampment, and Q. Curtius makes use of the same expression. "Nonis castris in regionem Arabitarum, inde totidem diebus in Gedrosiam perventum est." (Lib. 9. C. 10. Tom. 2.-737.) Raphelius, the editor of Arrian, observes "Σταθμῷ ab ἵστημι sto, est iter unius diei, quippe

times more, particularly when they croſſed Lydia for the Meander, where they only made three halts in a march of twenty-two [h] paraſengs, reckoning ſeven paraſengs and a third, before each halt. The ſame body of troops arriving at Iconium, a city of Phrygia, marched alſo twenty paraſengs with only three [i] halts, and directing their route to the left of the Euphrates, they even marched thirty-five paraſengs with only five [k] halts.

The marches of the ten thouſand Greeks, in their retreat after the battle of Cunaxa, differ little from thoſe, which they went through, under the orders of the younger Cyrus. Sometimes they were ſhorter on account of the difficulty of the roads, but at others, they were very long, as they marched thirty paraſengs with only five halts, in the territories of the Taochians; [l] and when they croſſed the country of the Chalybians, who hung upon their rear, and continually harraſſed them, even fifty paraſengs were paſſed with only ſeven halts. [m]

Xenophon,

quippe quo confecto agmen ſubſiſtit, ut fatigata corpora quiete leventur." (Ad Σταθμὸ τρεις. Arrian. Exped. Alex. Lib. 1. C. 2.--12.) I am not ſatisfied, I confeſs, with the expreſſion that I have introduced, but I yet flatter myſelf its meaning is not widely different. Heſychius and Suidas have defined the "Σταθμὸ, ϛρατιωτικη καταλυσις," which is ſubſtantially the ſame.

[b] Xenophon. Exped. Cyri. Lib. 1.--9.
[i] ——— Lib. 1.--17.
[k] ——— Lib. 1.--45.
[l] ——— Lib. 4.--328, 329.
[m] ——— Lib. 4.--334.

Xenophon, according to Mons' d'Anville, alludes to a parafeng of two thoufand two hundred and fixty-eight " toifes, which exclufive of a fraction, amount to forty-five ftadia. The ten thoufand Greeks marched therefore before their halts, two hundred and twenty-fix, two hundred and feventy-two, three hundred and feventeen, and even fometimes, three hundred and feventy ftadia, and confequently their marches equalled the longeft of the Macedonian army. There is even reafon to believe, that the ten thoufand Greeks marched beyond many of thefe ufual halts, in a day; and the Greek term, which Xenophon makes ufe of, does not fignify any given fpace which the troops marched in a day, but fimply the repofe allotted to them after having marched a certain diftance. Diodorus Siculus relates, that Demetrius the fon of Antigone having received intelligence that Ptolemy had invaded the ifland of Cyprus, and made an irruption into Cilicia paffed twenty-four of thefe ufual halts in fix° days; and Arrian affures us, that Ptolemy in the purfuit of Beffus reached ten of them in four days.ᵖ If the ten thoufand Greeks paffed many of them in a day, we may reafonably conclude, that their marches furpaffed thofe of Alexander, which were meafured fo exactly by Diognetus and Beton, the Prince's furveyors. Beton had particularly defcribed them in a work, from which Strabo, Arrian, and

Pliny,

ⁿ Traité fur les Mefures. Itin. 95.

° "Διελων γαρ απο Μαλλυ, εξ ημερας ϛαθμυς εικοσι κ̓ τεσσαρας." Diod. Sicul. Lib. 19. Tom. 2.--381.

ᵖ "Εν ημεραις τεσσαρσι ϛαθμυς δεκα." Arrian. Exped. Alex. Lib. 3. C. 29.--252.

Pliny,[q] borrowed very liberally.—Reflecting on the rapid marches of Ghengis Khan, and those of the Patans and Marattas,[r] all the marvellous in Alexander's expeditions vanishes at once, and there remains no longer any plausible pretence of attacking their possibility. "Our scepticism will not be sufficient" as Fontenelle judiciously observes, "if we doubt only of these extraordinary facts, we should doubt even if they were as extraordinary as they appear[s] to be."

[q] See Athenæus. Lib. 10. Tom. 1.--441.—And Casaubon's Observations on the passage.

[r] In our times the motions of Hyder Ali and Tippoo Saib's cavalry have been equally rapid. Detachments of them, when they were supposed to be at a considerable distance, have instantaneously appeared, and afterwards retreated with the same celerity.

[s] "Ce n'est pas entendre assez bien le Pyrrhonisme, que de douter des faits extraordinaires, il faut aller jusqu'a douter qu'ils soient aussi extraordinaires qu'ils le paroissent."——L'extrait du Mem. de Mr de Lisle sur les Mes. Geograph. des Anciens. Hist. de l'Acad. des Sciences. 1714.

END OF THE SECOND SECTION.

SECTION. III.

AN exact knowledge of Alexander's character can only be acquired by entering minutely into both his public and private life. The discussion will ascertain the degree of censure or approbation, that his disposition, his virtues and his vices severally merit, which will be determinate and certain, as it will be founded on the fixed and unerring rules of justice, the principle of all the virtues according to Aristotle,[a] or at least including them. It is not in the power of caprice to abrogate her laws: the most ingenious sophistry cannot obscure them. The philosopher is their interpreter, and there is an appeal to his impartial tribunal from the world at large, which is frequently actuated by passions, sometimes influenced by its partialities, and sometimes warped by its prejudices.

That

---

[a] "Και δια τϒτο πολλακις κρατιϛη των αρετων ειναι δοκει η Δικαιοσυνη· κ̓ ϐ̓'ἑσπερ@., ϐ̓'ἑως, ἑτω θαυμαϛ@.· κ̓ παροιμιασαζιμενοι φαμεν

Εν δε Δικαιοσυνη συλληβδην πασ'αρετη ϛι.'"

Theognis. 147.

"Και τελεια μαλιϛα αρετη, ὁτι της τελειας αρετης χρησις εϛι.'" De Moribus. Lib. 5. C. 3. Aristot. Opera. Tom. 3.--77. Folio. Paris. 1654.

That intellectual and internal virtue, without which the mind hath no valuable powers, and man is incapable either of commanding or conducting himself,[b] is in fact but strict and essential justice. It was thus that Plato[c] taught, when he refuted, under the borrowed name of Socrates, the strange maxims of Thrasymachus, which, in defiance of the virtuous efforts of philosophers in every age, have been unfortunately adopted by princes either vicious in themselves, or corrupted by long and continued success. —With the latter possibly Alexander is to be classed.—By a scrupulous and careful attention to the chronological order of events, we may perceive the variations in his character and conduct, and the gradual progress of his corruption will appear as distinctly marked, as the events from which it flowed. Prosperity had a fatal influence on the Macedonian Monarch's heart, and the regular and uninterrupted series of his conquests gave birth to a crowd of vices, which were fostered by flattery, and almost justified by the uncommon baseness of his parasites and minions.

Alexander was born almost immediately after Elpines became the Athenian Archon, in the first year of the 106th Olympiad, and

---

[b] "Ἀρ' ἐν ὥστε, ὦ Θρασύμαχε, ψυχὴ τὰ αὐτῆς ἔργα εὖ ἀπεργάσεται, ςερομένη τῆς οἰκείας ἀρετῆς; ἢ ἀδύνατον; Ἀδύνατον·" Plato. De Republicâ. Lib. 1. Platonis Opera. Tom. 2.--353. Folio. Pari. 1578.

[c] "φημὶ γὰρ ἐγὼ εἶναι τὸ δίκαιον οὐκ ἄλλο τι ἢ τὸ τοῦ κρείττονος ξυμφέρον." Plato. De Republicâ. Lib. 1. Platonis Opera. Tom. 2.--338.

the certainty of the fact is demonstrated by the cotemporary occurrences, which Plutarch mentions.[d]

Philip did not overlook any thing neceffary for his Son, and gave him an education every way fuitable to his birth and ftation. Leonides, a relation of Olympias, whofe rigid aufterity of morals was remarkable and well known, directed the education of the young Prince, but Lyfimachus the Acarnanian was appointed his preceptor, and he found out the method of captivating both the Father and the Son by the groffeft adulation. He gave the name of Achilles to his Royal pupil, that of Peleus to Philip, and had the affurance to apply that of Phœnix to himfelf,[e] We may reft affured that the young Prince's mind fuffered under fuch a tutor, and it may be reafonably prefumed, that the feeds of thofe vices were then fown in it, which in maturer life grew up, and threw a fickly fhade over the fplendid actions, from which he would otherwife

[d] "Εγενηθη δε ων Αλεξανδρος ισαμενυ μηνος Εκατομβαιωνος, ον Μακεδονες Λωοι καλυσιν, εκτη καθ' ην ημεραν ο της Εφεσιας Αρτεμιδος ενεπρησθη νεως· ———— Φιλιππω δε αρτι Ποτιδαιαν ηρηκοτι τρεις ηκον αγγελιαι κατα τον αυτον χρονον· η μεν, Ιλλυριυς ηττασθαι μαχη μεγαλη δια Παρμενιωνος· η δε, Ολυμπιασιν ιππω κελητι νενικηκεναι· τριτη δε, περι της Αλεξανδρυ γενεσεως." Plut. De Vit. Alex. Plutarchi Opera. Tom. 1.--665, 666.

[e] If we are to believe Plutarch, he had no other merit. "Αλλο μεν υδεν εχων αξιον, οτι δ' εαυτον μεν ονομαζειν Φοινικα, τον δε Αλεξανδρον, Αχιλλεα, Πηλεα δε, τον Φιλιππον, ηγαπατο, κ' δευτερον ειχε χωραν" (De Vit. Alex. Plutarchi Opera. Tom. 1.--667.) The rays of Royal bounty have been frequently directed on worthlefs and improper objects; but hiftory fcarcely furnifhes another inftance of a Favourite, that rofe into employment on fuch pretenfions.

wife have derived fuch immortal honour. Quintilian[f] unjuftly accufes Leonides, on the faith of Diogenes of Babylon, with the corruption of Alexander's mind; but he confounds the refpectable Leonides with Lyfimachus, and improperly terms him the pedagogue. Leonides had conftantly refufed the office of preceptor, as we learn from Plutarch, whofe expreffion[g] may have deceived the learned Rhetorician, and occafioned his reference of the lectures of Lyfimachus to Leonides, which undoubtedly obftructed Ariftotle's more virtuous fyftem. This great man was called by Philip to give leffons to his Son, under the magiftracy of Pythodotus, in the fecond year of the 109th Olympiad, and the Monarch warmly exhorted him to attend to the inftructions of fuch an able mafter, with the forcible admonition of avoiding, from his counfels, the errors of which he ferioufly repented.[h] ——Memorable words! which truth hath fometimes forced from the lips of princes and of kings, in thofe laft and awful moments of exiftence, when pride and vanity fink into humiliation, and flattery itfelf, having no longer any hopes, is filent.

Alexander

---

[f] "Leonides Alexandri pedagogus, ut a Babylonio Diogene traditur, quibufdam cum vitiis imbuit, quæ robuftum quoque et jam maximum regem ab illâ inftitutione puerili funt profecuta."
Quint. Inft. Orat. Lib. 1. C. 1.--7. Ed. Gefner. 4to Gotting. 1738.

[g] Some of the editors of Plutarch read "Αυτ⊙ μεν ὁ φευγων το της Παιδαγωγιας ονομα," but the "Μεν εν φευγων" of the Francfort edition, Folio, 1620, appears to be the true reading.
De Vit. Alex. Plut. Opera. Tom. 1.--667.

[h] "Εκελευσε δ'αυτον Αριστοτελει προσεχειν, ᾗ φιλοσοφειν, Ὁπως (εφη) μη πολλα τοιαυτα πραξης εφ' οις εγω πεπραγμενοις μεταμελομαι." Apothegm. Plut. Opera. Tom. 2.--178.

Alexander was then in his thirteenth year, and not the fifteenth, as Diogenes Laertius hath supposed, [i] who prolongs by his calculation the life of Alexander somewhat above two years. The Son of Philip was initiated into all the sciences, and ran through the circle of human knowledge under Aristotle's care. After a residence of eight years [k] at the court of Macedon, which Justin hath reduced to five, [l] the philosopher retiring to Athens, when Evenætus was Archon, parted with his Royal pupil to meet no more, though he survived him some years. [m]

In all probability the young Prince, agreeable to Plutarch's opinion,

---

[i] "Επι Πυθοδοτε δ'ελθειν προς Φιλιππον, τω δευτερω ετει της ενατης ϗ εκατοςης Ολυμπιαδ⊙, Αλεξανδρω ωεντεκαιδεκα ετη ηδη γεγονοτ⊙." Diog. Laert. Lib. 5. Segm. 10. Tom. 1.--274. Ed. Meibomii. 4to Amst. 1709.

[k] Apres avoir demeuré à la cour de Macedoine pendant dix-huit années." "Προς Φιλιππον ηχιτο, κατα Πυθοδοτον Αρχοντα, ϗ διετρεψε χρονον οκτα ετη παρ αυτω καθηγεμεν⊙ Αλεξανδρω." (Dion. Halicar. Epist. ad Amm. Tom. 6.--728.) These eight years are unaccountably magnified into eighteen.

[l] "Exactâ pueritiâ, per quinquennium sub Aristotele doctore inclyto omnium philosophorum, crevit." (Justin. Lib. 12. C. 16.--346.) Diogenes Laertius also suppofes Aristotle to have resided eight years at the Court of Macedon, as he came there in the second year of the 109th Olympiad, and quitted it, "Εις δ'Αθηνας αφικεσθαι τω δευτερω ετει της ενδεκατης ϗ εκατοςης Ολυμπιαδ⊙." Diog. Laert. Lib. 5. Segm. 10. Tom. 1.--274.

[m] "Le philosophe ne revit plus son disciple, et lui survêcut peu de tems." The Baron de St. Croix observes, in a note upon this passage, "Denys d'Halicarnasse———fait mourir ce philosophe sous l'Archonte Cephisodore la treizieme année après sa retraite de la cour de Macedoine." I trust the "Τω δε τρισκαιδεκτω μετα την Αλεξανδρω ΤΗΛΕΥΤΗΝ, επι Κηφισοδωρω αρχοντ⊙, απειρας εις Χαλκιδα, ποσω τελευτα, τρια προς εξηκοντα βιωσας ετη" (Dion. Hal. Epist. ad Amm. Tom. 6.--728.) will warrant the deviation, for which I am responsible.

opinion,[n] received lectures in politics and in morality from Aristotle, and was also introduced into the profound sanctuary of the Acroatic and Epoptic[o] doctrines, where persons were not usually allowed to penetrate. The Greek historian produces, as a proof of his opinion, a letter[p] written by Alexander to Aristotle, in which he laments the publication of his Acroatic works[q] with a jealousy, unworthy of a person of any genius, and more particularly a Sovereign. Can we possibly believe that the philosopher stooped to the meanness of assuring him, that the work in question would not be understood, except by a few adepts,[r] and that he

---

[n] "Εοικεν δε Αλεξανδρος ȣ μονον τον ηθικον κ̃ πολιτικον παραλαβειν λογον, αλλα κ̃ των απορρητων κ̃ βαρυτερων διδασκαλιων, ἁς ὁι ανδρες ιδιως ακροαματικας κ̃ ιποπτικας προςαγορευοντες, ȣκ εξιφερον εις πολλȣς, μετασχειν." Plut. De Vit. Alex. Plut. Opera. Tom. 1.--668.

[o] The mysterious language of initiation, hath been extremely well explained by Salmasius, in his notes added to the commentary of Simplicius, upon Epictetus. 14.

[p] The following is supposed to have been the laconic epistle.
"ΑΛΕΞΑΝΔΡΟΣ ΑΡΙΣΤΟΤΕΛΕΙ ΕΥ ΠΡΑΤΤΕΙΝ·
Οὐκ ορθως εποιησας, εκδȣς τȣς ακροαματικας των λογων· τινι γαρ δη διοισομεν ἡμεις των αλλων, ει καθ'ȣς επαιδευθημεν λογȣς, ἑτοι παντων εσονται κοινοι; εγω δε βȣλοιμην αν ταις περι τα πριςα εμπειριαις, η ταις δυναμεσι διαφερειν· ερρωσο." Plut. De Vit. Alex. Plut. Opera. Tom. 1.--668.

[q] Salmasius hath discussed with great learning, the Acroatic and Epoptic doctrines in the notes on Simplicius just referred to; (226----244.) and the editors of the new Deux-ponts edition of Aristotle in 8vo have very ingeniously given an epitome of them, which may be consulted with advantage.

[r] "Την φιλοτιμιαν αυτȣ παραμυθȣμενȣ· Αριστοτελης, απολογειται περι των λογων εκεινων, ὡς εκδεδομενων κ̃ μη εκδεδομενων· αληθως γαρ, ἡ μετα τα φυσικα πραγματεια, προς διδασκαλιαν κ̃ μαθησιν ȣδεν εχȣσα χρησιμον, ὑποδειγμα——τοις πεπαιδευμενοις απ'αρχης γεγραπται·" (Plut. De Vit. Alex. Plut. Opera. Tom. 1.--668.) Aulus Gellius hath preserved the supposed concise answer, of the Peripatetic philosopher, in which, as he remarks, there is the same "Brevitatis elegantissimæ filus tenuissimus."

"AP-

he might be therefore easy on the subject. An answer of this kind would sink Aristotle in the general esteem, and some justice is due to his injured reputation. In the dedication of his rhetoric to his Royal pupil,* he mentions the Prince's request that he would not communicate the work to any other person, as he wished alone to enjoy the advantage of it. The philosopher, in reply, informs the Prince, that authors had a sort of parental fondness for their works, and were not like the sophists, who seldom were at the trouble of any compositions, and satisfied themselves with the stipends from their scholars, whom they quitted without regret, and for whom they had no attachments. Aristotle concludes with an exhortation to Alexander to guard the precepts which were not sullied by venality, and would contribute to his future happiness and honour, whilst in their turn they would derive no inconsiderable share of lustre from his patronage. The philosopher thus artfully insinuates, that from a parental species of regard for his works, he took a pride in their publication, and that, exclusive of such motives, it was a duty, which he owed to his disciples. In the end, he hints to the Prince with great address, that he ought rather to profit by such useful and disinterested maxims, than envy the public in general a knowledge of them. To soften

" ΑΡΙΣΤΟΤΕΛΗΣ ΒΑΣΙΛΕΙ ΑΛΕΞΑΝΔΡΩ ΕΥ ΠΡΑΤΤΕΙΝ·

Εγραψας μοι περι των ακροατικων λογων, οιομεν῀ δειν αυτυς φυλαττειν εν απορρητοις· ισθι ᾱν αυτυς κ̀ εκδεδομενης, κ̀ μη εκδεδομενυς· ξυνετοι γαρ εισι μονοις τοις ἡμων ακυσασιν· ερρωσο." Aul. Gell. Lib. 20. C. 5.--877. Edit. Gronov. 4to L. B. 1709.

* " Εγραψας δε μοι διακελευομεν῀ ὁπως μηδεις των λοιπων ανθρωπων ληψιται τον βιβλιον τυτο·"
Rhet. Aristot. Opera. Tom. 3.--833.

soften the unpleasant part of the reply, he adds the compliment of supposing the Prince's notice of the precepts would be a strong recommendation in their favour, and that their reputation would be fully established by the honour of his adoption of them. Instead of approving of the little jealousy and self-interested views of Alexander, the master of the Lyceum excited his pupil to more generous actions, and encouraged him to diffuse, as far as he was able, the knowledge ᵗ with which he was acquainted. Addressing also his treatise of the world to Alexander, this great man added, "I consider it as highly glorious in you, who are one of the greatest of Monarchs, to turn your mind to the study of those sublime truths, which history and philosophy present to you, and to encourage the great men of your court to excel in all those things, wherein you have so peculiarly distinguished yourself!"ʷ

We may reasonably conceive Aristotle's answer was conveyed in terms of the same generous import, instead of the outrage to his memory, which hath been transmitted to posterity. But this imaginary letter, and those also at the end of his works, in which he exhorts Alexander to govern his subjects with lenity, and to distinguish himself by his virtues, are certainly of very dubious authority.

The

ᵗ " Ὅπως νεοι καθιϛοτες ὑπο μηδεν۞ χϱημασι διαϕθαϱηϛονται· κοσμιως δε μετα σε συμβαινϛαντες εις η̈́λικιαν ελθοντες'" (Rhet. ad Alex. Aristot. Opera, Tom. 3.—833.) Advice worthy of the sage who dictated it.

ʷ " Πϱεπειν δε οιμαι γε σοι ηγεμονων οντι αϱιϛω, την των μεγιϛων ἱϛοϱιαν μετιεναι, ϕιλοσοϕια τε μηδεν μικϱον επινοειν, αλλα τοις ταυτης δωϱοις δεξιεσθαι τοις αϱιϛοις." De Mundo. C. 1. Aristot. Opera, Tom. 1.—846.

The author of the treatife on elocution, falfely attributed to Demetrius Phalereus,[x] feems to intimate, that Ariftotle's letters were written in a fuperior ftyle, and refembled dialogues and differtations. That, at prefent under confideration, hath no characteriftic of this kind either in form or matter, and as Artemon had made a collection of them, which the rhetorician alludes to, if this pretended letter of the Peripatetic philofopher had been of the number, there can be no doubt, but he would have expreffed himfelf very differently concerning them.——Some later Sophift, having read the preface to Alexander's rhetoric, perhaps fabricated both Alexander's letter, which is at prefent the fubject of obfervation, and the anfwer to it. The writers of Pergamus and of Alexandria are well known to have been the authors of various works, which they paffed upon the public as productions of the Ancients, [y] and it is very probable, that Andronicus Rhodius, of the Peripatetic fect, who lived in the 180th Olympiad, and about 60 years before Chrift, felected from them thefe forged letters of Alexander and his ancient mafter,[z] which were afterwards haftily adopted by Aulus Gellius, and Plutarch. Alexander's letter indeed, as it correfponds with the general tenour of Ariftotle's

---

[x] "Αρτεμων μεν ων, ὁ τας Αριϛοτελυς αναγραψας επιϛολας φησιν, ὁτι δει εν τω αυτω τροπω, διαλογον τι γραφειν ᷀η επιϛολας· ειναι γαρ την επιϛολην, οἱον το ἱτερον μερ᷀· τυ διαλογυ." Demet. Phalereus. Sect. 231.

[y] Galen. De Hippocrat. Nat. Hom.

[z] "Exempla utrarumque literarum, fumpta ex Andronici philofophi libro fubdidi." Aulus Gellius. Lib. 20. C. 5.--877.

Ariſtotle's expreſſions, may be allowed, though forged, to contain the Macedonian Monarch's ſentiments; but his virtuous Preceptor had never difgraced himſelf by any proſtitution of his principles, notwithſtanding the ſhameful accuſations of Tertullian.[a]

The illuſtrious philoſopher inſpired his diſciple with a ſtrong partiality for Homer, whoſe beauties he explained to him, whilſt at the ſame time he enlarged upon the morality, which lent new charms to the harmony of verſe.[b] Alexander retained the whole Iliad by memory, and a great part of the Odyſſey, and frequently repeated different paſſages from theſe two poems.[c] He ſhewed alſo his diſcernment in the preference, which he gave as a Sovereign to Homer, in compariſon of Heſiod, whoſe works he thought more particularly calculated for paſtoral and rural life.[d] Under Alexander's pillow not only the Iliad of Homer was diſcovered, but even the Eunides of Cratinus,[e] a celebrated comic poet.

Harpalus

---

[a] "Ariſtoteles tam indecore Alexandro regendo potius adulatur, quam Plato Dionyſio ventris gratiâ venditatur." (Tertullian. Apologet. C. 46.--393. Ed. L. B. 8vo 1718.) The Baron de St. Croix obſerves that Tertullian, in his apology for Chriſtianity, hath tried, condemned, and executed all the great men of antiquity.——The African Preſbyter had certainly ſome of the fire of the climate in his conſtitution, and his zeal may have carried him farther than might be wiſhed; but allowances are to be made for the times, in which he wrote, and the perſecutions, under which the Chriſtian church was then ſmarting.

[b] Dion. Chryſoſt. Orat. 11. De Regno paſſim.

[c] Dion. Chryſoſt. Orat. 4. De Regno.—Dialog. Mortuorum. 12. Luciani Opera, Tom. 1. --384.

[d] Dion. Chryſoſt. Orat. 11. De Regno.

[e] Ptolem. Hephæſtion. Apud Hiſt. Poet. Scriptores. 326.

Harpalus had also a commission from the young Prince to send him the works of Philistus, the tragedies of Euripides and Sophocles, and the Dithyrambic works of Telestis and Philoxenus, Books being very scarce in the southern provinces of Greece.[f]

The Macedonian Monarch took great pleasure in tragical representations, and Athenodorus, in his presence, disputed with Thessalus the superiority of their theatrical talents. The latter having been the unsuccessful candidate for popular applause, the young Prince endeavoured to console him, and paid him the flattering compliment, that he would rather have lost a part of his dominions, than Thessalus should have been worsted.[g] As far as we can judge from a circumstance related by Athenæus, Alexander had not the same relish for comedy. Antiphanes, a comic writer of eminence, reading one day to him one of his pieces, and observing that the Prince was very inattentive to it, took the liberty of telling him, "that to enter into the spirit of such performances, a little acquaintance with comic life was necessary, and that he would have enjoyed their beauties, if he had often formed one of those parties, where a free currency of witticisms passed without restraint."[h] Yet this want of taste for comedy had no effect on his usual

---

[f] "Τῶν δὲ ἄλλων βιβλίων οὐκ εὐπόρων ἐν τοῖς ἄνω τόποις, Ἅρπαλον ἐκέλευσε πέμψαι· κᾀκεῖνος ἐπέμψεν αὐτῷ τάς τε Φιλίστου βίβλους, ᾗ τῶν Εὐριπίδε ᾗ Σοφοκλέες ᾗ Αἰσχύλε τραγῳδιῶν συχνὰς, ᾗ Τελέστε ᾗ Φιλοξένε διθυράμβες." De Vit. Alex. Plut. Opera. Tom. 1.--668.

[g] "Επεὶ δὲ ἐνίκησεν Ἀθηνόδορος, Ἐβελόμην ἄν, ἔφη, μᾶλλον ἀπολωλέναι μέρος τῆς βασιλείας, ἢ Θετταλον ἑωρακέναι ἡττημένον." De Fort. Alex. Plut. Opera. Tom. 2.--334.

[h] "Δεῖ γὰρ ἔφησεν, ὦ βασιλεῦ, τὸν ταῦτα ἀποδεξόμενον ἀπὸ συμβολῶν τε πολλάκις δεδειπνηκέναι, ᾗ περὶ

usual liberality, and Lycon of Scarphia, having artfully interwoven in one of his pieces some verses, in expectation of a gratuity, Alexander with a smile at his address, ordered him ten talents.[i] This generosity notwithstanding ought to have had its bounds, and should not have been showered down with the profusion upon Chœrilus, which Horace hath censured, though he seems to have exaggerated the anecdote.[k]—The agreement, which the Macedonian Monarch made with him, was certainly a singular one, and Chœrilus was to receive for every good verse, a piece of gold, with a box upon the ear, for every bad one; but for his consolation many modern poets, on the same terms, might have been exposed to a repetition of the punishment, without any recompence. Alexander was, however, aware of the mediocrity of Chœrilus, and he frequently declared he would have preferred being the Thersites of Homer to the Achilles of his own poet.[l]

With

περι ἑταιρας πλεοναχις κ̓ αληθιναι κ̓ διδωκεναι πληγας" (Athenæus. Lib. 13. Tom. 1.--555.) The mistress and the harlot made their appearance very frequently on the old comic stage, with both the Greek and Latin authors, and even the pruriencies of the British Drama were not effectually restrained at the opening of the present century. Antiphanes, from whom the anecdote is taken, was the author of no less than 260, or 365 comedies according to others. Fabricius, with persevering industry, hath given a list of them. Fabricii Biblioth. Græca. Tom. 1.--742 ---744.

[i] De Fort. Alex. Plut. Opera. Tom. 2.--334.

[k] "Gratus Alexandro Regi Magno fuit ille
    Chœrilus, incultis qui versibus et male natis
    Rettulit acceptos, regale numisma, Philippos."
            Horat. Epist. Lib. 1. 8.--232----234.

[l] "Chœrilus poeta fuit, qui Alexandrum Magnum secutus, bella ejusdem descripsit: cui Alexander

With these ideas, it may be asked, how the Macedonian Monarch could have retained at his court both Chœrilus, Agis of Argos,[m] Cleo of Sicily, and many others of the most wretched poetasters in the Grecian cities.——Their despicable abilities could not have recommended them to his protection, but having wormed themselves into favour by the basest adulation, they had corrupted his heart, without being able to seduce his understanding.——Few persons of a liberal education are ignorant of the freedom of Diogenes with Alexander, but the Prince could not help admiring the sarcastic boldness of the Cynic. Dion. Chrysostom[n] hath given the conversation of these two celebrated Personages, where the characters of the speakers in the dialogue are very well preserved, though we may wish the pleasantry, on Alexander's father Ammon, had been omitted,[o] as he did not pretend to pass for the son of this Deity before the Lybian expedition, which was long after this interview.

The Royal munificence, with which Alexander encouraged the labours

---

ander dixisse fertur, malle se Thersitem Homeri esse, quam hujus Achillem." Acro ad Horatii Art. Poet. V. 357.

[m] "Agis quidam Argivus pessimorum carminum post Chœrilum conditor, et ex Siciliâ Cleo; hic quidem non ingenii solum, sed etiam nationis vitio adulator; et cetera urbium suarum purgamenta, quæ propinquis etiam maximorumque exercituum ducibus a rege præferebantur." (Q. Curtius. Lib. 8. C. 5. Tom. 2.--594.) The Latin historian could not have divined a stronger expression than the "Purgamenta."

[n] Dion. Chrysost. Orat. De Regno. 4.

[o] Lucian hath avoided the dilemma, by laying the scene in the shades after Alexander's death. Dial. Mort. 13. Luciani Opera. Tom. 1.--389——394.

labours of Ariftotle,[p] ought to infure him the gratitude of men of letters, but his bounty was alfo extended to Xenocrates. A very confiderable fum was remitted to this philofopher for his immediate wants, which Plutarch fixes at fifty talents;[q] and for the honour of Xenocrates, the Greek hiftorian fhould have added, that he only accepted of thirty minæ.[r]——Pyrrho received of Alexander, according to Sextus Empyricus[s] ten thoufand pieces of gold for a poem in the Conqueror's praife. This dubious fact however is refuted by the joint teftimony of Ariftocles and Diogenes

[p] " La magnificence vraiment royale, avec laquelle Alexandre encouragea les travaux d'Ariftote, devroit feule lui meriter la reconnaiffance des gens de lettres." I could have wifhed that the Baron de St. Croix had fpecified fome of thefe acts of Royal magnificence, but not one fingle inftance is referred to. In the life of Ariftotle by Ammonius, we meet with the following paffage. " Ὁ δὲ γε Ἀριςοτελης ερχιται εν τη των Μακεδονων πολει, ενθα παιδευει Ἀλεξανδρον το Κτιςτι, ᾗ μεγα μερος γεγονε της τυτυ βασιλειας πολλα γαρ ιδυνηθη παρα τω βασιλει" but the only favour, I believe, on record, which he received, was that mentioned, fo much to his honour by Plutarch, and conferred upon him by Philip. " Μετεπεμψατο των Φιλοσοφων τον ενδοξοτατον ᾗ λογιωτατον, Ἀριςοτελην, καλα ᾗ περιποντα διδασκαλια τιμησας αυτω· την γαρ Σταγειριτων πολιν, εξ ἧς ην Ἀριςοτελης, αναςατον υπ᾽ αυτυ γεγενημενην, συνωκισε παλιν, ᾗ τυς διαφυγοντας η δελινοντας των πολιτων αποκατιςησιν·" (De Vit. Alex. Plut. Opera. Tom. 1.--668.) Alexander's Royal munificence refpecting the philofopher is therefore very problematical, and in the latter part of their lives, even every friendly intercourfe feems to have vanifhed.

[q] De Vit. Alex. Plutarchi Opera. Tom. 1.--668.

[r] Plutarch in his Apothegms hath notwithftanding mentioned the philofopher's refufal of the fifty talents: " Ὃς ουκ εδεξατο, μη δεισθαι φησας·" (Plut. Opera. Tom. 2.--181.) And Diogenes Laertius relates the circumftance with the philofopher's obfervation: Ἀλεξανδρυ γεν ᾗ συχνον αργυριον αποςειλαντ- αυτω, τρισχιλιας Ἀτλικας αφελων, το λοιπον απεπεμψεν, ειπων 'ΕΚΕΙΝΩ ΠΛΕΙΟΝΩΝ ΔΕΙΝ ΠΛΕΙΟΝΑΣ ΤΡΕΦΟΝΤΙ." Diog. Laert. Lib. 4. Segm. 8. Tom. 1.--232.

[s] Sextus Empyricus, adverfus Grammat. Ed. Fabricii. 278.

genes Laertius,[v] who affure us this Sceptic philofopher neither left any work behind him, nor ever wrote any.

Dandamis and Calanus[w] the celebrated Indian Gymnofophifts, were alfo treated in a diftinguifhed manner by the Macedonian Monarch, and the latter had very magnificent funeral obfequies beftowed on him. Callifthenes, Oneficritus, and Anaxarchus, enjoyed likewife Alexander's perfonal favour, and were honoured with many marks of his friendfhip and benevolence. Callifthenes indeed forfeited them, as will be mentioned afterwards, but Oneficritus and Anaxarchus continued to preferve their influence by the moft ignominious flattery. Suppofing they could not fufficiently difcharge by any other method their debt of gratitude, they failed in the duties, that truth impofes upon every writer, in comparifon of which every other obligation ceafes.[x]

The arts and fciences, when Alexander began to reign, flourifhed in Greece, and its tranquillity, which continued undifturbed during

---

[v] "Οἱ δ'ὅλως ἃ συνιγραψαν, ὥσπερ κατα τινας, Σωκρατης, Στιλπων, Φιλιππος, Μενεδημ⊕ Πυρρων." Diog. Laert. Proœmium Segm. 16. Tom. 1.--11.—See alfo Ariftonic. apud Eufeb. Præparat. Evangel. 718.

[w] Plut. De Vit. Alex. Plut. Opera. Tom. 1.--668.

[x] Intellectual flavery, which fetters the freedom of the mind, is affuredly of every fpecies of fubjection, the moft cruel and fevere. Quintilian obferves with fpirit, "Nihil eft periculofius acceptis beneficiis, fi in omnem nos adligant fervitutem," (Declam. 333.--687. 4to L. B. 1720.) and Man muft be indeed a degraded being that can accept of fuch fervices with fuch chains.

during the whole courſe of his conqueſts, contributed greatly towards the perfection of the public taſte.ʸ Artiſts of great talents in every denomination were encouraged by rewards, and the choice, which the Macedonian Monarch made of Lyſippus, Pyrgoteles, and of Apelles, is well known.ᶻ The manner in which he received Dinocrates, an eminent Macedonian architect,ᵃ proves that he found a pleaſure in extending his protection to perſons of abilities, though in the rejection of the architect's abſurd deſign of cutting mount Athos into a Coloſſal ſtatue to repreſent him, he diſcovered his own good ſenſe and the greatneſs of his mind.ᵇ A weaker underſtanding, as Lucianᶜ hath obſerved, might have been tempted by the offer, and would not have poſſeſſed perhaps ſufficient reſolution

---

ʸ See upon this ſubject, Winkelman Hiſt. de l'Art. Tom. 2.—who hath entered into it with the warmth and minuteneſs of a connoiſſeur.

ᶻ "Imperator edixit, ne quis ipſum alius, quam Apelles, pingeret: quam Pyrgoteles ſculperet: quam Lyſippus ex ære duceret." Plinii Nat. Hiſt. Lib. 7. C. 37. Tom. 2.--59, 60.

ᵃ "Dinocrates architectus pluribus modis memorabili ingenio." (Plin. Hiſt. Nat. Lib. 5. C. 10. Tom. 1.--561.) Plutarch gives him the name of Staſicrates.

ᵇ "Athon montem formavi in ſtatuæ virilis figuram, cujus manu lævâ deſignavi civitatis ampliſſimæ mænia, dextrâ pateram, quæ exciperet omnium fluminum, quæ ſunt in illo monte, aquam, ut inde in mare profunderetur. Delectatus Alexander ratione formæ ſtatim quæſivit, ſi eſſent agri circa, qui poſſent frumentaria ratione civitatem tueri. Cum inveniſſet non niſi tranſmarinis ſubvectionibus; Dinocrates inquit, attendo egregiam formæ compoſitionem, et eâ delector; ſed animadverto, ſi quis deduxerit eo loci coloniam, fore ut judicium ejus vituperetur." Vitruvius Præfat. ad Lib. 2.--17. Folio. Amſt. 1649.

ᶜ "Επηνει δε τον Αλεξανδρον της μεγαλοψυχιας, κȷ ανδριαντα μειζω τυτον τυ Αθω ελεγεν αυτυ ανεςχ ̓ναι, εν ταις των αει μιμησομενων διανοιας· υ γαρ μικρας ειναι γνωμης υπεριδειν ὑτω παραδοξυ τιμης." Lucian, pro Imagin. Tom. 2.--489.

refolution to have defpifed this exceffive and extraordinary honour. But a clear and correct delicacy of tafte, was, in this inftance, an effectual prefervative againft the delufions of vanity and pride. —Alexander, however, afterwards employed Dinocrates in the conftruction of Alexandria, and this artift both drew the plan and directed its execution.[d] Lucian then is in an error, when he advances, that Dinocrates loft the favour of his mafter by this fulfome piece of flattery, and was not afterwards confulted or employed by him.[e] The circumftantial detail, which Vitruvius[f] hath left us, of the means, which the artift made ufe of to introduce himfelf into Alexander's fervice, demonftrates inconteftably that he was a ftranger to him before this fingular propofal. From his refidence in the Eaft, the corruption of the Macedonian Monarch's tafte may be dated, and the multiplicity of the ornaments on the funeral pile of Hephæftion fully authorizes the obfervation. Perfians, Macedonians, fhips and boats, banners and other military trophies, were profufely introduced, and there was a ftrange

[d] "Cum Rex Alexander urbem in Ægypto conftituere vellet, architectus Dinocrates cum cretam non haberet, poler taque futuræ urbis lineamenta duxiffet, &c." (Val. Max. Lib. 1. C. 4.--46, 47.) "Alexandria enim vortex omnium eft civitatum : quam multa nobilitant, et magnificentia conditoris altiffimi, et architecti folertia Dinocratis." Amm. Marcellinus. Lib. 22. C. 16.--371. Ed. Gron. 4⁰ 1693.

[e] "Αλλα κολακα ευθυς ιπιγνης τον ανθρωπον, ουκ ιτ' ηδ'ις τα αλλα ομοιως ιχρητο." Lucian. Quomod. Hift. confcrib. fit. Tom. 2.--17.

[f] "Confpexit eum Alexander————interrogabatque quis effet : At ille, Dinocrates, inquit, architectus Macedo, qui ad te cogitationes et formas affero dignas tuâ claritate." Vitruvius. Præfat. Lib. 2.--17.

strange and inconsistent mixture of centaurs, lions and sirens.[g] Alexander's correct judgment therefore in the arts, which Horace[h] hath applauded, was only strictly true before his Asiatic conquests, and Oriental luxury produced afterwards a total change in it.

Nature had not refused to the Macedonian Monarch that exquisite sensibility, which in the Grecian climate was so common. Aristotle understood too well the advantages to be derived from music in the education of his pupil, to neglect any talents of this kind, that he discovered; but the rules, which he had laid down, did not admit of all the varieties of instrumental harmony, and the flute being proscribed,[i] it does not appear to have been used in the Prince's company.

---

[g] See l'Hist. de l'Academie des Inscript. &c. Tom. 31.--76. &c. &c.

[h] "Judicium subtile videndis artibus illud." Horat. Epist. 1.--242. Lib. 2.

[i] "Ουτε γαρ αυλοις εις παιδειαν ακτεον, ουτ'αλλο τεχνικον οργανον, οιον κιθαραν, καν ει τι τοιουτον ετερον εστιν, αλλα οσα ποιησει αυτων ακροατας αγαθες, η της μουσικης παιδειας, η της αλλης· ετι δε ουκ εστιν ο αυλος ηθικον, αλλα μαλλον οργανιστικον· ωστε προς τας τοιαυτας αυτω καιρους χρηστεον, εν οις η θεωρια καθαρσιν μαλλον δυναται, η μαθησιν προσθωμεν δε, οτι συμβεβηκεν εναντιον αυτω προς παιδειαν, κ̣ το κωλυειν τω λογω χρησθαι την αυλησιν· διο καλως απεδοκιμασαν αυτα οι προτερον την χρησιν εκ των νεων, κ̣ των ελευθερων·———Επει δε των τε οργανων κ̣ της εργασιας αποδοκιμαζομεν την τεχνικην παιδειαν· τεχνικην δε τιθεμεν την προς τους αγωνας (εν ταυτη γαρ ο πραττων, ου της αυτου μεταχειριζεται χαριν αρετης, αλλα της των ακουοντων ηδονης κ̣ ταυτης φορτικης·) διοπερ ου των ελευθερων κρινομεν ειναι την εργασιαν, αλλα θητικωτεραν." (Aristot. de Republicâ. Lib. 8. C. 6. Tom. 3.--611, 612.) A modern author, that I have somewhere met with, hath summed up every advantage to be reaped from music by saying it "is an elegant amusement." "It is a science however," he adds, "which employs no one useful faculty of the mind, and it often leads to company, which a gentleman would consider a disgrace, if he was not himself an Amateur." I will not say with Shakespeare that he

"———Is fit for treasons, stratagems and spoils."

This conjecture may serve to explain Alexander's emotions when Timotheus played something in the Orthian [k] style, till then unknown, and which inflamed the Macedonian Monarch in such a manner, that he hurried to his arms. Antigenides is also said to have agitated Alexander still more violently at an entertainment, with some Harmatian measures.[l] Plutarch, notwithstanding, tells us, that Alexander knew perfectly how to preserve his dignity, and by no means disgraced himself with the allowance of any improper freedoms, either from musicians, or the professors of any such accomplishments.[m] The Greek historian undoubtedly meant to allude to the time when the Son of Philip was under the tuition of Leonides and Aristotle, as he had, some pages before, mentioned Alexander's partialities for rapsodies, and the performers on the flute and harp. Festivals were instituted in which the Conqueror

---

[k] Suidas relates this anecdote at the word "Ορθιασματων," (Tom. 2.--713.) and he defines the "Ορθιον νομον" as follows, "Ανατεταμενοι δ'ησαν κ̣ ευτονοι Ομης&
Ενθα ϛαϛ'κυσε Θεα μεγα τε δεινον τε,
Ορθοι, Αχαιοισι."

[l] "Και γαρ αυτ&, Αντιγενιδυ ποτε τον αρματειον αιληντ& νομον, ετως παρεϛη κ̣ διεφλεχθη τον θυμον υπο των μελων, ωϛε τοις οπλοις αιξας, επιβαλειν τας χειρας εγ'υς παρακειμενοις" (De Fort. Alex. Orat. 2. Plut. Oper. Tom. 2.--335.) Suidas explains the "Αρματει& νομ&.———αρματειον μελ&, απο αρ-μᾰτ&· οπερ εποιησαν εφ'Εκτορι ελκομενω υφ'αρματ&·" ('Αρματει&. Tom. 1.--332.) Kuſter very curiously adds, as a note upon this passage, "Quid sit 'Αρματειον μελ& pulchre explicat etymologus, quem consule." The Baron de St. Croix hath rendered the "Τον αρματειον νομον" "Ce nom Harmatien," It must be allowed to be, at least, a literal translation.

[m] I am apprehensive the whole of this passage is founded on a mistake. Plutarch is referred to, but Philip's ideas have been transferred to Alexander. "Και τοις περι μυσικην, κ̣ τα εγκυκ-

queror of the East offered prizes and rewards to these different performers, and on the celebration of the marriages between the Macedonians and the Persians, the most celebrated practitioners were searched after and sent for. Some played on the flute, some on the harp, others accompanied them with their voices, and those who distinguished themselves were magnificently rewarded. The crowns and garlands, which were distributed on this occasion, amounted, according to Chares, to ten thousand five hundred talents, and even the singers, the tragic and comic characters, and the figure-dancers had a share in the donations.ⁿ

The Macedonian Monarch had been a great admirer from his infancy, as may be gathered from Dexippus,° of a variety of vigorous and athletic exercises. He excelled in running,ᵖ he wrestled with Crisson,ᑫ and amused himself at the ball with Aristonicus, to whom the Athenians erected a statue and gave the rights

---

λια παιδευταις ᴂ παιυ τι πιςτευων την επιςασιαν αυτη κ̣ καταςτισιν." De Vit. Alex. Plut. Opera. Tom. 1.-- 667, 668.

ⁿ "A dix mille talents." "Οἱ δε πεμφθεντες φησι στεφανοι ὑπο των πρεσβευτων κ̣ των λοιπων ταλαντων ησαν μυριων πεντακισχιλιων" (Athenæus. Lib. 12. Tom. 1.--539.) where there is a long and entertaining account of this splendid carousal.

° "Πασαν ασκησιν ησκημεν⊙ σωματικην'" Syncellus. 263.—Euseb. Chronic. 57.

ᵖ "Ελαφρ⊙ δε ων κ̣ ποδωκης." Plut. Apoth. Tom. 2.--179.

ᑫ Plutarch tells us, that this contest of the Macedonian Monarch with Crisson was in running. "Ὡσπερ Κρισσων ὁ Ἱμεραι⊙ απελειφθη διαθεων πρὸς Αλεξανδρον." (De Adulat. Tom. 2.--58.) See however Palmerius. Observat. in Auctor. Græc.--214.

rights and privileges of a citizen,' on account of his wonderful agility. Alexander entertained indeed such a sincere regard for him, that having perceived some likeness between him and Palamedes, in a picture of the latter at Ephesus, where he was represented expiring in the snares of his enemies, he was affected with the tenderest concern.' The Prince seemed also to have a similar regard for the pugilist Dioxippus' before the unmerited disgrace, which he fell into. Clitomachus, one of the unfortunate inhabitants of Thebes, who survived its ruin, and gained many prizes by his performances on the lute, and in the pancratium, prevailed upon the Conqueror, from these successes, to alleviate his captivity, though it is not true as Tzetzes reports," that Alexander rebuilt Thebes out of respect to him. These instances are sufficient to render doubtful what Plutarch relates of this Prince's aversion to the wrestlers.ˣ Yet we may, notwithstanding, believe with this historian,

---

ʳ "Αριστονικον, τον Καρυστιον τον Αλεξανδρυ σφαιριστην Αθηναιοι πολιτην εποιησαν δια την τεχνην κȷ ανδριαντα ανεστασαν." Athenæus. Lib. 1.--19.

ˢ "Περι Αλεξανδρυ τυ βασιλεως φησιν, ως εν Εφεσω θεασαμενȣ· Παλαμηδην δολοφονυμενον εν πινακι, εθορυβηθη· διοτι εωκει τω δολοφονυμενω Αριστονεικȣ· ο σφαιριστης Αλεξανδρυ." Ptol. Hephæst. Hist. Poet. Script. 305, 306. 8ᵛᵒ 1675.

ᵗ "Dioxippus Athenienfis pugil nobilis, et ob eximiam virtutem regi pernotus et gratus;" (Q. Curt. Lib. 9. C. 7. Tom. 2.--717, 718.) who seems to have copied the account of his fatal success from Diodorus Siculus, Lib. 17. Tom. 2.—237, 238.

ʷ Chilo. 139.

ˣ "Φαινεται δε κȷ καθολυ προς το των αθλητων γενȣ· αλλοτριȣ· εχων. πλειστες γε τοι θεις αγωνας ȣ μονον τραγωδων κȷ αυλητων κȷ κιθαρωδων, αλλα κȷ ραψωδων, θηρας τε παντοδαπης κȷ ῥαβδομαχιας, ȣτε πυγμης, ȣτε παγκρατιȣ μετα τινȣ· σπȣδης εθηκεν αθλον." De Vit. Alex. Plut. Opera. Tom. 1.-- 666.

torian, that it was with some reluctance he permitted the introduction of pugilism and the pancratium into the gymnastic games, in the spectacles, which he gave to his troops. This appears to be the fair and candid construction of the text of Plutarch, though the learned Monsieur Burette hath supposed, that the Macedonian Monarch "thought so little of both pugilism and the pancratium as not to give himself the trouble of allowing them a place amongst the other games, of which the public festivals were composed."[y] It is therefore very probable that Alexander's antipathy was only to the pugilists by profession, and those who devoted themselves to the pancratium, without any other occupation. We may easily conceive then, that in the games at Ecbatana, and in those, where the children only entered the lists,[z] the Conqueror might follow with less embarrassment his own inclinations; and as those games were not there very common, they might with less difficulty be varied. The Stadium or simple foot-race, and the Dolichus or long course, where children contended for the prize in Nemean, Asclepian, Ælean and Olympic games;[a] or even the Diaulus or double course,[b] in which children engaged at the Pythian

[y] "Il faisoit si peu de cas du pugilat et du pancrace, qu'il ne se mit jamais en peine de leur donner place parmi les autres spectacles, qui composoient ces sortes de fêtes publiques." Acad. des Inscript. Tom. 3.--263.

[z] This was sometimes the case, as may be learnt from Arrian. "Παιδων γαρ αγων ην εκεινη τη ημερα γυμνικ⊙." De Exped. Alex. Lib. 7. C. 14.--508.

[a] See an inscription found in the city of Tegæa. Corsini Dissert. 4.—And his observations on it.

[b] The Stadium was a simple foot-race, revived by Iphitus, taking its name from its length: the Diaulus

an games, might have been preferred to the pancratium and pugilism. Alexander, previous to his departure for Asia, offered the sacrifices to Jupiter Olympius, which had been instituted by Archelaus, one of his predecessors; and both celebrated the Olympic games at Ægæ,[e] and also treated the public with gymnastic exercises on every remarkable occasion.

The circumstances that have been mentioned, will have thrown some little light on Alexander's education, whose private life deserves as much attention as his victories. In following the different historians of his actions there is a philosophical kind of duty, which should not be forgotten. The Son of Philip hath been called the Great, but such an epithet hath been sometimes voluntarily prostituted by the vilest adulation, and at others compulsively extorted by arrogance and tyranny. Without being overawed by the authority of a great name, let us endeavour, by a cool and candid examination of the Macedonian Monarch's pretensions,

---

Diaulus was a double stadium, in which they ran from the barrier to the goal, (the modern Amateur of the turf will excuse an adherence to ancient terms) and returned to the barrier; and the Dolichus was a still longer course, consisting of seven, twelve, and sometimes twenty-four stadia. (Suidas ad Δολιχ⊙. Tom. 1,--214.) In the two former, speed was generally successful; but in the latter, both strength and speed, and, in the language of Newmarket, bottom, were absolutely necessary. Much curious information on the subject of the Grecian games may be collected from Corsini, (Dissert. Agonist.) who hath touched on almost every interesting particular that relates to them.

[e] "Celebra à Ægas les jeux Olympiques qui y avoient été etablis par Archelaus." The Baron de St. Croix refers to Arrian, and I have almost verbally translated him. "Διι τω Ολυμπιω την θυσιαν την απ'Αρχελαυ ετι καθιςωσαν ιθυσι, ᾑ τον αγωνα εν Αιγαις διεθηκε τα Ολυμπια." Exped. Alex. Lib. 1. C. 11,--45.

tenfions, to difcover if he had any right to the title. Juftin[d] reports that Alexander, before he fet out for Afia put all his ftep-mother's relations to death, and that every individual, the brilliancy of whofe talents might have raifed in them any royal expectations, was included in this profcription, but there is not a veftige of this calumny in the writings of the Ancients.

The reftoration of the privileges of the Grecian colonies in Afia, and the deftruction of an odious Oligarchy were the firft fruits of Alexander's victories.[e] His moderation and his juftice, were in many inftances undoubtedly confpicuous, but the hiftorians may have multiplied them, and they ought not to be admitted in a group without confideration.

We are informed by Q. Curtius, that Strato having been deprived of his dominions from his attachment to Darius, the Conqueror permitted Hephæftion to difpofe of the vacant diadem as he pleafed.[f] The Favourite caft his eyes upon two young men, who

---

[d] "Proficifcens ad Perficum bellum, omnes novercæ fuæ cognatos,————————interfecit. Sed nec fuis, qui apti regno videbantur, pepercit." Juftin. Lib. 11. C. 5.--265.

[e] "Και τας μεν ολιγαρχιας πανταχυ καταλιειν εκελευσε, δημοκρατιας δε γε εγκαθιςαναι, και τυς νομυς τυς σφων εκαςοις αποδυναι." Arrian. Exped. Alex. Lib. 1. C. 18.--68.

[f] "Regnabat in eâ Strato, Darii opibus adjutus; fed quia deditionem magis popularium, quam fuâ fponte fecerat, regno vifus indignus; Hephæftionique permiffum, ut quem eo faftigio e Sidoniis digniffimum arbitraretur, conftitueret regem. Erant Hephæftione hofpites clari inter fuos juvenes, qui factâ ipfis poteftate regnandi, negaverunt, quemquam patrio more in id faftigium recipi, nifi regiâ ftirpe ortum. Admiratus Hephæftio magnitudinem animi fpernentis, quod alii per

who were then his guests, but they declined the honour, and recommended to him Abdolominus, descended from their ancient kings, but reduced to a state of poverty, in which he laboured for a maintenance.[g]

Hephæstion confirmed their choice, but Justin seems to hint that the new monarch was not of a noble extraction,[h] and Diodorus Siculus transports the scene to Tyre after its capture, where he supposes Balonymus[i] to have succeeded Strato. The latter historian

---

per ignes ferrumque peterent. Vos quidem macti virtute, inquit, estote, qui primi intellexistis, quanto majus esset, regnum fastidire quam accipere. Ceterum, date aliquem regiæ stirpis, qui meminerit, a vobis acceptum habere se regnum. At illi quum multos imminere tantæ spei cernerent, singulis amicorum Alexandri, ob nimiam regni cupiditatem, adulantes; statuunt, neminem esse potiorem quam Abdolominum quemdam, longâ quidem cognatione stirpi regiæ adnexum, sed ob inopiam suburbanum hortum exiguâ colentem stipe." Q. Curt. Lib. 4. C. 1. Tom. 1. --156——158.

[g] If we could suppose, with Q. Curtius, the conversation between the new Monarch and his Royal Patron to have really passed, an instructive and useful lesson might be collected from it. "Admitti eum Rex protinus jussit; diuque contemplatus, 'corporis,' inquit, 'habitus famæ generis non repugnat: sed libet scire, inopiam quâ patientiâ tuleris?' Tum ille, utinam, inquit, 'eodem animo regnum pati possim: hæ manus suffecere desiderio meo: nihil habenti, nihil defuit.' " Q. Curtius. Lib. 4. C. 1. Tom. 1.--160.

[h] "Justin pretend que ce nouveaux roi etoit d'une naissance obscure." The Latin historian says nothing of the birth or family of Abdalonimus, and the construction, which the Baron de St. Croix hath put upon the passage, can only be inferred by implication. "Insignis præter cæteros fuit Abdalonimus, rex ab Alexandro Sidoniæ constitutus: quem Alexander, cum operam oblocare ad puteos exhauriendos, hortosque irrigandos solitus esset, misere vitam exhibentem, regem fecerat, spretis nobilibus, ne generis id, non dantis beneficium putarent." (Lib. 11. C. 10. --282, 283.) I have lowered the force of the French expression.

[i] "Της μεν Τυριων πολεως κατεςησε τον ονομαζομενον Βαλλωνυμον." Diod. Sicul. Lib. 17. Tom. 2. --195.

historian however, deceives himself, for Azelminus then reigned instead of Strato. The author of the second differtation on the fortune of Alexander, attributed to Plutarch,[k] assures us that this event happened at Paphos, which was at that time under the dominion of a vicious and tyrannical prince of the family of the Cinarides. After the tyrant had been dethroned by the Macedonian Monarch, a person of the fame Royal lineage was substituted in his room, who had lived till then unnoticed, from the produce of a garden, which he cultivated. On his accession to the throne, he took the name of Alunomus, but the circumstance of Hephæstion's recommendation is wanting.—The variation and disagreement of the different historians afford a strong suspicion of the anecdote, and the silence of Arrian renders it still more dubious. As Strato, in the absence of his father Gerostratus, the king of the Aradians, who had then joined Autophrodates with the Phœnician fleet, went to meet Alexander, and to put Aradus, Marathon, Mariamne, and the rest of his dominions under the Macedonian Monarch's protection,[l] the fable may be owing to his offer of obedience.

---

[k] "Παλιν εν Παφω, τȣ βασιλευοντ۞ αδικε κȣ πονηρȣ φανεντ۞, εκβαλων τȣτον Αλεξανδρ۞, ἑτεροι ἱςτει, τȣ Κινυραδων γενȣς ηδη φθινεν κȣ απολειπειν δοκȣντος· ἱα δ' ȣν εφασαν περιειναι παντα κȣ αδοξον ανθρωπον εν κηπω τινι παρημιλημενως διατρεφομενον· επι τȣτον ὁι πεμφθεντες ἡκον, ἑυρεθη δε πρασιας τινας επαντλων———αχθεις δε προς Αλεξανδρον εν ευτελει σινδονικη, βασιλευς ανηγορευθη, κȣ πορφυραν ελαβι, κȣ εις ην των ἑταιρων προσαγορευομενων· εκαλειτο δε αρα Αλινομ۞." Plutarchi Opera. Tom. 2. --340.

[l] Arrian. Exped. Alex. Lib. 2. C. 13.--144.

Moſt probably the ſame Hiſtorians have reprefented Alexander's conduct, in a more favourable, than correct light, reſpecting the Queen and mother of Darius, after the battle of Iſſus. The miſtake which Syſigambis made, when ſhe imagined Hephæſtion to have been the king, and the anſwer of the Macedonian Monarch are only given by Arrian as traditions,[m] which were neither taken notice of by Ptolemy nor Ariſtobulus. Yet he does not think they were entirely deſtitute of probability,[n] and he laviſhes much praiſe and commendation on Alexander's[o] virtue, which, he argues, muſt have been highly celebrated from the circulation of ſuch a vague and uncertain adventure.

Monſieur de Bougainville hath amply, as well as ably vindicated the honour of Statira,[p] whoſe character and conduct had ſuffered and been ſuſpected from the ambiguity and inaccuracy of Plutarch and Juſtin. His defence of this Princeſs is founded on the moſt ſagacious obſervations, and the ſubject is handled in ſuch a maſterly manner, that it wants no additions.

The

---

[m] "Λογ⊙ δι ιχη.————" Arrian. Exped. Alex. Lib. 2. C. 12.--141.

[n] "Και ταυτα εγω ὡϛ ἀληϑη, ετι ὡς παντη απιϛα ανεγραψα." Arrian. Exped. Alex. Lib. 2. C. 12.--141, 142.

[o] One of the fineſt eulogies upon Alexander that is to be met with in any language, may be found in Monteſquieu. "Qu'eſt-ce que ce conquerant, qui eſt pleuré de tous les peuples qu'il a ſoumis? qu'eſt-ce que cet uſurpateur, ſur la mort duquel la famille qu'il a renverſeé du trône verſe des larmes? C'eſt un trait de cette vie dont les hiſtoriens ne nous diſent pas que quelque autre conquerant puiſſe ſe vanter." De l'Eſprit de Loix. Lib. 10. C. 14. Tom. 1.--198. 4ᵗᵒ El. 1767.

[p] Hiſtoire de l'Academie des Inſcriptions. Tom. 25.--37.

The Macedonian Monarch's generofity to the Royal family of Perfia, which Tyriotes had related to Darius, induced him, according to Q. Curtius,[q] to fend ambaffadors to his more fortunate rival, and fue for peace. Neither Diodorus Siculus[r] nor Juftin[s] have fpoken of the pathetic converfation between Darius and Tyriotes, or Tyrcus, as he is called by Plutarch, though they have recorded the embaffy, which had the peace of Afia for its object. All the hiftorians, fix the time of this embaffy fome days after the battle of Gaugamele. Arrian ftates the converfation of the Perfian Monarch with his Eunuch to have been foon after the battle of Iffus, but he allows its certainty depended on very loofe reports,[t] and to fuch reports little credit can certainly be due.

One

---

[q] "Itaque quamquam pace fruftra bis petitâ, omnia in bellum confilia converterat; victus tamen continentiâ hoftis, ad novas pacis conditiones ferendas decem legatos cognatorum principes mifit." (Q. Curt. Lib. 4. C. 11. Tom. 1.--249.) The affecting interview between Darius and Tyriotes is luxuriantly defcribed in the preceding pages.

[r] "Παλιν εξεπεμψεν αλλους πρεσβεις, επαινων μεν αυτον επι τω καλως κεχρησθαι τη τε μετρι κ̀ τοις αλλοις αιχμαλωτοις, αξιων δε φιλον γενεσθαι, κ̀ λαβειν την εντος Ευφρατε χωραν, κ̀ ταλαντα αργυριυ τρισχιλια, κ̀ την ετεραν τε ἑαυτε θυγατερων γυναικα." Diod. Sicul. Lib. 17. Tom. 2.--202.

[s] "In itinere nuntiatur, uxorem ejus ex collifione abjecti partus deceffiffe, ejufque mortem illachrymatum Alexandrum, exfequiafque benigne profecutum, idque cum non amoris, fed humanitatis caufâ feciffe. Nam femel tantum eam Alexandro vifam effe, cum matrem filiafque ejus parvulas frequenter confolaretur. Tunc Darius fe ratus vere victum, cum poft prælia etiam beneficiis ab hofte fuperaretur, gratumque fibi effe, fi vincere nequeat, quod a tali potiffimum vinceretur. Scribit itaque et tertias epiftolas, et gratias agit, quod nihil in fuos hoftile fecerat. Offert deinceps majorem partem regni ufque flumen Euphraten et alteram filiam uxorem: pro reliquis captivis triginta millia talentum." Juftin. Lib. 11. C. 12.--287, 288.

[t] "Και τουτον κ̀ λογος κατεχει." Arrian. Exped. Alex. Lib. 4. C. 20.--308.

One of the first politicians of our age hath admitted, that Alexander was guilty of two difgraceful actions, the burning of Perfepolis, and the murder of Clitus. But Montefquieu appears to have been led into an error by Q. Curtius, who relates that the Conqueror of Afia, on the inftigation of Thais and flufhed with wine, at the end of an entertainment fet fire to the palace of Perfepolis, and that the city was entirely confumed."——The Latin hiftorian hath given, however, too extenfive a conftruction to the text of Diodorus Siculus, from which he feems to have borrowed his relation, as the Greek author merely tells us, that the environs of the palace were burnt.[x] Arrian fpeaks only of the

---

[w] Q. Curtius, with fome introductory fentences defcriptive of the Royal debauchery, gives the following detail of its deftruction. "Thais et ipfa temulenta, maximam apud omnes Græcorum initurum gratiam adfirmat, fi regiam Perfarum juffit incendi. Expectare hoc eos, quorum urbes barbari deleffent. Ebrio fcorto de tantâ re ferente fententiam, unus et alter, et ipfi mero onerati, adfentiunt. Rex quoque fuit avidior, quam patienter: quin igitur ulcifcimur Græciam, et urbi faces fubdimus? omnes incaluerant mero: itaque furgunt temulenti ad incendendam urbem, cui armati pepercerant. Primus rex ignem regiæ injecit; tum convivæ et miniftri, pellicefque. Multa cedro ædifica erat regia: quæ celeritâ igne concepto, late fudit incendium. Quod ubi exercitus, qui haud procul ab urbe tendebat, confpexit; fortuitum ratus, ad opem ferendam concurrit. Sed ut ad veftibulum regiæ ventum eft, vident regem ipfum adhuc adgerentem faces. Omiffâ igitur, quam portaverant, aquâ, aridam materiam in incendium jacere cæperunt. Hunc exitum habuit regia totius Orientis, unde tot gentes ante jura petebant: patria tot regum; unicus quondam Græciæ terror; molita mille navium claffem, et exercitus, quibus Europa inundata eft; contabulato mari molibus, perfoffifque montibus, in quorum fpecus fretum immiffum eft. Ac ne longâ quidem ætate, quæ excidium ejus fequuta eft, refurrexit. Alias habuere urbes Macedonum reges, quas nunc habent Parthi, hujus veftigium non inveniretur, nifi Araxes amnis oftenderet. Haud procul mœnibus fluxerat, inde urbem fuiffe XX ftadiis diftantem, credunt magis, quam fci. unt adcolæ." (Q. Curt. Lib. 5.--67. Tom. 1.--356, 357, 358.) The learned reader may confult Salmafius, (Plin. Exercit. 846.) on the Araxes.

[x] "Πας ὁ περι τα βασιλεια τοπ۞ κατεφλιχθη." Diod. Sicul. Lib. 17. Tom. 2.--216.

the disaster which befel the ancient palace of the kings of Persia,[y] and agrees in this particular with Strabo[z] and Clitarchus.[a] Plutarch even diminishes the conflagration, and we may collect from him, that this edifice was the sole building exposed to the flames, that a part of it was only burnt, and that Alexander, recovering from his Bacchanalian phrensy, ordered the flames to be extinguished.[b] The ruins of this celebrated palace are still subsisting,

---

[y] Thais does not appear in Arrian's narrative to have had any share in the transaction, and the Bacchanalian riot is totally suppressed. Parmenio opposed the Macedonian Monarch's intention with arguments drawn both from honour and prudence, but in vain; and the Royal palace of Persepolis, if we are to believe this Greek historian, suffered in retaliation for the Persian ravages in Greece. "Τα βασιλεια δε τα Περσικα ενεπρησε, Παρμενιωνος σωζειν συμβαλλοντος, τα τε αλλα κ̀ ὁτι ȣ καλον αυτȣ κτηματα ηδη απολλυναι, κ̀ ὁτι ȣχ 'ὡσαυτως προσεξησιν αυτω ὁι κατα την Ασιαν ανθρωποι, ὡς ȣδε αυτω εγνωκοτι κατεχειν της Ασιας αρχην, αλλ' απηλθην μονον νικηντα· ὁ δε, τιμωρησασθαι εθελειν Πέρσας εφασκιν, ανθ' ὡν επι την Ἑλλαδα ελασαντες, τας τε Αθηνας κατισκαψαν, κ̀ τα ἱερα ενεπρησαν, κ̀ ὁσα αλλα κακα τȣς Ἑλληνας ειργασαντο, ὑπερ τȣτων δικας λαβειν. Αλλ' ȣδ' εμοι δοκει συν τω δρασαι τȣτο γε Αλεξανδρον, ȣδε ειναι τις αυτη Περσων των παλαι τιμωρια." (Exped. Alex. Lib. 3. C. 18.--224, 225.) The evidence is unexceptionable from its conclusion.

[z] "Ενεπρησε δε ὁ Αλιξανδρος τα εν Περσαιπολει βασιλεια, τιμωρων τοις Ἑλλησιν, ὁτι κακεινων ἱερα κ̀ πολεις ὁι Περσαι πυρι κ̀ σιδηρω διεπορθησαν." Strabo. Lib. 15.--1061.

[a] "Ὁι δε μεγας Αλεξανδρος ȣ Θαιδα ειχε μεθ' ἑαυτȣ την Ατλικην ἑταιραν· περι ἡς φησι Κλειταρχος ὡς αιτιας γενομενης τȣ εμπρησθηναι τα εν Περσιπολει βασιλεια." Athenæus. Lib. 13.--576.

[b] Plutarch after mentioning the Bacchanalian entertainment, and the seductive appeal of Thais to Alexander's passions, adds "Ἁμα δε τω λογω τȣτω κροτȣ κ̀ θορυβȣ γενομενȣ δε παρακελευσεως των ἑταιρων κ̀ φιλοτιμιας, επισπασθεις ὁ βασιλευς κ̀ αναπηδησας, εχων στεφανον κ̀ λαμπαδα προηγειν· ὁι δε ἑπομενοι κωμω κ̀ βοη περιεσταντο τα βασιλεια· κ̀ των αλλων Μακεδονων ὁι πυνθανομενοι συνετρεχον μετα λαμπαδων, χαιροντες· ηλπιζον γαρ ὁτι τοις οικοι προσεχοντες εςι τον νȣν, κ̀ μη μελλοντας εν βαρβαροις οικειν, το συμπρησαι τα βασιλεια κ̀ διαφθειρειν· ὁι μεν ὁυτω ταυτα γενεσθαι φασιν, ὁι δε απο γνωμης· ὁτι δ' ȣν μετινοησιν ταχυ κ̀ κατασβεσαι προσεταξεν, ὁμολογειται." (De Vit. Alex. Plut. Opera. Tom. 1.--687.) The dubious anecdote of Thais was most probably adopted on the very disputable authority of Clitarchus, and the "Ὁι δε απο γνωμης" appears to strengthen Arrian's relation.

ing, but exclusive of this circumstance, such immense masses of stone of the astonishing thickness and strength, that Le Brun [d] hath described, could not have been so completely destroyed, that no remains of them were left. We may reasonably presume, that the fire, after having reduced every thing that was combustible into ashes, then gradually expired. Many writers [e] having adopted the opinion of Q. Curtius, it appears more necessary to exculpate Alexander, and to shew that the city of Persepolis existed ages after his death.

Diodorus Siculus speaks of a sacrifice by Peucestes, a Persian Satrap, to the Manes of Philip and of Alexander in the city of Persepolis, [f] some time after the death of the latter monarch; and Antiochus Epiphanes, according to the book of Maccabees, [g] attempted

---

[c] Mons[r] le Comte de Caylus, whose opinions are certainly respectable, thinks differently. See a long dissertation on the subject in the Hist. de l'Acad. des Inscript. Tom. 29.--139.

[d] Voyage de Le Brun. Tom. 4. C. 52.

[e] Salmasius. Exercit. Plin. 226, 228.—Bochart. Geograph. Sac. Lib. 2. C. 2.—Prideaux. Connect. of the History of the old and new Testament. Book 8. Vol. 1.--397. Folio. 1718.—Plin. Hist. Nat. Lib. 6. C. 26. Tom. 1.--710.

[f] " Ὡς δε ποθ'ήκον εις Περσεπολιν το βασιλειον, Πευκεςης μεν, ων ταυτης της χωρης Σατραπης κ͂ ςρατηγ⸿, θυσιαν επετιλεσε μεγαλοπρεπη τοις θεοις κ͂ Αλεξανδρω κ͂ Φιλιππω, μεταπεμψαμεν⸿ δε εξ ὁλης σχιδον της Περσιδ⸿ ιερειων κ͂ των αλλων των εις ευωχιαν κ͂ πανηγυριν χρησιμων πληθ⸿, ἱςιασι την δυναμιν." Diod. Sicul. Lib. 19. Tom. 2.--334.

[g] " Εισεληλυθει γαρ εις την λεγομενην Περσεπολιν, κ͂ επεχειρησεν ιεροσυλειν, κ͂ την πολιν συνεχειν· διο δη των πληθων ὁρμησαντων, επι την των ὁπλων βοηθειαν ετραπησαν· κ͂ συνεβη τρωπωθεντα τον Αντιοχον ὑπο των εγχωριων, ασχημονα την αναζυγην ποιησασθαι." 2. Maccab. C. 9. V. 2.

tempted to plunder its temple famous for its riches, but was repulsed by the inhabitants and put to flight, which proves both the opulence and population of the city, about 164 years before Chrift, the period of this attack.—Ptolemy the aftronomer, who lived under Hadrian and Antonine[h] reckons alfo Perfepolis amongft the principal cities of Perfia,[i] and Ammianus Marcellinus[k] fpeaks of it as exifting with eclat, as late as in the reign of Julian.

The total deftruction of this celebrated city is to be referred to the firft ages of Mahometifm, and its inhabitants having violated a treaty, which they had concluded with the Muffulmen, they were maffacred and their city ruined. Adula-Katil-Mich afterwards completed its entire deftruction,[l] and its remains were employed in the ftructure of Shiras, which was at no great diftance, and was founded in the 76th year of the Hegira, under the Ommiades. This was the real epoch of the total ruin of Perfepolis, called Iftakhar by the Orientals, and it now only offers to the traveller a few ragged hovels in the midft of immenfe wrecks of its ancient glory.[m]—But it may be perhaps objected, that Perfepolis had been

F F rebuilt

---

[h] Petav. Doctrina Temp. Tom. 2.--634.

[i] Ptolem. Lib. 6. C. 4.

[k] "Inter quæ Perfepolis eft clara." Ammian. Marcell. Lib. 23. C. 6.--407. Ed. Gronovii. 4to, L. B. 1693.

[l] Geograph. Turc. 488. A manufcript in the late French King's library.

[m] Voyage de la Bruyn. Tom. 4.--301.—See alfo, Voyages de Pietro della Valle, Tom. 5.--312.

rebuilt after it was burnt by Alexander. The sacrifice, however, of Peucestes was too near this supposed event, for the city to have risen from its ashes in so short a space of time. To add a more decided proof, Strabo, and Arrian tell us, that Alexander resided in this ancient capital of Persia after his Indian expedition, and mention also its flourishing state, and that it wanted only the palace of its ancient kings.[a] The palace of Persepolis was imagined to have been burnt 330 years before Christ, and Alexander's return to this city was 326 years before Christ, which leaves only an interval of four years, and they could not have been sufficient to have reinstated it in its former splendour.

The fame of Alexander's victories had been widely spread throughout the East, and Thalestris, the Queen of the Amazons, is said to have formed the romantic project of a journey to see him.—Q. Curtius and Justin[o] fix her arrival after the reduction of

---

[a] "Strabon et Arrien rapportent qu'Alexandre sejourna dans cette ancienne capital de la Perse au retour de son expedition des Indes, et ajoutent, en parlant de l'etat florissant où elle trouvoit, qu'il ne manquoit à sa splendour, que le palais de ses anciens rois." For the proof of this assertion, the Baron de St. Croix refers his reader to Strabo (Lib. 15.--501.) and Arrian, (Lib. 4. C. 30.) but after a minute examination, both personally and by proxy, I have not discovered a single sentiment in either of the books, referred to in these authors, with this import. Strabo, when he speaks of Persepolis, does not mention Alexander's return to it, after the expression "Ενπρησι ——— τα εν Περσαιπολει βασιλεια." (Lib. 15.--1061.) and Arrian does not even mention Persepolis, in the thirtieth chapter of the fourth book. There is, however, the following passage in Arrian: "Ενθεν δε ες τα βασιλεια ηει των Περσων, ὰ δη προσθεν κατεφλεξεν αυτ⊙." (Exped. Alex. Lib. 6. C. 30.--473.) which proves that the palace, or, at least, a part of it, was still in being.

[o] Q. Curtius (Lib. 6. C. 5. Tom. 1,--419———423.) hath given the galant adventure at full length:

of Hyrcania; Diodorus Siculus [p] after Alexander's second expedition into that country; Plutarch [q] after the passage of the Iaxartes; and Arrian introduces it amongst the events after the Indian campaign. The first three historians speak of this visit as of a fact, which had positively happened, and endeavour to assign the same motives of Thalestris for the journey. Plutarch hath preserved the names of the historians, who gave credit to this extraordinary adventure, in which, galantry according to their account, had a principal share, and they were Clitarchus, Policritus, Antigenes and [r] Ister. Anticlides, Philo the Theban, Philip of Theangela, [s] Hecateus of Eretria, Philip of Chalcis, and Duris of Samos, very properly rejected it as a fable; and as Alexander,

though

---

length: Justin hath abridged it. "Hyrcaniam Mardosque subegit. Ibi ei occurrit Thalestris sive Minithya, Amazonum regina, cum trecentis mulieribus, viginti quinque dierum inter infestissimas gentes itinere confecto, ex rege liberos quæsitura: cujus conspectus adventusque admiratione omnibus fuit, et propter insolitum feminis habitum, et propter expetitum concubitum. Ob hoc tredecim diebus otio a rege datis, ut visa est uterum implesse, discessit." Lib. 12. C. 3.--308, 309.

[p] "Επανελθοντ<i>ος</i> δ᾽αυτε παλιν εις την Υρκανιαν, ἡκε προς αυτον ἡ βασιλισσα των Αμαζονων, ονομα μεν Θαληςρις, βασιλευσα δε της μεταξυ τε Φασιδ<i>ος</i> κ᾽ Θερμωδοντ<i>ος</i> χωρας· ην δε τω τε καλλει κ᾽ τη τε σωματ<i>ος</i> ρωμη διαφερεσα, κ᾽ παρα τοις ὁμοεθνεσι θαυμαζομενη κατ᾽ανδρειαν· κ᾽ το μεν πληθ<i>ος</i> της ςρατιας επι των ὁρων της Υρκανιας απολελοιπυια, μετα δε τριακοσιων Αμαζονιδων κεκοσμημενων πολεμικοις ὁπλοις παρεγενομενη· τε δε βασιλευς θαυμαζοντ<i>ος</i> το, τε παραδοξον της παρεσιας, κ᾽ το αξιωμα των γυναικων, κ᾽ την Θαληςριν ερομενε, τινα χρειαν εχεσα παρεςιν, απεφαινετο παιδοποιας ἑνεκεν ἡκειν·" Diod. Sicul. Lib. 17. Tom. 2.--220.

[q] "Και τον Οριξαρτην διαβας ποταμον, ὁν αυτ<i>ος</i> ωετο Ταναιν ειναι ————ιππευχα δε προς αυτον κρ. κισθαι την Αμαζονα ὁι πολλοι λεγεσιν" De Vit. Alex. Plut. Opera. Tom. 1.--691.

[r] De Vit. Alex. Plut. Opera. Tom. 2.--691.

[s] I have adopted the emendation "Theangela," suggested by Langhorn, (Plutarch's Lives. Vol. 4.--286.) on the authority of Athenæus. Φιλιππ<i>ος</i> Θεαγγελευς. Lib. 6.--271.

though he mentioned in one of his letters to Antipater, the offer which the Scythian monarch made him of his daughter's hand, neither took any notice of the Amazons, nor of the Queen, they were confirmed in their opinion of its falfity.' Plutarch hath added, that Oneficritus reciting before king Lyfimachus the fourth book of his hiftory, in which this adventure of Thaleftris was included, the prince could not help laughing at its abfurdity and inquiring how it happened, that he had been fo long ignorant of it.ʷ——Arrian ˣ alfo affures us, that neither Ptolemy nor Ariftobulus, nor any one refpectable hiftorian had given it his fanction. To fhew that even the Amazons did not exift in Alexander's days, he reafons from the filence of Xenophon, who mentions the inhabitants of Colchis and Phafis, in his defcription ʸ of the retreat of the ten thoufand Greeks, without naming the Amazons, who were fuppofed to have formerly occupied that tract of country.

The

---

¹ "Και μαρτυρειν αυτοις ιοικιν Αλιξανδρ῀. Αντιπατρῳ γαρ απαντα γραφων ακριβως, τον μεν Σκυθην φησιν αυτω διδοναι την θυγατιρα πρός γαμον, Αμαζον῀ δε ουδε μνημονευει." De Vit. Alex. Plut. Opera. Tom. 2.--691.

ʷ "Λεγεται δι πολλοις χρονοις Ονησικριτ῀. ἱςερον ηδη βασιλευοντι Λυσιμαχῳ των β.βλων το τεταρτον αναγινωσκειν, εν ῳ γεγραπται περι της Αμαζον῀ τον εν Λυσιμαχον ατρεμα μειδιασαντα, Και που (φαναι) τοτε ημην εγω·" De Vit. Alex. Plut. Opera. Tom. 7.--691.

ˣ "Ταυτα δε ουτι Αριςοβελ῀, ουτι Πτολεμαι῀, ουτι τις αλλ῀ ανεγραψεν, ὁςις ικαν῀ υπερ των τηλικουτων τεκμηριωσαι." Arrian. Exped. Alex. Lib. 7. C. 13.--506.

ʸ "Ουδε δοκει μοι εν τω τοτε σωζισθαι το γεν῀ των Αμαζονων, ουδε τις προ Αλεξανδρη η Ξενοφων ανεμνησθη αυτων, Φασιανων τε μνησθεις κ̄ Κολχων, κ̄ ὁσα αλλα απο Τραπεζουντ῀ ὁρμωμενοι, η περι ις Τραπεζουντα κατελθειν οἱ Ελληνες επηλθον εθνη βαρβαρικα· ινα περ κ̄ ταις Αμαζοσιν εντιτυχηκισαι, ειπερ ετι ησαν Αμαζονες·" Arrian. Exped. Alex. Lib. 7. C. 13.--506, 507.

The chronicle of Paros,[z] refers this wonderful retreat to the Archonſhip of Lachis, 400 years before Chriſt, which was 44 years previous to the birth of Alexander.

The active and martial life, to which even the Sarmatian women were devoted, gave the Scythians undoubtedly the idea of the Amazons; a fiction which the Greeks adopted, and which correſponded ſo much with the taſte of their writers, that the hiſtories of many of their heroes were embelliſhed with it.[a] Strabo refutes with great judgment the ſtory of Thaleſtris, who was ſuppoſed to have travelled from the borders of the Thermodon and the Caſpian gates, which were more than ſix thouſand ſtadia diſtant from each other. This able geographer conſiders every thing as fabulous, that had been circulated reſpecting the Amazons;[b] and his authority is certainly preferable to that of the learned French Academician,

[z] Epoch. 67.

[a] Monſieur Freret ſuppoſes the Greeks to have invented the fable of the Amazons. Hiſt. de l'Acad. des Inſcript. Tom. 21.--106.

[b] "Strabon refute avec raiſon le voyage de Thaleſtris qu'on pretend etre venue des bords du Thermodon juſqu'aux portes Caſpiennes." "Κλειταρχ⊙· φησι την Θαλησριαν απο Κασπιων πυλων, κỳ Θερμωδοντ⊙· ὁρμηθεισαν ελθειν προς Αλεξανδρον· τισι δ'απο Κασπιων εις Θερμωδοντα ςαδιοι πλειες ἑξακισχιλιων·" (Strabo. Lib. 11.--771.) I have adhered to Strabo's copulative Και, which increaſes the improbability, that he criticiſed. The Baron de St. Croix ſeems to have miſtaken him. ——" Περι δε των Αμαζονων τα αυτα λεγεται, κỳ νυν, κỳ παλαι, τερατωδη τ'οντα, κỳ πιστεως πορρω· Τις γαρ αν πιστευσειεν, ὡς γυναικων στρατ⊙·, η πολις, η ἐθν⊙· συςαιη αν ποτε χωρις ανδρων; κỳ ου μονον γε συςαιη, αλλα κỳ εφοδυς ποιησαι επι την αλλοτριαν——— ——κỳ απιςως αποφαινονται· καθαπερ κỳ περι Θαλησριας, ἡν Αλεξανδρω συμμιξαι φασιν εν τη 'Υρκανια, κỳ συγγενεσθαι τεκνοποιιας χαριν, δυναςευεσαν των Αμαζονων· ου γαρ ὁμολογειται τουτο· αλλα των συγγραφιων τοσουτων οντων, οἱ μαλιςα της αληθειας φροντισαντες ουκ ειρηκασιν.

demician,' who subscribes to the vague reports of the Indians of Maragnon, and some other parts of South America, and hath attempted

σιν· ἐ δ'οἱ πιστευομενοι μαλιστα ἐδεν᾽ μεμνηται τυτων· ἐ δ'οἱ ειποντες τα αυτα ειρηκασι." (Strabo. Lib. 11.--770.) And Arrian gives as little credit to their existence. "Μη γινεσθαι μεν γαρ παντελως το γεν᾽ τυτων των γυναικων, ἐ πισον δοκει εμοιγε, προς τοσυτων κ᾽ τοιυτων ὑμνηθεν." Exped. Alex. Lib. 7. C. 13.--507.

c " Je sais, que tous, ou la plupart des Indiens del'Amerique meridionale sont menteurs, credules, entêtes du merveilleux; mais aucun de ces peuples n'a jamais entendu parler des Amazones de Diodore de Sicile et de Justin. Cependant il etoit deja question des Amazones parmi les Indiens du centre de l'Amerique, avant que les Espagnols y eussent penetrè, et il en a etè mention depuis chez des peuples qui n'avoient jamais vû d'Europeens. C'est ce que prouve l'avis donné par le Cacique à Orellana et à ses gens, ainsi que les traditions rapporteés par le pere d'Acuna, et par le pere Baraze. Croira-t-on que des sauvages de contreés eloignees se soient accordes à imaginer, sans aucun fondement, le meme fait; et que cette pretendue fable ait etè adoptèe si uniformement et si universellement à Maynas, au Para, à Cayenne, à Venezuela, parmi tant de nations, qui ne s'entendent point, et qui n'ont aucune communication." (Voyage de Condamine dans l'interieur de l'Amerique Meridionale. 111, 112.) The Baron de St. Croix observes that it was neither from Diodorus Siculus, nor Justin, nor even the Europeans, that these people received the fable of the Amazons; their own natural character, as they were declared to be "Menteurs, credules et entêtes de merveilleux," having suggested it to them; and he asks, with very forcible propriety, if the existence of the country of El Dorado is to be admitted, because the different inhabitants of Peru, Brazil, and Guiana, have believed it. The concurrence of traditions, whenever they are properly authenticated, under these circumstances, is certainly extraordinary; but two rules may perhaps be laid down, which, in a great measure, may serve for our general direction. When traditions of things, which were possible, are handed down to succeeding generations, in distant and unconnected nations, they undoubtedly carry with them an appearance of authority: where they run in a direct opposition to the known and immutable laws of nature, they can only be considered as repeated instances of weakness and credulity. Such a society as that of the Amazons, could not have subsisted without a total metamorphosis of the human species, and the annihilation of its wants and passions. To make use of Strabo's strong expression, it would be literally " Ὀχ αν ει τις λεγοι, τυς μεν ἀνδρας γυναικας γινομενες τυς τοτε, τας δε γυναικας ανδρας" (Lib. 11.--770.) Bryant (Analysis of Ancient Mythology. Vol. 3.--457——486.) hath blown away this historical chaff with uncommon ability, and industry: I cannot abridge his labours, without depriving them of strength, and paring off some beauty.

tempted to establish their existence. The female form is certainly too delicate to support the regular and severe labours of military service, and the two sexes, united by mutual desires and mutual wants, could not have separated without the violation of the strongest and most general laws of nature.——We are told, that Atropates, a Satrap of Media sent a hundred Amazons to Alexander, who directed them to return into their own country, and to inform their Queen that he intended paying her a visit. Arrian,[d] who relates the circumstance, conjectures very plausibly, that this Satrap ordered some of the Barbarian women to dress themselves like the supposed Amazons, on purpose to amuse the Macedonian Monarch, and that the episode of Thalestris was founded on this piece of pleasantry.

The conspiracy and death of Philotas, are related in the most interesting and pathetic manner by Q. Curtius, and the passage is indeed the most brilliant morsel of his work. There is a noble flow of eloquence in the speech of Philotas, and the affecting apostrophe to Parmenio, deserves the warmest admiration. "Must[e] you

---

[d] "Ενταυθα λεγουσιν οτι Ατροπατης ο της Μηδειας σατραπης γυναικας ἑκατον αυτω ἱδωκε, ταυτας φασκων ειναι των Αμαζονων· ᾗ ταυτας σκευη ανδρων ἱππιων εσταλμενας, πλην γε δι οτι πελεκεις αντι δοξατων εφορεν, ᾗ αντι ασπιδων πελτας·————Ει δε ἱππικας δη τινας γυναικας Ατροπατης εδειξεν Αλεξανδρω, βαρβαρης τινας αλλας γυναικας ἱππευειν ησκημενας δοκω οτι εδειξεν, ες τον λεγομενον δη των Αμαζονων εσταλμενας." Arrian. Exped. Alex. Lib. 7. C. 13.--506——508.

[e] "Ergo, carissime pater, et propter me morieris, et mecum. Ego tibi vitam adimo, ego senectutem tuam exstinguo! Quid enim me procreabas infelicem adversantibus Diis? an ut hos ex me

you then, my dear father, not only die for me, but also with me? I am the unhappy wretch, that take away your life, and put a period to your old age! Why did you beget me in the displeasure of the gods? I cannot determine whether my youth be more miserable, or your grey hairs: I am snatched away in the bloom of my years, and the executioner must put an end to your days, whom the course of nature would have taken out of the way, had fortune had but a little patience."[f] Yet these beauties would undoubtedly have been introduced with more propriety into any other work than history, which ought only to admit the cold and correct truth, and should convince by a rational appeal to the understanding, without attempting to dazzle and seduce it by any ornaments. Stripping the narrative of its adventitious decorations, are we to collect from it, that Philotas was really guilty of the treason, with which he was accused? his defence by the Latin historian apparently proves his innocence, notwithstanding we are afterwards told, that his execution did not merit the pity and commiseration of his friends.[g] It may be difficult to reconcile the cruel

---

me fructus perciperes, qui te manent? Nescio, adolescentia mea miserior est, an senectus tua: ego in ipso robore ætatis eripior; tibi carnifex spiritum adimet, quem si fortuna expectare voluisset, natura reposcebat." Q. Curt. Lib. 6. C. 10. Tom. 1.--461.

[f] Digby's Q. Curtius, Book 6. Vol. 1.--365, 366.

[g] It is fit that the Latin historian should be heard in his defence. "Parmenio et Philotas, principes amicorum nisi palam sontes, sine indignatione totius exercitus non potuissent damnari. Itaque anceps quæstio fuit: dum inficiatus est facinus, crudeliter torqueri videbatur: post confessionem, Philotas ne amicorum quidem misericordiam meruit." (Q. Curt. Lib. 6. C. 11. Tom. 1.--472.) The confession of the charge varied the whole face of the proceedings, whether real or imaginary.

cruel indifference to his fate with the regrets of the Macedonian army, at first extremely exasperated against Philotas, and afterwards very clamorous against the authors of his punishment.[h] Perhaps that sort of ostentatious vanity, which in the tide of prosperity is apt to assume an offensive aspect, and irritate the vulgar, though it may be despised by the Sage, was the only crime of the unfortunate General. Death cancelled in all likelihood the failing, and the Macedonian soldiers both forgot his foibles, and recollecting his virtues sincerely bewailed his loss.

---

[h] "Philotan ficut recentibus sceleris ejus vestigiis jure adfectum supplicio censuerant milites; ita postquam defierat esse, quem odissent, invidia in misericordiam vertit. Moverat et claritas juvenis; et patris ejus senectus atque orbitas. Primus Afiam aperuerat regi omnium periculorum ejus particeps; semper alterum in Acie cornu defenderat : Philippo quoque ante omnes amicus ; et ipfi Alexandro tam fidus, ut occidendi Attalum non alio ministro uti mallet. Horum cogitatio fubibat exercitum ; feditiofæque voces referebantur ad regem." (Q. Curtius, Lib. 7. C. 1. Tom. 2.--473, 474.) Popular clamours and prejudice, after the facrifice of their victim, have frequently been followed by Popular regret, and the

"Virtutem incolumem odimus
Sublatam ex oculis quærimus invidi."
Horat. Od. 24. Lib. 3.

is verified in almost every age. Livy speaking of Manlius, gives us one instance of it. "Populum brevi, postquam periculum ab eo nullum erat, per se ipsas recordantem virtutes, desiderium ejus tenuit." (Lib. 6. C. 20. Tom. 2.--350, 351. Edit. Drakenborch. 4to 1738.) and Corn. Nepos, in his life of Dion, supplies us with another. "Hujus de morte ut palam factum est, mirabiliter vulgi mutata est voluntas. Nam, qui vivum eum tyrannum vociarant, eundem liberatorem patriæ tyrannique expulsorem prædicabant. Sic fubito misericordia odio subcesserat, ut eum suo sanguine, si possent, ab Acheronte cuperent redimere." (Vit. Dion. C. 10.--325. Ed. 8vo L. B. 1773.) Velleius Paterculus, hath subscribed to the principle and explained the motive, " et his nos obrui, illis instrui credimus." (Lib. 2. C. 9. Tom. 1.--379. 8vo L. B. 1779.) though the seeds of the sentiment may be found, as Ruhnkenius observes, in Thucydides, (Lib. 2.--118.) and his imitator Sallust, Bell. Catil. C. 3.--35——37. 4to Amst. 1702.

In Alexander's addrefs to his troops he accufed Parmenio, according to Q. Curtius, of being an accomplice with his fon, who confeffed, on being put to the torture, that his father was the author of the plot, and to confirm the declaration, made a difcovery of the criminal projects of Hegelochus.[i] Arrian and Plutarch have not left a fyllable refpecting the charge againft Parmenio, and they are equally filent as to Hegelochus. But Diodorus Siculus, who furnifhed to all appearance Q. Curtius with the principal circumftance of this important accufation, affures us, that Parmenio was one of thofe condemned to death with his fon Philotas,[k] and the expreffion may have induced Juftin[l] to believe that he fuffered with him. The error, however, was a grofs one, for this great man was affaffinated a little afterwards in Media, by Cleander, Sitaces and Minidas, the obfequious minifters of the Macedonian Monarch's cruelty, who fufpected Parmenio to have been

---

[i] "Pater, inquit, meus Hegelocho quam familiariter ufus fit, non ignoratis. Illum dico Hegelochum, qui in acie cecidit: ille omnium malorum nobis caufa fuit. Nam quum primum Jovis filium fe falutari juffit rex, id indigne ferens ille, hunc igitur regem agnofcimus, inquit, qui Philippum dedignatur patrem? actum eft de nobis, fi ifta perpeti poffumus." (Q. Curt. Lib. 6. C. 11. Tom. 1.--466, 467.) Admitting this confeffion to have been made, there are ftill doubts of its truth, for we are told in the preceding fentence, "Philotas, verone an mendacio liberare fe a cruciatu voluerit, anceps conjectura eft, quoniam et vera confeffis, et falfa dicentibus, idem doloris finis oftenditur."—The ftrongeft of all arguments againft the ufe of Torture.

[k] "Πολλων δε ρηθεντων λογων, οι Μακεδονες κατεγνωσαν τε Φιλωτα κỳ των κατειτιχθεντων θανατον· εν οις υπηρχε Παρμινιων· Ὁ πρωτος ειναι δοκων των Αλεξανδρε φιλων, τοτε δε ε παρων, αλλα δοξας δια τε ιδιε ὑιε Φιλωτε πεποιησθαι την επιβολην·" Diod. Sicul. Lib. 17. Tom. 2.--222.

[l] "Parmenio quoque fenex, dignitate regi proximus, cum Philotâ filio, de utroque prius quæftionibus habitis, interficitur." Juftin. Lib. 12. C. 5.--312, 313.

been deeply involved in the conspiracy of Philotas. It is possible also that Alexander acted on political principles, however opposite to those of justice, and considered the experiment to be a dangerous one, of suffering the father to survive his son.ᵐ

Both Philotas and Parmenio, if we are to rely on Justin,ⁿ were put to the torture. It is certain, that the latter at least escaped this ignominious treatment; and notwithstanding the testimony of Diodorus Siculus,ᵒ Plutarch,ᵖ and Q. Curtius,ᑫ there are doubts, if even the son was exposed to it. Ptolemy and Aristobulus,ʳ who must

---

ᵐ "Επι Παρμενιωνα δε ςαλτναι Πολυδαμαντα, ινα των εταιρων, γραμματα φιροντα παρ Αλιξανδρα προς τας ςρατηγας τας εν Μηδια, Κλεανδρον τε, κ̃ Σιταλκην, κ̃ Μενιδην· ἁτοι γαρ επι της ςρατιας, ἡς ηρχε Παρμενιων, τεταγμενοι ησαν· Και προς τουτων αποθανειν Παρμενιωνα· τυχον μεν, ὁτι ου πιςον εδοκει ειναι Αλεξανδρω, Φιλωτα επιβουλευοντος, μη ξυμμετασχειν Παρμενιωνα τω παιδι τα βαλευματος· τυχον δι ὁτι ει κ̃ μη ξυμμετισχι, σφαλερος ηδη ην περιων Παρμενιων, τα παιδος αυτα ανηρημενου, εν τοσαυτη ων αξιωσει παρα τη αυτω Αλιξανδρω, κ̃ ες το αλλο ςρατευμα μη ὁτι το Μακεδονικον, αλλα κ̃ των αλλων ξενων·" Arrian. Exped. Alex. Lib. 3. C. 26.--243, 244.

ⁿ Lib. 12. C. 5.--213.--the passage already cited.

ᵒ "'Ο μεν εν Φιλωτας, βασανισθεις προτερον, κ̃ ὁμολογησας την επιβουλην, κατα το των Μακεδονων εθος μετα των συγκαταγνωσθεντων εθνατωθη·" Diod. Sicul. Lib. 17. Tom. 2.--222.

ᵖ "Ex τατα δε συλληφθεις ανεκρινετο, των εταιρων εφεςωτων ταις βασανοις, Αλιξανδρα δε κατακοοντ®. εξωθεν αυλαιας παρατεταμενης." (Plut. De Vit. Alex. Tom. 1.--693.) A striking instance of Royal feeling for one, who had been a confidential friend!

ᑫ "Per ultimos deinde cruciatus, utpote damnatus, et inimicis in gratiam regis torquentibus laceratur." Q. Curt. Lib. 6. C. 11. Tom. 1.--465.

ʳ "Oú ils rapportoient seulement que Philotas avoit eté percè de traits." Arrian had before mentioned some circumstances as related by Ptolemy and Aristobulus, but he drops Aristobulus,

and

must have been almoſt ſpectators of the dreadful application, omit it in their memoirs, and Ptolemy ſpeaks only of the death of Philotas, from his having been pierced with darts.

Juſtin' is again deceived, when he advances, that Alexander perſonally boaſted of his own exploits at the tragic end of the entertainment, when all the laurels of the Conqueror of Darius withered. Plutarch, on the contrary, informs his readers, that the diſpute aroſe from the recital of ſome verſes compoſed by one Pranicus or Pierio, in which he had made very free with the ancient Officers, who had been unſucceſsful againſt the Barbarians.' The Philoſophical

and gives the remaining particulars only on the faith of Ptolemy. "Πτολεμαιᾷ δε ὁ Λαγε λιγм. ———————Φιλωταν μεν προσακωτισθηναι προς των Μακεδονων, κ ὁσοι αλλοι μετεσχον αυτω της επιβελης." Exped. Alex. Lib. 3. C. 26.--243.

' "Solemni die amicos in convivium vocat. Ubi ortâ inter ebrios rerum a Philippo geſtarum mentione, præferre ſe patri ipſe, rerumque ſuarum magnitudinem extollere cælo tenus cæpit, adſentante majore convivarum parte. Itaque cum unus e ſenibus Clitus, fiduciâ amicitiæ regiæ, cujus palmam tenebat, memoriam Philippi tueretur, laudaretque ejus res geſtas, adeo regem offendit, ut telo a ſatellite rapto eumdem in convivio trucidaverit." Juſtin. Lib. 12. C. 6.--315, 316.

' "Ποτε δε νιανικα σιῤῥαγεντᾷ, ηδετο ποιηματα Πρανικε τινᾷ (ὡς δε φασιν ενιοι Πιεριωνᾷ) εις τους ςρατηγες πεποιημενα της ετυχχᾷ ητιμενες ὑπο των βαρβαρων, επ'αισχυνη κ χιλωτι' των δε πρεςβυτερων δυσχεραινοντων, κ λοιδορκντων τον τε ποιητην κ τον αδοντα, τε δε Αλεξανδρε κ των περι αυτον ηδεως ακροωμενων κ λεγειν κελευοντων' 'Ο Κλειτᾷ ηδη μιθυων, κ φυσει τραχυς ων κ αυθαδης ηγαναχτει, μαλιςα φασκων η καλως εν βαρβαροις κ πολεμιοις υβριζεσθαι Μακεδονας πολυ βελτιονας των γελωτων, ει κ δυςυχια κεχρηνται." (De Vit. Alex. Plut. Opera. Tom. 1.--693.) "Ce recit eſt confirmé par celui de Quinte Curce," concludes the French ſentence. I have omitted it, becauſe Q. Curtius neither mentions Pranicus, nor Pierio, and inſtead of agreeing with Plutarch, he confirms, as far as his authority hath any weight, the relation of Juſtin. "Sollemni et tempeſtivo adhibetur convivio. In quo rex quum multo incaluiſſet mero, immodicus æſtimator ſui, celebrare, quæ geſſerat, cœpit; gravis etiam eorum auribus, qui ſentiebant vera memorari." Q. Curt. Lib. 8. C. 1. Tom. 2.--568.

Philosophical historian aggravates what fell from Clitus, and endeavours to palliate the atrocity of Alexander's conduct by his provocation,* but this will be found, from attentive observation, to have been the precise period of the change in the Macedonian Monarch's disposition.

Man often struggles to advantage with distress, and rises superior to the malignity of fortune: in more favourable moments he frequently becomes its victim. Elate with happiness and swoln with prosperity, he is no longer the master of himself; the passions rage with augmented violence; and the resolution which exerted itself under the pressure of adversity, is totally overpowered by its new and more dangerous antagonists. Alexander, at the summit of earthly grandeur, and commanding, as it were the universe, soon ceased to be distinguished by the virtues, which had acquired him the public admiration and esteem, when he had a formidable rival in Darius, and his successes depended on the uncertain fate of war, and the precarious issue of numerous battles and engagements.

The historians of the Macedonian Monarch have not sufficiently attended to this change in his character, and are rather to be considered as his apologists. To Plutarch, the objection is more particularly applicable, but the Scripture hath marked with a juster and more impartial hand the progress of his vices, and after having

---

* De Vit. Alex. Plut. Opera. Tom. 1.---694. Q. Curtius (Lib. 8. C. 1. Tom. 2.--568 ---573.) gives a full account of the dispute, but as to the indiscreet language, which Clitus repeatedly made use of, he coincides with the Greek historian.

having touched on his conquests, hath recorded the melancholy effects, which they produced upon his mind.[x]

Human glory, like the great luminaries of the heavens, hath its phases and eclipses: at one time it is overshadowed by a few momentary indiscretions, at another it wholly disappears, and becomes obscured by a thick mass of vices. It is the peculiar province of history, to observe minutely these various revolutions, to give a faithful description of them, and to deliver down to posterity the real characters of the great men whose actions it relates, without either lessening, or adding to their merit.

The death of Callisthenes called for the tears of Theophrastus,[y] and indignation of Aristotle. Alexander, cruel and vindictive, now lent a ready ear to every injurious tale or slanderous accusation, and under the pretence of the conspiracy of Hermolaus, embraced the opportunity of ruining the disciple of his ancient master. Some satirical expressions and imprudent censures, which fell in an unguarded moment from the philosopher, irritated the Macedonian Monarch, and provoked his resentment.[z] Ptolemy and Aristobulus

---

[x] "Και ὑψώθη, ϗ̓ ἐπηρϑη ἡ καρδια αυτυ." 1. Maccab. C. 1. 3.

[y] "Ut Theophrastus interitum deplorans Callisthenis, sodalis sui." Cicero. Tuscul. Quest. Lib. 3. Sect. 10. Tom. 2.--307.

[z] "Παρρησιαςικωτερον λαλυντα τω βασιλει, ϗ̓ μη πειθομενον αυτω." (Diogen. Laert. Lib. 5. Tom. 1.--271. Ed. Meibom. 4to Amst. 1709.) "Gravitas viri et prompta libertas invisa erat regi, quasi solus Macedonas paratos ad tale obsequium moraretur." (Q. Curt. Lib. 8. C. 5. Tom.

lus[a] suppose, that Hermolaus and his accomplices had imbibed their rebellious principles from Callisthenes, whose lectures they had attended. All the other historians assure us, on the contrary, that his intimacy with Hermolaus was the sole reason for the suspicions of his loyalty, and that trivial and unfounded as they were, his enemies magnified them, by their hatred and malevolence, into proofs of guilt.[b] In the opinion of Q. Curtius, Callisthenes was innocent,[c] and his defence of Hermolaus, though it may be perhaps

---

Tom. 2.--596.) "Haudquaquam aulæ et adsentantium adcommodatus ingenio." (Q. Curt. Lib. 8. C. 8. Tom. 2.--618.) "Καλλισθενης λεγων μεν ην δυνατ۩, κỳ μεγας, νουν δε ουκ ειχεν." (Aristot. apud Plut. De Vit. Alex. Plut. Opera. Tom. 1.--695.) Such was the prevailing opinion, and there remains little doubt that Callisthenes owed his ruin to the rigid austerity of his manners, and a want of that supple and accommodating habit, which, like old age, as described by Catullus,

"Omnibus omnia annuit,"
209. Ed. Vulpii. 4to 1737.

and is an essential requisite in every corrupt and luxurious Court.

[a] "Αριστοβουλ۩ μεν λεγει, οτι κỳ Καλλισθενην επαρχι σφας εφασαν ες το τολμημα· κỳ Πτολεμαι۩ ωσαυτως λεγει." Arrian. Exped. Alex. Lib. 4. C. 14.--293.

[b] "Οι δε πολλοι ου ταυτη λεγουσιν, αλλα δια μισ۩ γαρ το ηδη ον προς Καλλισθενην εξ Αλεξανδρου, κỳ οτι ο Ερμολαους ες τα μαλιστα επιτηδει۩ ην τω Καλλισθενει, ου χαλεπως πιστευσαι τα χειρω υπερ Καλλισθενους Αλεξανδρον· Ηδη δε τινες κỳ τα κατεγραψαν, τον Ερμολαον προαχθεντα ες τους Μακεδονας ομολογειν τε επιβουλευσαι." Arrian. Exped. Alex. Lib. 4. C. 14.--293.

[c] "Initi consilii in caput regis innoxius: (Q. Curt. Lib. 8. C. 8. Tom. 2.--618.) but he admits that the philosopher lent a ready ear to some improper censures of his Sovereign. "Callisthenes non ut participem facinoris nominatum esse, constabat; sed solitum puerorum sermonibus vituperantium criminantiumque regem faciles aures præbere." (Q. Curt. Lib. 8. C. 6. Tom. 2.--607.) Plutarch, notwithstanding, hath effectually vindicated Callisthenes. "Και τοι των περι Ερμολαον ουδεις ουδε δια της εσχατης αναγκης του Καλλισθενους κατειπεν." De Vit. Alex. Plut. Opera. Tom. 1.--695.

haps too ingenious, leaves no doubt whatever of the injuflice that was done to him.[d]

The Latin hiftorian adds, that Callifthenes was condemned without being heard in his defence.[e] But this idea feems to be contradicted by the evidence of Ariftotle, and we learn that his ancient fcholar was condemned by the Macedonians,[f] who had preferved their right of trial for ftate crimes, and had carefully excluded the Royal authority from any fhare in their deliberations.[g] If the Macedonians tried Callifthenes, the fentence muft have been conformable to their laws, and the philofopher muft have been either ftoned to death, or pierced with darts,[h] inftead of expiring on the crofs, according to Ptolemy;[i] being confined in a cage,

---

[d] Q. Curt. Lib. 8. C. 7. Tom. 2.--608----612.

[e] "Callifthenes quoque tortus interiit.————————Itaque nullius cædes majorem apud Græcos Alexandro excitavit invidiam, quod præditum optimis moribus artibufque, a quo revocatus ad vitam erat, quum interfecto Clito mori perfeveraret; non tantum occiderit, fed etiam torferit indicta quidem caufa." Q. Curt. Lib. 8. C. 8. Tom. 2.--618, 619.

[f] "Οργιζομενε τε δημε————————πρασι γαρ γιγνονται, οταν εις αλλον την οργην αναλωσωσιν· οιον συνεβη επι Εργοφιλε· μαλλον γαρ χαλεπαινοντες, η Καλλισθενει αφησαι δια το Καλλισθενες τη προτεραια καταγνωναι θανατον·" Ariftot. Rhetor. Lib. 2. C. 3. Arift. Opera. Tom. 3.--751.

[g] "De capitalibus rebus vetufto Macedonum more inquirebat exercitus, in pace erat vulgi. Nihil poteftas regum valebat; nifi prius valuiffet auctoritas." Q. Curt. Lib. 6. C. 8. Tom. 1. --444, 445.

[h] Which were Macedonian punifhments, as we learn from Q. Curtius (Lib. 6. C. 11. Tom. 1.--470, 471.) and Arrian. Exped. Alex. Lib. 3. C. 26.--243.

[i] "Πτολεμαι۞ δε ὁ Λαγε ϛρεβλωθεντα κ̧ κρεμασθεντα αποθανειν." Arrian. Exped. Alex. Lib. 4. C. 14.--294.

cage, and dying from filth and vermin, by the report of others; and still less being exposed to a lion,[k] or shut up in a cavern after having the nose, lips, and ears cut off,[l] which were the common punishments of the Eastern and barbarous[m] nations. Aristobulus related that Callisthenes was carried a prisoner, and in chains, along with the army, and that he died a natural death;[n] and Chares confirms this account, and assures us, that he died in irons after a confinement of seven months, when Alexander besieged the city of the Malli.[o] The Prince in a letter to Antipater, informs him, "The Macedonians have stoned the young men to death. As for the Sophist I will punish him myself, and those that sent him too, nor shall the towns that harboured the conspirators

---

[k] "Εν σιδηρα περιηγετο γαλεαγρα, φθειριων κ̔ ακομιϛ᾽ κ̔ τιλϑ᾽ λιοντι παρακληθεις, ετω κατιϛριψιν" Diogen. Laert. Lib. 5. Tom. 1.--271, 272.

[l] Quippe cum Alexander Magnus Callisthenem philosophum, propter salutationis Persicæ interpellatum morem, insidiarum, quæ sibi paratæ fuerant, conscium fuisse iratus finxisset; eumque, truncatis credulitcr omnibus membris, abscissisque auribus ac naso labiisque, deforme ac miserandum spectaculum reddidisset: insuper cum cane in caveâ clausum ad metum ceterorum circumferret. &c." Justin. Lib. 15. C. 3.--396.

[m] See Diod. Sicul. Lib. 17. Tom. 2.--213.--Ammian. Marcellinus. Lib. 30. C. 8.--636. Ed. Gronov. 4to 1693.--Justin. Lib. 1. C. 10.--51.--Q. Curtius. Lib. 3. C. 8. Tom. 1. --108.

[n] "Καλλισθενην δε Αριϛοβυλ᾽ μεν λεγει δεδεμενον εν πεδαις ξυμπεριαγεσθαι τη ϛρατια, ιπειτα νοσω τελυτησαι." Arrian. Exped. Alex. Lib. 4. C. 14.--294.

[o] "Χαρης δε, μετα την συλληψιν επτα μηνας φυλατ̔εσθαι δεδεμενον, ως εν τω σινεδριω κριθεις, οχ̔, τ᾽ Αριϛοτελες· εν αις ημεραις Αλεξανδρ᾽ εν Μαλλοις Οξυδρακαις ετρωθη περι την Ινδιαν αποθανειν ἰπη παχυν γενομενον κ̔ φθειριασαντα." De Vit. Alex. Plut. Opera. Tom. 1.--696.

spirators escape."[r] Plutarch, who preserved this fragment of a letter, adds, that several authors believed, that Callisthenes finished his days by a natural death in prison.[q] The writers of antiquity, who have taken notice of the death of the philosopher, do not mention any extraordinary punishment, that he suffered,[r] and their silence seems to strengthen the opinion of Aristobulus and Chares. Alexander, with his consummate political knowledge, could not have been so inconsiderate as to display before the Macedonians, the refined modes of torture invented by the people, that they had conquered. From this prudential system the execution of Callisthenes was probably suspended, and the hazard of another insurrection of the troops avoided, who might have considered the philosopher as a victim sacrificed on account of his adherence and attachment to the customs of their country.

Alexander hath been accused with strict justice of shedding the blood of his best friends,[s] but malice may have augmented the number

---

[r] Langhorn's Plutarch. Vol. 4.--299. " Οἱ μὲν Παῖδες (φησιν) ὑπο των Μακεδονων κατελευσθησαν· τον δε σοφιστην εγω κολασω, κ̓ τυς εκπεμψαντας αυτον, κ̓ τυς ὑποδεχομενυς ταις πολεσι τυς εμοι επιβυλευοντας." De Vit. Alex. Plut. Opera. Tom. 1.--696.

[q] " Αποθανειν δε αυτον, οἱ μεν ὑπο Αλεξανδρυ κρεμασθεντα λεγυσιν, οἱ δε, εν νοσω δεδεμενον κ̓ νοσησαντα." De Vit. Alex. Plut. Opera. Tom. 1.--696.

[r] Dial. Mortuorum. 13. Luciani Opera. Tom. 1.--394.--Val. Max. Lib. 9. C. 3.--817.--Ed. Torrenii. 4to 1726.--Excerpta ex Polybio. Lib. 12.---Seneca. Quæst. Nat. Lib. 6. Tom. 2.--805. Ed. 8vo Amst. 1672.

[s] Plutarch. De Multitudine Amicorum. Tom. 2.--96.---Dialog. Mortuorum. 13, 14. Luciani Opera. Tom. 1.--394----396.---Tit. Liv. Lib. 9. C. 18. Tom. 2.--907.---Arrian. Exped. Alex.

number of thofe, who were fuppofed to have been put to death from his fufpicions and caprices. Juftin pretends, that Lyfimachus, who mounted the throne after Alexander's deceafe, had been expofed to a lion, on account of his connections with Callifthenes,[t] under whom he ftudied, and that he difpatched the ravenous beaft, by thrufting his arm, wrapped in his mantle, down its throat. The origin of this fable, which was adopted by feveral hiftorians, was clearly feen by Q. Curtius, who tells us, that Alexander, on a hunting party in Sogdia, was in great danger from a lion, and that Lyfimachus rufhed in to his affiftance.[w] This cirumftance might eafily have given rife to the fable, but far from being expofed to the wild beaft as a punifhment, the danger of Lyfimachus was both voluntary and accidental. Plutarch even reckons Lyfimachus amongft the perfons who accufed Callifthenes,[x] and on this

---

Alex. Lib. 7. C. 4.--483.---Dion. Chryfoft. Orat. Lib. 9.--598.--De Vit. Alex. Plut. Opera. Tom. 1.--697.

[t] "Lyfimachus, audire Callifthenem, et præcepta ab eo virtutis accipere folitus, mifertus tanti viri, non culpæ, fed libertatis pœnas pendentis, venenum ei in remedia calamitatium dedit. Quod adeo ægre Alexander tulit, ut eum objici ferociffimo leoni juberet. Sed cum ad confpectum ejus concitatus leo impetum feciffet, manum amiculo involutam Lyfimachus in os leonis immerfit, adreptàque linguà, feram exanimavit." (Juftin. Lib. 15. C. 3.--396, 397.) Valerius Maximus alfo hath the expreffion of "Lyfimachus leoni objectus." Lib. 9. C. 3.--817.

[w] "Alexander cum toto exercitu ingreffus agitari undique feras juffit. Inter quas quum leo magnitudinis raræ ipfum regem invafurus incurreret; forte Lyfimachus, qui poftea regnavit, proximus Alexandro, venabulum objicere feræ cœperat. Quo rex repulfo, et abire juffo, adjecit, tam a femet uno quam a Lyfimacho leonem interfici poffe. Lyfimachus enim quondam cum venaretur in Syriâ, occiderat eximiæ magnitudinis feram folus: fed lævo humero ufque ad offa laceratus ad ultimum periculum pervenerat." Q. Curtius. Lib. 8. C. 1. Tom. 2.--566.

[x] "Επειτα Λυσιμαχοι κỳ Αγνωνες επεφυοντο, φασκοντες πεπυσθαι τον σοφιςκ, ως επι κπλαλυσει τυραννιδος μεγα φρονωντα, κỳ συντρεχειν προς αυτον τα μειρακια, κỳ περιπειν, ως μονον ελευθερον εν τοσαυταις μυριασιν." De Vit. Alex. Plut. Opera. Tom. 1.--696.

this fuppofition, he could not have forfeited the Macedonian Monarch's favour from an undue partiality to the philofopher, and an improper intimacy with him.

The condemnation of Agathocles of Samos, refts only on the fame weak foundation. The tears, which he dropped over the afhes of Hephæftion, could not have been criminal in Alexander's eyes, who had fhed them in abundance on the fame occafion; befides, Lucian is the fingle author, that hath tranfmitted to us this dubious anecdote.[y]

Alexander felt fome poignant regret on the death of Clitus, it was, however, of fhort duration, and he foon abandoned himfelf again to the fame vicious exceffes, which have fo difgraced his character. Adoration was the firft object of his wifhes, but the manly eloquence of Callifthenes, had checked the criminal inclinations, which the tribe of his obfequious fycophants was well difpofed to gratify. Yet the motives of the Macedonians for refufing him their adoration, though perfectly proper, were not taken up on juft principles, or from found diftinctions. The Perfians had been always accuftomed to render their kings honours purely civil, and the Greeks deceived by this external fhew of veneration, which was ftill in ufe with the Eaftern nations, confidered

---

[y] "Τοτι κỳ Αγαθοκλης ὁ Σαμι®- ταξιαρχων παρ Αλιξανδρω, κỳ τιμωμεν®- παρ'αυτυ, μικρυ δειν συγκατεριχθη λιοντι, διαβληθεις ὁτι δακρυστι παριων τον Ηφαιςιων®- ταφον." Lucian. Calumn. non tem. cred. Tom. 3.--149.

sidered it as a mark of a religious and profane worship, with which they ought not to comply. This extraordinary homage, which the Persian monarchs appeared to receive from their subjects, arose from their peculiar tenets, and the belief that their kings, according to the Zend-Avesta, were animated with some particles of the sacred fire, which is perpetually burning in the presence of Ormazd. [a]——The great author of the spirit of laws, pretends that Alexander, "assumed the manners of the Persians, that he might not chagrin them too much by obliging them to conform to those of the Greeks, [a] and Arrian hath likewise apologized for the Macedonian Monarch's conduct on this occasion, [b] but it is still liable to

---

[a] Zend-Avesta. Tom. 3.--607. This sacred fire, immediately preceded the Persian monarchs in their processions, as may be learned from Xenophon: "Και πυρ οπισθεν αυτε επ'εσχαρας μεγαλης ανδρες εποντο φεροντες. Επι δε τετοις, ηδη α:τ℥. εκ των πυλων πρεφαινετο ὁ Κυρ℥." (Cyropædia. Lib. 8.--595.) and Ammian. Marcellinus informs us it was supposed to have originally fallen from heaven. "Feruntque si justum est credi, etiam ignem cælitus lapsum apud se sempiternis foculis custodiri, cujus portionem exiguam ut faustam præiisse quondam Asiaticis regibus dicunt." Lib. 23. C. 6.--406.

[a] Nugent's Translation. Vol. 1.--212. "Il prit les mœurs des Perses, pour ne pas desoler des Perses, en leur faisant prendre les mœurs des Grecs." Montesquieu, de l'Esprit des Loix. Lib. 10. C. 14. Tom. 1.--198.

[b] "Ὡς εμοιγε κ̣ ἡ Περσικη σκευη σοφισμα ειναι δοκει, προς τε τυς βαρβαρυς, ὡς μη παντη αλλοτριον αυτων φαινεσθαι τον βασιλεα· κ̣ προς τυς Μακεδονας, ὡς αποστροφην τινα ειναι αυτω απο της οξυτητ℥. τε κ̣ ὑβρεως Μακεδονικης." (Arrian. Lib. 7. C. 29.--544, 545.) Yet the Macedonian troops had openly expressed strong symptoms of dissatisfaction, at their Monarch's adoption of the Persian dress and luxury. "Hoc luxu et peregrinis infecta moribus veteres Philippi milites, rudis natio ad voluptates, palam aversabatur, totisque castris unus omnium sensus ac sermo erat, plus amissum victoria quam bello quæsitum esse. Tum maxime vinci ipsos, dedique alienis moribus et externis: tantæ moræ pretium, domos quasi in captivo habitu reversuros: pudere jam sui. Regem victis quam victoribus similiorem ex Macedoniæ imperatore Darii satrapen factum." (Q. Curtius. Lib. 6. C. 6. Tom. 1.--427, 428.) The reasons for their dissatisfaction, Q. Curtius had before explained

to objection. The adoption of the customs of a conquered nation, is a kind of insult on the victorious troops, and destroys at once the happy confidence of superiority, which is the life of military enthusiasm, and the first cause of those powerful exertions, which are generally decisive and successful. Asiatic luxury and the Eastern manners, could not fail of enervating the courage of the Macedonian army, and of stifling that noble ardour, which is fanned into a blaze by the reaction of the soul, on the objects, which have forcibly affected it. "It was not prudent," as an able politician hath observed, "to shock the Macedonians, in order to gratify the Persians. Wherever the manners of a conquered nation are adopted by the conquerors, their ruin follows, and is certain. Is it possible that Alexander was either ignorant of this common maxim, or considered the degradation and corruption of the Macedonians as the foundation of his power? the Asiatics, who had been used to creep under the yoke of despotism, might submit to their chains with some docility, but the Greeks must have required management." [c]

Alexander's historians have let only a few anecdotes escape from them, that bare to open to view the vices of their Hero, which
it

ed to us. "Persarum spolia gestare dicebat: sed cum illis quoque mores induerat: superbiamque habitus animi insolentia sequebatur." Lib. 6. C. 6. Tom. 1.--425.

[c] "Pour plaire aux Perses etoit-il prudent de choquer les Macedoniens? Donner aux vainqueurs les mœurs des vaincus, c'est preparer leur ruin: c'st la rendre certaine; et l'on veut qu' Alexandre, ignorant cette verite commune, ait regardé la corruption et l'avilissement des Macedoniens comme le fondement de sa puissance: les Asiatiques accoutumès à ramper sous les despotisme, devoient porter leur chaine avec docilité; les Grecs seuls meritoient des menagements."
Observ. sur l'Hist. de la Grece, par M. l'Abbe Mably. 225, &c.

it was their conftant ftudy to conceal. Arrian, though the leaft culpable [d] in this refpect, is not entirely excufable, but Ariftobulus hath the affurance to advance, that the Macedonian Monarch never exceeded in the pleafures of the table, except in compliment to his friends, and that he feldom made free with wine. [e] This is far from coinciding with the teftimony of many writers of Alexander's life, and the expreffions of Menander, [f] prove that the Prince's intemperance was even become proverbial. Chares of Mitylene relates, that the Macedonian Conqueror having ordered fome gymnaftic games on the funeral of Calanus, in which fome prizes were offered for the greateft drinkers, thirty-five of thefe heroes died in this honourable field of battle, and fix others expired a few moments afterwards in their tents. [g] Promachus carried off the firft prize which was a talent,

[d] Where Arrian could not defend, he has endeavoured to palliate.—See Exped. Alex. Lib. 7. C. 29, 30.--543——545.

[e] " Και δι ποτοι δι, ως λεγει Αριστοβυλ. Θ., ε τε οινε ενεκα μακροι κιτω εγιγνοντο (ε γαρ πινειν πολυν οινον Αλιξανδρον) αλλα φιλοφροσυνης της εις τες εταιρυς" (Arrian. Exped. Alex. Lib. 7. C. 29.--545.) " Ην δι κỳ προς οινον ητίον η εδοκει καταφερης· εδοξε δι δια τον χρονον· ον ε πινων μαλλον η λαλων ηλκιν, εφ' ικαστης κυλικ⊙· αιει μακρον τινα λογον διατιθιμεν⊙·, κỳ ταυτα, πολλης σχολης εσης." De Vit. Alex. Plut. Opera. Tom. 1.--677.

[f] " Μιναδρ⊙ δ'εν Κολακι φησι,
       Κοτυλας χωρων δεκα εν Καππαδοκια
       Κυθυλον χρυσων στεθια τρις επιον μεστον γε
       Αλιξανδρου πλιον πεπωκας τε βασιλεως·
       Ουκ ελατίον ε μα την Αθηνην μεγαγε"
                    Athenæus. Lib. 10.--434.

[g] " Χαρης δ'ο Μιτυληναι⊙ εν ταις περι Αλεξανδρον ιστοριαις, περ. Καλανε ειπων τε Ινδε φιλοσοφη,——ότι κỳ επι τω μνηματι αυτε διεθηκεν Αλιξανδρ⊙ γυμνικον αγωνα και μεσικον εγκωμιων· εθηκε δι φησι κỳ δια την φιλοινιαν των Ινδων, κỳ ακροποσιας αγωνα· κỳ ην αθλον τω μεν πρωτω ταλαντον, τω δε δευτερα τριακοντα

talent.——Nicobulus assures us also, that Alexander at a supper with Medius, drank as much as twenty other guests who partook of the entertainment, and that on retiring he fell into a profound sleep,[h] a strong symptom undoubtedly of sobriety.

Plutarch recedes the least from his professed character of Alexander's apologist, and he would have us to believe, that the Prince highly disapproved of the effeminacy of Agnon and Philotas.[i] Ælian in opposition tells us, that he had personally corrupted them,[k] and the opinion is confirmed by the testimony of Agatharcides of Gnidus,[l] and the letter, which Alexander wrote to the inhabitants

κοιτα μναις, κỳ τω τριτω δεκα· των αν πιοντων τον οινον παραχρημα μεν ετελευτησαν ὑπο τη ψυχης τριακοντα και πεντε· μικρον δε διαλιποντες εν ταις σκηναις εξ· ὁ δε πλειςον πιων κỳ νικησας επιι μεν ακρατα χοας τεσσαρας· εκαλειτο δε Προμαχ⊕· (Athenæus. Lib. 10.——436, 437.) The Χοαι τεσσαρες were something short of two gallons, but the prowess of Proteas was as remarkable. Athenæus. Lib. 10.——434.

[h] " Νικοβελη δε ———— φησιν, ὁτι παρα Μεδειω τω Θεσσαλω δειπνων Αλεξανδρ⊕., εικοσιν ησιν εν τω συμποσιω, πασιν προυπιε παρα παντων τα ισα λαμβανων, κỳ ανασας τε συμποσιη, μιτ' ε πολυ ανεπαιετο." Athenæus. Lib. 10.——434.

[i] " Επει δε της περι αυτον ἑωρα παντα πασιν εκτετρυφηκοτας, κỳ φορτικης ταις διαιταις, κỳ πολιτελειαις οντας, ὡςε Αγνωνα μεν Τηιον αργυρης εν ταις κρηπισιν ἡλης φορειν, Λεοννατω δε πολλαις καμηλοις απ' Αιγυπτη κονιν εις τα γυμνασια παρακομιζεσθαι, Φιλωτα δε, προς θηρας ςαδιων ἑκατον αυλαιας γιγονεναι, μυρω δε χρομενες ιεναι προς αλειμμα κỳ λετρον ὁσες ηδε ελαιω, τριπτας δε κỳ κατευνασας περιαγομενες· επιτιμησιν πραως, κỳ φιλοσοφως· (De Vit. Alex. Plut. Opera. Tom. 1.——688.) Athenæus gives nearly the same ostentatious account, (Lib. 12.——539.) from whom it descended most probably to Plutarch and Ælian.

[k] " Ὁτι διεθρυπτε της ἑταιρης Αλεξανδρ⊕., τερφαν επιχωρων αυτοις· Ειγε κỳ Αγνων χρυσης ἡλης εν ταις κρηπισιν εφορει." (Ælian. Var. Hist. Lib. 9. C. 3. Tom. 1.——570.) Whether these nails or studs were golden ones or silver ones, the vanity of Agnon was equally ridiculous.

[l] " Αγαθαρχιδης δε ὁ Κνιδι⊕. εν ογδοη Ασιατικων ιςορει, ὡς οι ιςιωντες Αλεξανδρον τον Φιλιππε των φιλων,

inhabitants of Ionia, and his orders for a quantity of purple, with which he meant to clothe his friends.ᵐ Inſtead of laying any reſtraint on luxury, it was authorized by his own example, and, according to Phylarchus, the daily expences of the Royal houſehold were enormous.ⁿ The Prince's tent alone contained a hundred beds, the pillars which ſupported them were incruſted with gold, and the ceiling was beautified and embelliſhed with the ſame extravagance.° When he gave audience, he was ſeated on a throne of gold, ſurrounded with numerous guards, and Iphippus of Olinthus adds, that the floor was ſprinkled with delicious liquors and perfumes, and that myrrh and all kinds of the moſt odoriferous incenſe were burnt before him.ᵖ This is certainly no

I i proof

λων, το μᾶλλον παρατεθησεσθαι των τρωγηματων περιχρυσων· οτε δε θελοιεν αναλισκειν, περιελοντες τον χρυ-σον αμα τοις αλλοις εξεβαλον, ινα της μεν πολυτελειας οι φιλοι διαται γινωνται, οι δε οικεται κυριοι.'' Athenæus. Lib. 4.---155.

ᵐ "Εγραψε δε κ τοτε Αλεξανδρς ταις εν Ιωνια πολεσιν, κ πρωτοις Χιοις, οπως αυτω πορφυραν αποςτιλω-σιν· ηθελε γαρ τυς εταιρυς απαντας αλυργας ενδυσαι ςολας.'' Athenæus. Lib. 12.---539, 510.

ⁿ Athenæus. Lib. 12.---539.

° "Αυτω δε Αλεξανδρω η μεν σκηνη ην κλιναι εκατον· χρυσοι δε κιονες πεντηκοντα διειληφεσαν αυτην, κ την οροφον αυτης ανειχον· Αυτθ δε ο οροφθ διαχρυσθ ην, κ εκπεπονητο ποικιλμασι πολυτελισι· κ πρω-τοι μεν Περσαι πεντακοσιοι, οι καλυμενοι Μηλοφοροι, περι αυτην εςτθ εςηκεσαν, πορφυρας κ μηλινας εσθημενοι ςολας· επ'αυτοις δε τοξαται χιλιοι, φλογινα ενδεδυκοτες κ ισγινοβαφη· προ δε τυτων οι αργυρασ-πιδες πεντακοσιοι Μακεδονες· Εν μεση δε τη σκηνη χρυσες ετιθετο διφρθ, κ επ'αυτυ καθημενθ Αλεξανδρθ εχρηματιζε, περιεςωτων αυτω παντοθεν των σωματοφυλακων. Περιηει δε την σκηνην περιβολθ, ενθα ησαν Μακεδονες χιλιοι, κ Περσαι μυριοι." (Ælian. Var. Hiſt. Lib. 9. C. 3.---571, 572, 573.) See alſo Athenæus. Lib. 12.---539.

ᵖ "Εθυεν δε ο Αλεξανδρς κ μυρω σπυδαιω, κ οινα ευωδη το δαπεδον εθυμιατο δε απ'τω συιερα, κ τα αλλα θυμιαματα." Athenæus. Lib. 12.---537, 538.

proof of Alexander's moderation in his pleasures, of which Arrian[q] wishes to persuade us, and is not calculated to authenticate what Montesquieu afferts. "He[r] was close and reserved in his private expences————In regulating his household, he was the private Macedonian."[s] It seems extraordinary, that this acute and penetrating writer should have imagined Alexander found the means of augmenting his power by his strict frugality, and of furnishing himself with resources from his private œconomy. Such perhaps might have been the case when he first commenced hostilities against the Persian empire, and his policy, and even his necessities pointed out to him a line of conduct very different from that, which he followed after the battle of Gaugamele. From this period of his life, he displayed a luxurious parade and pomp, which equally insulted the severer manners of his own country, and the misfortunes of the people that he had conquered. Nothing had perhaps hitherto reached the magnificence on the celebration of the marriages between the Macedonians and the Persian women. No less than ninety-two nuptial beds were prepared in one spacious chamber, and the coverture of each was valued at twenty minæ.[t]—Alexander's was distinguished by feet of

---

[q] "Χρημάτων δε ες μεν ηδονας τας αυτυ, φειδωλοτατ⊙· ες δε ευποιιαν των πελας, αφθονωτατ⊙·" Arrian. Exped. Alex. Lib. 7. C. 28.--543.

[r] "Sa main se fermoit pour les depenses privées————falloit-il regler sa maison? C'etoit un Macedonien." Montesquieu de l'Esprit des Loix. Livre 10. C. 14.--200.

[s] Nugent's Translation. Vol. 1.--214.

[t] 64ℓ. 11s. 8d. sterling.

of folid gold.—All the courtiers and a great number of ſtrangers were invited to the entertainment on this occaſion, and it was given in a tent, ſupported by columns nearly thirty feet in height, plated with gold and ſparkling with jewels and precious ſtones.ᵛ The ableſt tragedians and comedians, and moſt celebrated muſicians aſſiſted at the feſtival, and Athenæus hath preſerved their names which he extracted from Chares, as well as the particulars that have been mentioned.ʷ

Plutarch hath endeavoured to frame ſome little excuſe for Alexander's adoption of the manners and habits of the nations that he conquered, and attempts to juſtify him, by ſaying, the dreſs which he made uſe of was a medium between that of Perſia and of Media.ˣ

But

ᵛ "Χαρης δ'εν τη δεκατη των περι Αλεξανδρον ιστοριων, οτε φησιν, ηλε Δαρειον, γαμους συντελεσιν εαυτε, κ̣ των αλλων φιλων ενενηκοντα κ̣ δυο θαλαμης κατασκευασαμενϑ· εν τω αυτω τοπω· ην δε ο οικϑ. εκατοντακλινϑ., εν ω εκαστη την κλινη, κεκοσμημενη ςολη γαμικη εικοσι μνων αργυρων, η δε αυτε χρυσοπες ην· συμπεριλαϐι δε εις το συμποσιον, κ̣ τες ιδιοξενες απαντας· κ̣ κατεκλινεν αντιπροσωπες εαυτω τε κ̣ τοις αλλοις νυμφιοις την τε λοιπην δυναμιν, πεζην τε και ναυτικην, και τας πρεσϐειας, και τες παρεπιδημευντας εν τη αυλη. κατεσκευασο δε ο οικϑ. πολυτελως και μεγαλοπρεπως ιματιοις τε και οθονιοις πολυτελεσιν· υπο δε ταυτα πορφυροις και φοινικοις χρυσυφεσιν· τα δε μενειν την σκηνην υπεκειν το κιονες εικοσιπηχεις περιχρυσοι κ̣ διαλιθοι κ̣ περιαργυροι· περιϐεϐληντο δ'εν τω περιϐολω πολυτελεις αυλαιαι ζωντοι, και διαχρυσοι, κανονας εχουσαι περιχρυσους κ̣ περιαργυρες· της δε αυλης ην το περιμετρον σαδιοι τεσσαρες·" Athenæus. Lib. 12.—538.

ʷ "Les plus habiles hiſtoriens et les muſiciens celeb.es." The band, according to Athenæus, (Lib. 12.--538, 539.) conſiſted of the "Θαυματοποιοι, Ραψωδϑ., Φιλοκιθαρισαι, Αυλωδοι, Αυληται, Διονυσοκολακες, Αλεξανδροκολακες, Τραγωδαι, Κωμωδοι, Ψαλτης," and ſome chorus-ſingers and vocal performers. The hiſtorians are not mentioned, and I have omitted them. The Baron de St. Croix may have perhaps included them under the Ραψωδϑ.

ˣ "Ενεδυσατο την βαρϐαρικην ςολην, ειτε βελομενϑ. αυτον συνοικειων τοις επιχωριοις νομοις, ως μεγα προς εξημερωσιν ανθρωπων το συνηθες κ̣ ομοφυλον· ειτ'αποπειρα τις υδειτο της προσκυνησεως αυτη τοις Μακεδο-

But the Conqueror carried his extravagance much further, and Iphippus of Olinthus relates, that he sometimes appeared at thefe feſtive entertainments in purple, with the horns of Jupiter Ammon, and that he was drawn in a car with a Perſian mantle over his ſhoulders, and the quiver of Diana at his back. Amongſt his friends he appeared ſometimes like Mercury, with feathers to his heels and a Caduceus in his hand, which he exchanged for the lion's ſkin and club of Hercules.[y] "Hills and mountains," obſerves Plutarch, "are not eaſily taken by ſtratagem or ambuſcade, but a weak mind, ſwoln big and lofty by fortune, birth, or the like, lies naked to the aſſaults of every mean and petty aggreſſor."[z] Alexander was ſoon captivated with the groſſeſt flattery, and his deſpotic temper prevented his friends from approaching him either with freedom or ſincerity. Maximus Tyrius ſeems to indicate,

οτι, κατα μικρον ανεσχισθαι την εκδιαιτησιν αυτε κ̄ μεταβολην εθιζομενοις· 8 μην την γε Μηδικην περιηκατο παντάπασιν, βαρβαρικην κ̄ αλλοκοτον εσαν, εδε αναξυριδας, εδε κανδυν, εδε τιαραν ελαβεν, αλλα εν μεσω τινα της Περσικης κ̄ της Μηδικης, μιξαμενθ- ευπως, ατυφοτεραν μεν εκεινης, ταυτης δε σοβαρωτεραν εσαν." De Vit. Alex. Plut. Opera. Tom. 1.--690.

[y] "Εφ.ιππθ- δε φησιν, ως Αλεξανδρθ- κ̄ τας ιερας εσθητας εφορει εν τοις δειπνοις, οτι μεν την τα Αμμωνθ- πορφυριδα, κ̄ περισχιδεις κ̄ κερατα, καθαπερ ο Θεθ-· οτε δε κ̄ της Αρτεμιδθ-, ην κ̄ επι τα αρματθ- εφορει, πολλακις την Περσικην ςολην υποφαινων ανωθεν των ωμων, το τε τοξον κ̄ την σιβυνην· ενιοτε δε κ̄ την τα Ερμε τα μεν αλλα σχεδον——— ——εν δε τη συνεσια τα τε πεδιλα, κ̄ τον πετασον επι τη κεφαλη, κ̄ το κηρυκειον εν τη χειρι, πολλακις δε λεοντην κ̄ ροπαλον ωσπερ ο Ηρακλης." Athenæus. Lib. 12.--537.

[z] Plutarch's Morals. Vol. 2.--195. 8vo Edit. 1704. "Των μεν γαρ τοπων τα υψηλα δυσπροσοδα και δυσεφικτα γενοντο τοις επιβελιεσι· το δε εν ψυχη νεν εκ εχεσι δι'αυτυχιαν η δι'ευφυιαν υψθ- και φρονημα, τοις μικροις και ταπεινοις μαλιςα βατιμον εςι." Plutarch. De Adul. et Amic. Diſcrim. Tom. 2.--65.

cate, that this was one principal reason of the rapid progress, which adulation made amongst the Macedonians. "When fear and tyranny prevail, adulation," in the words of the philosopher, "regularly flourishes, and friendship descends into the grave."[a] Iphippus of Olinthus informs us, that Alexander's best friends were under the necessity of applauding what they could not approve; and in those riotous excesses, which tarnished the Prince's glory, they observed a profound silence, from the apprehension of increasing his outrageous passions, or affording him any pretext to indulge his favourite propensity of shedding human blood.[b] Lucian assures us likewise, that calumny and flattery had a ready access to the Macedonian Monarch;[c] and Anaxarchus, to console him for the murder of Clitus, defended in his presence the execrable maxim that justice had no other rule than the will of kings.[d] "This miserable Sophist was one of the most distinguished of the infamous band of Medeus, that arch parasite and enemy to the Macedonian nobility, and chief of all that numerous train which Alexander entertained in his court. This man taught his disciples

to

---

[a] "Οπυ γαρ δεος και εξυσια διασποτικη το αρχομενον αγχει αναγκη οιιρο κολακειαν μεν αυξειν, φιλιαν δε καταφωρυχθαι." Maximus Tyrius. Tom. 1.--393. Ed. Reiske. 8vo Lips. 1774.

[b] "Ευφημια τε και σιγη κατειχε παντας υπο δεος τας παροντας· αφορητ⊙ γαρ ην, και φονικ⊙." Athenæus. Lib. 12.--538.

[c] "Η γυν κολακεια και η διαβολη τοτε μαλιστα χωραν ισχε πρ⊙ το Αλεξανδρυ παθ⊙ συντιθεμεν." Lucian. Calumn. non tem. cred. Tom. 3.--150.

[d] "Την δικην εχει παρεδρον ο Ζευς, και την Θεμιν, ινα παν το παραχθεν υπο τυ κρατυντ⊙ θεμιτον η και δικαιον; τοιυτοις τισι λογοις χρησαμεν⊙ Αναξαρχ⊙, το μεν παθ⊙ εκυφισε τυ βασιλεως, το δε ηθος εις πολλα χαυνοτερον ϗ παρανομωτερον εποιησεν." De Vit. Alex. Plut. Opera. Tom. 1.--695.

to slander boldly, and push home their calumnies; for though the wound might probably be cured and skinned over again, yet the teeth of slander would be sure to leave a scar behind them: by these scars (or to speak more properly) gangrenes and cancers of false accusations, fell the brave Callisthenes, Parmenio, and Philotas, whilst he himself became an easy prey to an Agnon, Bagoas, Agesias and Demetrius, who tricked him up like a barbarian statue or antick, and paid the mortal, the adoration due to a God."ᵉ This gloomy picture of the effects of adulation on Alexander's conduct, must notwithstanding be correct, as it comes from the hand of Plutarch. It may be more easily relied on, as he is always disposed to palliate the Macedonian Monarch's excesses, and would willingly persuade us, that he courageously resisted the solicitations of Agnon and Philoxenus, when they would have seduced him into some unnatural sensualities.ᶠ But admitting these sycophants

to

ᵉ Plutarch's Morals. Vol. 2.--134, 135. "Ην δε ο Μηδιος τε περι Αλεξανδρον χορε των κολακων οιον εξαρχος, και σοφιστης κορυφαιος επι τους αριστους συντεταγμενος· εκελευεν αν θαρρυντας, απτεσθαι και δακνειν ταις διαβολαις, διδασκων οτι και θεραπευτε το ελκος ο δεδηγμενος, η υλη μενει της διαβολης. ταυταις μεν τοι ταις ηλαις, μαλλον δε γαγγραιναις, και καρκινωμασι διαβρωθεις Αλεξανδρος, απωλεσε και Καλλισθενη, και Παρμενιωνα και Φιλωταν· Αγνωσι δε και Βαγωαις και Αγησιαις και Δημητριοις αφειδως ενδωκεν εαυτον υποσκελιζεσθαι, προσκυνουμενος και καταστολιζομενος και αναπλαττομενος υπ' αυτων ώσπερ αγαλμα βαρβαρικον." (Plut. De Adult. et Amici. Discrim. Tom. 2.--65.) Monsieur de Theil hath added to his translation of this part of Plutarch's Works, some curious observations upon the ancient Parasites.

ᶠ "Φιλοξενος —————— εγραψε ειναι παρ' αυτω Θεοδωρον τινα Ταραντινον, εχοντα παιδας ωνιους δυο, την οψιν υπερφυεις, και συνδανομενος ει πριηται, χαλεπως ενεγκων, ίδοι πολλακις προς τους φιλους, ερωτων τι πωποτε Φιλοξενος αισχρον αιτω συνεγνωκως, τοιαυτα ονειδη προξενων καθηται· τον δε Φιλοξενον αυτον εν επιστολη πολλα λοιδορησας, εκελευεν αυτοις φορτιοις τον Θεοδωρον εις τον ολεθρον αποστελλειν· επεπληξεν δε και Αγνωνι νεανισκω, γραψαντι προς αυτον, ότι Κρωβυλον ευδοκιμενται εν Κορινθω, βελεται πριαμενος αγαγειν προς αυτον." De Vit. Alex. Plut. Opera. Tom. 1.--676, 677.

to have had the power of exciting the Prince to the destruction of his ablest generals, and most faithful friends, we may easily conceive their influence must have been as fatal, when they offered to him new symptoms of criminal debauchery.

The shameful passion of the Greeks for unnatural vices ᶻ was a matter of public notoriety, and little doubt can remain of the infamous commerce between the Macedonian Monarch and the Eunuch Bagoas. Dicearchus informs us, that he embraced him in the most lascivious and indecent manner in the theatre, before a crowded audience, which far from blushing at the scandalous transaction,

z Some learned men have endeavoured to rescue several of the great characters of Antiquity from this detestable suspicion, (See Toup. Appendicula Not. atque Emend. in Theocritum. 26. ---Potter's Grecian Antiq. Book 4. C. 2. Vol. 2.--390.---Philo. De vitâ contemplativâ.--- Max. Tyrius. Differt. 8, 9, 10, 11.---Hist. of Athens. 321.) and to explain away the appendant tribe of young men and boys, celebrated for their beauty, that constantly clung around them. Many virtuous individuals must certainly have risen superior to the general depravity, and the young men, under their patronage, must have been trained up to every thing that was good or great; but whilst such practices and such premiums existed, as Moschus and Theocritus have described,

" Και παιδων ιδιδασκε φιληματα·———"

Moschi Idyll. 3.--84.--28. Oxon. 8ᵛᵒ 1748.

" Αιεν δι περι τυμβον αολλεις παρι πρωτω
Κεροι εριδμαινεσι φιληματος ακρα φερεσθαι·
'Ος δε κε προσμαξη γλυκερωτερα χειλεσι χειλη
Βριθομενος στεφανοισιν ἱην προς μητερ'απηνθεν·
Ολβιος, όστις παισι φιληματα κεινα διαιτα·
Η πε τον χαροπον Γανυμηδεα πολλ' επιβωςρει,
Λυδιη ισον εχειν πιτρη στομα·———"

Theocrit. Id. 12.--30. Tom. 1.--55. Oxon. 4ᵗᵒ 1770.

it is in vain to combat, by any arguments, the " Ελληνικον τροπον" and the profligacy of those licentious times. Athenæus tells us, without equivocation, " Ολως δε τες παιδικες ερωτας των επι ταις θηλειαις προκρινεσι πολλοι," and he adds, to shew its notoriety, "Παρα γαρ ταις αλλαις ταις ενιομεμιναις πολισιν επι της Ελλαδος σπεδασθηναι το δε το ιδθ.." (Lib. 13. Tom. 1.--601.) There is not a more infamous acknowledgment upon Record!

transaction, testified its satisfaction by a very general applause.' The severe observations of Orsines, respecting this Eunuch, in Q. Curtius,' evidently prove the unnatural connection between his master and the Catamite; but the Latin historian, with unaccountable inconsistency, afterwards asserts, that Alexander in his sensual gratifications had not strayed beyond the bounds of nature, or wandered into forbidden paths.ᵏ

Alexander's humanity to the nations, that he conquered, hath been boasted of, but it is sometimes problematical. Many actions of his life demonstrate to a certainty, that in the latter period of his reign he had forgotten the clemency, with which in an early stage of glory and of victory, he had soothed the misfortunes of the different people, over whom he triumphed. Vanity and political finesse might have perhaps suggested to him

such

ʰ "Φιλοπαις δε ην εκμανως κỳ Αλεξανδρ⊕· ὁ βασιλευς· Δικαιαρχ⊕· γυν εν τω περι της εν Ιλιω θυσιας, Ηγωμα τε ευνουχη ετως αυτον φησι πρασθαι, ὡς εν οψει θεατρη ὁλη καταφιλειν αυτον ανακλασαντα, κỳ των θεατων επιφωνησαντων μετα κροτε εκ απειθησας, παλιν ανεκλασας εφιλησεν." Athenæus. Lib. 13. Tom. 1.--603.

ⁱ "Les reproches qu'Orsines fait dans Quinte Curce à cet eunuque." I have made a trifling alteration in the sense of this sentence, as the only reproach, which Orsines personally made to Bagoas was the " Audieram in Asiâ olim regnasse Feminas; hoc vero novum est, regnasse Castratum." (Q. Curt. Lib. 10. C. 1. Tom. 2.--755.) To a friend, who wished to put him on his guard against the Eunuch's machinations, with more caustic acrimony, he had previously observed, "Amicos regis, non scorta se colere." Q. Curt. Lib. 10. C. 1. Tom. 2.--752.

ᵏ "Veneris intra naturale desiderium usus, nec ulla nisi ex permisso voluptas." (Q. Curtius. Lib. 10. C. 5. Tom. 2.--786.) I am utterly unable to reconcile the "Naturale desiderium" with the " Bagoæ spadoni, qui Alexandrum obsequio corporis devinxerat sibi." Q. Curt. Lib. 10. C. 1, Tom. 2.--751.

such a laudable and advantageous line of conduct, at the outset of his military career, and the mask dropped when it was no longer neceſſary. True virtue, which really ſprings from the heart, ſeldom varies, but continues to animate the boſom, until it ceaſes to throb itſelf. The devaſtation of the country of Sambus,¹ and that of the Pathalians;ᵐ the burning of the city of the Agalaſſians;ⁿ the crucifixion of the Indian prince Muſicanus,ᵒ and the puniſhment

---

¹ "Εξης δε την τε Σαμ6ου βασιλειαν εξεπορθησε κ᾽ τας πλειςας πολεις εξηνδραποδισαμεν۞ κ᾽ κατασκαπ-σας, κατεκοψε των Βαρβαρων υπερ τας οκτω μυριαδας." Diod. Sicul. Lib. 17. Tom. 2.--239.

ᵐ "In proximam gentem Pathaliam perventum eſt. Rex erat Mœris, qui urbe deſerta in montes profugerat. Itaque Alexander oppido potitur, agroſque populatur." (Q. Curtius. Lib. 9. C. 8. Tom. 2.--729.) Under the ſame circumſtances, perhaps the modern rules of war would authorize the ſame treatment. Arrian gives a very different account of the buſineſs. " Ὁ δε κατα διωξιν των φευγοντων εκπεμψας της ςρατιας της κουφοτατας, επει τινες αυτων ξυνεληφθησαν, αποπεμπει τουτυς παρα της αλλυς, εντειλαμενος επαινεται θαρρυντας εναι γαρ αυτοις την τε πολιν οικειν ως προσθεν, κ᾽ την χωραν εργαζεσθαι κ᾽ επαπηλθον οι πολλοι αυτων" Exped. Alex. Lib. 6. C. 18.--443.

ⁿ "Των δε αλλων εγχωριων συναθροισθεντων, δισμυριοι μεν καταφυγοντας εις πολιν μεγαλην κατα κρατος ειλε· των δε Ινδων διαφραξαντων τας ςενωπας, κ᾽ απο των οικιων μαχομενων πυρωςως, βιαζομενος απεβαλε των Μακεδονων ουκ ολιγους· δια δε την οργην εμπρησας την πολιν, συγκατεκαυσε τυς πλειςας" Diod. Sicul. Lib. 17. Tom. 2.--235.

ᵒ This unfortunate Indian prince had neglected, according to Arrian, the following duties either to Craterus, or his Royal maſter, "Ουπω απηντηκει αυτω Μυσικανος, ενδιδους αυτον τε κ᾽ την χωραν, ουτε πρεσβεις επι φιλια εκπεμπει, ουδε τι ουτι αυτ۞ επιπομπει, ἁ δη μεγαλυ βαςιλει εικ۞, ουτε τι ητηκει εξ Αλεξανδρυ" (Exped. Alex. Lib. 6. C. 15.--439.) Theſe offences were however afterwards forgiven, on the ſeveral expectations being fully gratified, and the Prince had his territories reſtored to him. A citadel was notwithſtanding built in the Prince's capital, and Craterus had the command of it. "Οτι επιτηδειον αυτω εφανη το χωριον ες το κατεχεσθαι τα κυκλω εθνη φυλαττομενα" (Exped. Alex. Lib. 6. C. 15.--440.) Whether Muſicanus was diſſatisfied with, or ill treated by this Grecian garriſon, we are not told, but he withdrew himſelf and ſoon appeared in arms. The iſſue of the conteſt was ſoon decided, and the Indian prince was brought a priſoner by Pytho, who

punishment of many Brahmins, whose only crime had been that of encouraging their countrymen to defend their liberty and laws; and, in a word, the destruction of many Indian cities, which had the courage either to oppose or retard the projects of the Macedonian Monarch, are not the most decisive specimens of his clemency.

After having granted terms to one of these cities and accepted its surrender, he fell upon a part of the garrison in its march, and slaughtered the whole of the detachment. Plutarch, from whom the fact is borrowed, admits it to have been a disgraceful stain in his Hero's [p] life, and he confesses also, that the Macedonian Monarch put, with his own hand, Orsidates to death, who had revolted against him, by piercing him with darts. [q]

Alexander's

---

who had been sent against him. The remainder of his history, is summed up by Arrian in a few lines. " Και τουτον κρεμασαι Αλεξανδρ⊕ κιλιυει εν τη αυτη γη, κ̧ των Βραχμανων οσοι αιτιοι της αποςασιως τω Μυσικανω κατιςησαν" Exped. Alex. Lib. 6. C. 17.--442.

[p] " Apres avoir accordé la paix a une ville Indienne, ce prince retourne bientot sur ses pas entre dans cette malheureuse cité, et en massacre tous les habitans." The following passage in Plutarch is referred to, " Επει δε των Ινδων οι μαχιμωτατοι μισθοφορυντες επιρριπτων ταις πολεσιν, ιρρωμενως αμυνοντες, κ̧ κατα πολλα τον Αλεξανδρον κακοποιουν, σπεισαμεν⊕ εν τινι πολει προς αυτους, απιοντας εν οδω λαβων, απαντας απεκτεινεν κ̧ τυτο τοις πολεμικοις εργοις αυτυ, ταλλα νομιμως κ̧ βασιλικως πολεμησαντ⊕, ως κηλις προσεςιν" (De Vit. Alex. Plut. Opera. Tom. 1.--698.) I need not, I apprehend, point out the propriety of the alteration.

[q] " Και των αποςαντων Βαρβαρων Ορσοδατην αυτ⊕ κατετοξευσιν" (De Vit. Alex. Plut. Opera. Tom. 2.--697.) The Baron de St. Croix, in all likelihood, overlooked the passage in Plutarch, where Alexander ordered that quarter was not to be given, merely from political motives. " Φονον μεν ουν ενταυθα πολυν των αλισκομενων γενεσθαι συνεπεσεν" γραφει γαρ αυτ⊕ ως νομιζων αυτω τυτο λυσιτελειν, εκελευεν αποσφατεισθαι τυς ανθρωπυς." De Vit. Alex. Plut. Opera. Tom. 1.--686.

OF ALEXANDER THE GREAT. 251

Alexander's cruelty is strongly marked by the pointed energy of the Scriptural expression, which hath lost much of its original force in its transition into another language.' The profane writers have, notwithstanding, concealed and kept back from public view the representation of the bloody scenes, which passed at a distance, though the truth sometimes escapes them, and Arrian honestly avows his inclination for very severe, as well as disproportionate punishments.'

The Gentoo annals mention the Conqueror of Asia, and have bestowed on him the terms of "most mighty robber and murderer;" but most of the Oriental traditions have supposed him to have been beneficent and humane. Yet the Indians in all probability formed their opinions from comparisons, and the misery, which

they

' "Interfecit" is employed by the Vulgate, and our English version hath, " he flew the kings of the earth." Neither of these expressions may possibly convey the full sense of the "ισφαξι," the Greek word "σφαζω" or "σφαττω" being properly rendered, "macto, jugulo, immolo."

' "L'inclination qu'Alexandre avoit pour les executions sanguinaires." "Ου μη αλλα κ αυτ<i>-Αλεξανδρ<i>- οξυτις<i>- λεγεται γινεσθαι εν τω τοτε ες το πιςευσαι τε τοις επικαλουμενοις, ως πιθανοις ον εν παντι ουσι' κ ιπι το τιμωρησεσθαι μεγαλως τες επι μικροις εξελεγχθεντας." Arrian. Lib. 7. C. 4.—483.

' "Mhaabah, Dukkoyt é Kooneah." (Holwell's interesting Events relative to the Provinces of Bengal, Part 2, 4.) We learn also from Chardin, that "les Parses ou Guebres au lieu d'admirer ce Prince, et de reverer son nom, comme font tant d'autres peuples, le mepiisent, le detestent, le maudissent, le regardent comme un pirate, un brigand, comme un homme sans justice et sans cervelle, né pour troubler l'ordre du monde et pour detruire une partie du genre humain." Voyages en Perse. Tom. 2.--185. Ed. 4to

they personally suffered, might have recalled their attention from that, which their ancestors had experienced under the Macedonian arms. Since the reign of Mahmoud in the eleventh age, who subdued India, and treated the natives with the rigour of an exasperated conqueror, and the inhumanity of a fanatic, these mild and inoffensive people have been accustomed to the horrid ravages of war, and to an unvarying repetition of pillage, flames, and bloodshed. Such were the certain and terrible effects of the different invasions of their country, and reasoning from these scourges of human life, they considered Alexander as a conqueror of extraordinary moderation, and even attributed to him the most remarkable and magnificent monuments in that vast country.* The Persians, however, had serious and substantial reasons to consecrate the Macedonian Monarch's memory in their annals. When he became possessed of the Persian empire, prosperity had not corrupted him with its baneful influence, and the Conqueror of Darius treated his new subjects with a gentleness and lenity, till then unknown, under any violent change of government. But the condition of Persia was not improved, and it received no benefit or advantage whatever from the Grecian conquest. It continued to be governed by a despot, and suffering the vexations of rapacious officers, was also exposed to every shock of the succeeding revolutions, without having either its chains loosened, or their galling weight diminished.

Q.

---

* Zend-Avesta, par Anquetil. Tom. 1.--392.

Q. Curtius hath been accused,[x] with injustice, of having written the panegyric of Alexander rather than his life, as the ingenious writer hath both frequently brought forward, and stated with impartiality, his faults and crimes. The Prince, he says, abandoned himself, after the change in his character, to a system of voluptuousness, and though the Persians could not prevail against him, he was conquered by his own vices.[y] Feasts, festivals, and games, became the common occupations of the Conqueror of Asia, who passed whole nights in drunkenness and debauchery.[z] The same historian, in another part of his work, informs us, that Alexander's character was totally altered, and that the moderation and continence, which he had professed, were succeeded by intemperance and pride. His palace was filled with three hundred and sixty concubines, and the guard of the seraglio was composed of a troop of Eunuchs.[a] These anecdotes, and others of the same tendency, that are suppressed, are not usually introduced into a panegyric; and

---

[x] Clerici Judicium de Q. Curtio. 9.

[y] " Sed ut primum instantibus curis laxatus est animus, militarium rerum quam quietis otiique patientior ; excepere eum voluptates ; et quem arma Persarum non fregerant, vitia vicerunt."
Q. Curt. Lib. 6. C. 2. Tom. 1.--395.

[z] " Intempestiva convivia, et perpotandi pervigilandique insana dulcedo, ludique et greges pellicum.————intempestivis conviviis dies pariter noctesque consumeret ; satietatem epularum ludis interpolabat." Q. Curtius. Lib. 6. C. 2. Tom. 1.--395.

[a] " Hic vero palam cupiditates suas solvit, continentiamque et moderationem, in altissimâ quâque fortunâ eminentia bona, in superbiam ac lasciviam vertit. Patrios mores disciplinamque Macedonum regum salubriter temperatam, et civilem habitum, velut leviora magnitudine suâ ducens ; Persicæ regiæ, par Deorum potentiæ fastigium æmulabatur. Jacere humi venerabundos pati cœpit.

and we cannot rationally suppose from them, that Alexander, even in the conflagration of his passions, was conducted by the flash of reason, that Montesquieu[b] hath spoken of, "which those who would fain make a romance of his history, and whose minds were more corrupt than his, could not conceal from our view."[c]

Q. Curtius is undoubtedly alluded to, and he little deserves such a sarcastic animadversion, for having faithfully exposed the conduct of this Prince.

Notwithstanding the charge of an unjustifiable partiality for the Macedonian Monarch in Q. Curtius, he may be suspected, on the contrary, of having imagined some circumstances, that have affected his reputation. The death of Orsines is of the number. This illustrious Persian, of high birth and dignity, made some presents, as we are told, to the Conqueror of Asia, and the principal courtiers, amongst whom Bagoas was either omitted or forgotten. The exasperated Eunuch could not pardon the indignity, and in revenge for the supposed affront, he accused Orsines of the pillage

---

cæpit.————superbiamque habitus animi insolentia sequebatur.——Pellices C. C. C. et sexaginta, totidem qui Darii fuerant, regiam implebant, quas spadonum greges, et ipsi muliebria pati adsueti, sequebantur." Q. Curtius. Lib. 6. C. 6. Tom. 1.--424——426.

[b] "Qui ceux qui avoient voulu faire un Roman de son histoire, et qui avoient l'esprit plus gâté que lui n'ont pu nous derober." L'Esprit des Loix, Lib. 10. C. 13. Tom. 1.--196.

[c] Nugent's Translation, Vol. 1.--210.

pillage of the tomb of Cyrus, and assured his Royal Master, that the embezzled plunder, amounted to three thousand talents. The funeral monument was directed to be opened, and as it contained only two Scythian bows, a sabre, and a crown of gold, the Eunuch had the address to persuade Alexander of the truth of his assertions, and the unfortunate Persian was led to execution.[d]

The relation however of Q. Curtius, does not agree with that of any of the other historians.——Plutarch informs us, that Polymachus was condemned to death for the pillage of the tomb of Cyrus[e]; and Strabo believes a band of robbers were the authors of the crime, as they destroyed what they could not carry off.[f] Arrian pretends, that the Magi, who had the care of this monument, underwent the torture, though no discoveries were derived from it.[g] The last historian speaks afterwards of the punishment of Orsines, who had the government of Persia after the death of Phrasaortes, and was convicted of extortion, and of having plundered

---

[d] The story is told at some length, and with many interesting circumstances, by Q. Curtius. Lib. 10. C. 1. Tom. 2.--751——755.

[e] "Επειτα τον Κυρη ταφον διορωρυγμενον, απεκτεινε τον αδικησαντα· Και τοι Πελλαι‐ ην ου των ασημοτατων ὁ πλημμελησας, ονομα Πολυμαχ‐." De Vit. Alex. Plut. Opera. Tom. 1.--703.

[f] "Προνομευταν εργον ην, ουχι του Σατραπου, καταλιποντων ἁ μη δυνατον ην ῥᾳδιως εκκομιζι·"
Strabo. Lib. 15.--1061, 1062.

[g] "Αλεξανδρ‐ δε ξυλλαβων τυς Μαγυς τυς φυλακας τυ ταφυ εςρεβλωσιν, ὡς κατειπειν τυς δρασαντας· οἱ δε ουτε σφων ουτε αλλυ κατειπον ςρεβλυμενοι, υδε αλλη πη ξυνηλεγχοντο ξυνειδοτες τω εργω." Arrian. Exped. Alex. Lib. 6. C. 29.--473.

dered the temples and Royal tombs at Perſepolis,[h] monuments at a diſtance from that of Cyrus, who had choſen Paſagardis[i] for the place of his interment. Ariſtobulus hath given a deſcription of the place of ſepulchre, and Arrian[k] hath preſerved it.

The tomb of Cyrus was ſituated in a ſacred wood, watered by ſprings, that fertilized the earth, which was covered with thick rich graſs, and equalled that of the moſt beautiful meadows. In the midſt of the ſhady trees of this ſacred grove, a little edifice aroſe, to which only a narrow entrance opened. The aſhes of Cyrus were depoſited in a golden caſe within the building, and it contained alſo a couch with golden feet, a throne of gold, ſome ſplendid garments, and carpets of exquiſite workmanſhip, ſwords, collars, and jewels ſet in gold. A collection of ſuch riches is far from coinciding with the ſenſe of the epitaph, which Plutarch[l] hath

---

[h] "Κατα Οξεινε πολλοι λογοι ελιχθησαν προς Περσων, ὁς πεξι Περσων, επηδε Φρασαηρτης επιλευσε· κͅ εξηλεγχθη Οξεινης ιερα τι ότι σεσυληκε, κͅ ταφες βασιλικας, κͅ Περσων πολλας ότι ε ξυν δικη απεκτεινε· τετον μεν δη όις εταχθη ὑπο Αλεξανδρε εκρεμασαν." Arrian. Exped. Alex. Lib. 6. C. 30.--473.

[i] "Εις πασαργαδας ἡκε· κͅ τετο δ'ην βασιλειον αρχαιον· ενταυθα δε κͅ τον Κυρε ταφον ειδεν εν παραδεισω." Strabo. Lib. 15.--1061.

[k] "Περι αυτον αλσ⸫ εμπεφυτευσθαι δενδρων παντοιων, κͅ ὑδατι ειναι καταρρυτον κͅ ποαν βαθειαν πεφυκεναι εν τω λειμωνι ——————— ανωθεν δε οικημα επειναι λιθινον ειργασμενον, θυριδα εχον φερεσαν εσω ςενην, ως μολις αν ενι ανδρι ε μεγαλω, πολλα κακοπαθεντι παρελθειν· εν δε τω οικηματι πυελον χρυσην κεισθαι, ινα το σωμα τε Κυρε ετεθαπτο, κͅ κλινην παρα τη πυελω· ποδας δε ειναι τη κλινη χρυσας σφυρηλατες, κͅ ταπητα επιβλημα των Βαβυλωνιων, κͅ καινακας πορφυρες ὑποςρωννυσθαι· επειναι δε κͅ κανδυς, κͅ αλλες χιτωνας της βαβυλωνια εργασιας· κͅ αναξυριδες Μηδικαι κͅ ςολαι ὑακινθινοβαφες λεγει ότι εκειτο —————— κͅ ςρεπτοι κͅ ακινακαι, κͅ ενωτια χρυσα τι κͅ λιθων κολλητα· κͅ τραπιζα εκειτο." Arrian. Exped. Alex. Lib. 6. C. 29.--470, 471.

[l] "Ω ΑΝΘΡΩΠΕ, ΟΣΤΙΣ ΕΙ, ΚΑΙ ΠΟΘΕΝ 'ΗΚΕΙΣ ('ΟΤΙ ΜΕΝ ΓΑΡ 'ΗΕΕΙΣ ΟΙΔΑ) ΕΓΩ ΚΥΡΟΣ

hath tranfmitted to us. "Whoever thou art, and whenfoever thou comeſt, for come thou wilt, I am Cyrus, the founder of the Perſian empire; envy me not the little earth that covers my remains!" The modeſty of this infcription, in all probability, fuggeſted to Xenophon a hint for his fpeech of Cyrus, a few moments before he expired.ᵐ "My children, when I am no more, neither encloſe my body in gold nor filver, commit it as foon as poſſible to the earth, for there cannot be a greater happineſs than to mingle with the duſt."

By the Perſian cuſtoms, their kings had only the honour of fepulchres,ⁿ and their tombs, which are ſtill exiſting, are fituated to the Eaſt of the mountain of Iſtakhar, and have no refemblance with that, which Ariſtobulus hath defcribed, no more than thoſe of Naxi-Ruſtan.º The facred wood, with which he furrounds the tomb of Cyrus, betrays the falſity of the defcription. This mode

---

ΚΥΡΟΣ ΕΙΜΙ 'Ο ΠΕΡΣΑΙΣ ΚΤΗΣΑΜΕΝΟΣ ΤΗΝ ΑΡΧΗΝ· ΜΗ ΟΥΝ ΤΗΣ ΟΛΙΓΗΣ ΤΑΥΤΗΣ ΓΗΣ ΦΘΟΝΗΣΗΣ, 'Η ΤΟΥΜΟΝ ΣΩΜΑ ΠΕΡΙΚΑΛΥΠΤΕΙ." (De Vit. Alex. Plut. Opera. Tom. 1.--703.) Strabo (Lib. 15.--1062.) and Arrian (Lib. 6. C. 29.--472.) vary the concluding fentence of this epitaph. The former reads "Μη ϑ φϑονησεις," and the latter "Μη ϑ φϑονει μοι τϑ μνηματϑ·" which is more confiſtent with the relation of Ariſtobulus. Perhaps, however, the whole is a mere fiction.

ᵐ "Το δ'εμον σωμα, ω παιδες, οταν τελευτησω, μητε εν χρυσω, ϑητι, μητε εν αργυρω, μηδε εν αλ-λω μηδενι· αλλα τη γη ὡς ταχιςα αποδοτι· τι γαρ τϑτϑ μακαριωτερον, τϑ γη μιχϑηναι." Xenophon. Cyropædia. Lib. 8.--658. 4ᵗᵒ Oxon. 1727.

ⁿ Hyde. De Religione Veterum Perſarum. C. 34.

º See the obfervations of Monfieur Caylus, Hiſt. de l'Acad. des Infcriptions. Tom. 29.--144. —Voyages de Le Bruyn. Tom. 4.--393.—Chardin. Tom. 2.--162.

mode of burial was not in use in Persia, and the Grecian custom of interring their dead in shady groves [p] is introduced amongst a people, who were utter strangers to such rites. The pretended riches in the tomb of Cyrus have also been imagined from the common tales, which Aristobulus incautiously adopted. Q. Curtius hath taken care to undeceive us, and we are told by him, that Alexander expressed his surprise, on finding such a powerful monarch as Cyrus, had been interred with so little magnificence and pomp. [q]

Arrian informs us, that Cambyses committed the custody of his father's Mausoleum to the Magi, who received a daily allowance of a sheep, a measure of flour, and one of wine, and every month a horse, which composed the sacrifices to the shades of Cyrus. [r] This

---

[p] Vangoens. Diatribe de Cepotaph. C. 4, 5, 6.

[q] "Auro argentoque repletum esse crediderat, quippe ita fama Persæ vulgaverant; sed præter clypeum ejus putrem, et Arcus duos Scythicos, et acinacem, nihil reperit. Ceterum corona aurea imposita amiculo, cui adfueverat ipse, solium, in quo corpus jacebat, velavit; miratus tanti nominis regem, tantis præditum opibus, haud pretiosius sepultum esse, quam si fuisset e plebe." (Q. Curt. Lib. 10. C. 1. Tom. 2.--754.) I have omitted the "Alexandre, selon cet ecrivain, en reconnut la sausseté," as I am not able to discover any direct authority for this opinion, and such an acknowledgment would have left Alexander no pretext whatever for the punishment of Orsines, which Q. Curtius immediately relates. The crafty Eunuch naturally took advantage of his Master's surprise, which might arise even from his disappointment, and the unity of the piece, whether real or fictitious, is by these means preserved.

[r] "Ειναι δε εντ⊙ τε περιβολε, προς τη αναβασει τη επι τον ταφον φερεση, οικημα σμικρον τοις Μαγοις πεποιημενον, οι δε εφυλασσον τον Κυρε ταφον, ετι απο Καμβυσε τε Κυρε, παις παρα πατρ⊙ εκδεχομενοι την φυλακην. Και τουτοις προβατον τε ες ημεραν εδιδετο εκ βασιλεως, κ αλευρων τι κ οινε τεταγμενα, κ ιππ⊙ κατα μηνα ες θυσιαν τω Κυρω." Arrian. Exped. Alex. Lib. 6. C. 29.--471.

This account is certainly erroneous. The Persians never admitted their departed heroes into the number of their Deities, but their religious opinions are as incorrectly spoken of in Q. Curtius. Darius there sacrifices to the local Divinities of Cilicia,[*] and Arrian[†] is equally exceptionable, when he supposes Jupiter to have been addressed by the Persians, who were neither acquainted with his name nor worship. In their defence, it may be observed, that they were perhaps seduced by the most celebrated authors of antiquity, who were as ignorant and mistaken on the subject of the religion of this people.[‡]

Harpalus escaped by flight, and avoided the punishment which Orsines suffered. This Macedonian officer, during the life of Philip, had been intimately connected with his Son, and when Alexander mounted the throne, he had the treasury under his direction.

[*] "Ipse in jugum editi montis adscendit, multifque conlucentibus facibus patrio more sacrificium Diis praesidibus loci fecit." Q. Curt. Lib. 3. C. 8. Tom. 1.--110.

[†] "Επι τοις δε ανατειναι Δαρειον ες τον Ουρανον τας χειρας, κ̧ ευξασθαι ωδε. Αλλ'ω Ζευ βασιλευ, οτω επιτετραπται νεμειν τα βασιλεων πραγματα εν ανθρωποις, συ νυν μαλιστα μεν εμοι φυλαξον Περσων τε κ̧ Μηδων την αρχην, ωσπερ ουν κ̧ εδωκας." Arrian. Exped. Alex. Lib. 4. C. 20.--308.

[‡] The Greeks, as the Baron de St. Croix very justly observes, wished to impose their religious tenets ("Faire hellenifer en matiere de religion" is his expression) on all the nations of the earth. In the happy possession of arts, sciences, and literature, with a singular absurdity, they both invented and propagated the strangest inconsistencies; and with a few grains of allowance, the reproach of Lactantius, to one of their first-rate authors may be transferred, without much apprehension of impropriety, to their writers of almost every class. "Quorum laevitas instructa dicendi facultate et copia incredibile est quantas mendaciorum nebulas excitaverit." (De Falsa Religione. Lib. 1.) If we are to believe the modern travellers, the Greeks of our days have not degenerated.

direction. But the gratitude of Harpalus was not equal to the new Monarch's patronage and confidence, and liftening to the pernicious counfels of Taurifcus, he mifbehaved in fuch a manner, that, from apprehenfions of perfonal danger, he fled to Megaris, a little before the battle of Iffus.[x] Alexander pardoned him, prevailed on him to return,[y] and after placing him at the head of his finances, again intrufted him with the treafury at Ecbatana.[z] It is neceffary to ftate thefe facts with accuracy, which Arrian hath preferved, becaufe they throw a degree of light on the conduct of Harpalus, with which the other hiftorians have not furnifhed us. All of them fupprefs his firft offence, which fhould be fpecified, to prevent its being confounded with the crime, of which he was afterwards guilty. The news of the rigid and exemplary chaftifement, that Alexander had inflicted on the governors, convicted of extortion and oppreffion in the provinces during his abfence, had already reached the ears of Harpalus, whofe conduct was not free from cenfure and fufpicion. Unable to face the gathering

---

[x] "Ολιγον δε προσθεν της μαχης της εν Ισσω γενομενης, αναπεισθεις προς Ταυρισκου Άρπαλ⊕, ϛευγη ξυν Ταυρισκω." Arrian. Exped. Alex. Lib. 3. C. 7.--192.

[y] "'Αρπαλω δε εν τη Μεγαριδι φυγη ην· αλλ'Αλιξανδρ⊕ πειθει αυτον κατελθειν, πιϛεις δους ουδεν αυτω μειον εσοθαι επι τη φυγη· ουδε εγενετο επανελθοντι, αλλ'επι των χρηματων αυθις εταχθη 'Αρπαλ⊕." Arrian. Exped. Alex. Lib. 3. C. 7.--192.

[z] "Προσεταξε τα χρηματα τα εκ Περσων κομιζομενα, εις την ακραν την εν Εκβατανοις καταθεσθαι, κ) 'Αρπαλω παραδουναι." (Arrian. Exped. Alex. Lib. 3. C. :9.--227.) It is difficult to decide on the greatnefs of the indifcretion, or the generofity of fuch a confidence: we might be tempted, in the words of Valerius Maximus, to make the vigorous exclamation, "O! fiduciam non folum fortem fed pene etiam temerariam, quæ,——acerrimis odiis latera fua cingere aufa eft, ufumque minifterii vix tutum in amicis, e finu inimicorum petere fuftinuit." Lib. 3. C. 7.

thering ftorm, this guilty and ungrateful minifter again fled with an efcort of fix thoufand men, that he entertained in his pay, and took refuge at Athens, with a part of the immenfe treafures that he had embezzled.[a] Q. Curtius relates,[b] that the Macedonian Monarch "received letters of advice, that Harpalus had indeed entered Athens, and by large fums gained the chief citizens; notwithftanding which, in an affembly of the people, he had been commanded to leave the town, whereupon he retired to the Greek foldiers, who feized him, and that he was afterwards treacheroufly killed by a certain traveller."[c] It is extraordinary that a prifoner, and furrounded by a body of troops, fhould have been affaffinated by an unknown traveller, and little credit is certainly due to fuch an anecdote.

Harpalus was undoubtedly obliged to quit Athens, as Diodorus Siculus affures[d] us, and we may eafily conjecture from the circumftances,

[a] "Ἁρπαλ⊙ δε των εν Βαβυλωνι θησαυρων κ̅ των προσοδων την φυλακην επιπιςευμιν⊙, επειδαν ταχιςα ὁ βασιλευς εις την Ινδικην εςρατευσεν, απεγνω την επανοδον αυτυ· δυς δ'ἑαυτον εις τρυφην,———————το μεν πρωτον εις ὑβρεις γυναικων κ̅ παρανομυς ερωτας Βαρβαρων εξερραπη· κ̅ πολλα της γαζης ακ̅αλιςατοις ἡδοναις κατηναλωσεν·————τυ δε Ἀλεξανδρυ μετα την εξ Ινδων επανοδον πολλυς των σατραπων κατηγορηθεντας ανελοντ⊙., φοβηθεις την τιμωριαν, κ̅ συσκευασαμεν⊙. αργυριυ μεν ταλαντα πεντακισχιλια, μισθοφορυς δ'αθροισας εξακισχιλιυς, ανηρεν εκ της Ασιης, κ̅ κατεπλευσεν εις την Αττικην·" (Diod. Sicul. Lib. 17. Tom. 2.—245.) The five thoufand talents, according to Lempriere's calculation, amount to £968,750, of our money.

[b] "Literæ ei redduntur; Harpalum intraffe quidem Athenas, pecunia conciliaffe fibi principum animos: mox concilio plebis habito juffum urbe excedere, ad Græcos milites perveniffe, a quibus interceptum et trucidatum a quodam viatore per infidias." Q. Curt. Lib. 10. C.2.—760.

[c] Digby's Q. Curtius. Vol. 2.—174, 175.

[d] "Ἐξαιτεμεν⊙. δε ὑπ' Ἀντιπατρυ κ̅ Ὀλυμπιαδ⊙., κ̅ πολλα χρηματα διαδυς τοις ὑπερ αυτυ δημηγορυσι ρητορσι, διεδρα·" Diod. Sicul. Lib. 17. Tom. 2.—245.

stances, which Plutarch mentions on the exile of Demosthenes, that he was not attended by his men to Athens.[e] When he left this city, he joined them at Tænarus in Laconia, where they had been stationed,[f] and he afterwards retired into the island of Crete, where Thimbron, one of his associates, who afterwards possessed himself of Cyrene, retaliated his treason on him, and slew him.[g] This Thimbron was certainly the traveller of Q. Curtius, and he is guilty of an anachronism, in fixing the death of Harpalus before that of Alexander. Arrian asserts, that the faithless treasurer of the Macedonian Monarch survived his master, and Diodorus Siculus may possibly add some strength to his evidence.[h] The saying

[e] It is a reasonable inference from Plutarch's silence, who mentions only Harpalus. The history of his reception at Athens merits some attention. "Οἱ μεν αλλοι ῥητορες ευθὺς ὑποφθαλμιασαντες πρὸς τον πλετον, ἐβοηδεν, καὶ συνεπειδοντες Αθηναιες διχισθαι καὶ σωζειν τον ἱκετην· ὁ δε Δημοσθενης πρωτον μεν απελαυνην συνεβολευς τον Ἁρπαλον, καὶ φυλαττεσθαι μη την πολιν εμβαλωσιν εις πολεμον, εξ ουκ αναικαιας καὶ αδικε προφασεως." Twenty talents, however, (£3974) and a cup of great value, totally changed the question, and the trimming Orator, by a convenient hoarseness, had the next day lost his voice. The wits of Athens termed it a Silver Quinsy. "Και μεθ' ἡμεραν τω καὶ καλως τριοις καὶ ταινιαις κατα τε τραχηλου καταλιξαμενῷ, εις την εκκλησιαν προηλθε· καὶ κελευοντων ανιςασθαι καὶ λεγειν, διενευεν ὡς αποκεκομμενης αυτω της φωνης· ὁι δ'ευφυεις κλευαζοντες, ουκ ὑπο συναλκης εφρασον, αλλα απ' ΑΡΓΥΡΑΓΧΙΗΣ ειληφθαι νυκτωρ τον Δημαγωγον." De Vit. Demost. Plut. Opera. Tom. 1.--857.

[f] "Κατηρεν εις Ταιναρον προς τες μισθοφορους"------He had before expressly said, "τες δε μισθοφορους απελιπε περι Ταιναρον της Λακωνικης." Diod. Sicul. Lib. 17. Tom. 2.--245.

[g] "Διαλαμβανει δε ὡς Θιβρων ὁ Λακεδαιμονι. Ἁρπαλον (τον τα Αλεξανδρε χρηματα, ζωντ. εκεινου, ἁρπασαντα, καὶ φυγοντα προς τας Αθηνας) τετον εκεινῷ αποκτεινας, καὶ ὁσα απειλιπετο λαβων χρηματα πρωτα μεν επι Κυδωνιαν την επι Κρητης εςαλη." Photii Biblioth. 217.

[h] Diodorus Siculus. Lib. 18. Tom. 2.—The Baron de St. Croix's expression is, "Il est demontre par le temoignage de Diodore et d'Arrien." I have been under the necessity of lowering its import, as Diodorus Siculus does not demonstrate what the Baron de St. Croix imagined. He takes up again the history of Harpalus in the eighteenth book, but without fixing the precise time

saying also of Diogenes, who died in the same year with Alexander, which Cicero[i] hath left us, confirms the account of the Greek historian. The Cynic philosopher made a practice of citing Harpalus, as an instance of the inattention of the Gods, and reproached them with their long connivance at the happiness and good fortune of the traitor.——The expulsion of Harpalus from the Attic territories, may be dated in the third year of the 113th Olympiad, in the Archonship of Chremes,[k] two years before the death of Alexander. Usher[l] supposes, with some probability, the assassination of Harpalus to have happened the year after his Master's death, and 323 years before Christ, when Cephisodorus was Archon. The Jesuit Petau[m] includes the flight and death of Harpalus in the same year, but he relies on Arrian and Diodorus Siculus for his authority, and Arrian directly contradicts him.— Alexander's intention of returning into Europe, is not mentioned by

time of the events which he relates. "Ἁρπαλα ηχε τον εκ της Ασιας δρασμον ποιησαμενα, ᾗ κατιλυσαντ⊖· εις Κρητην μετα των μισθοφορων, καίπερ ει τη περι ταυτης βιβλω δεδηλωκαμεν; Θιμβρων ὁ των φιλων νομιζομεν⊖·, ἀποφανησας τον Ἁρπαλον, κυριος εγενετο των χρηματων ᾗ των στρατιωτων οντων ἑπτακισχιλιων." (Lib. 18. Tom. 2.--272.) From this passage it might even be supposed that Harpalus was assassinated soon after his escape into Asia.

i " Diogenes quidem Cynicus, dicere solebat, Harpalum, qui temporibus illis prædo felix habebatur, contra Deos testimonium dicere, quod in illâ fortunâ tam diu viveret." Cicero de Naturâ Deorum, Lib. 3. Tom. 2.--514.

k Corsini. Fast. Attic. Tom. 4.--40.

l Usserii Annales. 215. Folio. Genev. 1722.

m Petav. Doct. Temp. Lib. 13. Tom. 2.--597. " L'autorité de Diodore et d'Arrien sur lesquels il s'appuye lui sont absolument contraires." I have varied the expression for it was not warranted.

by any hiftorian, Q. Curtius excepted, and its execution muft have been at that time very prejudical to the Prince's intereft, who had juft met with a fevere misfortune in the lofs of Hephæftion, and was in great affliction for him. We are told by fome authors that Glaucias, the unfortunate phyfician was crucified,[n] that Alexander conducted in perfon the car, which conveyed Hephæftion's remains to the tomb, and that the temple of Æfculapius at Ecbatana, was by his orders razed to the ground. It is alfo faid, that the Oracle of Jupiter Ammon was applied to, and confulted on the propriety of divine honours to the Favourite.[o] It is however doubtful, if Æfculapius was known at Ecbatana, and Arrian hath judicioufly rejected thefe abfurd marks of regret, which he confiders as indecent in a Sovereign, and more adapted to the character of a Barbarian.[p]

Plutarch and fome other writers,[q] appear to have compiled thefe

---

[n] "Οι δε, κ̃ τον ιατρον Γλαυκιαν οτι εκριμασι, κ̃ τουτον ως εφι φαρμακω κακως δοθεντι·————οι δε τ̃ το σωμα εφ'οτω το σωμα εφεριτο, αυτ@. εςιν οτε ηνιοχει τουτο·————αλλοι δι, οτι κ̃ του Ασκληπιου το ιδος εν Εκβατανοις κατασκαψαι εκιλευσε·" Arrian. Exped. Alex. Lib. 7. C. 14.--509, 510.

[o] "Οι δε λεγυσιν οτι κ̃ εις Αμμων@. επεμψεν, ερησομενες τον Θεον, ει κ̃ ως Θεω θυειν συγχωρει Ἡφαιστιωνι·" Arrian. Exped. Alex. Lib. 7. C. 14.--510.

[p] "Οιδαμη πισον εμοιγε λεγοντες————Βαρβαρικον δη τυτο, κ̃ εδαμη Αλεξανδρω προσφορον." (Arrian. Exped. Alex. Lib. 7. C. 14.--509. 510.) Ælian and Plutarch, whilft they report the facts, admit their impropriety. "Αλλ'ενταυθα επινθι Βαρβαρικως Αλεξανδρ@. ηδη." (Ælian. Var. Hift. Lib. 7. C. 8. Tom. 1.--486.) "Ταυτα μεν ει————ευφημιας χαριτ@. ην ευδε τι μης, οικυ δε Βαρβαρικυ, κ̃ τρυφης κ̃ αλαζονειας επιδειξις εις κενα κ̃ αζηλα την περισσιαν διατιθεμινως." (De Vit. Pelopid. Plut. Opera. Tom. 1.--296, 297.) Juftin hath alfo "Quem contra decus regium Alexander diu luxit." Lib. 12. C. 12.--335.

[q] Ælian. Var. Hift. Lib. 7. C. 8. Tom. 1.--483-487.--Luc. Calumn. non tem. cred. Tom. 3.--147, 148.

these fables without any judgment, but the Greek philosophical historian assures us also, that Alexander levelled the battlements and parapets on the walls of the neighbouring cities, and cut off the hair of the horses and mules.' This last species of mourning is not in the least improbable, as it was a Persian custom, which he might have followed, and the army of Mardonius, from the same respectful motives, clipped their horses and other beasts of burthen on the death of Masistius.' Diodorus Siculus' informs us, that Alexander went still farther, and commanded the Asiatics to extinguish their sacred fire, which was only customary on the decease of the kings of Persia. This writer adds likewise, that Hephæstion died from the consequences of intemperance at Ecbatana,ʷ and not at Babylon,

---

* "Ἀλέξανδρος ὁ μέγας, Ἡφαιςιωνος ἀποθανοντος, ε μονον ἱππες εκειρε κὶ ἡμιονες, αλλα κὶ τας ἐπαλξεις αφειλε των τειχων, ὡς ἂν δοκοιεν ἁι πολεις πενθειν." (De Vit. Pelopid. Plut. Opera. Tom. 1. --296.) "Τετο εδενι λογισμω το παθος Ἀλεξανδρος ἠνεγκεν, αλλ'ευθυς μεν ἱππες τε κειρας πασας επι πενθει, κὶ ἡμιονες εκελευσεν, κὶ των περιξ πολεων αφειλεν τας επαλξεις." De Vit. Alex. Plut. Opera. Tom. 1.--704.

ˢ "Απικομενης δε της ἱππε ες το ςρατοπεδον, πενθος εποιησαντο Μασιςιε πασα τε ἡ ςρατιη κὶ Μαρδονιος μεγιςον· σφεας τε αυτες κειροντες, κὶ τες ἱππες κὶ τα ὑποζυγια, οιμωγη τε χρεωμενοι απλιτω." Herod. Lib. 9.--702.

ᵗ "Πασι δε τοις κατα την Ασιαν οικεσι προσεταξε το παρα τοις Περσαις ἱερον πυρ καλεμενον επιμελως σβεσαι, μεχρι ἂν τελεση την εκφοραν· τετο δε ειωθισαν ὁι Περσαι ποιειν κατα τας των βασιλεων τελευτας." Diod. Sicul. Lib. 17. Tom. 2.--250.

ʷ "Διηγυσιν εις Εκβατανα της Μηδιας·------εν ὁις Ἡφαιςιων ακαιροις μεθαις χρησαμενος, κὶ περιπεσων αρρωςια, τον βιον κατελιπεν" (Diod. Sicul. Lib. 17. Tom. 2.--247.) Plutarch is rather more circumstantial. "Ὡς δε ἡκεν εις Εκβατανα της Μηδιας------ετυχε δε περι τας ἡμερας εκεινας Ἡφαιςιων πυρεσσων· οἱα δε νεος κὶ ςρατιωτικος, ε φερων ακριβη διαιτην, αλλα τω τον ιατρον Γλαυκον απελ-
θειν

Babylon, which was reported,[x] as appears from Polyænus.[y] The details, into which Diodorus Siculus hath entered, refpecting the pompous funeral, that Alexander beftowed on his Favourite, and the fumptuous monument, which he erected to his memory, are liable to lefs objection, as they agree with the rules of art.[z] Iphippus of Olinthus, compofed a work on the deaths of Alexander and Hephæftion,[a] and Diodorus Siculus appears to have extracted his information from it.

The Conqueror of Afia advanced towards Babylon, and the deputies of numerous and diftant nations, met him with congratulations on his different fuccefies. Lybians, Carthaginians, Brutians, Lucanians, Tufcans, Scythians, Celts, and people, who had fcarcely ever heard of the Macedonian name, haftened to offer their homage [b] to the Conqueror of the Eaft, or rather to his fortune.

θεὶν εἰς τὸ θέατρον περὶ ἄριστον γινομένƟ, κ̃ καταφαγων αλεκτρυονα ὶϛδον, κ̃ ψυκτηρα μεγαν εκπιων οινε, κακως ισχιν, κ̃ μικρον διαλιπων απεθανεν." De Vit. Alex. Plut. Opera. Tom. 1.--704.

[x] "Comme Juftin et Polyen l'ont fauffement avance." I have been again under the difagreeable neceffity of deviating from the French fentence. With refpect to Juftin, the charge is totally without foundation. "Dum hæc aguntur, unus ex amicis ejus Hephæftion decedit," (Lib. 12. C. 12.--335.) is his account of the Favourite's death, in which Babylon, is neither mentioned nor referred to.

[y] "Ἥκειν τις ἀγγέλλων Ἡφαιϛιων εν Βαβυλωνι τεθνηκειν." (Polyænus. Lib. 4. C. 3.--354.) I flatter myfelf the " Ἵκαν τις ἀγγέλλων" will juftify the alteration that I have made.

[z] Diod. Sicul. Lib. 17. Tom. 2.--250, 251.—Hift. de l'Acad. des Infcriptions. Tom. 31.--76. Their confufed ornaments, the Baron de St. Croix hath, notwithftanding, already criticifed.

[a] Athenæus. Lib. 4. Tom. 1.--146.

[b] "Babylonem ad Alexandrum ex omnibus fere orbis terrarum partibus legati venerunt. Nam præter eos quos Afiæ nationes, civitates et principes miferant; etiam multi ex Africâ et Europâ legati

fortune. Diodorus Siculus[c] declares in general terms, that the inhabitants of the extensive country, between the northern sides of the Adriatic gulph and the pillars of Hercules, dispatched ambassadors to him. Aristus and Asclepiades,[d] have left an account of the audience given to the Roman envoys, and tell us, that Alexander, having learnt from them many particulars, relating to their government and manners, predicted the future greatness of the Roman empire. Clitarchus adopted, with his usual credulity, the embassy.[e] 'Arrian suspects it with reason,[f] and gives

little

---

gati accesserunt. Ex Africâ, ab Hammoniis, Æthiopibus, Carthaginiensibus cæterisque Pœnis, et cunctis qui mare usque ad Columnas Herculis accolebant. Ex Europâ, a Græcorum civitatibus et Macedonibus, Thracibus, Illyriis et Scythis, Brutiis quoque Lucanis, ac Tuscis Italiam colentibus, Siciliæ et Sardiniæ insulis; ab Hispanis etiam ac Gallis, quorum nomina ac cultum tum primum Macedones cognoverunt." Usserii Annales. 207.

[c] "Χωρις γαρ των απο της Ασιας εθνων, κ᾽ πολεων, ετι δε δυνασων πολλοι κ᾽ των εκ της Ευρωπης κ᾽ Λιβυης κατηντησαν· εκ μεν Λιβυης Καρχηδονιοι κ᾽ Λιβυφοινικες, κ᾽ παντες οι την παραλιον οικουντες μεχρι των Ηρακλειων στηλων." Diod. Sicul. Lib. 17. Tom. 2.--249.

[d] "Αριϛ. δε κ᾽ Ασκληπιαδης των τα Αλεξανδρε αναγραψαντων, κ᾽ Ρωμαιως λεγουσιν οτι επρεσβευσαν· κ᾽ τυχοντα ταις πρεσβειαις Αλεξανδρον υπερ Ρωμαιων τι της εσομενης ες το επειτα δυναμεως μαντευσασθαι, τον τε κοσμον τον ανδρων ιδοντα κ᾽ το φιλοπονον τε κ᾽ ελευθεριον, κ᾽ περι τα πολιτευματ᾽ αμα διαπυνθανομενον." Arrian. Exped. Alex. Lib. 7. C. 15.--514.

[e] "Clitarchus————legationem————ad Alexandrum missam." Plin. Hist. Nat. Lib. 3. Tom. 1.--324.

[f] "Και τουτο ουτι ως ατρεκες, ουτε ως απιϛον παντη κατεγραψα· πλην γε δη οτι τις Ρωμαιων υπερ της πρεσβειας ταυτης, ως παρα Αλεξανδρον σταλεισης, μνημην εποιησατο τινα, ουδε των τα Αλεξανδρε γραψαντων (οις τισι μαλλον εγω ξυμφερομαι) Πτολεμαιος ο Λαγυ κ᾽ Αριϛοβελος· ουδε τω Ρωμαιων πολιτευματι επεοικος ην, ελευθερω δη τοτε ες τα μαλιϛα οντι, παρα βασιλεα αλλοφυλον, αλλως τε κ᾽ ες τοσονδε απο της οικειας πρεσβευσαι, ουτε φοβω εξαναγκαζοντ᾽, ουτε κατ᾽ ελπιδα ωφελειας, μισει τι, ειπερ τινας αλλους, τε τυραννικε γενες τε κ᾽ ονοματ᾽ κατεχομενους." (Arrian. Exped. Alex. Lib. 7. C. 15.--514.) Titus Livy is of opinion, that even the Fame of Alexander's exploits, had not reached Rome. "Quem ne fama quidem illis notum arbitror fuisse." Lib. 9. C. 18. Tom. 2.--908.

little credit to this ſtrange catalogue of people, ſuppoſed to have ſent deputies to Alexander, which he only ſpeaks of as a common report, deſerving no attention in his work. The refutation of fables does not fall within the province of hiſtory, it ought to be founded only on an aſſemblage of truth or probabilities: a critical examination of facts, is the ſcaffolding of the building.

Amongſt the projects, which Alexander had in view after his return from his Indian expedition, Q. Curtius ſuppoſes one very appoſite to the character of the Macedonian Monarch, but the means of carrying it into execution, can only have been imagined by the Latin hiſtorian. The governors of Meſopotamia, as we are told by him, were ordered to cut down the wood on mount Libanus, from whence it was to be tranſported to Thapſacus. A number of ſeven oared veſſels were deſigned to be conſtructed there, and they were afterwards to drop down to the ſea by Babylon, [g] and to form a Macedonian fleet. Thapſacus was ſituated on the Euphrates, at the diſtance of four thouſand eight hundred ſtadia from Babylon, according to the calculations of Hipparchus, but Eratoſthenes reduces the diſtance,[h] and the former writer afterwards

[g] "Meſopotamiæ prætoribus imperavit, materia in Libano monte cæſa, deveſtaque ad urbem Syriæ Thapſacum, ingentium carinas navium ponere: ſeptiremes omnes eſſe, deducique Babylonem." Q. Curt. Lib. 10. C. 1. Tom. 2.--749, 750.

[h] "Απο Βαϲιλων̅ος εις Θαψακον ειναι ϛαδιυς τετακισχιλιυς οκτακοσιυς" (Strabo. Lib. 2.--130.) This ſeems to have been the opinion of Hipparchus: Eratoſthenes differs with him. "Ουτ' απιϕηιατο ηδαμυ Ερατοϲθενης την Θαψακον της Βαϲυλων̅ος ϖρος αρκτυς κειϲθαι ϖλειοσιν η τετρακισχιλιοις κ̅ ϖεντακοσιοις

wards reckons three thousand stadia, from Babylon to the mouths of the Euphrates.[i] Reasoning from nautical principles, on the proportions, which the ancients allowed to their seven oared gallies,[k] they must have drawn thirty-nine feet eight inches of water, nearly what the modern three deckers of 100 guns require, and it is not possible to believe that in the Euphrates, at such a distance from the sea, there could have been a depth of water for vessels of that burthen. At this distance also from the sea, the assistance of the tide to float them must undoubtedly have been wanting. Polybius[l] informs us, that the Euphrates was very low in winter, though it was increased in the summer-months from the melting of the snow upon the mountains; but as the water of the river, during the heat of summer, was diverted into a thousand channels, for the purpose of refreshing the country, the stream of the Euphrates could be scarcely navigable, and still less adequate to the transport of troops, and the various stores and implements of war.

The

πεντακοσιοις σαδιοις." (Strabo. Lib. 2.--131.) The Baron de St. Croix supposed them to have agreed.

[i] "Εντευθεν δ'επι τας ικϐολας τυ Ευφρατυ————τρισχιλιες." Strabo. Lib. 2.--134.

[k] Scheffer. De Milit. Nav. Vet. Lib. 1. C. 4.

[l] "Συμϐαινει, την υπεναντιαν φυσιν εχειν τυτον τοις πλειςοις των ποταμων· τοις μεν γαρ αλλοις αυξεῖχι το ρευμα, καθ'ους αν πλειυς διαφερονται τοπυς· κ᾽ μεγιςοι μεν εισι κατα τον χειμωνα, ταπεινοτεροι δε κατα την ακμην τυ θερυς· ετ᾽ δε κ᾽ πλεις᾽ γινεται τω ρευματι κατα Κυν᾽ επιτολην, κ᾽ μεγις᾽ εν τοις κατα Συριαν τοποις· αει δε προιων ελατἰων αιτιον δε τυτων, οτι συμϐαινει, την μεν αυξησιν υκ εκ της συρρυσιως των χειμεριων ομϐρων, αλλ'εκ της ανατηξεως των χιονων γιγνεσθαι· την δε μειωσιν δια τας εκτροπας τας επι την χωραν, κ᾽ τον μερισμον αυτυ τον επι τας αρδιυσεις. Η κ᾽ τοτε βραδειαν συμϐαινει γινεσθαι την κομιδην των δυναμεων, ατε καταγομων μεν οντων των πλοιων, ταπεινοτατυ δε τυ ποταμυ, κ᾽ τελευς εςεχυ τι συνεργυσης της τυ ρευματ᾽ βιας προς τον πλυν." Polybius. Lib. 9. C. 43. Tom. 3.--181.

The Armenians, on this account, when they descended as low as Babylon, made use of little osier boats which they covered with skins,[m] and even in the place, intended for the dock-yard of the seven oared gallies, there was a ford, when the Macedonian army crossed the Euphrates to enter Mesopotamia.[n] The whole therefore proves, that the project instead of being Alexander's, was only the imaginary one of Q. Curtius.[o]

The predictions of Calanus, of the soothsayer Pythagoras, and those of the Chaldæans, as well as a multitude of other presages, which announced the dissolution of the Conqueror of Asia, have been

---

[m] "Τα πλοια αυτοισι εστι τα κατα τον ποταμον πορευομενα ες την Βαβυλωνα ιοντα κυκλοτερεα, παντα σκυτινα· επεαν γαρ εν τοισι Αρμενιοισι τοισι κατυπερθε Ασσυριων οικημενοισι νομεας ιτεης ταμωμενοι ποιησωνται, περιτεινουσι τουτοισι διφθερας στεγαστριδας εξωθεν, εδαφεος τροπον, ουτε πρυμνην αποκρινοντες ουτε πρωρην συναγοντες, αλλ' ασπιδος τροπον κυκλοτερεα ποιησαντες, κ̣ καλαμης πλησαντες παν το πλοιον τουτο, απιασι κατα τον ποταμον φερεσθαι, φορτιων πλησαντες." Herod. Lib. 1.--92.

[n] "Il y avoit au milieu de ce fleuve un gué, lorsque l'armee Macedonienne traversa l'Euphrate pour entrer dans la Mesopotamie." The Baron de St. Croix, for the proof of this assertion, refers his readers to the seventh chapter of the third book of Arrian. I cannot pretend to reconcile either the "Καταλαμβανει δυσιν γεφυραιν εζευγμενον τον πορον·" or the "Και εσι τω δε ου ξυνεχης ἡ γεφυρα τη εζευγμενη ες τε δε επι την αντιπεραν οχθην, τοις Μακεδοσι δειμαινουσι μη επιθοιντο οι αμφι Μαζαιον τη γεφυρα, ἱνα επαυετο" with his construction. The "Και τυθυς ὡς εφυγε Μαζαιος, επεβληθησαν αἱ γεφυραι τη οχθη τη περαν, και διεβη επ' αυτων ξυν τη στρατια Αλεξανδρος." (Arrian. Exped. Alex. Lib. 3. C. 7.--193.) is in a more peremptory style of contradiction.

[o] Yet Aristobulus relates, according to Arrian, the descent of some vessels of burthen from Thapsacus to Babylon. "Κατελαβε δε εν Βαβυλωνι, ὡς λεγει Αριστοβουλος, και το ναυτικον, το μεν κατα τον Ευφρατην ποταμον αναπεπλευκος απο θαλασσης της Περσικης·——το δε εκ Φοινικης ανακεκομισμενον, πεντηρεις μεν δυο των εκ Φοινικων, τετρηρεις δε τρεις, τριηρεις δε δωδεκα, τριακοντορους δε ες τριακοντα· ταυτας ξυντμηθεισας κομισθηναι επι τον Ευφρατην ποταμον εκ Φοινικης ες Θαψακον πολιν· εκει δε ξυμπηχθεισας αυθις καταπλευσαι ες Βαβυλωνα." Arrian. Exped. Alex. Lib. 7. C. 19.--522, 523.

been reprefented in melancholy and fombre colours by the hiftorians, to render, according to Plutarch's ideas,[p] the laft concluding fcene of Alexander's life more ftriking and pathetic, and to give it a tragical effect, both productive of terror and of pity. Such attempts are, notwithftanding, more proper for the ftage, as Polybius hath ably remarked in his obfervations on the death of Agathocles,[q] and the hiftorians who related it. The fame obfervations are applicable to the writers of the life of Alexander, though they may be entitled to fome indulgence. The incertitude of all fublunary things, hath been, in every age, a favourite fubject of mournful declamation, and the fudden and inftantaneous exchange of a throne for the dreary grave, is frequently dwelt upon with a gloomy confolation, as it levels all diftinctions, and reduces the monarch and the fubject to the fame equality.

The difaftrous omens, which preceded the death of the Conqueror of Afia, were not invented by the hiftorians, and Plutarch is not juftified in fuch fuggeftions. The different predictions, to which fuperftition lent afterwards its aid, were circulated with officious induftry, by almoft all the governors of the conquered provinces; in fome inftances from motives of intereft, in others from apprehenfions for their perfonal fecurity. Confcious of many acts of extortion and
oppreffion,

[p] "Ὥσπερ δράματος μεγάλου τραγικὸν ἐξόδιον κ̀ περιπαθὲς πλασαντες." De Vit. Alex. Plut. Opera. Tom. 1.--706.

[q] Polybius. Lib. 15. C. 33, 34. Tom. 3.--562. The fentiments of Polybius will not admit of abbreviation: by an introduction of them at length, I might offend againft the very rules, which the judicious author lays down, in the paffages that are referred to.

oppreſſion, that Alexander in ſimilar employments had ſeverely puniſhed, they naturally wiſhed to keep their maſter at a diſtance, and to prevent, as long as they were able, his return to the capital, where his leiſure would have afforded him an opportunity of inveſtigating their conduct, from which they had every thing to fear. Under theſe circumſtances, Appolodorus of Amphipolis, who had the command at Babylon, prevailed upon his brother Pythagoras the ſoothſayer to favour his deſigns, and he diſcovered, with obſequious ingenuity, portentous appearances in the entrails of the victims, which forbade the Macedonian Monarch's entry into the city.'

The Chaldæan prieſts had alſo ſerious reaſons of alarm, and they ſeconded the governor's endeavours from the ſame principles, which Arrian hath explained to us. Xerxes, on his return from his unfortunate expedition againſt Greece, had deſtroyed the Temples of every denomination at Babylon, and even the celebrated one of Belus, which was immenſely rich, had not eſcaped the general deſtruction. To this Temple of Belus, the kings of Aſſyria had annexed conſiderable demeſnes, and a great revenue was ſet apart to defray the expences of the prieſts and ſacrifices. From the time of its deſtruction, however, the Chaldæan prieſts continued in quiet and undiſturbed poſſeſſion of the ſums, appropriated

for

' "Μηνυσεως γινομενης κατα Απολλοδωρε τε ςρατηγε της Βαβυλων⊙, ως μη περι αυτε τεθυμεν⊙, μαλη Πυθαγοραν τον μαντιν· εκ αρημενε δε την πραξιν, ερωτησε των ιερων τον τροπον· φησαντ⊙ δε οτι το υπαρ ην αλοβον, Παππε (επεν) ισχυρον το σημειον." De Vit. Alex. Plut. Opera. Tom. 1--705.

for its use; and though Alexander had given orders for the rebuilding of the temple, the work proceeded very flowly in his abfence. To give more rapidity to the execution, he had determined to employ his troops in it, and the Chaldæan priefts, fearful, both, of being called to account for the fums, which they had received, and being deprived of their future revenues, publifhed many predictions, that the entry of Babylon would be fatal to its new Mafter, and invented likewife many omens, with the hopes of preventing his approach.'

If Alexander had appeared to have given credit to thefe prophecies and prefages, he muft have weakened the belief of his Divinity, which he wifhed to propagate. His ambition was to pafs for an Immortal, and fully fenfible of the advantages to be reaped from fuch a received opinion, both in Greece and Afia, he was little folicitous whether death deftroyed the illufion, provided the fuppofition of it, in his life, imprefled the world with awe, and affifted him in the completion of his great defigns. Q. Curtius, in Alexander's fpeech to Hermolaus, hath extremely well developed the Macedonian Monarch's conduct. "It' was ridiculous

---

' " Επιιοντα γαρ εξ Ινδων ες Βαβυλωνα μετα τη ςρατη, κ̓ πλησιαζοντα ηδη παρεκαλουν οἱ Χαλδαιοι την ησοδον εαισχην εν τω παροντι" (Appian. de Bell. Civil. Lib. 2. Tom. 2,--853.) " Τηχς εντεχειν αυτω Χαλδαιυς, παραινουντας απεχισθαι Βαβυλων& τον Αλεξανδρον." De Vit. Alex. Plut. Opera. Tom. 1.--705.

' "Illud pene dignum rifu fuit, quod Hermolaus poftulabat a me, ut adverfarer Jovem, cujus oraculo agnofcor. An etiam quod Dii refpondeant, in meâ poteftate eft ? Obtulit nomen filii mihi:

lous enough in Hermolaus, that he would have had me oppofe Jupiter, who thought fit by his Oracle to own me for his fon: Do the anfwers of the Gods depend on me? he was pleafed to offer me the title of Son; and I thought, to receive it, would very much contribute to the fuccefs of what I had in view; I wifh the Indians could be perfuaded that I was a God; for war depends much upon Fame, and fometimes a falfe report believed has had the effect of a truth." ʷ

The Conqueror of the Eaft often employed the means of Superftition, when they were likely to be ferviceable to him, and had frequently recourfe to them with fuccefs. When he defired to remove a fubject, whofe fidelity was fufpicious, Ariftander interpreted one of the Prince's dreams agreeable to his inclination, and Alexander the fon of Ærope was difmiffed.ˣ The accidental appearance of an eagle was fufficient to reject the opinion of Parmenio,ʸ and to counteract the influence of this old and able general with the troops. The Greeks were to be intimidated, and their anxiety appeafed: a thoufand prefages immediately announced the deftruction of Thebes.

mihi: recipere ipfis rebus, quas agimus, haud alienum fuit. Utinam Indi quoque Deum effe me credant. Fama enim bella conftant; et fæpe etiam, quod falfo creditum eft, veri vicem obtinuit."
Q. Curt. Lib. 8. C. 8. Tom. 2,--615, 616.

ʷ Digby's Q. Curtius. Vol. 2.--90.

ˣ The dream, and the interpretation may be found in Arrian. Exped. Alex. Lib. 1. C. 25. --90, 91.

ʸ Arrian. Exped. Alex. Lib. 1. C. 18.--70, 71.

Thebes.[z] Alexander's emissaries undoubtedly augmented these prodigies, and increased their number in proportion to the effects, which they were intended to produce, but the historians of his life cannot be charged with the invention of them. They might adopt them incautiously without considering how they originated, and they may have applied them to the Macedonian Monarch without examination, but it is time to return to the circumstances which attended his death.

In a fragment of the Ephemerides preserved by Arrian,[a] and copied incorrectly by Plutarch,[b] we have a daily account of the progress of the Macedonian Monarch's last malady, and its symptoms are so accurately stated, as to render a mistake impossible on the cause of its fatal termination.

Having passed the day with Medius in play, notwithstanding he had a feverish complaint, he indulged himself in eating in the evening.[c] Aristobulus relates, that being in a high and burning fever, with a great thirst, he still made free with wine, and a delirium following in consequence of this imprudence, he died the twenty-

---

[z] Ælian. Var. Hist. Lib. 12. Tom. 2.--821——823.—Diod. Sicul. Lib. 17. Tom. 2.--167, 168.—Pausanias. Lib. 9. C. 6.--724.

[a] Arrian. Exped. Alex. Lib. 7. C. 25.--537, 538.

[b] De Vit. Alex. Plut. Opera. Tom. 1.--706.

[c] " Δειπνησας προς Μηδιον κυβευων· ειτ'οψε λουσαμενω-, ϗ τα ιερα τοις Θεοις εϖιθεις, εμφαγων, δια νυκτος επυρεξεν" De Vit. Alex. Plut. Opera. Tom. 1.--706.

twenty-eighth day of the month Dæſius.[d] This account agrees in general with the Ephemerides, with that of Diodorus Siculus,[e] and many other authors, though Q. Curtius and Juſtin perſuade us, that Alexander was poiſoned. The two Latin hiſtorians pretend, that Alexander's ſucceſſors had power ſufficient to ſtifle the proofs of their guilt, and prevented the communication of it to poſterity.[f] But a different concluſion may, perhaps, be more rationally

[d] "Ἀριϛοβȣλ۞ δε φησιν αυτον πυρέιτοντα μανικως, διψησαντα δε σφοδρα, πιειν οινον· εκ τουτου δε φρενητιασαι, ϗ τελευτησαι, τριακιδι Δαισιουμηνος." De Vit. Alex. Plut. Opera. Tom. 1.--706.

[e] "Diodorus Siculus mentions the entertainment given by Medius, and adds, that Alexander drank off an Herculian bumper, and was immediately taken violently ill. "Παρεκληθη προς τινα των φιλων Μηδιον τον Θετ]αλον επι κομον ελθειν· κακει πολυν ακρατον εμφορηθεις, επι τελευτης Ἡρακλεȣς μεγα ποτηριων πληρωσας εξεπιεν· αφνω δε, ωσπερ ὑπο τινος πληγης ισχυρας πεπληγμεν۞ ανεϛεναξε μεγα βοησας, ϗ ὑπο των φιλων απηλλατ[ετο χειραγωγȣμεν۞." (Diod. Sicul. Lib. 17. Tom. 2.--252, 253.) Plutarch formally contradicts this aſſertion, "Ουτε σκυφον Ἡρακλεους εκπιων, ουτε αφνω διαλγης γενομεν۞ το μεταφρενον, ωσπερ λογχη πεπληγως·" (DeVit.Alex. Plut. Opera. Tom. 1.--706.) and Seneca believes it. (Epiſt. 83.--Tom. 2. 345. 8ᵛᵒ 1672.) Athenæus is more circumſtantial, "Αλεξανδρ۞ γȣν αιτησας ποτε ποτηριον διχουν, ϗ πιων προυπιε τω Πρωτεα· ϗ ὁς λαβων ϗ πολλα ἱμνησας τον βασιλεα, επιεν ως ὑπο παντων κροταλισθηναι· ϗ μετ'ολιγον το αυτο ποτηριον αιτησας ὁ Πρωτεας, ϗ παλιν πιων προυπιε τω βασιλη· Ὁ δε Αλεξανδρ۞ λαβων εϛπασι μεν γενναιως, ου μην επηνεγκεν, αλλ' επεκλινεν επι το προσκεφαλαιον, αφεις των χειρων το ποτηριον· ϗ εκ τουτου νοσησας απεθανε·" (Lib. 10.--434.) The "ποτηριον διχοȣν" is ſuppoſed to have been nearly equal to two gallons.

[f] "Veneno necatum eſſe credidere plerique : filium Antipatri inter miniſtros, Jollam nomine, patris juſſu dediſſe.————Hoc per Caſſandrum adlatum, traditumque fratri Jollæ, et ab eo ſupremæ regis potioni inditum. Hæc utcumque ſunt tradita, eorum, quos rumor adſperſerat, mox potentia extinxit." (Q. Curt. Lib. 10. C. 10. Tom. 2.--811----813.) "Amici cauſas morbi, intemperiem ebrietatis diſſeminaverunt : re autem vera inſidiæ fuerunt, quarum infamiam ſucceſſorum potentia oppreſſit." (Juſtin. Lib. 12. C. 13.--338.) Diodorus Siculus alſo relates the ſame received opinion, and the ſuppoſed reaſons for the ſuppreſſion of it. "Φασι γαρ Αντιπατρον————δια τȣ ιδιȣ ὑιȣ, τεταγμενȣ περι τον κυαθον, δȣναι πιειν θανασιμον φαρμακον τω βασιλει· μετα δε την τελευτην πλειϛον ισχυσαντ۞ των κατα την Ευρωπην, ϗ μετα ταυτα Κασσανδρȣ τȣ ὑιȣ διαδεξαμενȣ,

onally drawn from such silence. Their mutual dissentions would most probably have given birth to mutual accusations, and each Pretender to the throne would doubtless have found his interest in ruining the character, and blasting the reputation of his rival.

Q. Curtiusf hath given us notwithstanding a detail of this imaginary conspiracy. Alexander had been long dissatisfied with Antipater, and

διαδεξαμενη την βασιλειαν, πολλης συγκρισεως μη τολμαν γραψαι περι φαρμακειας·" (Diod. Sicul. Lib. 17. Tom. 2.--253.) Pliny mentions it, and adds with becoming asperity, that Aristotle was very shamefully a Privy Counsellor on the occasion. " Ungulas tantum mularum repertas, neque aliam ullam materiam, quæ non perroderetur a veneno Stygis aquæ, cum id dandum Alexandro Magno Antipater mitteret, memoria dignum est magna Aristotelis infamia excogitatum:" (Plin. Hist. Nat. Lib. 30. Tom. 4.--769, 770.) For an account of the Stygian water, see Vitruvius. Lib. 8. C. 3.--163. Amst. 1649.

ᶠ Q. Curtius. Lib. 10. C. 10. Tom. 2.--811——813. Justin hath entered into it more fully. "Auctor insidiarum Antipater fuit, qui cum carissimos amicos ejus interfectos videret; Alexandrum Lyncistam, generum suum occisum; se magnis rebus in Græciâ gestis, non tam gratum apud regem, quam invidiosum esse ; a matre quoque ejus Olympiade variis se criminationibus vexatum. Huc accedebant ante paucos dies supplicia in præfectos devictarum nationum credulitér habita. Ex quibus rebus se quoque a Macedoniâ non ad societatem militiæ, sed ad pœnam evocatum arbitrabatur. Igitur ad occupandum regem, Cassandrum filium dato veneno subornat, qui cum fratribus Philippo et Jollâ ministrare regi solebat : cujus veneni tanta vis fuit, ut non aëre, non ferro, non testâ contineretur, nec aliter ferri, nisi in ungulâ equi potuerit ; præmonito filio, ne alii quam Thessalo et fratribus, crederet. Hac igitur ex causâ apud Thessalum paratum, repetitumque convivium est. Philippus et Jollas præguftare ac temperare potum regis soliti, in aquâ frigidâ venenum habuerunt, quam præguftatæ jam potioni supermiserunt." (Just. Lib. 12. C. 14.--338, 339.)——A late noble Author, who, finished his Political career, after basking in the warm sunshine of a Court, by passing through the Torrid Zone of Ministerial Persecution, into the Frozen Region of Oblivion, hath touched in his usual animated manner on the Macedonian Monarch's character and end. "Alexander had violent passions, and those for Wine and Women were predominant, after his ambition. They were spots in his character, before they prevailed by the force of habit : as soon as they began to do so, the King and Hero appeared less, the Rake and Bully more. Persepolis was burnt at the instigation of Thais, and Cli-

and was believed to have sent Craterus with orders to destroy him. The Macedonian governor escaped the blow, and delivered to Cassander a mortal poison, which he was directed to give his brother Ioalas, the Royal cup-bearer, who was to introduce it into the Monarch's cup. This fable hath afforded grounds for many writers [h] to suspect that he died by a violent death, but Arrian [i] relates the conspiracy, rather that he might not appear to have been ignorant of it, than from any idea of its authenticity.—According to Plutarch, there were not any suspicions that Alexander fell by poison at the time of his death, and they were most probably first circulated by Olympias, who had vowed an eternal hatred to Antipater. Eight years after the death of her Son, to overwhelm with infamy the memory of Antipater, she scattered in

---

tus was killed in a drunken brawl. He repented indeed of those two horrible actions, and was again the King and Hero upon many occasions; but he had not been enough upon his guard, when the strongest incitements to vanity and sensual pleasures offered themselves, at every moment, to him: and when he stood, in all his easy hours, surrounded by Women, Eunuchs, by the Panders, Parasites and Buffoons of a voluptuous Court, they, who could not approach the King, approached the Man, and by seducing the Man, they betrayed the King. His faults became habits. The Macedonians, who did not, or would not see the one, saw the other; and he fell a sacrifice to their resentments, to their fears, and to those factions, that will arise under an odious government, as well as under one that grows into contempt." (Idea of a Patriot King. Lord Bolingbroke's Works. Vol. 3.--112, 113. 4to 1777.) Whether the Conqueror of Asia died in consequence of his own intemperance, or fell by poison, is one of those Problems, on which there may be still much Argument exhausted without conviction.

[h] Ælian. De Nat. Animal. Lib. 5. C. 29. Tom. 1.--272. 4to 1744.—Dion. Chrysost. Orat. De Fort.—Sext. Emp. contra Grammat. Lib. 1. C. 12.—Pausanias. Lib. 8.--636.—Tacitus. Annal. Lib. 2. Tom. 1.--121, 122. 4to Paris. 1771.

[i] "Καὶ ταῦτα ἐμοὶ, ὡς μὴ ἀγνοεῖν δοξαίμι μᾶλλον ὅτι λεγόμενα ἐστιν, ἢ ὡς πιστὰ ἐς ἀφήγησιν ἀναγεγράφθω." Arrian. Exped. Alex. Lib. 7. C. 27.--542.

in the wind the afhes of Ioalas, who had been unjuftly accufed of having diftributed the fatal potion.[k] Under the pretence alfo of punifhing his accomplices, fhe put to death a multitude of perfons, equally the victims of her vengeance and caprice.

The Royal diary reports the death of Alexander, on the twenty-eighth day of the month Dæfius, of the Macedonian year, which anfwers to the month Thargalion, the laft of the Attic year.[l] This important event may be then afcertained to have happened at the end of the firft year of the 114th Olympiad, when Hegefias was Archon, 430 years after the foundation of Rome, and 324 before Chrift. Alexander was thirty-two years, ten months, and twenty-two days old, when he died, inftead of thirty-two years and eight months, three days excepted, according to Ariftobulus,[m] and he reigned twelve years and eight months.[n] The Jefuit Petau fixes, without authority, the death of Alexander, at the commencement of the firft year of the 114th Olympiad.[o] Corfini[p] hath

---

[k] "Φαρμακειας δε υποψιαν αυτικα μεν ουδεις εσχεν. Εκτω δε ετει φασιν μηνυσεως γενομενης, την Ολυμπιαδα πολλους μεν ανελειν, εκριψαι δε τα λειψανα του Ιολα τεθνηκοτος, ως τουτου το φαρμακον υγιαντος." De Vit. Alex. Plut. Opera. Tom. 1.--707.

[l] "Ετελευτα μεν δη Αλεξανδρος τη τεταρτη και δεκατη και εκατοστη Ολυμπιαδι, επι Ηγησιου Αρχοντος Αθηνησιν." Arrian. Exped. Alex. Lib. 7. C. 28.--542.

[m] "Εβιω δε δυο και τριακοντα ετη, και του τριτου μηνας επιλαβειν οκτω, ως λεγει Αριστοβουλος." Arrian. Exped. Alex. Lib. 7. C. 28.--542.

[n] "Εβασιλευσε δε δωδεκα ετη." Arrian. Exped. Alex. Lib. 7. C. 28.--542.

[o] Petavius De Doctrin. Temper. Tom. 2.--859.

[p] Corfini. Faft. Attic. Tom. 4.--50——54.

hath refuted the opinion with great ability, and with a force of reasoning that wants no assistance.

Are we to believe the writers of Alexander's life, who have assured us, that he did not name a successor, and that he replied only in general terms, when his inclinations were consulted on the future government of his empire, that he left it to the most worthy and deserving?[q] A declaration of this kind appears at first to be contradicted by the Book of Maccabees, but the disagreement may possibly be explained away, without either doubts of that part of the sacred writings, or a violation of critical consistency.

We learn from the Book of Maccabees, according to the Vulgate,[r] with which the Greek text[s] and the Syriac version correspond,

---

[q] "Quærentibus his, cui relinqueret regnum? respondit ei, qui esset optimus." (Q. Curt. Lib. 10. C. 5. Tom. 2.--781.) "Οι δε και ταδε ανεγραψαν, ερεσθαι μεν της εταιρης αυτον, οτω την βασιλειαν απολειπει· τον δε υποκρινασθαι, οτι τω Κρατιςω." (Arrian. Exped. Alex. Lib. 7. C. 26. --540.) "Cum deficere eum amici viderent, quærunt, quem imperii faciat hæredem. Respondit, dignissimum." (Justin. Lib. 12. C. 15.--341.) "Των δε φιλων επερωτωντων, τινι την βασιλειαν απολειπεις; ειπε, τω Κρατιςω." Diod. Sicul. Lib. 17. Tom. 2.--253.

[r] "Et post hæc decidit in lectum et cognovit quia moreretur. Et vocavit pueros suos nobiles, qui secum erant nutriti a juventute, et divisit illis regnum suum, cum adhuc viveret." 1. Maccab. C. 1.--5, 6.

[s] "Και μετα ταυτα επεσεν επι την κοιτην, και εγνω οτι αποθνησκει· Και εκαλεσε της παιδας αυτου της ενδοξης της συντροφης αυτου απο νεοτητος, και διειλεν αυτοις την βασιλειαν αυτου ετι ζωντος αυτου." (1. Maccab. C. 1.--5, 6.)—For an explication of the "Παιδας" or "Pueros," see Menochius. Comment. Script. Tom. 2. Ed. Aven. 356.

spond, that Alexander, "fell sick, and perceived that he should die. Wherefore he called his servants, such as were honourable, and had been brought up with him from his youth, and parted his kingdom among them, while he was yet alive."[t]

The general meaning of this passage hath been differently understood by various commentators; but it may be placed, notwithstanding, in a new light, by a few simple observations. The expression, "he parted his kingdom among them," may be taken in a more restricted sense than it hath usually been understood, and may signify that Alexander divided his empire amongst his great men as Satraps, without any intention of distributing to them their respective districts, as Sovereigns of so many little and detached kingdoms.——We read in the eighth and ninth verses of the first chapter of the first Book of Maccabees, that, "His servants bare rule every one in his place. And after his death they all put crowns upon themselves."[w] This account perfectly ascertains the conduct of the Macedonian Monarch's successors, who first extending their power, secured themselves by the deaths of their competitors, and then proclaiming themselves kings, usurped the Royal diadem. The text of Scripture clearly discriminates two facts. Alexander's choice of many of his grandees to govern the different parts of the kingdom, and their usurpation

---

[t] 1. Maccabees. Chap. 1. Verses 5, 6.

[w] "Και επικρατησαν οι παιδες αυτυ εκαςος εν τω τοπω αυτυ· Και επεθεντο παντες διαδηματα μετα τo αποθανειν αυτον, κ̣ οι υιοι αυτων οπισω αυτων ετη πολλα·" 1. Maccab. C. 1.--8, 9.

pation of Royalty, after the death of the Macedonian Monarch, who had no ideas of wrefting the fceptre out of the hands of his defcendants. If the author of the Book of Maccabees had intended to infinuate, that Alexander's choice carried along with it the right of mounting the throne, he would not undoubtedly have diftinguifhed in fuch a decided manner the emblems of Royalty, which they fo prefumptuoufly arrogated. The inheritance of a crown, and its ufurpation by the fame individual, include a contradiction.

The firft of thefe facts is not literally mentioned in any profane author, but it appears to be a neceffary confequence of the events, which they relate, as they fuppofe it to have happened. It is ftrengthened alfo by a tradition, the veftiges of which, are to be found both with the Ancients, and all the nations of the Eaft.

Aridæus the brother of Alexander, mounted the throne, on the death of the Conqueror of Afia,* and after a reign of fome years died; but the Macedonian Monarch's generals, who had only the authority which they exercifed under his name, and that of his children, did not ftill venture to declare themfelves kings. Roxana and her fon having been put to death by the order of Caffander,

---

* "Ευθυς δε βασιλια κατεςησαν τον Φιλιππε υιον Αρρεδαιον, ᾳ μετωνομασαν Φιλιππον" (Diod. Sicul. Lib. 18. Tom. 2.---258.) Juftin hath given more at large a detail of the immediate difputes on Alexander's death, which ends with the "In Aridæum regem confentiunt. Servata eft portio regni Alexandri filio, fi natus effet." (Juftin. Lib. 13. C. 2, 3, 4.---351———355.) And Q. Curtius hath entered into them ftill more fully, Lib. 10. C. 7, 8, 9. Tom. 2.---788———807.

fander,[y] and Hercules the fon of Barcine by Polyperchon,[z] the ambition of Antigonus was no longer reftrained by any bounds, and finding his duplicity no further neceffary, he openly laid claim to the title and ornaments of Royalty.[a] His rivals foon followed the example. Till this period, the different governors and generals had ufurped the power, and extended the territories of their mafter, under the fpecious pretext of his fervice, and obedience to his commands.[b] Seleucus had fubmitted indeed with impatience to this artifice, and though he had always fears and apprehenfions of appearing before the Macedonians with any external marks of Royalty, he had not fcrupuloufly confined himfelf to

---

[y] "Κασσανδρ⊕. δε ὁρων Αλεξανδρον τον εκ Ρωξανης αυξανομενον, κ κατα την Μακεδονιαν λογυς ὑπο τινι διαδιδομενυς, ὁτι καθηκει προαγειν εκ της φυλακης τον παιδα, κ την πατρωαν βασιλειαν παραδιδοναι, φο- ϐηθεις ὑπερ ἑαυτυ, προσεταξε Γλαυκια τω προσηκοτι της τυ παιδ⊕. φυλακης την μεν Ρωξανην κ τον βασιλεα κατασφαξαι, κ κρυψαι τα σωμαλα, το δε γεγον⊕. μηδενι των αλλων απαγγειλαι· ποιησαντ⊕. δ'αυτυ το προσταχθεν, ὁι περι Κασσανδρον, κ Λυσιμαχον κ Πτολεμαιον, ετι δ'Αντιγονον, απηλλαγησαν των ὑπο τυ βασιλεως προσδοκωμενων φοϐων." Diod. Sicul. Lib. 19.--398, 399.

[z] "Αμα δε τυτοις πραττομενοις, Πολυσπερχον, μει ηθροικως δοξαν δυναμιν, κατηγαγεν επι την πατρωαν βασιλειαν Ἡρακλεα τον Αλεξανδρυ κ Βαρσινης—————δησας ὁ Κασσανδρ⊕. μηποτι φυσει προς μεταϐολην οντει οξεις ὁι Μακεδονες αυτομολησωσι προς τον Ἡρακλεα, διεπρεσϐευσατο προς Πολυσπερχοντα." The iffue of the embaffy follows in a few words. "Περας δε, πολλαις κ μεγαλαις επαγγελιαις πεισας τον Πολυσπερχοντα, κ συνθηκας εν απορρητοις συνθεμενος, προετρεψατο δολοφονησαι τον βασιλεα." Diod. Sicul. Lib. 20. Tom. 2.--425.

[a] Diodorus Siculus however informs us, that Antigonus took the favourable moment of fome military fuccefs againft Ptolemy to declare himfelf King. "Ὁ δ'Αντιγον⊕., πυθομεν⊕. την γενομενην νικην, κ μετεωρισθεις επι τω μεγεθει τυ προτερηματ⊕., διαδημα περιεθετο, κ το λοιπον εχρηματιζε βασιλευς." (Diod. Sicul. Lib. 20. Tom. 2.--445.) And Plutarch confirms the fuppofition. Vit. Demet. Tom. 1.--896. And Juftin alfo, Lib. 15. C. 2.--395.

[b] "Quippe paulo ante regis miniftri, fpecie imperii alieni procurandi, finguli ingentia invaferant regna." Q. Curt. Lib. 10. C. 10. Tom. 2.--809.

to such restrictions, when he gave audience to foreigners, and strangers.[c] If Alexander had distributed the full Sovereignty of the different provinces to the great men, that he made choice of, his orders would have been at least in part executed, and they would not have failed to publish their titles to the high stations, which they occupied. Instead of any proclamations of this kind, the Royal family continued to be respected, and enjoyed its rights as long as any branch of it existed,[d] and till the death of Perdiccas and of Eumenes, who were considered as its protectors,[e] had left an open field for the disputes of the contending parties. It may perhaps be objected, that the Macedonian grandees parcelled out the empire,[f] but we may easily discover, that the credit and authority of the several Pretenders were the only obstacles, that counteracted Alexander's last wishes.

In

[c] "Καὶ γὰρ Λυσίμαχος ἤρξατο φορεῖν διάδημα, κ̀ Σέλευκος ἐντυγχάνων τοῖς Ἕλλησιν· ἐπεὶ τοῖς γε Βαρβάροις πρότερον, ὕτως ὡς βασιλεὺς ἐχρημάτιζε." De Vit. Demetrii. Plut. Opera. Tom. 1.--896.

[d] "Hujus honoris ornamenta tamdiu omnes abstinuerunt, quamdiu filii regis sui superesse potuerunt. Tanta in illis verecundia fuit, ut, cum opes regias haberent, regum tamen nominibus æquo animo caruerint, quoad Alexandro justus hæres fuit." Justin. Lib. 15. C. 2.--395.

[e] "Alexandro Babylone mortuo, quum regna singulis familiaribus dispartirentur, et summa rerum tradita esset tuenda eidem, cui Alexander moriens annulum suum dederat, Perdiccæ : ex quo omnes conjecerant, eum regnum ei commendasse, quoad liberi ejus in suam tutelam pervenissent." (Corn. Nep. de Vit. Eumenis. C. 2.--505—507.) "Petiit autem ab Eumene absente, ne pateretur, Philippi domus et familiæ inimicissimos stirpem quoque interimere, ferretque opem liberis Alexandri. Quam veniam si sibi daret, quam primum exercitus pararet, quos sibi subsidio adduceret. Id quo facilius faceret, se omnibus præfectis, qui in officio manebant, misisse literas, ut ei parerent, ejusque consilio uterentur." Corn. Nepos. de Vit. Eumenis. C. 6.--525.

[f] Q. Curtius. Lib. 10. C. 10. Tom. 2.--807——809.———Diod. Sicul. Lib. 18.

In that species of military anarchy, which followed Alexander's death, power naturally prevailed over right, and became the only rule of the illegal and unequal division of the empire, that ensued. It is possible, that Perdiccas, who presided at the numerous deliberations, in which the fate of the empire [g] was decided, might, either from caprice or interested views, have made some changes in the directions of his master, from whom he received a ring as a sort of appointment to the offices of executor of his orders, of protector of the kingdom, and of guardian to his children. [h] It is natural to imagine, that this general, who was attached to Alexander by the ties of blood, [i] might be the person that he had in contemplation, when he answered, "to the most worthy and deserving," on being asked how he wished to dispose of the kingdom; and that he intended only to vest the regency in him, during the minority of his children, without the remotest idea of altering the succession, and giving him the power of transmitting it to his family, in preference to his own immediate descendants. Perhaps also the Macedonian Monarch, leaving only children in a state of infancy, by widows or daughters of the natives of the countries,

that

---

[g] "Perdicca, perducto in urbem exercitu, consilium principum virorum habuit, in quo imperium ita dividi placuit." (Q. Curt. Lib. 10. C. 10. Tom. 2.--807.) "Ουτῶ δὲ παραλαβων την των ὁλων ἡγεμονιαν, κ̄ συνεδρευσας μετα των ἡγεμονων, Πτολεμαιω μεν τω Λαγω την Αιγυπτον ιδωκε, Λαομεδοντι δε τω Μιτυληναιω Συριαν, &c. &c. &c." Diod. Sicul. Lib. 18. Tom. 2.--258.

[h] "Επιμελητην δε της βασιλειας Περδικκαν, ὡ κ̄ ὁ βασιλευς τον δακτυλιον τελευτων εδιδωκε." Diod. Sicul. Lib. 18. Tom. 2.--258.

[i] "Κυναν Φιλιππω θυγατηρ ——— γημαμενη δε Αμυντα τω Περδικκω." Polyæni. Strat. Lib. 8. --816.

that he had conquered, was cautious of declaring them in exprefs terms his fucceffors, from the fear of infulting the Macedonians. Such might have been his reafons, and with thefe fentiments he might have confidered it prudent, to leave his grandees the liberty of choofing out of his own family, the fucceffor moft capable, in their opinions, of fuftaining the weight of empire, and filling up the void by his lofs. The laft words of the Macedonian Monarch will plaufibly admit of this explication, and by the diftribution of his conquefts, as Satrapies, he might flatter himfelf the ambition of the great men would be fatisfied, and that their veneration of his memory would preferve to his children the Supreme power and Sovereignty. Yet there is a poffibility that even the laft words of Alexander have been fuppofed by his officers, and this fuggeftion is rather favourable to the Book of Maccabees. The doubts of the Prince's intention exculpated in the minds of the troops their tumultuous behaviour, and were fome excufe for the different pretenfions, in the fupport of which torrents of blood were foon fhed.[k] From the fame motives, the expiring Monarch

---

[k] "Orofius in a profufion of metaphor, opens his narrative of the Macedonian diffentions with, " At ego nunc revocor, ut per hæc eadem tempora——— quæ inter fe bella gefferint Macedonum duces, revolvam qui mortuo Alexandro diverfas fortiti provincias, mutuis fe bellis confumpferunt, quorum ego tumultuofiffimum tempus ita mihi fpectare videor, quafi aliqua immenfa caftra per noctem de fpeculâ montis adfpectans, nihil in magno campi fpatio præter innumeros focos cernam : ita per totum Macedoniæ regnum, hoc eft per univerfam Afiam et plurimam Europæ partem, Lybiæque vel maximam, horrendi fubito bellorum globi colluxerunt ! Qui cum ea præcipue loca, in quibus exarfere, populati funt, reliqua omnia terrore rumoris, quafi fumi caligine, turbaverunt. ———Alexander per duodecim annos trementem fub fe orbem ferro preffit. Principes vero ejus quatuordecim annis dilaniaverunt, et veluti opimam prædam a magno leone proftratam avidi difcerpfere

OF ALEXANDER THE GREAT. 287

Monarch is imagined to have forefeen the fatal diffentions, that his death would produce, and the very extraordinary funeral games that would attend¹ it.

We are told by many ancient authors, whofe entire works have not reached us, that Alexander diftributed by a will the different provinces of his empire. The expreffions of Q. Curtius on this fubject are by no means equivocal, and they agree with the Book of Maccabees. We are not to conclude, however, with the Latin hiftorian, that thefe traditions were falfe,ᵐ and, on the contrary, it may be reafonably prefumed, that Alexander's fucceffors might influence the pens of their cotemporary writers, and prevent a publication of the Prince's teftamentary difpofitions. Political fagacity pointed out to them, that, without having been chofen, the title of Royalty, which firft arofe from the powers, which Alexander had confided to the great men around him, " whilft he was yet alive," and which they afterwards ufurped on the death of the different branches of the Royal family, was literally extinct, and that the people, oppreffed by their defpotic governments, might

---

difcerpfere catuli: feque ipfos invicem in rixam irritatos prædæ æmulatione fregerunt." Orofius. Lib. 3. C. 23.---201. 4ᵗᵒ L. B. 1767.

¹ "Ceterum providere jam ob id certamen, magnos funebres ludos pararifibi." (Q. Curt. Lib. 10. C. 5. Tom. 2.--781.) "Αποθνησκων δε, προς τας εταιρας ιδων, εφη, Μεγαν ορω μη τον επιταφιον εσομενον." Plutarch. Apothegm. Tom. 2.---181.

ᵐ "Credidere quidam teftamento Alexandri diftributas effe provincias; fed famam hujus rei, quamquam ab auctoribus tradita eft, vanam fuiffe comperimus." Q. Curtius, Lib. 10. C. 10. Tom. 2.--809.

might have seized the pretext to emancipate themselves. Q. Curtius is not the only writer of antiquity, who mentions the last dispositions of the Macedonian Monarch. Diodorus Siculus assures us, that he had deposited with the Rhodians, a testament, containing his directions concerning his empire," and Ammianus Marcellinus speaks also of this will, in which he had named his successor.° Moses of Chorene,ᴾ a writer of the fifth century and of some authority, hath not forgotten also the division of the Eastern empire, nor the last dispositions of the Conqueror. Malalaᑫ tells us in his chronicle, that Alexander just before he expired, gave directions that the governors, whom he appointed in the different provinces, should reign in them, and the author of the chronicle, of which Scaliger publishedʳ an extract, agrees with Malala, but the testimony of these writers of the middle age deserves little credit, for they have in fact but copied the Book of Maccabees.

The

" "Τον δε πλεισον ισχυαντα των μνημονευομενων Αλεξανδρον, προτιμησαντ'αυτην μαλιsα των πολεων κ͵ την υπερ ολης της βασιλειας διαθηκην εκει θεσθαι." Diod. Sicul. Lib. 20. Tom. 2.--464.

° " Ut bella pretereamus Alexandri, et testamento nationem omnem in successoris unius jura transtatam." Amm. Marcellinus. Lib. 23. C. 6.--398.

ᴾ "Igitur Alexander ille Macedo————totius orbis imperio potitus, cum regnum suum inter plures testamento partitus est, ita tamen ut Macedonum imperium generatim univerfeque appellaretur, ipse e vita excessit." Hist. Armen. ex Vers. Whiston. Lib. 2. C. 1.--82, 83.

ᑫ "Μελλων δε τελευταν ὁ αυτ᷎ Αλεξανδρ᷎, διεταξατο ὡsε παντας τυς συν αυτω ὑπεραsπιsας κ͵ συμμαχυς βασιλευειν της αυτης χωρας, οπυ ην αυτυς εαsας, κ͵ κρατειν των εκεισε τοπων." Malal. Chronic. Lib. 8.--82. Apud Byzant. Script. Tom. 23. Ed. Venet.

ʳ Chronic. 72.

The Eastern nations have preserved in their writings, some remains of the traditions respecting the partition of the empire, which Alexander made, and the Tarikh-Montekheb intimates, "that the King divided, a little before his death, the provinces of Persia amongst the descendants of the princes, that he had stripped of them, on the condition of their doing him fealty and homage."¹ Sangiac-Tharikele adds, that after Alexander's death, these Feudatory or tributary princes became independent Sovereigns. But the division of Persia, amongst the issue of the dethroned princes is an error, and by the Feudatory princes, these authors undoubtedly meant Satraps, who had almost as extensive an authority, as the vassals of the ancient European monarchs. Cyrus, to supply the wants of his vast empire, and to relieve himself and his successors from the fatigues of such an extended government, created the office of Satraps, to whom he delegated his authority. These Satraps exercised indeed powers almost without bounds. They had the right of levying taxes and impositions, and they were even charged with the payment of the troops in their governments,¹ which were given in Apanage to the sons of the Persian monarchs. Hystaspes the son of Xerxes, held Bactria as Satrap,ʷ and the younger Cyrus enjoyed under the same title.

P p

---

¹ Herbelot. Bibliotheque Orientale. 318.—See also Mirkhoud. Sect. 21.

¹ "Σατραπας πιμψει μοι δοκει, οιτινες αρξουσι των ενοικουντων, ᾗ τον δασμον λαμβανοντες τας τε χωραις δωσουσι μισθον, ᾗ αλλο τελεσωσιν οἱ τι αν δεη." Xenoph. Cyropædia. Lib. 8.--637. 4ᵗᵒ 1727.

ʷ "Ὑσασπης, αποδημῶ. ων, κατ'εκεινον τον καιρον· ειχε γαρ την εν Βακτροις σατραπειαν" (Diod. Sicul. Lib. 11. Tom. 1.--457.) The Baron de St. Croix styles Hystaspes " fils d'Artaxerxes,"

the government of Afia Minor. We may judge from the preliminaries of his campaign, which terminated with the battle of Cunaxa, of the great and important powers intrufted to a Satrap, and how dangerous the office was in the hands either of an ambitious perfon, or one with military abilities of any confequence.

Alexander not only adopted the manners of the Perfians, but even their principles and form of government, and eftablifhed Satraps in all his empire. Moft of the hiftorians, who have fpoken of the divifion of it, which he made at his death, have intended by Satrapies to fpecify the portions which fell to the fhare of each of his generals, and gave the titles of Satraps to the governors of them. Appian,[x] in mentioning the events, which followed the Macedonian Monarch's death, informs us, that thefe generals from being Satraps became Kings. Yet this was by an abufe of their power. When Alexander made the partition of his kingdom, "whilft he was yet alive," he undoubtedly was not aware of the danger attending fuch appointments, which were originally little different from thofe, that Cyrus juft before his death conferred upon his friends, who appeared to him moft proper to be intrufted with the government of his kingdom.[y] The fame confequences might

---

but he was the fon of Xerxes, according to Diodorus Siculus, (Lib. 11. Tom. 1.--456.) and I have rectified the error.

[x] "Καὶ βασιλῆες ἅπαντες ἐκ Σατραπῶν ἐγίγνοντο·" (Appian. de Bell. Syriac. Tom. 1.--197. 8vo Amft. 1670.) Juftin hath the fame idea, "Sic reges ex præfectis facti." Lib. 8. C. 4.--361.

[y] "Ἔπειτα δὲ ὡς ἐγίγνωσκε τῶν φίλων ἐπὶ τοῖς ἑρημένοις ἐπιθυμοῦντας εἶναι, ἐκλεξάμενος αὐτῶν τοὺς δοκοῦντας ἐπιτηδειοτάτους εἶναι, ἐπέμπε Σατράπας·" Xenoph. Cyropædia. Lib. 8.--638.

might have flowed from them, if Cyrus, like Alexander, had only left a brother of inferior talents, and children in a state of infancy, or likely to be born.——The Prophecy of Daniel, respecting the Macedonian Conqueror, authorizes the explication, that hath been given of the seventh verse of the first Book of Maccabees, and agrees with the relation of the profane writers.ᵃ After having announced that, "aᵃ mighty king shall stand up, that shall rule with great dominion, and do according to his will,"ᵇ the Prophet continues his predictions in the following terms, "andᶜ when he shall stand up, his kingdom shall be broken, and shall be divided toward the four winds of heaven; and not to his posterity, nor according to his dominion which he ruled: for his kingdom shall be plucked up even for others besides these."ᵈ Daniel wished to indicate by these expressions, that the united empire of the Macedonian Monarch should after his death be divided, and the event justifies the prediction. Not only the conquests of the Macedonian Monarch were split into four great detached kingdoms, but even strangers according to the Vulgate,ᵉ or simply other individuals,

---

ᵃ Arrian. De rebus post Alexandrum apud Photium. 215.—Diod. Sicul. Lib. 18. Tom. 2. --258.—Dexippus apud Photium. 202.—Justin. Lib. 13. C. 7.--357——361.

ᵃ "Και αναστησεται βασιλευς δυνατ®· κ̃ κυριευσει κυριας πολλης, κ̃ ποιησει κατα το θελημα αυτε."
'Daniel. C. 11. V. 3.

ᵇ Daniel. Chap. 11. Verse 3.

ᶜ "Και ως αν ςη η βασιλεια αυτε, συντριβησεται, κ̃ διαιρεθησεται εις τες τεσσαρας ανιμες τε ερανε, κ̃ εκ εις τα εσχατα αυτε, εδε κατα την κυριαν αυτε, ην εκυριευσε, οτι εκτιληθεται η βασιλεια αυτε, κ̃ ἑτεροις εκτ®· τουτων." Daniel. C. 11. V. 4.

ᵈ Daniel. Chap. 11. Verse 4.

ᵉ "Lacerabitur enim regnum etiam in externos exceptis his." Daniel. C. 11. V. 4.

dividuals, agreeable to the Hebrew text and Septuagint,[f] had a share in the dismemberment, and proclaimed themselves kings. Arrian, Diodorus Siculus, Dexippus and Justin, have furnished us with the names of many of the great men[g] who filled these employments, and in the distant provinces, they took advantage of the Macedonian dissentions to establish their authority and independence. Theodotus of Bactria, first shook off the Macedonian yoke, and the example was soon followed by the neighbouring nations.[h]

---

[f] "Και ιτεροις εκτ⊙ τυτων." Daniel. C. 11. V. 4.

[g] "Arrien, Diodore, Dexippe et Justin, nous apprennent que plusieurs Satrapes des provinces eloignées de l'Orient profiterent des dissentions des Macedoniens, pour se soustraire à leur domination." The Baron de St. Croix in support of the assertion, refers his readers to Photii Biblioth. 215, 216.—Diod. Sicul. Lib. 18. Tom. 2.--258.—Justin. Lib. 13. C. 4.--355——361.—But these authors, in the passages referred to, principally confine themselves to the distribution of the provinces after Alexander's death.

[h] "Theodotus mille urbium Bactrianarum præfectus, defecit, regemque se appellari jussit : quod exemplum secuti totius Orientis populi a Macedonibus defecere." Justin. Lib. 41. C. 4. --686.

END OF THE THIRD SECTION.

SECT.

SECTION IV.

" —Orbis situm dicere aggredior, impeditum opus, et
facundiæ minime capax."
P. Melæ Procemium.

THE ancient hiftorians, collected with great labour and attention the materials for their works. The moderns have been reproached with compiling in their clofets and at their eafe memoirs of the facts with which they are acquainted, and fupplying, by the help of imagination, any chafm that might remain to be filled up. Reports, often faithlefs and commonly infufficient, concerning the countries, which have been the theatres of the events, that they pretend to defcribe, are almoft the whole refource of this clafs of authors.—Polybius fcaled the fummit of the Alps, to trace out with fidelity the march of Hannibal, and he matured his hiftory, by adding to his own reflections the advantages acquired from a knowledge of the world, which he reaped from his travels. The wifdom of the plan was indeed caught from Herodotus, whofe defcriptions are fo very exact, as to be in general preferable to

thofe

those of the later writers, and, in the inftances refpecting Alexander's expeditions, even to the geographical details of the Conqueror's own hiftorians.

The knowledge of the terreftrial globe, was undoubtedly extended by the companions of the Macedonian Monarch's arms, but, without allowing themfelves time for cool and ferious reflection, they took up every thing from its firft impreffion, which is frequently inaccurate, and their cotemporaries, dazzled with their profperity, fell into their errors.

Of ASIA MINOR.

The learned Salmafius[a] hath well obferved, that Q. Curtius[b] confounds the Marfyas, which paffed by Celæne, a city deftroyed, and afterwards rebuilt at fome diftance from its original fituation, under the name of Apamea, by Antiochus Soter,[c] with the Lycus, which bathed the walls of Laodicea. Thefe two rivers threw themfelves

---

[a] Salmafii Exercit. Plin. 582.

[b] "Ad urbem Celænus exercitum admovit. Mediam illâ tempeftate interfluebat Marfyas amnis." .Q. Curt. Lib. 3. C. 1. Tom. 1.--51, 52.

[c] Strabo. Lib. 12.--866.

themselves into the Meander, at the distance from each other of more than five hundred stadia, from the North to the South-East, in Pacatian Phrygia.[d]

Q. Curtius, speaking of Alexander's arrival at Gordium, the capital of Phrygia, and which had been formerly the residence of Midas, assures us, that this city was situated on the river Sangaris, and at an equal distance from the seas of Pontus and Cilicia.[e] Gordium, which was reduced to an insignificant village in the time of Strabo,[f] was afterwards restored under the reign of Augustus, and had the name of Juliopolis.[g] Monsieur d'Anville,[h] places it twenty-five leagues from the Pontus Euxinus, and eighty-four from the sea of Cilicia, equivalent to the Latitude of forty degrees and ten minutes, agreeable to Ptolemy,[i] and the situation is authorized also by the distance between Juliopolis and Constantinople, according to the itinerary of Antonine.[k] Q. Curtius hath therefore

---

[d] See la Carte de l'Asie Minor par d'Anville.

[e] "Tunc habebat quondam nobilem Midæ regiam ; Gordium nomen est urbi, quam Sangarius amnis interfluit, pari intervallo Pontico et Cilicio mari distantem." Q. Curt. Lib. 3. C. 1. Tom. 1.--55, 56.

[f] "Ουδ'ιχνη σωζοντα πολεων, αλλα κωμαι, μικρω μειζυς των αλλων." Strabo. Lib. 12.--852.

[g] Plin. Nat. Hist. Lib. 5. C. 39. Tom. 1.--624.—Strabo. Lib. 12.--860.

[h] La Carte de l'Asie Minor par d'Anville.

[i] Geograph. Lib. 5. C. 2.

[k] Antonini Itin. Ed. Wesseling. 142——141.

therefore fixed this city, twenty-seven leagues farther Southward than he ought to have done.[l]

The Latin historian is guilty of a more considerable error, in giving to the isthmus of Asia Minor the Longitude of Gordium, though it is formed by that portion of land situated between the gulph of Amisus and that of Tarsus, near the mouth of the Cydnus.[m] It is therefore five degrees to the East nearer Gordium.[n] Something may perhaps be discovered in the text of Q. Curtius to justify him, but it will, notwithstanding, be very difficult to make any sense of the following passage.[o] "These seas almost unite, having but a small neck of land to part them, each sea striving to encroach upon the land, and reducing it into a narrow strait. But yet though it reaches the Continent, and as it is almost surrounded with water, it seems to represent an island; insomuch, that were it not for this slender partition, these seas would join."[p]—The isthmus, which joins that part of Asia Minor to the great

---

[l] Yet Titus Livy seems to entertain the same opinion as to the situation of Gordium. "Postero die ad Gordium pervenit. Id haud magnum quidem oppidum est, sed plus, quam Mediterraneum, celebre et frequens emporium, tria maria pari ferme distantia intervallo habet." Lib. 38. C. 18. Tom. 5.--191.

[m] Strabo. Lib. 14.--990.

[n] La Carte de l'Asie Minor par d'Anville.

[o] "Inter hæc maria angustissimum Asiæ spatium esse comperimus, utroque in artas fauces compellente terram. Quæ quia Continenti adhæret, sed magnâ ex parte cingitur fluctibus, speciem insulæ præbet; ac nisi tenue discrimen objiceret, maria, quæ nunc dividit, committeret." Q. Curt. Lib. 3. C. 1. Tom. 1.--56.

[p] Digby's Q. Curtius. Vol. 1.--149.

great Continent of this quarter of the world, and the country between the gulphs of Amifus and Tarfus, was divided into three great kingdoms, Pontus, Cappadocia, and Cilicia, embracing an extent of twenty degrees of Latitude, and is defcribed, as one might have fuppofed, that of Corinth would have been.

Arrian hath confounded the Greater Phrygia,[q] watered by the Sangaris, of which Galatia, where the ancient Gordium flood, was once a part, with the Leffer Phrygia; more diftinguifhed by Phrygia above the Hellefpont, in which the Troad was included.[r] This error, as Cellarius[s] remarks, produced many others.—— Alexander marched from Gordium to Ancyra, a city of Galatia, according to Arrian.[t] It is certain that Ancyra, in the time of this hiftorian, was a city of Galatia, but in the age of Alexander, this country which was only inhabited by the Gauls, about two hundred and fifty years before Chrift, and took afterwards its name from them, was then called the Greater Phrygia. In the itinerary therefore of the Macedonian Monarch's army, the term of Greater Phrygia fhould be preferved.

---

[q] "Το δε Γορδιον εςι μεν της Φρυγιας της εφ᾽ Ἑλλησποντω, κειται δε επι τω Σαγγαρια ποταμω." Arrian. Exped. Alex. Lib. 1. C. 29.--100.

[r] Ptolemy (Lib. 5. C. 2.--117.) fuppofes the Leffer Phrygia to have been the fame with the Troad, though it was only a part of it. (See Strabo. Lib. 13.) Strabo allows that he has entered into a defcription of the Troad, with fome prolixity. Lib. 13.--871——878, &c.

[s] Geograph. Ant. Tom. 2.--97.

[t] Arrian. Exped. Alex. Lib. 2. C. 4.--111.

We find a similar miftake in Q. Curtius, and we are told, that Amphoterus and Hegelochus, reduced under fubjection the iflands between Achaia and Afia.* Achaia was fituated on the North of the Peloponnefus, and as it comprifed at that time no greater extent than in the days of Herodotus,* it ought not to be confidered as the Continent oppofite to Afia, though its boundaries were enlarged under the Roman empire, and the term might then be a proper one.

The ancient geographical writers are not free from miftakes of this kind, which they fell into from their inattention to hiftory, which ought always to be connected with geography, and indeed renders it only ufeful. On this account the migrations of different nations, the various revolutions, and the limits and names of countries, that were either conquered, or exchanged their mafters, fhould be difcriminated, and the different periods of thefe feveral changes marked in a chronological manner. Stripped of thefe precautions, geography will be found a dry catalogue of names, which fatigues the memory without improving the underftanding, and a number of anachronifms and contradictions muft inevitably follow. Afia Minor in particular was fubject to many revolutions, which, in the defcription of this part of the world, are abfolutely neceffary to be known; and Strabo, who joined to the views of the philofopher

great

---

* "Amphoterus et Hegelochus centum fexaginta navium claffe infulas inter Achaiam atque Afiam in ditionem Alexandri redegerunt." Q. Curt. Lib. 4. C. 5. Tom. 1.--193, 194.

* Herodotus. Lib. 1.--71, 72.

great geographical information, hath not overlooked them. "The migrations of the Greeks after the Trojan war," fays the judicious writer, "that of the Treres, the Cimmerians, Lydians, and thofe afterwards of the Perfians and Macedonians, and laftly that of the Galatians have created great difficulties and confufion. The removal of nations has not only been the caufe of much obfcurity, but the different authors, who have written of the fame places, have given them different names, and do not agree with each other. Phrygians are called Trojans, and with the licence of the tragic poets, the Lycians, Carians.

Notwithstanding thefe impediments, every poffible advantage ought to be endeavoured to be obtained, and where the darknefs of ancient hiftory cannot be diffipated, (as the duty of the geographer is not folely confined to it) the actual fituation of places fhould be explained."[y] Thefe obfervations point out to us not only the changes that have happened in Afia Minor, and the miftakes, which they have occafioned, but fhew us the route that we fhould take in our refearches, and the ufe and benefit of them.

---

[y] "Μετα δε τα Τροικα αι τε των Ελληνων αποικιαι, και αι Τηρων, και αι Κιμμηριων εφοδοι, και Λυδων, και μιτα ταυτα Περσων, και Μακεδονων, τελευταιον Γαλατων, ιταραξαν παντα, και συνεχεαν· Γεγονε δε η ασαφεια, δια τας μεταβολας μονον, αλλα και δια τας των συγγραφεων ανομολογιας, περι των αυτων ε τα αυτα λεγοντων· τες μεν Τρωας καλευντων Φρυγας, καθαπερ οι τραγικοι, τες δε Λυκιες Καρας, και αλλες ότως.— ————————Ομως δε καιπερ τοιετων οντων, πειρατεον διαιταν εκαςα εις δυναμιν, ο, τι δ'αν διαφυγοι της παλαιας ιστοριας, τετο μεν ιατεον (ε γαρ ενταυθα το της γεωγραφεως εργον) ταδε μεν οντα λεκτεον." Strabo. Lib. 12.—859, 860.

OF ÆGYPT AND LYBIA.

Little is to be gleaned refpecting Ægypt in the hiftory of Alexander's campaigns, which Diodorus Siculus hath left us. On the divifion of the Satrapies after the Macedonian Monarch's death, he fpeaks very fuperficially of the provinces, which formed his immenfe empire, and the following paffage hath neither a claim to accuracy nor precifion.[z] "All the extremities of Cælo-Syria and the neighbouring deferts, through which the Nile flows, feparating Ægypt from Syria." Short as this fentence is, it may be ftill difficult to conceive a juft idea of what the Greek author meant. Cælo-Syria, properly fo called, was fituated in the middle of the country between Libanus and Anti Libanus,[a] and it extended under the reign of Alexander's fucceffors to all the Southern part of Syria, as far as the frontiers of Ægypt and Arabia.[b] Diodorus Siculus hath adopted the whole extent, and hath confounded alfo Arabia Petrea with the Arabia of Heroum, confined

---

[z] "Παρα δε τα περατα της κοιλης Συριας κ̓ την συνεχως κειμενην ερημον, καθ' ην ὁ Νειλ۞ φερεμεν۞ ὁριζει Συριαν τε κ̓ την Αιγυπτον." Diod. Sicul. Lib. 18. Tom. 2.--261.

[a] "Κοιλοσυρια καλειται ιδιως δ' η τω Λιβανω κ̓ τω Αντιλιβανω αφωρισμενη." Strabo. Lib. 13. --1097.

[b] See the commentary of Euftathius on Dionys. Perieges. V. 970.--123. Ed. Steph. 4to 1577.

confined to Ægypt, whose limits were bounded by the lake Serbonis, near the promontory Kas Kazaron or cape Delkas,[c] and the mount Cassius of the Ancients.[d] The Ionians reduced Ægypt as far as the Delta, and pretended that the country to the East of the mouth of the Pelusiacus made part of Arabia, as the tract beyond that of the Canopus, was annexed to Lybia. This opinion, ably refuted by Herodotus,[e] was the source of all the errors of Diodorus Siculus, and also led him to stretch even to the Nile, that portion of Syria which ended at the lake Serbonis, and had the Arabia of Heroum to the South.——If Diodorus Siculus hath however extended too far to the limits of Syria, Arrian hath compressed them, when he tells us that Gaza was the last town on the road to Ægypt.[f] Syria had notwithstanding many other remarkable cities, and amongst them, Anthedon, Bethaila, Jenysus, Raphea and Rhinocolura, according to Pliny,[g] the

---

[c] Ægypte Ancienne et Moderne par d'Anville. 99.

[d] Herodotus. Lib. 2.--106.

[e] Herodotus. Lib. 2.--110, 111. Where the Point is well argued.

[f] "Εσχατη δε ωκητο, ως επ'Αιγυπτε εκ Φοινικης ιοντι." (Arrian. Exped. Alex. Lib. 2. C. 26.--174.) The Baron de St. Croix hath rendered the "Εσχατη δε ωκητο" by "La derniere ville habitée" and Dr. Gillies (History of Greece. Vol. 2.--629.) as well as Rooke, the translator of Arrian, have understood the expression in the same sense. May I be permitted to doubt, whether Arrian did not rather mean to intimate, that Gaza was the city last built and peopled on the road to Ægypt.——By this construction, the inadvertency, with which the Baron de St. Croix hath charged Arrian, is at an end, and Pliny's apparent contradiction will be no longer visible.

[g] "Telles qu'Anthedon, Bethaila, Jenysus, Raphia, et Rhinocolura, celleci, le dernier lieu de cette province felon Pline." I cannot comprehend how the "Oppida Rhinocolura, et intus Raphea :

the laſt of which ſtood on the confines of Syria towards Ægypt, and was nearly four hundred Olympic ſtadia from Gaza.

Q. Curtius informs us, that the country of Ammon was terminated to the Eaſt by the Æthiopians; to the South by the Troglodite Arabians, whoſe territories reached the Red Sea; to the Weſt by the Æthiopian Scenites, and to the North by the Nafamons.[h] We may collect ſome ideas of the accuracy of the Latin hiſtorian, from a compariſon of his poſition of theſe different nations with thoſe both of the ancient and modern geographers.

The Oracle of Jupiter Ammon, in Marmarica,[i] and not in the Cyrenaic, as Pliny[k] and Pomponius Mela[l] have advanced, had Lybia on the North, whoſe coaſts were inhabited, if we are to believe

---

Raphea: Gaza, et intus Anthedon," (Plin. Lib. 5. Tom. 1.--566.) can warrant ſuch a ſentence. I have releaſed Pliny from the weight of the obligation, and made the Baron de St Croix accountable for his own aſſertions.

[h] "Adcolæ ſedis ſunt ab Oriente proximi Æthiopum: in meridiem verſus Arabes ſpectant, Troglodyti cognomen eſt: quorum regio uſque ad rubrum mare excurrit. At qua vergit ad Occidentem, alii Æthiopes colunt, quos ſcenitas vocant: a ſeptentrione Naſamones ſunt, gens Syriaca." Q. Curtius. Lib. 4. C. 7. Tom. 1.--212, 213.

[i] I doubt whether the "Οἱ Μαρμαριδαι προσχωρευντες επι πλιον τη Κυρηναια, ᾗ παρατεινοντες μεχρι Αμμων⸫," (Strabo. Lib. 17.--1195.) will include the Oracle. See however Cellarii Geograph. 68.

[k] "Cyrenaica, eadem Pentapolitana regio illuſtratur Hammonis oraculo, quod a Cyrenis abeſt C. C. C. C. M. paſſuum." Plin. Nat. Hiſt. Lib. 5. C. 5. Tom. 1.--541.

[l] "Cyrenaica provincia eſt; in câque ſunt Hammonis oraculum, fidei inclytæ: et fons, quem Solis appellant." P. Mela. Lib. 1. C. 8.--46. 8vo L. B. 1748.

believe Herodotus,[m] by a wandering and unsettled nation; Ægypt on the East; on the South the Nobates and Garamantians, though Herodotus places them twenty days' journey to the West of the Ammonians; and the Inner Lybia on the West. The Troglodites, who were situated on the Western coast of the Arabian gulph, to the South of Ægypt,[n] cannot be included in the list of the neighbouring nations of the Oracle, nor the Æthiopian Scenites and Nomades, residing near the island of Meroe,[o] whose position to the South of Thebes is well known.——According to the ancient geographers, the Nasamons resided near the Great Syrtes, and the borders of Cyrene and Carthage, distinguished by the Aræ Philenorum.[p] Herodotus throws back the Southern frontiers of Lybia, as far as Augila,[q] ten days' journey from Ammon, whose Latitude will not then differ more than one degree and ten minutes, from that of the country of the Nasamons. Q. Curtius scarcely merits a reproach, for such a trifling mistake, but Diodorus Siculus is unpardonable, for having placed this Lybian nation to the South of the Oracle.

OF

[m] Herodotus. Lib. 4.---360.

[n] Strabo. Lib. 1.---71.

[o] Herodotus. Lib. 2.--116.

[p] Strabo. Lib. 2.---193.—Plin. Hist. Nat. Lib. 5. C. 5. Tom. 1.---543.—Scylacis Peripl. 111. 4to L. B. 1700.—Eustath. Comm. ad Dionys. Perieg. V. 209.--31. 4to 1577.—P. Mela. Lib. 1. C. 7.---40.

[q] Herodotus. Lib. 4.---361.

Of the COUNTRIES beyond the EUPHRATES.

We learn from Arrian, that the Macedonian army on leaving the banks of the Tigris, in their march to Gaugamele, had the Sogdian mountains on the left.[t] The error muſt have ariſen from the negligence of the copyiſt, who probably, inſerted Sogdian inſtead of Gordian or Corduan, as both Palmer[s] and Holſtenius[t] have obſerved. The neceſſity of this correction is indeed evident, from the march of Alexander's army. The Gordian or Corduan mountains, were ſituated to the North of Arbela, and conſequently the Macedonian troops muſt have them on the left. Strabo,[w] Q. Curtius,[x] and Plutarch,[y] unite their teſtimony in ſupport of this emendation; but inſtead of endeavouring to diſcover in the text of Arrian, a ſolution of the difficulty, in which he is involved,

Monſieur

---

[t] "Εν αριςερα μεν εχων τα Σογδιανων ορη." Arrian. Exped. Alex. Lib. 3. C. 7.--195.

[s] Exercitat. in Auctores Græcos. 238.

[t] Ad. Not. in Steph. Byzant.

[w] Strabo. Lib. 11.--802.

[x] "Secundâ vigiliâ caſtra movit: dextrâ Tigrim habebat; a lævâ montes, quos Gordæos vocant." Q. Curt. Lib. 4. C. 10. Tom. 1.--242.

[y] "Πεδιον το μεταξυ τυ Νιφατυ κ͵ των ορων των Γορδυαιων." De Vit. Alex. Plut. Opera. Tom. 1.--683.

Monfieur Freret[e] is difpofed to fuppofe he gave the name of Sogdian, a term fignifying, in his opinion, a valley, to all the country round about Arbela. This learned writer hath notwithftanding, inconfiftently advanced in his memoir on the chronology of Affyria, "that[a] the name of Sogdian was ufually applied to any mountainous country."—Abulfeda, however, leaves little doubt upon the fubject. Soghd, according to this Arabian author, is the name of an extenfive province of Trans-Oxiana, of which Samarcand was the capital.—Alfragan[b] reckons Sogdiana as a province of the Khorafan, and the other Oriental writers, from whom Monfieur Freret appears to have taken up his conjectures, are not favourable to him. Herbelot alfo contradicts him.

Alexander croffing Mefopotamia, in the direction of North to South, from Gaugamele to Memnium or Memin, left a great part of the country on the right. Q. Curtius affures us, that the Macedonian army had on the left Arabia Felix,[c] which is to the South-Eaft of the Defert, near the Euphrates and Babylon,[d] and, thus miftaking "Arabia Deferta" for "Arabia Felix," he places on the left, what was upon the right. But indeed the account of this

---

[e] Obfervat. fur la Cyrop. Hift. de l'Acad. des Infcriptions. Tom. 4.--611, 612.

[a] Hift. de l'Academie des Infcript. Tom. 5.--190.

[b] Element. Aftronom. C. 9.

[c] "Euntibus a parte lævâ, Arabia, odorum fertilitate nobilis regio." Q. Curt. Lib. 5. C. 1. Tom. 1.--302.

[d] Strabo. Lib. 16.--1112.

this historian, might induce us to believe, that Alexander had Arabia on the right during the whole of his march, which was the case only during a short part of it.

An alteration of a single word, in a geographical description, may sometimes occasion considerable errors, and Justin furnishes us with an instance of it. The Lycus, a river which flows through the plains of Arbela, is termed the Cydnus, a river of Cilicia, which washes the walls of Tarsus.[e] We may reasonably suppose this was owing to negligence in the copyist, but it has notwithstanding bewildered P. Orosius, who follows the exact footsteps of the abbreviator of T. Pompeius, and, with the greatest absurdity, states Alexander's last decisive engagement with Darius to have been fought near Tarsus.[f]

The Tigris and the Euphrates are said by Q. Curtius to cross both Media and Gordiana:[g] on the contrary, these rivers direct their course to the West of Media, and to the South and West of Gordiana. Diodorus Siculus may possibly have been the author of

---

[e] Justin. Lib. 11. C. 14.--293. Vossius, however, in opposition to Q. Curtius (Lib. 4. C. 16. Tom. 1.--293.) and Arrian, (Exped. Alex. Lib. 3. C. 15.--214.) maintains the present reading of Justin, and supposes the Cydnus and Lycus to have equally disgorged themselves into the Tigris.

[f] "Apud Tarsum bellum opponit." (Orosius. Lib. 3. C. 17.--184.) The error is indefensible.

[g] Q. Curtius. Lib. 5. C. 1. Tom. 1.--305.

of the error, for he makes the Tigris and the Euphrates, to water Media and Paraetacene,[h] a Northern province of Persia.[i]

In the letter, which Q. Curtius suppofes Darius to have addreſſed to Alexander, he informs the Macedonian Monarch, that "he[k] would find himſelf obliged to paſs the Euphrates, the Tigris, the Araxes, and the Hydaſpes, which were like ſo many bulwarks to his dominions."[l] Theſe expreſſions would naturally lead us to imagine, that the Perſian empire lay beyond the Hydaſpes. The Araxes appears alſo to be tranſported to the Eaſt of the Tigris. Perhaps however a river of that name, which paſſed by Perſepolis, might be alluded to; though from the circumſtance of the Araxes being mentioned amongſt the other great rivers of Aſia, it might be ſuſpected to be the river, which diſcharges itſelf into the Caſpian ſea.—Alexander in his anſwer to Darius, informs him, that his intention was to make himſelf maſter of Perſepolis, the capital of the Perſian monarch, and afterwards of Bactra, and Ecbatana. Q. Curtius mentions Ecbatana the laſt,[m] as if it had been beyond Bactra.

---

[h] "Ενιχθεντες δε δια Μηδιας κ{αι} Παραιτακηνης, εμβαλλυσιν εις την Μεσοποταμιαν." Diod. Sicul. Lib. 2. Tom. 1.--125.

[i] Herodotus. Lib. 1.--52.

[k] "Tranſeundum eſſe Alexandro Euphraten, Tigrimque et Araxen, et Hydaſpen, magna munimenta regni fui." Q. Curt. Lib. 4. C. 5. Tom. 1.--191.

[l] Digby's Q. Curtius. Vol. 1.--212.

[m] "Perſepolim caput regni ejus, Bactra deinde et Ecbatana." Q. Curt. Lib. 4. C. 5. Tom. 1.--192.

The Macedonian army, in its march from Sufa to penetrate into the interior provinces of the East, was obliged according to Diodorus Siculus [n] to pafs the Tigris. This error is probably but the confequence of the former miftake, which he had made, refpecting the courfe of this river, and which hath been already noticed. The judicious Palmer [o] hath not perceived it, becaufe he wifhed to fubftitute the Pafitigris for the Tigris, which often occurs in the text of Diodorus Siculus. The repetition itfelf proves that the common reading is correct, and to vary the paffages of the ancient writers upon frivolous pretenfions, would be to expofe them inceffantly to the caprice of critics and grammarians. The opinion that the Tigris, from its receiving the waters of Sufia, and the different channels of the Euphrates, took afterwards the name of Pafitigris, [p] feems to be confirmed by the navigation of Nearchus, [q] and fome expreffions of Pliny. [r] Alexander's hiftorians have, notwithftanding, confounded the Pafitigris with the Orates or Oroatis, [s] which feparates Perfia from Sufia, and

---

[n] Diodorus Siculus. Lib. 17.--211.

[o] Palmer. Exercit. apud Auctores Græcos, 138, 139.

[p] Recherches Geograph. fur le Golfe Perfique par d'Anville.—Hift. de l'Acad. des Infcriptions. Tom. 30.--173, &c.—See alfo Strabo. Lib. 15.--1060.

[q] Arrian. Hift. Ind. C. 42.--633.

[r] "Ubi remeavere aquæ, Pafitigris vocatur." Plin. Hift. Nat. Lib. 6. C. 27. Tom. 1--716.

[s] Yet Strabo tells us, "Πασιτιγριν απο τε Οροατιδ⊕ διηχει περι δισχιλιυς ςαδιυς." Lib. 15. --1060.

and which in all probability Diodorus Siculus hath taken for the Tigris.

After the death of Darius, Alexander purſued the Perſian monarch's aſſaſſins, and the remains of the Perſian army, and preſſed forward into that part of Aſia near the Caſpian ſea, and beyond the Iaxartes, which was an important diſcovery to the Greeks, who had only been till then acquainted with the countries to the Weſt of the Tigris and Euphrates. The Athenian orators were ſtruck with the rapid conqueſts of the Macedonian troops, and the tribune reſounded with harangues on the aſtoniſhing relations of their exploits. Æſchines cried out[t] in the midſt of one of the popular aſſemblies, "that[w] Alexander was at a diſtance farther than the Pole, almoſt beyond the limits of the habitable world."[x] Such was the impreſſion that the diſcoveries of the Macedonian Monarch made upon his cotemporaries. The orator may indulge himſelf in a paroxyſm of enthuſiaſm, but the philoſopher will ſcrutinize more calmly the hiſtory of events, and ſanction only thoſe, which have the ſupport of reaſon, and are authorized by truth.

Of

[t] "Eſchine s'ecria." I give the French expreſſion to juſtify the correſponding paſſage. One part of the Athenian Senate, either in the pay or intereſt of Alexander, or from views of oppoſition, might find their purpoſe in magnifying the victories of the Macedonian Monarch, but the Greek orator, in the ſentence alluded to, reaſons merely from the diſtance, which then ſeparated them.

[w] "Ὁ δε Αλεξανδρ⊙ εξω της Αρκτε ϗ της οικυμενης ολιγυ δειν πασης μεθεστηκει." Æſchines contra Cteſiph. Demoſt. Opera. 454. Folio. Franc. 1604.

[x] Leland's Orations of Æſchines and Demoſthenes, Vol. 3.--100. 8vo

Of the CASPIAN SEA.

The ancient Perſians had ſome correct notions of the Caſpian ſea, though they were not ſufficiently acquainted with the whole of its ſhape and figure, as we may gather from Herodotus. This Greek hiſtorian moſt probably borrowed his ideas from the Perſians, who neither puſhed their knowledge very far, nor acquired that degree of certainty, which might have been expected from them, owing to the abhorrence of all maritime expeditions, which they derived from their religious inſtitutions.[y] They were perſuaded alſo, that the coaſts of theſe ſeas were frequented by evil Genii, of whom they had fears and apprehenſions.[z]——The Greeks, who ſucceeded them in the empire of the Eaſt, ſailed generally to the Southward, and the Eaſterly and Weſterly winds,[a] which blew almoſt inceſſantly in thoſe roads, with the want of proper and convenient ports,[b] prevented them extending their voyages on ſuch

---

[y] We are told by Pliny, ſpeaking of Tiridates, "Navigare noluerat, quoniam exſpuere in maria, aliiſque mortalium neceſſitatibus violare naturam eam fas non putant." Hiſt. Nat. Lib. 30. C. 2. Tom. 4.--730.

[z] Memoires de Monſieur Anquetil. Hiſt. de l'Acad. des Inſcriptions. Tom. 31.--373.

[a] Q. Curtius informs us, that there is alſo a great and heavy ſea, which ſets in from the North. "A Septentrione ingens in litus mare incumbit." Lib. 6. C. 4. Tom. 1.--410.

[b] "Onne atrox, ſævum, ſine portubus, procellis undique expoſitam; ac belluis magis quam cetera

such stormy coasts. They relied on the neighbouring nations for information, and what they picked up from them was the source of numerous and multiplied errors. It is to the Russians that we are indebted for the present geographical system, and they have at last dissipated that mist of ignorance, in which this part of the world was enveloped. By repeated observations, the greatest length of the Caspian sea hath been demonstrated to be from North to South,^c and that it has neither any communication with the Ocean, nor adjoining seas.

The ancient geographers were divided in opinion respecting the figure of the Caspian sea. By some, it was supposed to be of an oblong shape:^d others concluded that it was round. It is astonishing, however, that the sentiments of Herodotus were not universally admitted. We understand from him, that an oared vessel might sail in fifteen days from end to end, and might cross it in eight.^e If we reckon, according to the calculation of many of the ancient authors, and even of Herodotus, the track of this vessel at

five

---

cetera refertum, et ideo minus navigabile." (P. Mela. Lib. 3. C. 5.--267.) The "Belluæ" might be the evil Genii of the Persians.

^c Memoire de Monsieur de l'Isle. Hist. de l'Acad. des Sciences. 1741.--245.

^d Μνοειδης ησα, κατα δε τινας κ̣ ϖρομηκης." Agathemerus. Lib. 1. C. 3.--184. Ed. Gronov. 4to L. B. 1700.

^e " 'Η δε Κασπιη, εϛι ετερη επ'ἑωυτης, ηϭα μηκ῀ μεν πλου, ειρεϭιη χρεωμενω, ϖεντι κ̣ δεκα ἡμερε- ων' ευρ῀ δε, τη ευρυτατη εϛι αυτη ἑωυτης, οκτω ἡμερεων." Herod. Lib. 1.--96.

five hundred stadia, ⁱ which ought in fact to be eight hundred or a thousand, the length of the Caspian sea, will be found within nearly five hundred stadia of that given to it in the modern discoveries, though the eight days' passage cannot be reconciled with any correct chart. The calculation of Agathemerus is more moderate, and he reduces it to two thousand five hundred stadia, ᵍ the extent which it really has on the Southern side; but the measure of eight thousand two hundred stadia, which he allows to the coasts of the Caspian sea, from the mouth of the Cyrus to that of the Iaxartes, is not equally just and accurate.

Eratosthenes had collected with care the observations of different persons, on the distance and extent of the coast of the sea, which bordered Albania and the country of the Cadusians, for the space of five thousand four hundred stadia; the country of the Mardi, as far as the mouths of the Oxus, for four thousand eight hundred; and from thence to the Iaxartes, which again took in two thousand four hundred stadia, ʰ amounting in the whole

---

ⁱ "Ἀπὸ δὲ Ἡλιουπολῖος ἐς Θηβας ἐστι διαπλοος ἐννεα ἡμερεων· στάδιοι δὲ της ὁδου ἑξηκοντα κ͂, οκτακοσιοι κ͂, τετρακισχιλιοι." (Herodot. Lib. 2.--107.) These four thousand eight hundred and sixty stadia allow five hundred and ninety for each day's sail, and the calculation appears to be adopted in general by the ancient authors. The turbulence of the Caspian sea might however reduce the reckoning.

ᵍ "Πλατ͂ος δὲ πλεισον β. φ. μιλιων δὲ τ. λ. δ." Agathemerus. Lib. 2. C. 14.--243.

ʰ "φησι δ'Ερατοσθενης τον ὑπο των Ἑλληνων γνωριμον περιπλευτης θαλατίης ταυτης, τον μεν παρα της Αλβανης, κ͂, της Καδυσιης, ειναι πεντακισχιλιων κ͂, τετρακοσιων· τον δὲ παρα τον Αναριακων, κ͂, Μαρδων, κ͂, Ἱρκανων, μεχρι τ͂, στομᾷος τ͂, Οξ͂, ποταμ͂, τετρακισχιλιων κ͂, οκτακοσιων· ενθεν δ'επι τε Ιαξαρτε δισχιλιων τετρακοσιων." Strabo. Lib. 11.--773.

whole to twelve thoufand fix hundred ftadia. Artemidorus computed the diftance at fifteen hundred and feventy-five, [i] which is not widely different from the prefent ideas, though they are not ftill as accurate as might be wifhed. Strabo affures us, that the Cafpian fea was little known beyond the Iaxartes, and that too much caution cannot be taken, in giving credit to any accounts of the Northern part of it, [k] with which the Ancients had but a very dubious acquaintance. The name indeed of the Cafpian fea, according to Pliny, did not extend beyond the Cyrus. [l]

It appears from the different computations, which have been already alluded to, that many authors of antiquity were aware, though their notions were far from being perfect, that the greateft extent of the Cafpian fea was from North to South. Ptolemy, however, hath totally difregarded the opinion, and allows twenty-three degrees and a half from Weft to Eaft, which is four times its extent. [m]

[i] "Eratofthenes ponit et menfuram: ab exortu et meridie, per Cadufiæ et Albaniæ oram quinquies mille C. C. C. C. ftad. Inde per Anariacas, Amardos, Hyrcanos, ad oftium Oxi fluminis, quatuor mille D. C. C. C. ftad. Ab eo ad oftium Iaxartis M. M. C. C. C. C. ftad. Quæ fumma efficit quindecies centena feptuaginta quinque M. paffuum." (Plin. Hift. Nat. Lib. 6. C. 13. Tom. 1.--668, 669.) The calculation therefore was that of Eratofthenes, and Pliny is only refponfible for the reduction of the ftadia to the Roman meafure.

[k] "Δει δε περι των εν τη μεριδι ταυτη, κ͵ τοις επι τουτων εκτετοπισμενοις απλυςερον αχμειν, κ͵ μαλιςα περι των διαςημματων." Strabo. Lib. 11.--774.

[l] "A Cyro Cafpium mare vocari incipit: accolunt Cafpii." Plin. Hift. Nat. Lib. 6. C. 13. Tom. 1.--670.

[m] See the obfervations on the Cafpian fea. Hiftoire de l'Academie des Sciences, 1721.--247.

The result of this extensive and undue extent in Longitude has been, that all the countries of Asia, within the twentieth and fortieth degrees of North Latitude, have been stretched to one hundred and ninety degrees of Longitude, and by this means, China is placed six hundred leagues more Easterly than it ought to be,[a] and the position of the different nations hath been thrown farther to the East. The Western regions have been equally misplaced, and a part of Albania, the Caspians, the Caducians, and the Geles, instead of occupying the Western shore of the Caspian sea, have been transported to the South.[o] Monsieur de Buffon, attributes the origin of this error to a supposition, that the lake Aral was considered as a part of the Caspian sea. "We shall find," this great Naturalist informs us, "that the Western coast of the Caspian sea, to the Eastern shore of the lake Aral, extends to a greater length than the distance from the Southern coast to the Northern coast of the same sea."[p] The best modern charts do not agree with this system, and on measuring the space of which Monsieur de Buffon speaks, it will be found, on the contrary, that the Caspian sea will have a third more of Latitude than Longitude. Besides the ancient geographers have not in the least confounded the lake Aral with this sea, and the Orientals, who have given us some

---

[a] Hist. de l'Academie des Inscriptions, Tom. 25.--45.

[o] Ptolem. Lib. 6. C. 2.

[p] "On trouvera encore que la longueur, depuis le bord Occidental de la mer Caspienne, jusqu'au bord Oriental du lac Aral est plus grande que la longueur depuis le bord meridional jusqu'au bord septentrional de la meme mer." Hist. Nat. Tom. 2.--41. Ed. 12mo

some very particular information relative to this lake, have been equally deceived as to the extent of the Longitude of the Caspian sea.

Abulfeda, an Arabian prince, and an author in the early part of the fourteenth century, relates the opinion of Kotiddin, who fixed the Longitude of the Caspian sea, at two hundred and seventy parasengs.[q] Ali-Kohesgi, a celebrated Oriental astronomer of the fifteenth century, included twenty-two parasengs in a degree, with a fraction of two thirds of a mile, three miles forming a paraseng.[r] According to this calculation, Kotiddin will only have allowed eleven degrees a third and two miles of Longitude to the Caspian sea, which reduces it more than one half of Ptolemy's computation.

It is probable that the extent of the Caspian sea was not always the same, on the Eastern, Western, and Southern shores, and that it hath been subject to many changes. Perhaps even the Caspian sea might have once covered the sandy surface which now separates it from the lake Aral, and indeed its waters must have been much more considerable, as many great rivers, which formerly opened into it, have had their courses turned and flow into it no longer. Mr. Hanway's journal proves, that many alterations have happened

---

[q] "Tradit Kotiddinus ejus Longitudinem ab Oriente ad Occidentem 270 Parasengas." Abulfeda ex Versione Ask.

[r] D'Anville Mesures Itin. 96.

happened in the neighbouring countries, and this fagacious traveller remarks, that on entering the bay of Aftrabad, on the South fide' of the Cafpian fea, it had gained fo much on the coaft and eaten it away, that in many parts of it, trunks of trees blocked up the fhore and made it difficult to land. When the Ruffians firft navigated the fea, they pretend that they found only five feet of water, during nine leagues to the South and South-Eaft of Chiterie Bogorie; but for the laft thirty years, the water hath deepened fo much, that Mr. Hanway could not meet with any foundings at fome diftance from the coaft, with a line of four hundred and fifty fathoms.ᵗ

Perhaps thefe alterations may have been the reafon of the uncertainty of the figure of the Cafpian fea, with which the Orientals were as little acquainted as the Ancients. The former have fometimes fuppofed that it was round or oval, at other times that it was triangular, and like the fail ufually carried by one of their oared veffels. The obfervations made in the reign of Czar Peter the firft, at laft determined its figure, ʷ though not exactly with geometrical

---

' Hanway's Hiftorical Account of the Britifh Trade over the Cafpian fea. Vol. 1. C. 25.---164. C. 26.---166.

ᵗ Hanway's Hiftorical Account of the Britifh Trade over the Cafpian fea. Vol. 1. C. 24.---155.

ʷ For the Honour of GREAT BRITAIN, the Moderns are indebted, as Dr. Robertfon obferves, (Hiftorical Difquifition on India. 205.) to Anthony Jenkinfon for the firft correct idea of the Cafpian fea. The following is what Hakluyt terms "a notable defcription" of it. "The Cafpian fea (to fay fomething of it) is in length about two hundred leagues, and in breadth one hundred

geometrical precision, for the chart of Monsieur d' Anville, published in 1754, differs in many particulars from the Czar's laid down by de l'Isle. The gulph of Jemba, which forms a bay, whose shores are the most Northern parts of this sea, hath changed its shape in the chart of Monsieur d' Anville, and advances a degree and a half to the South.

The point with the name of Mertovit Kultuk, is there extended in Longitude more than any part of it in Monsieur de l'Isle's chart. The figure of the bay of Balkan hath experienced a similar variation, and in short Monsieur d' Anville's observations, have induced him to alter many of his predecessor's positions and bearings on the borders of this sea.——Herodotus assures us, that the Caspian sea had no communication with the neighbouring ones,[*] and Aristotle describes it as a lake, situated at the foot of mount

hundred and fifty, without any issue to other seas: to the East whereof, joyneth the great desert countrey of the Tartars, called Turkemen; to the West, the countreys of the Chyrcaffes, the mountaines of Caucasus, and the Mare Euxinum, which is from the said Caspian sea a hundred leagues. To the North, is the river Wolga, and the Land of Nagay, and to the South part joyne the countreys of Media and Persia. This sea is fresh water in many places, and in other places as salt as our great ocean. It hath many goodly rivers falling into it, and it avoideth not it selfe except it be under ground. The notable rivers that fall into it, are first the great river of Wolga, called in the Tartar tongue Edell, which springeth out of a lake in a Marrish or plaine ground, not farre from the citie of Novogrode in Russia, and it is from the spring to the sea, above two thousand English miles. It hath divers other goodly rivers falling into it, as out of Siberia, Yaic and Yem: also out of the mountaines of Caucasus, the rivers of Cyrus and Araſk, and divers others."
Hakluyt's Collection of Voyages, Vol. 1.--394.

[*] "Ἡ δὲ Κασπιη θαλασσα ἐςι ιπ' ἑωυτης, ȣ συμμισγȣσα τη ἑτερη θαλασση." Herodot. Lib. 1. --96.

mount Caucasus, and adds that they called this lake, which was circumscribed by the habitations of different people, a sea.[y]

Alexander's conquests, instead of confirming the want of a communication in the Caspian sea with the neighbouring ones, gave birth to a multitude of errors or lent them fresh credit and support. Diodorus Siculus[z] is the only one of the Conqueror's historians, that embraced the opinion of Herodotus; and though Plutarch confesses that the Macedonian Monarch could learn nothing certain of this sea, he still hath no scruples of advancing that it was a gulph of the Northern ocean.[a] This erroneous conclusion was adopted by most of the Greek and Latin writers,[b] whose names it is unnecessary to mention; and even the judicious Strabo[c] is not to be excepted, who criticises unjustly Polycletus, on his having termed the Caspian sea a lake. Monsieur de l'Isle believes, that the Ancients were deceived by the great resemblance between the

---

[y] "Ἀλλ' ἥ γε ὑπο τον Κασπιον λιμνη, ἥν καλουσιν οἱ ἐκεῖ θαλασσαν." Arist. Meteor. Lib. 1. C. 13. Tom. 1.--770. Folio. 1654.

[z] Diod. Sicul. Lib. 18.--260, 261.

[a] "Αὐτὸς δὲ μετα της ακμαιοτατης δυναμεως εἰς Ὑρκανιαν κατεβαινε κ᾽ πελαγος ἰδων κολπον, οὐκ ἐλαττονα μεν του ποντου φανεντα, γλυκυτερον δε της αλλης θαλαττης, σαφες μεν οὐδεν ἰσχυεν πυθεσθαι περι αὐτου, μαλιστα δε εἰκασε της Μαιωτιδος λιμνης ανακοπην εἰναι· κ᾽ τοι τους γε φυσικους ἀνδρας οὐκ ἐλαθε ταληθες, αλλα πολλοις ἐτεσιν ἐμπροσθεν της Ἀλεξανδρου στρατειας ἱστορηκασιν ὅτι τεσσαρων κολπων εἰσικοντων ἀπο της ἐξω θαλασσης, βορειοτατος οὗτος εστιν, το Ὑρκανιον πελαγος κ᾽ Κασπιον ὁμου προσαγορευομενον." De Vit. Alex. Plut. Opera. Tom. 1.--690.

[b] Plin. Nat. Hist. Lib. 6. C. 15. Tom. 1.--668, 669, &c. &c.--P. Mela. Lib. 1. C. 2. --Dionys. Perieg. V. 722. Eustath. Comment. 96. Ed. Steph. 4to 1577.--J. Solinus. C. 21.

[c] Strabo. Lib. 11.--777.

the strait, by which they supposed this sea opened into the Northern ocean, and the mouth of the Volga. This river runs from the North in a Southerly direction, and widens at its entrance into the Caspian sea, which receives many rivers without ever overflowing. The phænomenon may be perhaps explained on the principles of evaporation, by which a quantity of water passes off, equal to that, which the sea receives.[d]

A conjecture, not less probable, arises from the route of the Scythians, when they formerly engaged in commerce on the Northern ocean. They mounted the Volga and the Kama, and to reach the Petzora, which throws itself into this sea, they carried their merchandise about half a league over land, though it was not mentioned, being only a trifle in comparison of their tedious passage by water.[e] We have another example of this mode of executing a long voyage principally on rivers, in the chart of Japan, which Kœmpfer brought along with him into Europe, and deposited in Sir Hans Sloane's museum. It hath been since published by Monsieur de Guignes.[f] The Saghalion, is there represented as united by the lake Paikal or Baikalmore to the Lena, notwithstanding there are two carrying-places in this route. The North

---

[d] See the very ingenious theory of Dr. Halley. Philosoph. Transact. 1687.--186. 202. Perry (State of Russia) hath even calculated the quantity of water, which the Caspian sea received from the Volga every minute.

[e] Considerat. Geograph. par Mons. Buache. 147.

[f] Hist. de l'Acad. des Inscriptions. Tom. 28.--503.

North American Indians, entertain nearly the same ideas with the Japanese, on the junction of their respective lakes and rivers, as may be gathered from a comparison of the chart, traced by Ochagach the Indian, before the French officers sent to make discoveries, and the observations, which they had personally made.[g] Champlain, to whom the French establishment in Canada owed its origin, related that the Indians informed him by mounting the Saguena, in forty or fifty days he might arrive at the Northern ocean. We know decidedly that this river receives that of the Chefoumatau, by which there is a passage, with one carrying-place to the lakes of the Miffaffins, and from these lakes they descend by the Kiche-Kupitan, or the great opening into Hudson's bay.

Objects frequently present themselves under the same aspect to those people, whose knowledge is very limited, and to those, who are not civilized. The Scythians were the Savages of the ancient Continent, and it is from their accounts, that Scymnus of Chio, in all likelihood, hath related that the Tanais derives its source from the Araxes,[h] which is the Rha or Volga. But the Araxes was a term applied by the Ancients to many rivers, notwithstanding Herodotus principally designs by it the Volga, which approaches very near the Twia, at the distance of eight leagues from the Tanais,

[g] Considerat. Geograph. de Mons. Buache. Chart 8.

[h] "Εις ην ὁ Ταναις απο τε ποταμε λαβων
Το ρευμ' Αραξιως επιμισγιται."
Scymni Fragm. 128, 129. Geog. Vet. Script. Min. Græc. Tom. 2.--50.

Tanais,[i] of which it was suppofed by Ariftotle to be a branch.[k] The Scythians, who navigated the two rivers, circulated a report that they joined each other, juſt as the Cafpian fea was imagined to have had a communication with the Ocean. A paffage of Artemidorus, publifhed a few years[l] fince, confirms this explanation, and we learn from it, that the Tanais had two openings, by one of which it fell into the Palus Mæotis, and by the other flowed into Scythia. The Rha or Wolga is to be underſtood by the latter, that croffes Afiatic Scythia before it throws itfelf into the Cafpian fea, which Artemidorus after Ariftotle's opinion, adopted alfo by Ptolemy, confiders as a branch of the Tanais.

This is not, however, the only example in geography of fuch communications,[m] which may be traced to the Scythians. The whole fpace of country between the Euxine and Cafpian feas being inhabited by thefe people, the Phafis, Araxes, and many other rivers, which on a junction with them loſt their own names, ferved to connect them with the different tribes of their extended nation,

---

[i] The Baron de St. Croix obferves alfo that even this diſtance is reduced by two other rivers, one of which runs into the Don, and the other into the Wolga. See likewife Perry's State of Ruffia.

[k] "Καὶ ὁ Ἀράξης· τυτυ δ' ὁ Τάναις αφοσχιζεται μερῶ ων." Ariſtot. Meteor. Lib. 1. C. 13. Tom. 1.--768.

[l] Vangoens Notes on Porphyrius de Antro Nympharum. 87.

[m] There is a very curious and intelligent memoir of Monfieur Buache, on the fuppofed communications of different rivers and feas, which have in our times difappeared. Hiſt. de l'Acad. des Sciences.

tion, and with a very ſhort paſſage over land, which they do not mention, they generally moved by water. Their relations might then have very naturally eſtabliſhed the ſuppoſed junction of the Phaſis and Araxes with the Lycus, of which Apollonius Rhodius [n] hath ſpoken. That of the Iſter with the Ionian ſea or Adriatic gulph and the Pontus Euxinus, which we are told of by the ſame author, have no other origin. The Greek poet adopted the opinion of Timagetes,[o] who aſſures us that the Argonauts on mounting the Iſter reached the ſea, which bathes the ſides of Italy[p] and part of Greece. We know the Danube, at ſome diſtance from its riſe,

[n] "————————Παρα προχοησι Λυκοιο,
'Ο τ'αποκιδναμεν⊙ ποταμα κελαδοντ⊙ Αραξεω
Φασιδι συμφερεται ιερον ῥοον· οι δε συν αμφω
Καυκασιην αλαδ'εις εν ελαινομενοι προχεεσιν."

Apoll. Rhod. Lib. 4. V. 132————134.
See alſo the Scholia. Ed. Hoelzlin. 398. 8vo L. B. 1641.

[o] "Ce poete a ſuivi l'opinion de Timoſthenes." "Τιμαγητ⊙ δε εν α περι λιμενων, τον Ιςρον φησι καταφερεσθαι εκ των Κελτικων ορων· ειτα εκδιδονεναι εις Κελτικην λιμνην· μετα δε ταυτα εις δυο σχιζεσθαι το υδωρ, ᾑ το μεν εις τον Ευξεινον ποντον εισβαλλειν, το δε εις την Κελτικην θαλασσαν· δια δε τοτο τα ςομα⊙ πλευσαι τας Αργοναυτας, ᾑ ελθειν εις Τυρρηνιαν· κατακολυθει δε αυτω ᾑ Απολλωνι⊙." (Scholia. ad Apoll. Rhod. Lib. 4. V. 258. Ed. Hoelzlin. 409.) The Baron de St. Croix for Timagetes hath boldly ſubſtituted Timoſthenes, who had, he ſays, the command of the fleet of Ptolemy Philadelphus, and was the author of ſome geographical details in ten books. The name, however, of Timagetes again occurs in the commentary on the 284th Verſe of the 4th Book of Apollonius Rhodius, and I have reſtored it. From the repetition of the words, it cannot be ſuppoſed to be an error.

[p] "Ενθα διχη το μεν ενθα μετ'Ιονιην αλα βαλλει
Τηδ'υδωρ, το δ'οπισθε ζαθεν δια κολπον ιησι
Σκιζομεν⊙ ποντε Τρινακριυ εισανεχοντα."

Apoll. Rhod. Lib. 4.--289————291.

rife, approaches the Adriatic gulph, with which a communication might eafily be opened, if a junction of it was formed with the river, which runs into the Adriatic gulph near Aquilea, and which is only feparated from the Danube by a narrow tract of country.

It is then very probable that Patroclus, who commanded the fleets of Seleucus and Antiochus, might more eafily have taken the mouths of the Volga for a ftrait,[q] as the miftake was fupported by the opinions of the natives, and they went by water to the Northern ocean. This navigator would naturally lofe no time in publifhing his pretended difcovery, or rather the confirmation of the report of the Macedonians, who followed Alexander; and from this circumftance we may date the errors of the cotemporary and later writers. P. Mela hath reprefented this ftrait, which ferved as a communication with the Cafpian fea and that of the Northern ocean, as long, very narrow, like a river, and continuing its courfe in a direct line, as it approached its opening[r] into the fea. Under this defcription the Volga cannot be miftaken.

Ptolemy, with the advantage of various relations, comes over to the fentiments of Herodotus, Ariftotle, Diodorus Siculus and Polycletus, and he tells us in his geography, that the Cafpian fea is

---

[q] Strabo. Lib. 2.

[r] "Mare Cafpium, ut angufto, ita longo etiam freto, primum terras, quafi fluvius, irrumpit."
P. Mela. Lib. 3. C. 5.--266.

is surrounded on all sides by land, and that it resembles, when compared to the Continent, an island in the midst of the waves.'

In the number of events and revolutions, which Providence hath brought about in different ages of the world, though they may have been fatal to the inhabitants of the countries that were immediately exposed to them, the circle of human knowledge was certainly extended. By one of these political convulsions, the opinions respecting the Caspian sea were reduced to a certainty, and its supposed communication with the Ocean proved to have been imaginary. Under the Arabian Caliphs the Northern regions were explored, and their conquests and incursions are clearly ascertained by the medals of these Sovereign princes, that are often found in the ancient tombs which are so numerous on the borders of Petzora.' It was then generally known, that the Caspian sea had no communication whatever with the Northern ocean, and Abulfeda indeed with the other Oriental geographers were never ignorant of it."—Arrian,˟ however, and Q. Curtius ʸ have
notwithstanding

' Ptolem. Lib. 7. C. 5.

' Strahlenberg's Hist. Geographical Description of the North and Eastern part of Europe and Asia. Sect. 6.--117.

ʷ "Nec conjungitur cum mari ambiente, nec cum alio ex maribus de quibus sermo præcessit."
Abulfeda ex Versione Ask. Eldrisi. Geog. Nub. 243.

˟ Arrian. Lib. 5. C. 26.--396.

ʸ "Quidam credidere, non Caspium mare esse; sed ex Indiâ in Hyrcaniam cadere." Q. Curtius. Lib. 6. C. 4. Tom. 1.--411, 412.

notwithstanding declared that the Caspian sea had a communication with the Indian ocean, by which the tract of land between the two seas must be considerably narrowed. This erroneous idea of the two historians perhaps induced Artemidorus to believe, that the Caspian sea was at no great distance from the Ocean,[a] and that the Caspians, who dwelt upon its shores, were the borderers of Persia; from which, that part of Asia situated between the Caspian sea and Indian ocean, the later including the whole expanse of water that washes the Southern side of Asia, was diminished five degrees in Latitude, and all the nations, that occupied this space of country, are made to disappear.

We learn from Polycletus,[a] that the water of the Caspian sea was fresh, and Plutarch[b] and Q. Curtius[c] have adopted the opinion, which is not altogether destitute of truth. Abulfeda relates, after a traveller, whose name he does not mention, that the water of this sea changes its colour on the Northern shore, and that it is freshened so much by the river Atal or Atalcus, which is the modern Volga, as to be serviceable even at the distance of a day's sail,

---

[a] "Περι της Κασπιης θαλασσης ιστορει Αρτεμιδωρος εν τη επιτομη των γεωγραφεμενων· εστι δε πλησιον τε Ωκεανε." Schol. ad Appol. Rhod. Lib. 3. V. 858. Ed. Hoelzlin. L. B. 8vo 1641.

[a] "Πολυκλητος δε κ̓ πιστεις προσφερεται περι τε λιμνην ειναι την θαλατίαν ταυτην——— κ̓ υπογλυκυ ειναι το υδωρ." Strabo. Lib. 11.--777.

[b] "Γλυκυτερον δε της αλλης θαλατης." De Vit. Alex. Plut. Opera. Tom. 1.--690.

[c] "Mæotim paludem in id cadere putant: et argumentum adferunt: aquam, quo dulcior sit quam cetera maria, infuso paludis humore mitescere." Q. Curtius. Lib. 6. C. 4.--410.

fail, which may be calculated at nearly twelve leagues.[d] Father Avril on the contrary limits its effects, and assures us that the fresh water extends only two leagues from the shore.[e] The Ancients, who seldom ventured out of the sight of land, concluded that the rest of the Caspian sea was like that, which they had before their eyes, but Le Bruyn[f] and many other travellers[g] have not forgotten to mention the singularity. Perhaps we may be tempted to suppose, with Monsieur de Buffon,[h] that it became only salt slowly, and by degrees. The rivers, that lose themselves in this sea, have continually brought along with them salts, which they detached from the earth in their passages, and these salts have not been dissipated by evaporation. It is possible also, that the difference between Abulfeda and Father Avril, may be owing to the observations made on the different parts of the coasts, on which they landed. The freshness of the Caspian sea could not have been always the same at an equal distance from the coast, but must

[d] "Mercator, qui in hoc mari navigavit, ita dicens, cum ad finem illius maris ad septentrionem pervenimus, illam aquam falsam ac limpidam colore mutatam comperi; tunc dictum fuit mihi illam aquam esse fluminis Atalci maris aquis mixtam, cumque ex illâ bibissem eam dulcem esse deprehendi, et ita prope diem per mare dulce navigavimus." Abulfeda ex Vers. Alk.

[e] Voyages en divers Etats d'Europe et d'Asie. 86.

[f] Voyages de Le Bruyn. Tom. 3.--459. Ed. 4to

[g] Voyages d'Olearius. 513.

[h] Histoire Naturelle. Tom. 2.--176. Ed. 12mo The Baron de St. Croix observes that Pliny appears to strengthen Monsieur de Buffon's system. "Præterea apud Bactros amnes Ochus et Oxus, ex appositis montibus deferunt salis ramenta." Plin. Hist. Nat. Lib. 31. C. 7. Tom. 4. --805. 4to 1685.

must have varied according to the quantity of water, which the neighbouring rivers poured into it, and the velocity with which it was discharged, as it would be conveyed to a distance proportionable with its rapidity. Strabo reproaches the companions of Alexander's arms with the invention of many falsities on the subject of the Caspian sea,[i] and with having confounded it with the Palus Mæotis: Plutarch[k] and Q. Curtius[l] inform their readers that this lake of European Scythia joined the Palus Mæotis, but this error may be attributed to the incorrect notions of the Ancients relative to the lake Aral, which they imagined to be the Palus Mæotis.—Herodotus relates that the country inhabited by the Chorasmians, the Hyrcanians and some other people, was watered by the river Aces or Akes. The precise place, where it disgorged itself, was between two mountains:[m] being banked up and secured with locks by the orders of the king of Persia, its course was thus stopped, and it formed a spacious lake, covering the plain between the two mountains.[n] The whole country became very

---

[i] "Προσεδοξάσθη δὲ κ̣ περι της θαλατης πολλα ψευδη δια την Αλεξανδρη φιλοτιμιαν—————εις ἐν συνηγον την τε Μαιωτιν λιμνην την δεχομενην τον Ταναιν, κ̣ την Κασπιαν θαλατίαν." Strabo. 11. --777.

[k] "Μαλιςα δε εικασι της Μαιωτιδ⸻ λιμνης αναχοπην ειναι." De Vit. Alex. Plut. Opera. Tom. 1.--690.

[l] "Mæotim paludem in id cadere putant." Q. Curtius. Lib. 6. C. 4. Tom. 1.--410.

[m] The Baron de St. Croix observes these Locks are termed by Sherefeddin "Coluga," or the "Iron Gate." Hist. de Timur. Lib. 3. C. 2. Lib. 6. C. 23.

[n] "Τας διασφαγας των ὀρεων ευδειμας ὁ βασιλευς, πυλας ιπ'εκαςη διασφαγι ιςησι· αποκεκλημενυ δε τυ ὑδατ⸻ της εξοδυ, το πεδιον το εντ⸻ των ὀρεων, πελαγ⸻ γινεται." Herod. Lib. 3.--256.

very clamorous on the occasion, and the Persian monarch, throwing down the mound, which he had ordered to be erected, the Akes or Aces returned into its old channel, and on the usual tribute being paid, was again permitted to fertilize the country.* In this description the Oxus is clearly ascertained, and the pass of Dehani-Chir, where the river is compressed into a narrow compass is exactly pointed out. We need not be astonished that Herodotus, who took up his information from report, should have confounded this pass with the lake formed by the waters of the Oxus, which is in fact the Aral. The mountains or bold steep sides, with which it is surrounded gave some reason for the mistake, and the Greek historian had certainly some proper ideas of this lake, known afterwards under the name of the Oxian lake, though all of them were not correct. In the remotest antiquity indeed, the Oxus always in some measure ran into this lake, and augmented it with at least some part of its waters.

The Turkish geographer informs us, that the Dgeihoun, which is the Oxus, on quitting the sands, which will be hereafter taken notice of, divides itself into many streams; those of Kiahvare, Hezar-Asb, Kierdan Kierb, and Hare, supply the whole country with

* " Επιαν ων μιδεν σφι παραδιδωται τυ ὑδατ©., ελθοντες ες τας Περσας αυτοι τε κ̓ γυναικες, ξαντες κἀτα τας θυρας τυ βασιλι©., βοωσι ωξυνμενοι· ὁ δε βασιλευς τοισι διομενοισι αυτεων μαλιϛα εντελλεται ανοιγειν τας πυλας τας ες τυτο ξεξυσας· επιαν δε διακορ©. ἡ γη σφιων γινηται πνευσα το ὑδωρ, αυται μεν ἁι πυλαι αποκληιονται, αλλας δ'εντελλεται ανοιγειν αλλοισι τοισι διομενοισι μαλιϛα των λοιπων· ὡς δ'εγω οιδ'ακυσας, χρηματα μεγαλα πρησσομεν©. ανοιγει, παρεξ τυ φορυ." Herod. Lib. 3.--256.

with water and are navigable.[p] Some of the branches of the Dgeihoun throw themselves into the lake Kharefm or Aral, whilft this river paffes along the valley of Kierlave, roaring fo as to be heard to the diftance of two leagues, and afterwards difcharges itfelf into the Cafpian fea near Kahlkahl, ten days' journey from Charefmus.

Thefe details ferve to illuftrate the text of Ptolemy, from whom we learn that many ftreams rife in the Sogdian mountains, fituated between two rivers. Thefe two rivers can only be the Oxus and Iaxartes, that receive the tributary ftreams, of which one forms the Oxian lake.[q] Ammianus Marcellinus, who hath often tranflated Ptolemy, and fometimes appears to have added to him, gives us fome idea of the Oxian lake by the expreffion of "far and widely extended,"[r] which can only agree with the lake of Aral. Pliny alfo mentions it by name, but he is miftaken in the fuppofition of its being the fource of the Oxus,[s] that Ptolemy fixes in the thirty-ninth degree of Northern Latitude,[t] the lake being in

---

[p] Geograph. Turc. 821, 822. and 884, 885.

[q] "Ον ὡς ποιεῖ την Ὀξιανην λιμνην." Ptolem. Lib. 6. C. 12.

[r] "Oxiam nomine paludem efficiunt longe lateque diffufam." (Ammian. Marcell. Lib. 23. C. 6.--410, 411. 4to L. B. 1693.) The Baron de St. Croix remarks that Ammianus Marcellinus hath tranflated the Greek word "λιμνην" of Ptolemy by "paludem" whereas it fignifies both a lake and a marfh or fen, and that the former term would have agreed better both with the actual ftate of the Oxian lake, and the text of the Greek geographer.

[s] "Oxus amnis, ortus in lacu Oxo." Plin. Hift. Nat. Lib. 6. C. 16. Tom. 1.--676.

[t] Ptolem. Lib. 6. C. 12.

the forty-fifth, which perfectly corresponds with the modern observations. It is true that the Greek geographer allows this Latitude to the middle of the lake, which should have been given to the Northern side of it, but the error is the result of the Ptolemean system, which throws back all the part of Asia beyond the Paropamisus, much farther North than it really is. Monsieur de l'Isle hath remarked, with great propriety, that the mouth of the Volga, which ought to be placed at the forty-sixth degree, is to be found at the forty-ninth, and the Southern shore of the Caspian sea at the fortieth degree instead of the thirty-seventh,* an inaccuracy of great consequence and moment. With these errors, it is extraordinary that Ptolemy should have so nearly approached the true Latitude of the Aral or Kharesm, which is still called Ogouz by the Tartars. Its ancient name of Oxian was derived from the Oxus, of which the Aces or Akes was probably a corruption, and the affinity of the Oxus with the modern Ogouz is easily perceptible.

In the Calmuck and Mungal tongues, Ongon signifies the Gift of God, and Ogouz seems to be derived from this word. The Carakalpak Tartars, that inhabit the country near the lake Aral, conduct a thousand little streams from it over their sandy plains, and when the water is evaporated, their surface is covered with a sort of crystallized salt, which is the only one these Tartars as well as those of Casastichia-Orda, and of Charesmus are able to procure.

---

* Memoire sur la mer Caspienne, Hist. de l'Acad. des Sciences, 1721, 248.

procure. From the great advantages which all these nations receive from the Aral, its Tartar name may have been given to it on principles of gratitude, and they might confider it as one of the immediate gifts of heaven. On the whole, it may be reasonably inferred, that the Oxian lake is that of the Ogouz or Aral, which was known to the ancient geographers, though the contrary hath been supposed.[x]

Polycletus[y] had confounded the Palus Mæotis with the Caspian sea, which received into it, according to Plutarch[z] and Q. Curtius,[a] this species of lake, whose true position Arrian[b] hath established in his history of Alexander's expeditions. From this circumstance, however, the Periplus of the Erythrean sea appears to have been falsely attributed to this Greek historian, as its author hath

---

[x] The Baron de St. Croix observes, though Monsieur de Buffon assures us before the conquest of Peter the 1st "On ignoroit jusqu'à l'existence du lac Aral, qui en est eloigné (de la mer Caspienne) vers l'Orient, d'environ cent lieus, ou si on connoissoit quelques unes des cotés de ce lac Aral, on croyoit que c'etoit une partie de la mer Caspienne," (Hist. Nat. Tom. 2.--160. Ed. 12mo) that Eldrisi, who composed his Work in the 527th year of the Hegira, which answers to the 1149th and 1150th of the Vulgar Era, expressly mentions the lake of Aral, Kharem, or Chouarasm, according to the Maronite orthography, and that it is accurately distinguished from the Caspian sea. (Climat. 3. Part. 8.--138. Ed. 1619.) Abulfeda also speaks of this lake under the name of the Chourasmian lake, which opens into the Dzeihoun or Gihon. Descript. Chorasm. Geograph. Minor. Tom. 3.--23.

[y] Strabo. Lib. 11.--777.

[z] De Vit. Alex. Plut. Opera. Tom. 1.--690.

[a] Q. Curtius. Lib. 6. C. 4. Tom. 1.--410.

[b] Arrian. Exped. Alex. Lib. 3. C. 30.--254. See also Dodwell. Dissert. in Script. Geograph. Minor. Tom. 4.--85.

hath advanced, that the Palus Mæotis and Caspian sea discharge their waters together into the Ocean.[c]

These errors, respecting the communication of the two seas, possibly afforded reason for Clitarchus[d] to believe, that the Caspian sea and the Pontus Euxinus were the same. Q. Curtius perhaps adopted the opinion,[e] but he is little solicitous as to any consequences, which depend upon his sentiments, and both relates contrary hypotheses, and admits them without caution or distinction. The name of Tanais given to the Iaxartes, from a corruption of the word Iksærte, which in the Mungal language conveys the idea of a great river, may have strengthened the opinion. Diodorus Siculus,[f] Justin,[g] and Q. Curtius[h] have confounded these two

---

[c] "Καθ' ἥν." Geograph. Minor. Tom. 1.--37.

[d] "Qui a crù que la mer Caspienne etoit la meme que celle du pont Euxin." The Baron de St. Croix supports the assertion by a reference to "Nam et irrumpit e Scythico oceano in aversa Asiæ, pluribus nominibus accolarum appellatum, celeberrimis duobus, Caspio et Hyrcanio. Non minus hoc esse quam Pontum Euxinum, Clitarchus putat." (Plin. Hist. Nat. Lib. 6. C. 13. Tom. 1.--668.) Of the validity of the evidence the reader will judge.

[e] "Opinion adoptée par Q. Curce." The Baron de St. Croix directs his readers to the following passages. "Cum vero venti a Pontico mari spirant quidquid sabuli in campis jacet converrunt." (Q. Curt. Lib. 7. C. 3. Tom. 2.--509.) "Asiæ omnia fere flumina, alia in Rubrum, alia in Caspium mare, alia in Hyrcanum et in Ponticum decidunt." (Q. Curt. Lib. 7. C. 3. Tom. 2.--501.) On the former, Cellarius hath defended the Latin historian, though weakly, and argues that the wind blows, in the same direction, both from the Euxine and Caspian seas towards Bactria: in the latter, Q. Curtius seems to have distinguished them. I have added the hypothetical "Perhaps."

[f] Diod. Sicul. Lib. 18. Tom. 2.--261.

[g] Justin. Lib. 12. C. 5.---315.

[h] Q. Curt. Lib. 7. C. 6. Tom. 2.--525. Lib. 7. C. 7. Tom. 2.--531, 532.

two rivers, which Plutarch[l] and Arrian[k] have difcriminated, though the pride and vanity of the Macedonians wifhed to unite them.[l]

Ptolemy[m] knew the difference, but bowing with fubmiffion to the authority of the hiftorians of the Conqueror of Afia refpecting the altars, which this Prince erected on the banks of the Iaxartes in memory of his conquefts, the Greek geographer hath tranfported them near the river Tanais, where, after running in a Southerly direction from its fource, it approaches the Rha, and then turning to the Weft, ftretches to the Palus Mæotis, in which it lofes itfelf.

The Greek geographer following the fame guides, hath multiplied the Scythians, as well as the Aorfes and Agathyrfes. Thefe nations inhabited one fide of the Tanais, where Ptolemy places them,[n] but he reckons them, notwithftanding, a fecond time amongft

---

[l] De Vit. Alex. Plut. Opera. Tom. 1.--691.

[k] Arrian. Exped. Alex. Lib. 3. C. 30.--251.

[l] " Επειδη γαρ ὁμολογητο, ὁτι εκ παντων διεεργει την Ασιαν απο της Ευρωπης ὁ Ταναις ποταμ۞, το δε μεταξυ της θαλατίης, ἡ τε Ταναιδ۞ πολυ μερ۞ της Ασιας ον, ὑχ'ὑπιπιπτε τοις Μακιδοσι." Strabo. Lib. 11.--777.

[m] Ptolemy. Lib. 3. C. 5. The Baron de St. Croix accufes the editor of Ptolemy with a wilful intention of mifunderftanding him, and of removing the altars in oppofition to the Text of Ptolemy, to the foot of the Riphæan mountains.

[n] Ptolem. Lib. 3. C. 5.

amongſt the Aſiatic Scythians.° If Pliny ᵖ appears to have not entirely avoided this miſtake, he diſtinguiſhes at leaſt by additional names the people of European Scythia, that he places near the Caſpian ſea, and underſtands the Aorſes by the Naſotiani, and the Arimaſpians by the Cacidari.ᑫ But perhaps theſe Aſiatic Scythians were colonies of the European Scythians, and preſerved their names after their migrations.

The ignorance of Q. Curtius equalled his credulity. Deceived by the name of the Tanais, improperly given to the Iaxartes, he ſweeps from the ſurface of the earth all Aſia ſituated between theſe two rivers, and ſpeaks of Bactria as the laſt province of Aſia, and ſeparated only from Europe by the Tanais, which he conſiders as the boundary of theſe two quarters of the world.ʳ In direct contradiction to ſuch a declaration, he pretends in another part of his work, that the Scythians, who lived above the Cimmerian

---

° Ptolem. Lib. 6. C. 14.

ᵖ "Ultraque Choraſmii, Candari, Attaſini, Paricani, Sarangæ, Parrhaſini, Maratiani, Naſotiani, Aorſi, Gelæ, quos Græci Caduſios appellavere, Matiani." Plin. Hiſt. Nat. Lib. 6. C. 16. Tom. 1.--675, 676.

ᑫ "Ariſmaſpi antea Cacidari." Plin. Hiſt. Nat. Lib. 6. C. 17. Tom. 1.--678.

ʳ "Tanais Europam et Aſiam medius interfluit." (Q. Curt. Lib. 6. C. 2.--398.) "Bactrianos Tanais ab Scythis, quos Europæos vocant, dividit. Idem Aſiam et Europam finis interfluit. ———— Si vero Tanaim tranſierimus——— Quis dubitavit patere etiam Europam victoribus ? ———— unus amnis interfluit, quem ſi trajicimus, in Europam arma proferimus." Q. Curt. Lib. 7. C. 7. Tom. 2.--531——535.

merian Bosphorus, belonged to Asia.' The region, which extends above the Bosphorus and Palus Mæotis, is notwithstanding to the West of the Tanais, and consequently situated in Europe, and is inhabited by the Roxolanes and Iazyges, two nations of European Scythians.' Q. Curtius hath fallen into this error, from having varied the situation of the mouths and the course of the Tanais, and advanced the Longitude five degrees. He adds afterwards, that the Scythians, from whom the Parthians sprung, did not come originally from the Bosphorus, but out of Europe." In this manner he removes the Cimmerian Bosphorus into Asia, whilst the strait, by which the Palus Mæotis discharges itself into the Pontus Euxinus, forms the separation of Asia and of Europe, whose limits have been so strangely described.

The false and erroneous position of many nations is a necessary consequence. The Cercetes, the Mosynœcians, and the Chalybians, are placed on the left of the Caspian sea, and the Leucosyrians and the Amazons on the right.' But the ancient geographers

---

¹ "Qui super Bosphorum colunt, adscribuntur Asiæ." Q. Curt. Lib. 6. C. 2. Tom. 1.--398.

¹ Ptolem. Lib. 3. C. 5.

ʷ "Nec dubitatur, quin Scythæ, qui Parthos condidere, non a Bosphoro, sed ex regione Europæ penetraverint." Q. Curt. Lib. 6. C. 2.--398.

ˣ "Cercetæ, Mosyni, et Chalybes a lævâ sunt; ab alterâ parte Leucosyri et Amazonum campi; et illos qua vergit ad septentrionem; hos ad occasum conversa prospectat." Q. Curt. Lib. 6. C. 4. Tom. 1.--409.

phers have uniformly established the Mosynœcians, the Chalybians, and their neighbours the Cercetes, called in later times the Apaites, in the mountains near the Pontus Euxinus,ʸ and the Leucosyrians were the inhabitants of Cappadocia,ᶻ whose situation is well known, as well as the country of the fabulous Amazons, who were supposed to have occupied the plains of Themiscyra,ᵃ on the banks of the Thermodon. A single error in geography is the parent of many others, and Q. Curtius again justifies the observation. This Latin historian, after having varied the position of the Chalybians, adds that they were neighbours to the great cities of Sinope and Amisus.ᵇ Amisus was at the distance of twelve hundred Olympic stadia to the North-East of the Chalybians,ᶜ and Sinope, a celebrated

---

ʸ Strabo. Lib. 12.--825.--Scylax. 79.--Dionys. Perieg. V. 768.--Et Eustathii Comment. ad Loc.--Xenophon. Exped. Cyri. Lib. 5.--379. 4ᵗᵒ Oxon. 1735. These Mosynœci were also called Mossuni, and the learned reader may consult on the etymology of the name, Apollonius Rhodius. Lib. 2. V. 1018. &c. with the Scholia on it, and also on Lib. 5. V. 379.--Bochart. Phaleg. 3.--12.

ᶻ Herodotus. Lib. 1.--35. All the tract washed by the river Halys seems to be called, by the ancient authors, indiscriminately, Syria, Assyria and Leucosyria. See Apoll. Rhod. 947——966. with the Scholia.--Dionys. Perieg. V. 733.--Strabo. Lib. 12.--819.--Plin. Hist. Nat. Lib. 6. C. 3. Tom. 1.--651.

ᵃ Strabo. Lib. 12.--823.--P. Mela. Lib. 1. C. 19.--108, 109.

ᵇ "Cet historien, apres avoir changè la situation des Chalybes, ajonte que ce peuple etoit vois in de deux villes celebres, Sinope et Amisus." The Baron de St. Croix must be responsible for his own assertion, for though he refers his readers to the fourth Chapter of the sixth Book of Q. Curtius, not a syllable respecting either Sinope or Amisus is to be found in it.

ᶜ See the Chart of Asia Minor by d'Anville.

brated city of Paphlagonia, was twelve hundred ftadia to the North-Weft of Amifus.[d]

Of the PEOPLE and COUNTRIES of HIGHER ASIA.

Pharafmanes the king of the Chorafmians came, according to Arrian, to meet Alexander, and he affured him, that he was a neighbour of Colchis and the Amazons, which is an abfurd miftake, and originated like that of Q. Curtius, already noticed. The Chorafmians refided on the banks of the Oxus, to the Eaft of the Cafpian fea, a pofition, which Ptolemy hath accurately marked,[e] who is far from multiplying this nation, as hath been unjuftly objected to him.[f] The name of Kharefm or Khoarefm, which hath been preferved with its ancient pofition by the Orientals,[g] fufficiently

[d] Marcian of Heraclea, (Geograph. Minor. Tom. 1.—74.) the Baron de St. Croix remarks, only reckons three hundred and fifty ftadia between Sinope and Amifus, and he fuppofes an error in the numerical letters. Inftead of the "τ ν" he reads "α ν," which will then agree with the calculation of the author of the Periplus Euxinus. "Απο δε Σινωπης εις Καρυσαν πεντηκοντα κ̂ ἱκατον (ςαδιοι.)————ενθενδε εις Ζαγωρα αλλοι αυ πεντηκοντα κ̂ ἱκατον· ενθενδε εις τον Ἁλυν ποταμον, τριακοσιοι————απο δε Ἁλυ⊙ ποταμου ες Ναυςαθμον, ςαδιοι ενενηκοντα————ενθενδε εις Κωνωπειον αλλην λιμνην, αλλοι αυ πεντηκοντα; Απο δε Κωνωπειω εις Ευσηνην ἱκατον κ̂ εικοσι· ενθενδε εις Αμισον ἱκατον κ̂ ἑξηκοντα." Arrian. Peripl. Pont. Euxin. 127, 128. 8vo Amft. 1683.

[e] Ptolem. Lib. 6. C. 12.

[f] Hift. de l'Acad. des Infcriptions. Tom. 25.—52.

[g] Abulfeda. Geograph. Min. Tom. 3.—20.—Eldrifi. Geog. Min. 138.

ciently demonstrates the situation of this Scythian people, a tribe of the Saques or rather Sacæs, who were an Abian colony.

Alexander's historians have been accused of transporting the Abians of Europe into Asia,[h] but carrying our inquiries far back, they may possibly be justified. The Scythians have in fact occupied almost all the Northern regions of the ancient Continent, or with a greater accuracy of expression, the uniformity of manners and modes of life, so visible in the different tribes of people, who inhabited that extensive tract of country, gave the Greeks some reasons to comprise them under the general name of Scythians. Their proper name, we are told by Herodotus, was that of the Scolotes, derived from one of their kings:[i] they were considered only as one people, and in this sense is Thucydides also to be understood, when speaking of their force and power.[k] Superior in numbers to any other nation in Europe or in Asia, when united they were irresistible, and in reality they both peopled many countries, and spread themselves almost over the face of the whole earth.

The geographers distinguished the Scythians by the European and Asiatic Scythians, but the term is too vague and comprehensive. They may

---

[h] Hist. de l'Acad. des Inscriptions. Tom. 26.--50.

[i] "Συμπασι δε ειναι ονομα Σκολοτυς, τυ βασιλιως επωνυμιην· Σκυθας δε Ἑλληνες ωνομασαν." Herodot. Lib. 4.--282, 283.

[k] "Ταυτη δε αδυνατα εξισουσθαι ουχ' οτι τα εν τη Ευρωπη, αλλ'ουδ'εν τη Ασιη εθνος εν προς εν ισιν ὁ, τι δυνατον Σκυθαις ομογνωμονουσι πασιν αντιστηναι." Thucydides. Hist. Lib. 2.--163.

may be more properly claſſed in the two ſeparate diviſions of the Nomades or wandering Scythians, and the Scythians who had fixed dwelling-places, and cultivated the country on which they ſettled. Ephorus has adopted the diviſion.¹ In the origin indeed of ſociety, it is perhaps the only one of any ſervice in aſcertaining the different nations of the world. Both the progreſs of civilization, which always ſtrikes at the root of morality, and the foundation of towns and cities, that conſtantly increaſe at the expence of the ſurrounding countries, whoſe inhabitants they regularly ſwallow up, whilſt at the ſame time they introduce a luxury, that ſoon renders contemptuous the ſober duties of rural life, have always put an end to theſe two claſſes, which for the happineſs of every people, were originally their ſole diſtinctions.——With the ancient Perſians there was indeed no other,ᵐ and they ſtill ſubſiſt amongſt the Tartars, who are the deſcendants of the Scythians. The powerful tribe of the Uſbeck Tartars is divided into the Oulagets, who rove from place to place, and are ſhepherds by profeſſion, and the Bukhars or Særtes, who live in villages, and have fixed habitations.ⁿ The ſhepherds or wandering Scythians were the moſt numerous, and included the Abians, a name which was given to any wandering nation, and which related to their form of life, that

---

¹ Strabo. Lib. 7.--463, 464.

ᵐ Herodotus. Lib. 1.--62, 63.

ⁿ Strahlenberg's Deſcription of the North and Eaſtern part of Europe and Aſia.

that Horace has deſcribed,[o] and in which, detached from thoſe poſſeſſions that ſometimes have an influence on the probity of the heart, they acquired a character of integrity, which even Homer celebrates.[p]

Ariſtarchus pretends that the name of Abians was confined to a particular nation,[q] and this opinion in ſome meaſure may agree with that which hath been adopted, and is authorized by the concurrent teſtimony of a crowd of writers, geographers, hiſtorians, and grammarians.[r] This appellation, after having been applied in general to all the wandering nations, was afterwards reſtrained to thoſe particular people, whoſe manners and way of life correſpond moſt with the idea repreſented by the term of Abians. A paſſage of Scymnus of Chios, ſeems to ſet the ſubject in a clear light. The

[o] "Quorum plauſtra vagas rite trahunt Domus."

Horat. Carm. Lib. 3.--24.--10.

Silius Italicus hath condenſed the hiſtory of their life into the narrow compaſs of two lines.

"Nulla domus; plauſtris habitant: migrare per arva,
Mos, atque errantes circumvectare Penates."

[p] "Γλακτοφαγων, Αβιων τε, δικαιοτατων ανθρωπων." Hom. Iliad. 13. V. 6.

[q] Apoll. Lexic. Tom. 1--13. And the ingenious conjecture of Monſieur de Villoiſon on the name of this people. 14.

[r] "Τους ανεφιους και τους ἁμαζοικους." Strabo. Lib. 7.--455.—Euſtathius. ad V. 6. Homer. Iliad. 13.—Nicol. Damaſc. de Mor. Gent. ad Calcem. Repul. Lac. Crag. 548. Ουβιαιοι, Δικαιοτατους.—Heſych. in Voc. Αβιων.—Apoll. Lexic. 13, 14.—Etymol. Mag. Ed. Sylb. 232, 233.—Steph. Byzant. 6, 7.

The geographical poet, after having mentioned the Scythians who had fixed dwelling-places, and cultivated the country that they occupied, following Ephorus his guide, adds, " many other people, who have no particular names, are shepherds, and from their religious principles treat their flocks with tenderness. They drink mares' milk like the Scythians, and have only one common property. Anacharsis is said to have been born amongst these people, celebrated for their moral character, and many of these Scythians are supposed to have passed into Asia, and there formed settlements, where they took the name of Saces."[s] The same passage is likewise extracted from the fourth book of Ephorus, in the fragment of the Periplus of the Pontus Euxinus, published by Vossius.[t] Strabo after having cited it from Ephorus, joins to it the verses of the poet Chærilus, in which he says, that "the Saces were shepherds

---

[s] "Τον Παντικαπη διαξαντι Λιμναιων εθνᾳ,
'Ετερα τε πλειονα ε διωνομασμενα,
Νομαδικα δε επι καλυμενα ευσεβη πανυ
'Ως ηδεν εμψυχων αδικησαι ποτ'αν,
Οικοφορα δ'ως εςηκε κ᾽ σιτυμενα,
Γαλακτι, ταις Σκυθικαις τε ιππομολγιαις
Ζωσι δε την τε κτησιν αναδεδεχοτες
Κοινην απαντων την τε ολην υσιαν·
Και τον σοφον Αναχαρσιν εκ των Νομαδικων
Φησι γενεσθαι των σφοδρ᾽ευσεβεςατων.
———————— κ᾽ κατοικησαι τινας
Εις Ασιαν ελθοντας, ὡς δη κ᾽ Σακας
Καλωσιν·
Scymni Chii Fragm. 111-123. Geog.Vet. Script. Græc. Min. Tom. 2. -49-50.

[t] Added to Scylax. 138. Ed. Gronovii. 4to L. B. 1700.

herds of Scythian origin, celebrated for their integrity, who inhabited Afia, a fertile country," [w] and he confirms the opinion of Ephorus.

We learn from Herodotus [x] and Pliny, [y] that the Perfians included all the Scythians under the Saces, becaufe this people agreeable to the ideas of the Roman Naturalift, was the neareft to their empire. But perhaps they might have other reafons, and the term had probably a different origin.

A knowledge of the old Runic tongue, the Sclavonian dialects, and of the language of Thibet or Tangut, as well as of the Perfian and Turkifh idioms, would afford us undoubtedly great affiftance in the explication of many Scythian names, but the fureft and moft ufeful would be the Mungal, which was fo widely fpread

in

---

[w] "Μηλονομοι τε Σακαι, γενια Σκυθαι αυταες ινειον
Ασιδα πυροφορον· νομαδων γε μεν ησαν αποικοι
Ανθρωπων νομιμων."
        Strabo. Lib. 7.--464.

[x] " Ὁι γαρ Περσαι παντας τυς Σκυθυς καλεσι Σακας." Herod. Lib. 7.--540.

[y] "Ultra funt Scytharum populi Perfæ, illos Sacas in univerfum appellavere a proximâ gente, antiqui Aramæos." (Plin. Hift. Nat. Lib. 6. C. 17. Tom. 1.--678.) The Greeks, the Baron de St. Croix remarks from Ariftophanes, applied the term of "Saces" to thofe, who had no fixed place of refidence, and were not Citizens of any town.

"Ἱμεις γαρ, ω'νδρες, ὁι παροντες εν λογω,
Νοσον νοσυμεν την εναντιαν Σακα·
Ὁ μεν γαρ ων ουκ αστος, εισβιαζεται."
        Ariftoph. Aves. 30----33.

in Afia.[a] The word Saki imports in it "I maffacre," and it is very probable, that the Scythians in their bloody engagements with the Perfians, cried out, when their enemies gave way, Sakib, Sakib,[a] kill or maffacre, and that the nation, whofe language was not underftood, took its name from the impreffion, which fear had profoundly graven on the heart, and the term, which it ufed itfelf in its combats. From Sakib or Saki the derivation of the Saces is naturally eafy,[b] who were alfo called Amourgians,[c] according to Herodotus, from one of their kings, of whom Ctefias[d] fpeaks, and not from Margus a river of Margia, as Monfieur Freret[e] conjectures. The Saces in reality never inhabited this country, and differed but little from the Afpaciafquians or rather Afpaciacians, as will be hereafter mentioned: but it may be firft neceffary to fix the pofition of the Abians.—Strabo fpeaks of the Saces as the moft Eaftern tribe of the Scythians beyond the Cafpian fea, and he places them, like Marcian of Heraclea, on the fame line with the Sogdians, near a ford of the Iaxartes, which facilitated their communication

---

[a] Strahlenberg. Defcription of the North and Eaftern part of Europe and Afia.

[a] Sakib in the Imperative, fee the Mungal grammar in Thevenot.

[b] Steph. Byzant. 580. Reland, according to the Baron de St. Croix, hath traced the etymology of the word up to the Arabians. (Differt. de Vet. Ling. Perfarum in voce Sacæ.) The German extraction however of Wachter, in his Gloffary, (1336) "Saka, nocere, vulnerare, damnum inferre," the Baron de St. Croix apprehends to be more legitimate.

[c] "Τυτυς δε ιοντας Σκυθας Αμυργιυς, Σακας εκαλεον." Herod. Lib. 7.—540.

[d] Phot. Bibl. 108.

[e] Obfervations fur la Cyropedie. Hift. de l'Acad. des Infcriptions, Tom. 7.—436.

communication with the Maſſagetes.[f] Agathemerus aſſures us, that on coming from the Weſt we find Sogdia and afterwards the Saces.[g] Ptolemy enters into more ſatisfactory details, and informs his readers that the Saces had to the Weſt, Sogdiana, and Scythia to the North, which was extended in a parallel line to the place where the Iaxartes changed its courſe,[h] and after having run from Eaſt to Weſt, turned towards the North-Weſt. The country of the Saces, who were ſupported by their flocks, and never inhabited any towns, according to Ammianus Marcellinus, joined Sogdia,[i] and a diſtrict immediately contiguous to this province on the Eaſt, preſerves even at this day the name of Sakita,[k] which ſeems to have a near affinity with the ancient name of the Saces, and to point out the identity of the true poſition of theſe people.

Diodorus Siculus pretends, that all Scythia beyond the Edmodus or Emodus to the North of India, was occupied by the Saces;[l] but we may eaſily diſcover that he was deceived, by the extent of territory, which the Perſians allowed to this nation. Eratoſthenes is

not

---

[f] "Τῆς δὲ προσίως τούτων μᾶλλον Μασσαγίτας, κỳ Σακας ονομαζεσι." Strabo. Lib. 11.--778.

[g] "Ειτα Σογδιανα, ητα Σακια." Agathemerus. Lib. 2. C. 6. 4ᵗᵒ L. B. 1700.

[h] Ptolem. Lib. 6. C. 13.

[i] "His contigui ſunt Sacæ, natio fera, ſqualentia incolens loca ſolo pecori fructuoſa, ideo nec civitatibus culta." Amm. Marcell. Lib. 23. C. 6.--411. 4ᵗᵒ L. B. 1693.

[k] Geographe Ancienne de Monſieur d'Anville. Tom. 2.--319.

[l] "Την δὲ προς τας Αρκτυς το Ημωδον ορ@ διειργει της Σκυθιας, ἣν κατοικυσι τῶν Σκυθῶν οἱ προσαγορευομενοι Σακαι." Diod. Sicul. Lib. 2. Tom. 1.--148.

not less reprehensible, who separates the Scythians and the Sogdians by the Iaxartes,[m] and we may judge of the accuracy of this geographer, respecting the North of Asia, from the position, which he gives to the Aracosians and Massagetes, on the banks of the Oxus near Bactria. Eratosthenes seems to consider these two nations as adjoining ones, whilst one was to the North of the Iaxartes, and the other to the West of the Paropamisus, and consequently about three thousand Olympic stadia from the Oxus.

As the Saces were a colony of Abians to the East of Sogdia, the historians of Alexander have incurred no just cause of censure from their transportation of this wandering tribe out of Europe into Asia, where some of them actually settled. Yet Arrian is not entirely unexceptionable, when he mentions towns belonging to these hordes,[n] who had no fixed and determinate place of residence, passing a vagrant life with their cars and waggons, and stopping only where they found a sufficiency of pasturage for their flocks and cattle. The foundation indeed of towns cannot be reconciled with the Scythian mode of life in general, and more particularly clashes with that of the Abian Saces. The series of events, which Arrian hath described, appear to indicate that the Scythians, who defended the passage of the Iaxartes were Abians,[o] though we have more reason to believe that he meant the Massagetes,

---

[m] "Διείργειν δὲ Σάκας μὲν, κὴ Σογδιανὰς τὸν Ἰαξάρτην." Strabo. Lib. 11.--782.
[n] Arrian. Exped. Alex. Lib. 4. C. 1.--258.
[o] ——————— Lib. 4. C. 4.--264——267.

getes, whose situation, to the North of the river, made it more immediately necessary for them to oppose the progress of the Macedonian Monarch. They attended Spitamenes in his expedition against Bactria,[p] after his irruption into Sogdia, in which he had been reduced to the necessity of raising the siege of Marcanda, and of retreating to take refuge amongst the wandering Scythians. Pharnuces, who pursued him, imprudently got into the midst of these people before he was aware of them,[q] and this circumstance evidently proves, that they were the tribes of Abian Scythians. A body of troops might enter their country without having the difficulty of passing any river, and the Massagetes had the Iaxartes for a barrier. Pharnuces had been led on to a distance by the facility of his march, and when he was attacked by the Abian Saces, who had assisted Spitamenes, he was obliged to fly with all his cavalry.[r] Arrian therefore ought not to have distinguished the Saces from the Asiatic Saces,[s] and his opinion has been improperly adopted by many other writers. Ptolemy was undoubtedly led astray by their authority, who reckons the Abians the most Northern of the tribes of Scythians beyond mount Imaus.[t]

The

---

[p] "Σπιταμενης τε κ̃, συν αυτω των Σογδιανων τινες φυγαδων, ες των Σκυθων των Μασσαγιτων καλεμενων την χωραν ξυμπιφευγοντες, ξυναγαγοντες των Μασσαγιτων ιππεας εξακοσιες, αφικοντο προς τι φρυριον των κατα την Βακτριανην." Arrian. Exped. Alex. Lib. 4. C. 16.--299.

[q] Arrian. Exped. Alex. Lib. 4. C. 5.--268, 269.

[r] ——————— Lib. 4. C. 5.--269.

[s] ——————— Lib. 4. C. 1.--257, 258.

[t] Ptolem. Lib. 6. C. 15.

The Oxus separated Bactria from Sogdia, but Polybius tells us, that this river having risen in Caucasus, by which the Paropamisus is to be understood, rolls through Bactria, where it is augmented by numerous streams, that discharge themselves into it.[w] It is certain however, that the Oxus received almost as many rivers, which opened into it from Sogdia as from Bactria. The expressions of this able historian, might induce us to suppose that he placed the Oxus in the centre of Bactria, since it is in Bactria, that he supposed it to be principally swoln by the various rivers that run into it. Dionysius the geographer hath stated a supposition nearly as erroneous, and makes the Oxus to cross Sogdia,[x] whilst it serves from its source to separate the two provinces of Bactria and Sogdia.[y] Polybius farther informs us, that the Aspasiacian Scythians, residing between the Tanais, which throws itself into the Palus Mæotis, and the Oxus, whose stream loses itself in the Caspian sea, crossed the latter river to make incursions into Hyrcania.[z] But the Greek historian must have been deceived by the improper name given to the Iaxartes, and has in consequence fallen into the

same

---

[w] "Ὁ γὰρ Ὀξὸς ἔχει μὲν ἐκ τοῦ Καυκάσου τὰς πηγάς· ἐπὶ πολὺ δ' αὐξηθεὶς ἐν τῇ Βακτριανῇ, συρρεόντων εἰς αὐτὸν ὑδάτων, φέρεται διὰ πεδιάδος χώρας, πολλῷ καὶ θολερῷ ῥεύματι." Polybius. Lib. 10. C. 48. Tom. 3.--303, 304. 8vo Lips. 1790.

[x] "Τοῖς δ' ἐπὶ πρὸς βορέην Χορασμίοι· οἷς ἐπὶ γαῖα
Σογδίας, ἥς διὰ μέσσον ἑλίσσεται ἱερὸς Ὦξος.
Ὅστε λιπὼν Ἠμωδὸν ὄρος, μετὰ Κασπίδα βάλλει."
Dionys. Perieg. 746----748.

[y] "Ὃς ὁρίζει τὴν τε τῶν Βακτρίων, καὶ τὴν τῶν Σογδίων." Strabo. Lib. 11.--786.

[z] "Περαιωμένοι τὸν Ὦξον, εἰς τὴν Ὑρκανίαν ἔρχονται." Polyb. Lib. 10. C. 48.--303.

same errors with the historians of Alexander's life and actions. The remainder of his narrative proves decisively, that this Scythian nation, which he meant by the Aspasiacians were the Saces: the term Aspasiacians might be an additional appellation to some particular tribe of them.[a] The Aspasiacian Scythians, we are told, had the Oxus only to pass in their irruptions into Hyrcania, and if their country was situated between the Oxus and the real Tanais, it must have included an immense tract of country, and a multitude of rivers must have opposed their numerous barriers to them, instead of which Polybius only takes notice of the Oxus. This river rolled over rocks, and formed according to some authors a kind of natural bridge of a stadium in length, over which the Scythians passed without difficulty;[b] but others supposed, that they took advantage of the place, where the Oxus disappears and runs under ground for some distance. The first of these opinions may not have been totally fictitious, as the Dgeihon or Amu, the Oxus of the Ancients, separates into many branches in the cantons of Balk and Termed, and afterwards collecting again its divided streams, passes between two mountains, by a narrow chasm called Dehani-Chir

[a] Ptolemy, in the Baron de St. Croix's opinion, hath distinguished, without any authority, the Aspasians or Aspasiacians from the Saces, and given the Aspasians a position too far North.

[b] "Διὰ δὲ τητε τε τοπε φασι τες Ασπασιακας παρ αυτην την πετραν υπο την καταφοραν τε ποταμε πηξειτιν μετα των ιππων εις την Υρκανιην· Ὁ δ᾽ ἑτερ̃ λογ̃ επιπικιςεραν εχει τε προσθεν την αποφασιν· τε γαρ υποκειμενε τοπε μεγαλες εχοντ̃ πλαταμωνας, εις ες καταρρακτει, τετες φασι τη βια τε ρευματ̃ εκκοιλαινοντα ᾗ διαρρηγνυντα κατα βαθ̃, υπο γην ϕερεσθαι τοπον ε πολυν, ειτ᾽αναφαινεσθαι παλιν· τες δε βαρβαρες δια την εμπειριαν κατα τον διαλειποντα τοπον ποιεισθαι, την διοδον επι των ιππων εις την Υρκανιαν." Polyb. Lib. 10. C. 48. Tom. 3.--304.

Chir or the Lion's mouth,' with scarcely an opening of fifty yards, which may be easily supposed to have been the natural bridge of the Oxus.—Polybius seems to have adopted the second idea, and it appears more probable. The Dgeihon beyond Dehani-Chir runs into a plain of sand of two leagues in length, where it loses itself. This plain might formerly have been very passable, but at present it is too hazardous to be attempted: at the end of it the Dgeihon again appears, and resumes its course towards Kharesm. The circumstance of rivers burying themselves, in this part of the world, within the bosom of the earth is not extraordinary, and Strabo is not justified in disputing the relation of Aristobulus,[d] who assures us, that the Polymetus, the Sogd of the Orientals, after having watered the valley of Marcanda lost itself in the sand, without discharging itself into the Caspian sea, as Ptolemy[e] hath related, which was physically impossible. The course of the Polymetus would in that case have been intercepted by the Oxus, which stretched from the South to the North-West.—The passage of the Afpasiacians near Termed, according to the real position of these places, proves that the Scythians made their incursions into

---

[c] Voyage d'Otter. Tom. 1.--236. The Turkish geographer, according to the Baron de St. Croix, enters into some interesting details relative to the course of the Oxus, 882, 883, 884 and 885. And Eldrisi, in a Maronite interpretation, describes the pass in the following manner. "————Ubi abscondit se sub magno quodam monte, super quem transeundi est quasi pontem."
                                    Geog. Nub. Clim. 3. P. 8.--138.

[d] Strabo. Lib. 11.

[e] Ptolem. Lib. 6. C. 14.

into that part of Hyrcania, between the Ochus and the Oxus. Monfieur d'Anville reckons the Ochus to be the Northern limit of this province, and this able geographer, it is to be fuppofed, had good reafons for abandoning the fentiments of Strabo [f] as well as Ptolemy,[g] who throw back the frontiers of Hyrcania beyond the Ochus. This river, which anfwers to the modern Thus, that runs near Nefa, which took its name from Næfia a province of the ancient Hyrcania,[h] continues its courfe, like the Thus, into the Cafpian fea.—Strabo relates the opinion of the writers, who imagined the Ochus and Oxus to form a junction,[i] and Q. Curtius hath been led into an error by it: Alexander, according to this hiftorian, paffed both thefe rivers to arrive at the city of Marginia,[k] where he pitched upon fituations for fix other towns. If the Macedonian Monarch, in his route from Bactria to Marginia, had met with the Ochus, it muft have opened into the Oxus, or its courfe muft have been lengthened from Eaft to Weft, which fuppofitions are equally falfe. The river to which Q. Curtius hath given the name of Ochus was the Margus, which runs in a parallel line with the Arius, and is ftill called by the Perfians, Marg-Ab.

[f] "Διαιρειται δε και ποταμοις η Ύρκανια τω τε Οχω και τω Οξω." Strabo. Lib. 11.--776.

[g] Ptolem. Lib. 6. C. 9.

[h] Strabo. Lib. 11.--776.

[i] —— Lib. 11.--776.

[k] "Superatis deinde amnibus Ocho et Oxo, ad urbem Marginiam pervenit." Q. Curtius. Lib. 7. C. 10. Tom. 2.--556.

Ab.[l] Pliny[m] informs us, that Antiochus the fon of Seleucus rebuilt on the banks of the Margus one of the towns, which Alexander founded, and which had been deftroyed by the Barbarians, but this king of Syria called it Antiochia, which proves the miftake of Q. Curtius. It may be perhaps conjectured, that Q. Curtius meant another river, which had alfo the name of Ochus, and agreeable to Ptolemy united itfelf to the Dargomanis,[n] and then joined the Oxus, but the Greek geographer is here lefs exact than even the Latin hiftorian.

Beffus received fome fuccours from the Dahes, who refided, according to Arrian,[o] beyond the Tanais or Iaxartes, but he places them much too far Northward. The Xanthians, Piffurians, Aparnians or Parnians, ferved to diftinguifh three tribes of this nation,[p] and the Aparnians were fettled next Hyrcania and the borders of the Cafpian fea. The Xanthians and Piffurians extended themfelves along the fhore and fides of the fea, in the Latitude of the ancient Aria. It is evident that Strabo, with whom Ptolemy[q] agrees, is accurate

---

[l] Geog. Ancienne par Monfieur d'Anville. Tom. 2.--297.

[m] "Alexander Alexandriam condiderat. Quâ dirutâ a Barbaris, Antiochus Seleuci filius, eodem loco reftituit Syriam. Nam interfluente Margo, qui corrivatur in Zotale, is maluerat illam Antiochiam appellari." Plin. Nat. Hift. Lib. 6. C. 16. Tom. 1.--674, 675.

[n] Ptolem. Lib. 6. C. 11.

[o] "Δαας τας επι ταδε τα Ταναιδ۞ ποταμυ οικειτας," Arrian. Exped. Alex. Lib. 3. C. 28.--249.

[p] Strabo. Lib. 11.--779.

[q] Ptolem. Lib. 6.

rate in his position of these people on this side of the Oxus, and that Arrian hath incorrectly transported them to the banks of the Iaxartes. Monsieur d'Anville hath placed them to the South of the Ochus, which seems to have been their true residence, pointed out by Strabo. This Greek geographer relates, that Arsaces governed the Dahes, called Parnians,' who had not absolutely any fixed settlement, but occasionally varied their residence, without quitting the environs of the Ochus. These Scythians are believed to have been a colony of the Dahes, that once occupied a tract of country above the Palus Mæotis,' and took the names of Aparnians, Xanthians, and Pissurians, in consequence of a migration like that of the Abians, who transplanting themselves into Asia were called the Saces, Amurgians and Aspasiacians. Herodotus considers the Mardes as a Persian people,' and he classes also another nation of the Mardes in the nineteenth Satrapy, with the Mossynœcians and Tibarenes." It is probable, that the name of Mard was given as a general term to the inhabitants of the mountains, who owed their liberty to the inaccessible ramparts of their country, Mard signifying in the Persian tongue a brave man, and Marad in the Hebrew, a revolt. The Mardes, according to Herodotus, were a wandering people,

' "Αρσακης ανηρ Σκυθης των Δαων τινας εχων τους Παρνους καλουμενους Νομαδας, παροικουντας τον Οχον,'
Strabo. Lib. 11.--783.

' "Φασι δε τους Παρνους Δαας μεταναστας ειναι εκ των υπερ της Μαιωτιδος Δαων," Strabo. Lib. 11. --784.

‡ Herodot. Lib. 1.--63.

" ——— Lib. 3.--246.

people, and principally shepherds,[x] an employment and mode of life in some measure connected with their situation, which must have been the Uxian mountains. We learn in fact from Q. Curtius, that this nation was near the Uxians,[y] and Mard might perhaps have been the name, which the Persians gave to a part of the inhabitants of the Uxian mountains, who had never been subdued: those who cultivated the plains, and were subject to the Persian Satrap, were not distinguished by this particular appellation, and were simply called Uxians.[z]——Q. Curtius[a] and many other writers have doubled the Mardes, and have introduced two different wars of Alexander with these people. Arrian adopts these opinions in his narrative concerning India,[b] though he only takes notice of a single nation of this name,[c] in his history of the Macedonian Monarch, and relates an expedition against them after the death of Darius, in which Diodorus Siculus[d] and Justin[e] agree with him.

---

[x] "Οἱ δὲ ἄλλοι νομάδες, Δάοι." Herodot. Lib. 1.--63.

[y] "Quinte Curce nous dit effectivement que cette nation etoit voisine des Uxiens." In the passage referred to by the Baron de St. Croix, the Mardes are only mentioned in the following manner. "Ventum est in Mardorum gentem bellicosissimam, et multum a ceteris Persis cultu vitæ abhorrentem." Q. Curt. Lib. 5. C. 6. Tom. 1.--353, 354.

[z] Arrian. Exped. Alex. Lib. 3. C. 17.--219.

[a] Q. Curtius. Lib. 5. C. 6. Tom. 1.--353, 354. The passage just cited, "Mardorum erat gens confinis Hyrcaniæ, cultu vitæ aspera, et latrociniis adsueta." Q. Curt. Lib. 6. C. 5. Tom. 1.--417.

[b] "Σύσιοις δὲ προσοικοι ὅτι εἰσιν οἱ Οὔξιοι, λέλεκται μοι· κατάπερ Μάρδοι μὲν Πέρσησι προσεχεῖς οἰκιῶσι." Arrian. Hist. Ind. C. 40.--630.

[c] Arrian. Exped. Alex. Lib. 3. C. 24.--238, 239.

[d] Diod. Sicul. Lib. 17. Tom. 2.--219.

[e] Justin. Lib. 12. C. 3.--308.

The Mardes, strictly speaking, were a Scythian people, who resided in the mountains of Deilam, to the South of the Caspian sea, and they were more properly called the great Mardes or Amardians from the Amardus, which watered their country. These Mardes or Amardians, were doubtless the people that Phraates, the first king of the Parthians, obliged to inhabit the city of Rages, which from that time became one of the greatest cities of Media.[f] Pliny ought not therefore to have distinguished the Amardians from the Mardes, "a rough and unconquered nation."[g] But the Latin Naturalist may have been deceived by the name of Mard, which the Persians gave in general to the inhabitants of mountains, and particularly to the inhabitants of those between Susia and Persia. He seems also to have multiplied them, and reckons five nations of them: one near Colchis,[h] of which Herodotus[i] also speaks; a second between Armenia and Media,[k] which appears to be the Gordians or Corduans; a third in Susia,[l] which is the Uxians in question, and the fourth is the Mardes,[m] which Pliny distinguishes very improperly from the Amardians or great Mardes, which he makes the fifth.[n]

The

---

[f] Isidori Characeni. Mans. Parth. 6. Geograph. Vet. Script. Min. Græc. Tom. 2.

[g] "Gens Mardorum, fera, sui juris." Plin. Hist. Nat. Lib. 6. C. 16. Tom. 1.--675.

[h] Plin. Hist. Nat. Lib. 6. C. 5. Tom. 1.--658.

[i] Herodot. Lib. 1.--63.

[k] Pliny's expression is "Circa Mardos et Armenios." Hist. Nat. Lib. 31. C. 7. Tom. 4.--805.

[l] Plin. Hist. Nat. Lib. 6. C. 27.--718.

[m] ——————— Lib. 6. C. 16.--675.

[n] ——————— Lib. 6. C. 19.--678.

X The hiſtorians of Alexander ſeized with a kind of tranſport on the reſemblance between the Agriaſpians or Ariaſpians, according to Ptolemy,° and the Arimaſpians, a people of European Scythia, celebrated both from the fables, that Ariſteas of Proconneſus ᵖ circulated of them, and alſo from the ſuccours given by them to the Argonauts, on which they had the name of Evergetes.ᵠ Theſe writers termed the Agriaſpians, who inhabited the South of the Aria Palus, or the modern lake Zera, Arimaſpians; and weakly imagined they had rendered the ſame ſervices to Cyrus,ʳ that the Arimaſpians afforded the Argonauts, though the Perſian Monarch was perhaps never in their country. Diodorus Siculus, equally miſtaken from the ſimilitude of theſe ſervices and the names of the two nations, does not likewiſe ſcruple to apply to the Ariaſpians the term of Arimaſpians.ˢ

The

° Ptolem. Lib. 6. C. 19.

ᵖ Herodot. Lib. 4.--286, 287, 288.

ᵠ Steph. Byzant.

ʳ "Αφικνεται ες της παλαι μεν Αγριασπας καλυμενυς, ύςερον δε Ευεργεται επονομασθεντας, ὁτι Κυρῃ τω Καμβισε ξυνεπιλαβοντο της ες Σκυθας ελασεως." Arrian. Exped. Alex. Lib. 3. C. 27.--246.

ˢ "Diodorus Siculus hath pretended to ſtate the preciſe relief, which they afforded Cyrus in his diſtreſs. "Ανεζευξε μετα της δυναμεως επι της προτερον μεν Αριμασπυς, νυν δ'Ευεργετας ονομαζομενυς, δια τοιαυτας τινας αιτιας. Κυρος ὁ την Μηδων αρχην μηλησησας εις Περσας, εν τινι ςρατεια περιληφθεις εν ερημω χωρα και πασῃ σπανει των αναγκαιων, ηλθε μεν επι της εσχατης κινδυνης, δια την ενδειαν της τροφης αναγκαζομενων των ςρατιωτων αλληλυς σαρκοφαγειν. Των δε Αριμασπων τρισμυριας ἁμαξας σιτα γεμεσας παρακομισαντων, σωθεις παραδοξως ατελειαις τε και αλλοις δορεαις ετιμησε το εθνος, και την προπαρχυσαν προσηγοριαν αφιλομενος, προσηγορευσε Ευεργετας." Lib. 17. Tom. 2.--222.

The Etymander waſhed the country of the Ariaſpians,[t] and opened into the Aria Palus. Monſieur d'Anville ſuſpects Ptolemy of concluding this river deſcended into the Southern ocean:[v] the Greek geographer however takes no notice of the river Etymander, and mentions only a people of this name.[x]

After having taken a view of the courſe of the rivers, and the ſituation of the different tribes of Scythians, compriſed in the Northern part of Aſia that Alexander's army overſpread, it may be neceſſary to attend to the provinces, of which Aſia was itſelf compoſed.

Though Sogdia makes a conſiderable figure in the hiſtory of Alexander's expeditions, Q. Curtius ſpeaks of its inhabitants as hardly known,[y] and places them according to his own erroneous ideas near the real Tanais and Caucaſus. Stephanus Byzantinus appears to place Sogdia, in the ſituation that Bactria ſhould have occupied, near Paropamiſus,[z] yet the error may poſſibly be owing to the copyiſt.—Golius[a] hath made a ſimilar excuſe for Ptolemy,

where

---

[t] Arrian. Exped. Alex. Lib. 4. C. 6.--273.

[v] Geograph. Anc. Tom. 2.--289.

[x] Ptolem. Lib. 6. C. 17.

[y] "Sogdianos et Arachoſios, nomine tantum notos." Q. Curt. Lib. 4. C. 5. Tom. 1.--191.

[z] Steph. Byzant. Σογδιανη.

[a] Golius. Not. in Alfer. 171.

where he transports Marcanda the capital of Sogdia into Bactria, but as this city is still falsely placed as to its Latitude,[b] we cannot so readily acquiesce in the idea of any mistake in the text of the Greek geographer, and suppose the transcriber to have been alone responsible for it. Monsieur d'Anville[c] hath acutely remarked, that this inaccuracy arose from a false reckoning in the itinerary measures, and "by the allowance of too much space to them, it inevitably followed, that Ptolemy gave in general a greater extent to the country than it really occupied, and Sogdia in particular was pushed much too far."

Bactria, if we are to believe Q. Curtius, formed a third part of Asia.[d] The Latin historian must have confounded Bactria in the time of Alexander, with the kingdom of Bactria formed afterwards by his successors, 255 years before Christ. Menander, one of the most illustrious of these princes, crossed the Hypanis and reduced many nations under his dominion, which the Macedonian Monarch had not conquered. Demetrius, the son of Euthedemus, also possessed himself not only of Patalene, but of many of the provinces on the coast of India,[e] and of the territories of Sigertes. Q. Curtius therefore

---

[b] Ptolem. Lib. 6. C. 11. Lib. 8. Tab. 7.

[c] "Auxquelles attribuant trop d'entendue, il devoit s'ensuivre que (Ptolemee) donna en general plus d'espace au pays qu'il n'en occupe, et que la Sogdiane en particulier fût poussèe beaucoup trop loin." Eclaircissement. Geograph. sur la Carte de l'Inde. 23.

[d] "Tertiam partem Asiæ tenet." Q. Curt. Lib. 5. C. 10. Tom. 1.--367.

[e] "Δημητριᾠ ὁ Ευθυδημε υἱᾠ τε Βακτριων βασιλεως, ε μονον δε την Παταληνην κατεσχον, αλλα κ̣ της αλλης παραλιας την τε Τεσσαριοσε καλεμενην, κ̣ την Σιγερτιδᾠ βασιλειαν. Καθαλε δε φησιν εκεινᾠ της συμπασης Αριανης προσχημα ειναι την Βακτριανην· κ̣ δη κ̣ μεχρι Σηρων, κ̣ Φαυνων εξετειναν την αρχην." Strabo. Lib. 11.--786.

therefore alludes to the boundaries of Bactria extended by its kings, who had united to it Aria, and part of India.

Perhaps however, the Latin historian may be in some measure excused, by supposing with Monsieur Freret [f] that the Persian word Bakter, from which in all probability Bactriana was derived, equally applied to all the country to the East of Persia. The learned academician is supported by Herbelot in the following terms. "From this word comes the name of the province, which we call Khorasan, and to which the Ancients gave the name of Bactriana from its being situated to the East of Persia." [g] Khorasan implies also like Bakter the East, or literally the place where the sun rises, agreeable to Abulfeda [h] and the Turkish geographer, who is much indebted to the Arabian prince for information. These writers allow a great space to the Khorasan, which comprehends not only the ancient Bactriana, but also Sogdiana, Margiana, Parthia and Aria. [i] In the summary description,

that

[f] Observations sur la Cyroped. Hist. de l'Acad. des Inscriptions. Tom. 4.--607.

[g] "De ce mot vient le nom de la province que les Anciens ont appellee Bactriane a cause qu'elle est situeè a l'Orient de la Perse, nous l'appellons aujourdhui le Khorassan." Bib. Orient. 164.

[h] "Porro Khorassam solis locus interpretatur, nam Kor solem, et Asam locum denotat." Abulfeda, ex Vers. cit. Geograph. Turc. 670.

[i] "Khorassam plurimas plagas complectitur. Afferunt Caldæi Khorassam protensam esse a Rai usque ad ortum solis. Alii autem existimant eam a monte Halwam ad locum nomine ortum solis patere.———Limites vero ejus hi sunt, nempe ad Occidentem Khorassam deserto, quod eam inter et mediam et Girgian interjectum est, ad Austrum pariter deserto, quod eam a Perside et Kumas

that Alfragan sketched of the different climates of the world, this astronomer includes in the Khorasan even Balk and Samarcand, which agree in situation with Bactria and Marcanda, the ancient capitals of Bactriana and Sogdiana in the province of Khorasan.[k] Yet the city of Balk must not be confounded with the country of that name, which is a single and separate canton, governed by a particular Khan of its own, who hath always preserved his independence, even in the midst of powerful neighbours, and hath chosen the city of Balk for his residence.[l]

The Oriental geographers supply us with useful explanations of some parts of ancient geography, and are principally of service respecting the real situation of places, and their modern as well as ancient names. Yet the testimony of the more ancient writers as to the limits of the different countries, can only be weakened by the contrary evidence of some cotemporary author. Admitting even that the Oriental writers have not properly distinguished the canton of Balk from the rest of the Khorasan, even the whole of this extensive province might not be able to give us the true limits of the ancient Bactriana, which, according to Ptolemy,[m] on the West had

---

mas sejungit, ad Orientem autem Segestam et India, ad septentrionem denique terminatur plagis Mawarannahr, seu quæ sunt ultra flumen Oxum, et aliquâ etiam parte Turchistam-Khorassam. Itaque continet multas provincias, quarum una quæ integram regionem adæquat." Abulfeda, ex Versione cit.

[k] Alferg. Elem. Astron. C. 9. Clim. 4, 5.   Golii Not. 166.

[l] Voyage d'Otter. Tom. 1.--240.

[m] Ptolem. Lib. 6. C. 10. Lib. 6. C. 11.

had Margiana; and fhould have included the Oxus, and Sogdiana on the North; a part of it as well as the Sacæ on the Weſt; and the Paropamifus and a part of Afia to the South. We learn from Q. Curtius[n] that the Tanais, which was the Iaxartes, feparates the Baɛtrians from the Scythians, and by this means he confounds Baɛtriana with Sogdiana. Even the defcriptions of the manners and modes of life of the inhabitants, which Alexander's hiſtorians have left us, prove thefe people to have been very different.

Baɛtra, called fometimes Zariafpe, is placed by Q. Curtius under the mountains of Paropamifus,[o] though it was in faɛt at fome diſtance from them. The refemblance of the ancient fituation of this town with the aɛtual pofition of Balk, Balch, or Balck agreeable to fome manufcripts, demonſtrates almoſt to a certainty this error of the Latin hiſtorian. According to Achmet[p] in his twenty-fecond climate, cited by Abulfeda, Balk is fituated in the middle of the Khorafan, and if any credit is due to Ibn-Haukal, it is built upon a flat furface in a plain, about four leagues from a mountain,

[n] "Baɛtrianos Tanais ab Scythis, quos Europæos vocant dividit." Q. Curt. Lib. 7. C. 7. Tom. 2.--531.

[o] "Ipfa Baɛtra, regionis ejus caput, fita funt fub monte Paropamiſo." Q. Curtius. Lib. 7. C. 4. Tom. 2.--510.

[p] "Ex Acmeto fapiente————Balk in medio Khoraſſam fitam effe traditur————Ex Ibn-Haukal Balk————ca in folo æquabile fita eſt, itaque a monte illi proximo quatuor paras diſſi-ta." (Abulfeda ex Verfione cit. Geograph. Turc. 698.) This city is fuppofed to be eight leagues, the Baron de St. Croix obferves, from the Dgeihoun or Oxus, according to Sherefeddin. Hiſt. de Timur. Lib. 1. C. 2.

mountain, which may have occasioned the mistake of Q. Curtius, and might be taken for a part of the Paropamisus. The situation of Balk on the river Dahas, which bathes its walls, ascertains the identity of this city with the Zariaspe or Bactra of the Ancients, and the learned Golius [q] produces many other corroborating proofs of it, in his observations upon Alfragan.

When the Macedonian army returned out of India by Gedrosia, Alexander directed Craterus to conduct a body of troops into the interior part of Ariana,[r] and to reduce it. But is this country understood to be the same with the Aria to the South of Hyrcania and Margiana, and to the North of the Dranges and a part of Media? Strabo clears away the difficulty, and dissipates the obscurity, which has been spread over this subject in Alexander's marches. Whilst this judicious geographer allows only to Aria itself a length of two thousand stadia, and reckons its breadth at three hundred,[s] he extends the limits of Ariana, from the frontiers of Bactriana and Sogdiana, as far as Media and Persia, and he includes in them Arachosia, Carmania, and the whole country to the Indus.[t] Dionysius the geographer hath allotted to Ariana an extent almost as considerable, and he comprises all the people near Paropamisus,

3 A   as

---

[q] Golius. Notes on Alfragan. 175, 176, 177.

[r] Strabo. Lib. 15.--1055.

[s] "Μηκ☾ δε της Αρης οσον διοχιλιοι ϛαδιοι, πλατ☾ δε τριακοσιοι τυ πιδιυ." Strabo. Lib. 11.--785.

[t] Strabo. Lib. 2.--131.

as well as the Arbians, Orites, and the inhabitants on the shores of the Erythrean sea, under the general name of Arianians,[w] a term which was at first used to distinguish them from the Arians, with whom they were afterwards confounded.

It seems probable that the term Aria was derived from the Calmuck or Mungal word Are, which signifies a man, and still subsists in Herah, Herat and Heri, the Aria of the Ancients;[x] or it may be deduced from Eri or Ære, which has the same signification with the Tartars. The Arians were distinguished for their knowledge and their police, as may be inferred from Strabo,[y] who compares them with the Indians, the Romans and the Carthaginians, and would willingly withdraw them from the disgraceful denomination of Barbarians. The Arians, had their name from Are or Ære, "men,"

[w] "Η τοι μεν δυνοντ℺ επι κλισιν η ελιοιο,
Ωριτας τ', Αριβας τε, λινοχλαινυς τ'Αραχωτας,
Σατραιδας θ', ὁσσυς τι παρα ωἱυχι Παρπανισοιο
Ξυνη ὁμως μαλα παντας επωνυμιην Αριανυς"
Dionys. Perieg. V. 1095——1098.

Moses of Chorene, according to the Baron de St. Croix, hath confounded the limits of Ariana, with those of the ancient kingdom of Bactriana, and supposed Aria to comprehend the whole country between the Caspian sea and the Indies, including twenty-six provinces, amongst which were Hyrcania, Parthia, Bactria, &c. &c. "Aria sive Chasti-Chorasania Mediæ ac Persiæ finitima est, atque ad Indiam pertinet, Hyrcanumque mare attingit. Ilæ autem provinciæ numerantur, Comsia, Hyrcania, &c. &c. &c." Mos. Chor. Geograph. ad Calcem. Hist. Armen. 365. Ed. Whiston.

[x] Herbelot. Biblioth. Orient. 448.

[y] "Και των Βαρβαρων αριυς, καθαπερ Ινδυς κ̣ Αριανυς· ιτι δι Ρωμαιυς κ̣ Καρχηδονιυς, ετω θαυμασως πολιτευομινυς." Strabo. Lib. 1,--116.

"men," to mark their decided superiority over the neighbouring nations, like the people of Paropamisus and the Mardes,[z] whose rude and savage life was but little removed from that of the common tribe of animals.

The ancient Medes had the name of Arians, according to Herodotus,[a] but it seems that they were not the Arians, of whom the Greek historian speaks in his division of the Satrapies.[b] The latter nation, which had a great affinity in language and manners with the Assyrians, was formerly very powerful. Most probably all the countries that formed their empire, were known under the general term of Ariana,[c] perhaps also Aria, and many other countries being conquered by the Persians, might be united in the same Satrapy under the name of Ariana, and from this circumstance Hellanicus may have supposed it to have been a province of Persia.[d] Stephanus Byzantinus, after having related the passage of this ancient historian, appears to be desirous of distinguishing Aria from Ariana, which was only an extension of it, and of mak-

---

[z] "Specus in montibus fodiunt, in quos seque ac conjuges et liberos condunt: pecorum, aut ferarum carne vescuntur. Ne feminis quidem pro naturæ habitu molliora ingenia sunt." Q. Curt, Lib. 5. C. 6. Tom. 1.--354.

[a] "Εκαλεοντο δε παλαι προς παντων Αριοι." Herodot. Lib. 7.--539.

[b] "Αριοι." Herodotus. Lib. 3.--245.

[c] See Cellarii Geograph. Antiq. Tom. 2.--515, 516.—Geograph. Ancienne de Monsieur d'Anville. Tom. 2.--285. &c. &c.—Vossius ad P. Melam. Lib. 1. C. 2.

[d] Apud Steph. Byzant. Αρια.

ing these countries inhabited by different people. Copying Apollodorus, he styles " Ariana a nation bordering on the Caduseans,"[e] and Pomponius Mela adopts this erroneous suppofition.[f] Pliny[g] is equally incorrect in placing Aria to the Weſt of Parthia, and the Arianians and Carmania to the South. Julius Solinus[h] hath united the Arians and Arianians, and places them to the Eaſt of the Parthians, which may ſerve to correct the text of Pliny,[i] whoſe errors have been to all appearance increaſed by the ignorance of his tranſcribers.

Of the PAROPAMISUS.

Conſidering the Paropamiſus as one part of the great chain of mountains, which, rifing on the ſides of Lycia, Pamphylia, and Cilicia,

[e] "Αριανια, ιθ۞ προσεχις τοις Καδυσιοις· Απολλοδωρ۞ δευτερω." Steph. Byzant. Αριανια.

[f] "Uſque ad Caſpium ſinus poſſident. Indis proxima eſt Ariane deinde Aria." P. Melam. Lib. 1. C. 2.--19, 20.

[g] "Habet ab ortu Arios, a meridie Carmaniam et Arianos." Plin. Hiſt. Nat. Lib. 6. C. 25. Tom. 1.--709.

[h] "Ab ortu Arios Arianoſque, Carmaniam a medio die." Julius Solinus. C. 59.

[i] By which, the Baron de St. Croix would read "Habet ab ortu Arios et Arianos, a meridie Carmaniam."

OF ALEXANDER THE GREAT. 365

Cilicia,[k] ſtretch acroſs Aſia from Weſt to Eaſt, and after receiving the different names of Taurus, Paropamiſus, Imaus and Edmodus, terminate at the ſea that waſhes China, we may diſcover a near reſemblance with the Caucaſus of Scythia, which is itſelf only a part of another chain of mountains, running from the Pontus Euxinus to the ſea of Tartary. Theſe two great tracts of mountainous country are connected by intermediate chains, in a direction from South to North, and are in fact only links of thoſe, which connect the North and South of Aſia.

Diodorus Siculus[l] diſtinguiſhes exactly theſe two chains of mountains, but like the other ancient authors, he has not turned his thoughts towards the communication that unites them, and is to appearance the frame that ſupports all Aſia. Arrian[m] and Q. Curtius[n] have ſimply advanced, that the Caucaſus and Taurus made a part of the ridge of mountains, which croſs that immenſe Continent. The term of Taurus is derived from a Chaldæan word, ſignifying

[k] Arrian. Exped. Alex. Lib. 5. C. 5.--349.

[l] "Ἀπο τοινυν τȣ κατα Κιλικιαν Ταυρȣ συνεχες ορ⊙- δι ολης της Ασιας διηκει, μεχρι τȣ Καυκασȣ ϰ͂ τȣ προς ανατολας ωκεανȣ· τȣτο δε παντοδαποις αναστημασι λοφων διειλημμενον, ιδιας καθ'εκαστον εχει προσηγοριας· τȣτον δε τον τροπον εις δυο μερη διαιρȣμενης της Ασιας, Το μεν προς τας Αρκτȣς αυτης νενȣκε, Το δε προς την μισημβριαν." Diod. Sicul. Lib. 18. Tom. 2.--260.

[m] Arrian. Exped. Alex. Lib. 5. C. 5.--349.

[n] "Caucaſum montem, cujus dorſum Aſiam perpetuo jugo dividit, ———————Taurus ſecundæ magnitudinis mons committitur Caucaſo, &c." Q. Curt. Lib. 7. C. 3. Tom. 2.--500, 501.

ſignifying a mountain,[o] and Eratoſthenes as well as Arrian have applied it alſo to the ſecond chain of mountains,[p] though they regularly change their appellation in the different countries.—— Caucaſus is an alteration of Groucaſum, which in the ancient Scythian language expreſſed a place covered with ſnow,[q] and the Barbarians called the mountains to the North of India, Imaus, which has the ſame import.[r]—The name of Muſtag or mountain of ice, by which the Tartars[s] diſtinguiſhed the Paropamiſus, furniſhes a ſignification nearly ſimilar. The Perſians indeed ſtill call a part of the ſame mountains Koh-Kaſer,[t] "impious" "treacherous mountain," more literally Koh-Kaf, "frothy mountain," in alluſion to the ſnow, which generally covers it; or according to Bayer, Khoo-Kafer, "the loſs of men," from its rigorous climate; but it is ſometimes only called Kaf, which is employed by the Arabs to deſcribe many mountains, but in particular thoſe of Paropamiſus.

[o] Hiſtoire du Commerce et de la Navigation des Anciens. 207. Which contains much valuable information.

[p] Arrian. Hiſt. Ind. C. 3.--552.

[q] "Et Caucaſum montem, Groucaſum, hoc eſt nive candidum." Plin. Hiſt. Nat. Lib. 6. C. 17. Tom. 1.--678.

[r] "Terme qui Pline rend par celui de nivoſum." I have varied the expreſſion, for Pliny has not applied the epithet "nivoſum" to the Imaus, though he frequently mentions theſe mountains.

[s] And alſo Imuſſahr, for Mus or Maus ſignifies with them Ice, to which they prefix, in the pronunciation, the vowel I, but Tag denotes mountains: thus the whole word ſignifies Icy or Snowy Mountains, whence the corrupt word Imaus takes its origin. Strahlenberg's Geograph. Deſcript. of the North and Eaſtern Part of Europe and Aſia, 416.

[t] Bayer de Regn. Bact. 8.

ropamifus."—It may be reafonably fuppofed, that the companions of Alexander's arms were ftruck with the analogy of founds, and catching with pleafure at the refemblance of the etymology of the name, which diftinguifhed the real Caucafus and that of the Paropamifus, made no fcruple of calling both thefe mountains equally Caucafus. Their own vanity and the flattery of their Sovereign might alfo have fome influence with them, in the application.—— Some fuch apology might have excufed the Macedonians, if they had fatisfied themfelves with only the adoption of the name, but they have confounded thefe two mountains, and have attributed to one, the characteriftic circumftance, which alone ought to have diftinguifhed the other. Like another Philoctetes, they have imagined they difcovered in the Paropamifus the cave in which Prometheus was faftened, and from which he was at laft delivered by Hercules. Arrian, with his ufual good fenfe, ftates thefe reveries as fabulous,[w] though Diodorus Siculus adopts them with credulous fimplicity, and relates that in the middle of Caucafus, called Paropamifus by fome, the natives ftill fhew a rock of ten ftadia in circumference and of four in height, where the eagle's neft and the

---

[w] Herbelot. Biblioth. Orient. "Thus likewife the denomination of Caucafus, called by others Caf, Caph or Caco: Caho and Cobo fignifies, in the Perfian, no more than mountains in general." Strahlenberg's Geographical Defcription of the North and Eaftern Part of Europe and Afia. 416. See alfo Reland. Differt. 8. De Vet. Ling. Pers. 155.

[x] "Καὶ γὰρ κὴ σπηλαιον λεγει ιδοντας εν Παραπαμισαδαις τες Μακεδονας, κὴ τινα μυθον επιχωριον ακουσαντας, η κὴ αυτες ξυνθεντας, φημισαι οτι τουτο αρα ην το Προμηθεως το αντρον, ινα εδεδετο· κὴ ὁ αετος ὁτι εκεισε εφοιτα, δαισομενος των σπλαγχνων τε Προμηθεως." Arrian. Exped. Alex. Lib. 5. C. 3.— 343, 344.

the marks of the fetters of the daring adventurer were yet an object of curiosity.[y] These fables, which can only refer to the real Caucasus, have been copied by Q. Curtius,[z] who draws from them very strange consequences. The Latin historian after having spoken of the fatigues, that the Macedonian Monarch's army experienced in its passage across the Paropamisus, which, according to his ideas, was to the West joining Bactria, with the Indian ocean to the South,[a] adds, that after the Prince's troops had recovered their march,[b] " he moved towards mount Caucasus, which with its long ridge of hills stretches itself through Asia, having on one side of it the Cilician sea, and on the other the Caspian sea, the river Araxes, and deserts of Scythia. Mount Taurus, which holds the second rank for bigness, joins to mount Caucasus: it takes its rise from Cappadocia, and running across Cilicia joins itself to the mountains of Armenia, so that all these mountains being united, form one continued

---

[y] "Κατα δε μεσον τον Καυκασον εςι πετρα δεκα ςαδιων εχεσα την περιμετρον, τετλαςων δε ςαδιων το υπ-σθ-, εν η κ, το Προμηθεως σπηλαιον εδεικνυθ' υπο των εγχωριων, κ, η τε μυθολογηθεντθ- αιτυ κοιτη, κ, τα των δεσμων σημεια." Diod. Sicul. Lib. 17. Tom. 2.--224.

[z] Q. Curt. Lib. 7. C. 3.--493----501.

[a] "Bactrianis ad Occidentem conjuncti sunt: Meridiana regio ad mare Indicum vergit." Q. Curt. Lib. 7. C. 3. Tom. 2.--493, 494.

[b] "Inde agmen processit ad Caucasum montem, cujus dorsum Asiam perpetuo jugit dividit: hinc simul mare, quod Ciliciam subit; illinc Caspium fretum, et amnem Araxem, aliaque regionis Scythiæ deserta spectat. Taurus secundæ magnitudinis mons committitur Caucaso, a Cappadociâ se adtollens Ciliciam præterit, Armeniæque montibus jungitur. Sic inter se tot juga velut serie cohærentia perpetuum habent dorsum, ex quo Asiæ omnia fere flumina, alia in rubrum, alia in Caspium mare, alia in Hyrcanum et Ponticum decidunt. XVII. dierum spatio Caucasum superavit exercitus." Q. Curt. Lib. 7. C. 3. Tom. 2.--500, 501.

tinued ridge, out of which almost all the rivers of Asia flow, some emptying themselves into the Red sea, others discharging themselves into the Caspian sea, while others again fall into the Hyrcanian and Pontick sea. The army passed over mount Caucasus in seventeen days."[c] It would be difficult to find either an ancient or modern historian, who has to answer for so many errors in such a short compass.——Q. Curtius undoubtedly intended to speak of the real Caucasus, since he joins it to the Taurus, and places the Caspian sea on the left: this however is the least of his mistakes. After a description of Alexander's march in the country of Paropamisus, he supposes this Prince to reach Caucasus, which must in consequence be situated between Paropamisus and the Indian ocean. But is this situation to be reconciled with the account, which he gives afterwards of this mountain? The Caucasus, he tells us, hath on one side the Caspian sea, the Araxes and Scythia, and on the other, the sea which bathes the coast of Cilicia, placed under the same parallel with the Caspian sea, and by these means the whole of Asia Minor with the Pontus Euxinus is thrown too far Northward. Q. Curtius hath given also a Latitude too far Southward to the Caspian sea, and brings it within seven degrees of the Equator. If we admit the ideas, which the Ancients entertained of the Longitude of the Caspian sea, to have been just and accurate, it then becomes parallel to that of Cilicia and Asia Minor.—These influences are fairly deducible from the text of Q. Curtius, who is accustomed very frequently to contradict himself, and may even be

[c] Digby's Q. Curtius. Book. 7. Chap. 3. Vol. 2.—18.

be believed to have imagined the Caucasus to run from North to South.—Arachosia, likewise, is placed to the West of Caucasus, and near the Pontus Euxinus, and consequently we must not be surprised to meet with its inhabitants near the Euxine sea.[d]—To complete the confusion and obscurity, the Latin historian appears to distinguish the Hyrcanian sea from the Caspian sea.

Q. Curtius mentions the climate of Paropamisus in the following terms.[e] "The snows are here so deep, and so congealed with the frost, that no footsteps or traces of beast or bird appear in all the country. The light is so obscure, that it may be compared to the dimness of the night, so that those things that are nearest at hand are hardly discernable."[f]—This is most certainly an overcharged description, which may be considered as a commentary on Diodorus Siculus, who tells us, when he speaks of this country, that it was situated under the Pole.[g] Q. Curtius therefore transports into it

---

[d] "Arachosios, quorum regio ad Ponticum mare pertinet." Q. Curt. Lib. 7. C. 3. Tom. 2.--492.

[e] "Adeo altæ nives premunt terram, gelu et perpetuo pene rigore constrictæ, ut ne avium quidem, feræve ullius vestigium extet. Obscura cœli verius umbra, quam lux, nocti similis premit terram: vix ut quæ prope sunt conspici possint." Q. Curt. Lib. 7. C. 3. Tom. 2.--498.

[f] Digby's Q. Curtius. Book 7. Chap. 3. Vol. 2.--17.

[g] "Ἡ δε τυτων χωρα κειται μεν ὑπ' αυτας τας Αρκτυς, χιονοβολειται δε πασα,————απασα δ' ἡ της χωρας φυσις ετι χλωραν εδ' ἡμερον εχει προσοψιν, αλλα λευκην ᾗ αντανγη την χιονα ᾗ των εν αυτη πηγνυμενον κρυσταλλον· διοπερ, ετ' ορνεα προσκαθιζοντ⊛, ετι θηριε διοδευοντ⊛, αξενα ᾗ απηιβατα παντα τα μερη της χωρας ὑπηρχιν." (Diod. Sicul. Lib. 7. Tom. 2.--223.) Churchill's Muse, in an irritated

it the inhabitants of Paropamifus, or rather appears to be wholly ignorant, that the nearer we approach to the Equator, the nearer we find day and night to be equal to each other. But it is an excefs of abfurdity to imagine that a country, only ten degrees from the Tropic of Cancer, fhould in the winter be plunged into one continued night.

Monfieur Bonami takes notice of the expreffions of Diodorus Siculus, and Q. Curtius, and then obferves, "that notwithftanding this frightful country is fituated towards the thirty-fifth degree of Northern Latitude, in a climate where the heat is more fenfible than cold, they have not only tranfported thither mount Caucafus and the Tanais, but alfo frofts and ice."[h] To this objection, however

---

irritated moment, feems to have painted, in fimilar and exaggerated colours, a part of GREAT BRITAIN, which, from Party principles, had been the invidious object of his refentment.

"Far as the eye could reach, no tree was feen,
Earth, clad in ruffet, fcorn'd the lively green.
The plague of locufts they fecure defy,
For in three hours a grafshopper muft die.
No living thing, whate'er its food, feafts there,
But the Chamelion, who can feaft on air,
No birds, except as Birds of Paffage, flew,
No bee was known to hum, no dove to coo,
No ftreams as amber fmooth, as amber clear
Were feen to glide, or heard to warble here."

Prophecy of Famine. Churchill's Poems. Vol. 1.—10. 8vo 1766.

[h] "Cependant ce pays fi affreux eft fitué vers le 35 degré de Latitude feptentrionale, c'eft à dire, dans un climat où la chaleur fe fait plus fentir que le froid.————en y tranfportant le mont Caucafe et le Tanais, ils y ont tranfporté les glaces et les frimats." Hift. de l'Academie des Infcriptions. Tom. 25.--22.

however, it may be anſwered that the hoar of a winter's froſt is ſometimes to be met with upon mountains in the Southern regions, the Pike of Teneriffe, which is ſeven degrees South of Paropamiſus being covered with ſnow, and inacceſſible even in the months of July and Auguſt.[i] The intenſe cold, ariſing from continual falls of ſnow, is likewiſe ſo very ſevere on the Cordilleras and Andes, in the Audience of Quito, near the Equator, that theſe mountains are not only uninhabitable, but neither plants nor animals are to be found upon them.[k] The climate of Paropamiſus produces alſo examples of the common phænomenon ariſing from the rarefaction of the air. Father Deſideri, who traverſed in 1715 the mountains of Cachemir, which are a part of the ancient Paropamiſus, and lie nearly in the ſame Latitude with the route of Alexander's army, expreſſes himſelf as follows. " The ſummit of the higheſt mountains is always covered with ſnow and ice.—I ſay nothing of the extreme cold, which I had to ſuffer.———Theſe mountains are a true image of deſolation, horror and even death."[l] Bernier's deſcription,

[i] Hiſtoire general de Voyages. Tom. 6.--189——220. Ed. 12. The Baron de St. Croix was perfectly correct in his expreſſion, for the difficulties were ſuppoſed to include an impoſſibility of ſucceeding in the attempt. Lieutenant Rye, with wonderful perſeverance, and not without ſome danger, hath ſince ſcaled this tremendous mountain in the month of April. See his Account of the Pike of Teneriffe. 4to 1793.

[k] Voyage de l'Amerique par D. G. Juan et D. Ulloa. Tom. 1.--351.

[l] "Le ſommet des plus hautes montagnes eſt toujours couvert de neige et de glace.———Je ne parle point du froid extrème qui j'ai eu à ſouff'rir———Ces montagnes ſont une vraie image de la triſtreſſe, de l'horreur, de la mort même." (Lettres Edifiantes et Curieuſes. Rec. 15.--185——193.) Much curious information may be extracted from this voluminous collection, but ſome attention will be requiſite to ſeparate the droſs, and the "Eſprit du corps" cannot be too much guarded againſt.

scription,[m] who had passed through the same country fifty years before, is substantially the same, and this celebrated traveller adds, that on the mountain of Pir-Penjal, the changes in the atmosphere were very violent and sudden, and that in less than an hour there was a transition from summer to winter.

Without wasting any time on the etymologies of the name of these mountains, which seem to confirm the relation of Alexander's historians, some of the circumstances of Tamerlane's march towards mount Ketuer, beween Badafchan and Cachemir, may be entered into with propriety. "Notwithstanding the season (the sun was then in Gemini) there was such a quantity of snow upon this mountain, that most of the horses, that attempted to ascend, could not keep their feet and fell. Some, however, after the frost in the night, which was severe, made some little progress, and when the sun arose, they were stopped, and covered with clothes, as it became impossible to proceed from the glassy ice. With great difficulty and great fatigue, the summit of the mountain was at last gained, and the place reached where the Siapoufch resided."[n] The country inhabited by this band of robbers

---

[m] Voyages de Bernier. Tom. 2. 270. "Nous entrames dans les montagnes, pour voir un grand lac ou il a de la glace, dont les vents font et defont des monceaux comme une petite mer glaciale." Voyage de Kachem. Tom. 2.--302.

[n] "Malgre la faison, (le soleil etoit alors dans les Gemaux) on trouva sur cette montague une si grande quantité de neige, que les pieds de la plupart des chevaux qu' on voulut y faire monter, tomberent; quelque-uns cependant, à la faveur de la gelée, qui etoit tres fort pendant la nuit, ne laifferent pas d' avancer, et lorsque le soleil paroiffoit, on s' arretoit et on couvroit de feutre les chevaux, parceque il etoit impoffible de marcher, tout etant remple de verglas. On parvint ainfi, après

bers was little more than three degrees to the North of Cachemir, and its mountains formed part of the chain, which stretched across the centre of Asia. From this body of evidence we may conclude, that the historians of Alexander's actions have not imposed upon us, when they spoke of the cold, which the Prince's troops suffered in the Paropamisus, though these mountains are in such a Southerly part of the world. Strabo,[*] who was not prejudiced in favour of these historians, expressly mentions the rigorous severity of the climate, and Q. Curtius is only reprehensible, when he states the length of the nights in this country, where the shortest day in the whole year consists of ten hours and a half.

The mountains, which cover the North of India have many passages, and that of Candahar is one, which is most travelled, especially by the caravans of Agra and Ispahan. The Macedonian army took the direct route from Bactra to Paropamisus, and there cannot be a doubt that Alexander entered India by this passage. Strabo is the writer of antiquity, that hath best illustrated the distressing march of the Macedonian army over these mountains. It was the second time that Alexander had conducted his troops into the country: the first was when he pursued the assassins of Darius.—" He came," says the judicious geographer, "by Ariana

---

pres beaucoup de fatigues, jusqu' au sommet de la montagne, où etoient les Siapoufch." Hist. des Huns, par Monsieur de Guignes. Tom. 5.--42.) Sherefeddin hath given, the Baron de St. Croix remarks, a similar detail of this march. Hist. de Timur. Voc. Lib. 6. C. 3.

[*] Strabo. Lib. 15.

na into the borders of India, and leaving it on the right, and Paropamifus to the North, he paffed into Bactriana. Having reduced under his fubjection all the territories under the Perfian dominion, and many other countries, he directed his march towards India, of which many things had been faid, though without any certainty. In his return he took the fhorteft route over the fame mountains, leaving India to the left. He then came back again and paffed its Weftern borders, croffing the rivers Cophes and Choafpes."[p]

Of INDIA.

The immenfe regions of India have been divided by the ancient geographers into Occidental India, which they call Send, and Oriental India, termed Hend,[q] inhabited by a people, whofe religion, manners and police, give them the ftrongeft pretenfions to antiquity. This rich and fertile country bears the name of Sindou[r] and of Zomboudipo

---

[p] " Ἥκει μεν ων της Ἰνδικης πλησιον δι᾽ Ἀριανων· ἀφεις δ᾽ αὐτην εν δεξια, ὑπερεβη τον Παροπαμισον εις τα προσαρκτια μερη, καὶ την Βακτριανην· καταςρεψαμεν⊙ δε ταχει παντα ὁσα ἠν ὑπο Περσαις, καὶ ετι πλειω, τοτ᾽ ηδη καὶ της Ἰνδικης ωρεχθη· λεγοντων μεν περι αὐτης πολλων, ȣ σαφως δε· Ανεςρεψε δ᾽ ȣν, ὑπερβας τα αὐτα ορη, κατ᾽ ἀλλας ὁδȣς ἐπιτομωτερας, εν ἀριςερα εχων την Ἰνδικην, εἶτ᾽ ἐπεςρεψεν ευθυς ἐπ᾽ αὐτην, καὶ τȣς ορȣς τȣς ἑσπεριȣς αὐτης, καὶ τον Κωφην ποταμον καὶ τον Χοασπην." Strabo. Lib. 15.--1021.

[q] Abulf. Climat. Al-Hend-Al-Send. Rec. de Voyages par Thevenot. Tom. 1.

[r] Bagavadam, Lib. 4.--91.

Zomboudipo' in their early records, which are written in the Sanfcreet language, but it muft be acknowledged that it was little known by the reft of the univerfe before the days of Alexander. The relations of Ctefias and the crude and imperfect notions of Herodotus can afford only a fmall portion of fatisfaction to any rational mind, and little confidence can be repofed on any information that may be gathered from them. The latter hiftorian affures us, that Darius the fon of Hyftafpes penetrated the fartheft into the Eaft of all the Perfian kings, but he cannot avoid acknowledging, that the Indians at a diftance and to the South were never fubject to the Perfian power.' Strabo pretends, that Cyrus in his expedition againft the Maffagetes ought to be confidered as the only one that approached this country, from which the Perfians were fatisfied with drawing fome auxiliaries, in general furnifhed by the Hydrachians. We learn alfo from the Greek geographer, that even the Perfians had not any knowledge of India, which had been enveloped in the darkeft obfcurity till Alexander's conquefts."
Megafthenes, who was well verfed in Indian antiquities, from his long refidence with Porus and Sandracotta, is of opinion, ' that
no

' Ezour-vedam. Lib. 1. C. 3.

t " Ουτοι μεν των Ινδων ικαστερω των Περσιων οικεασι, ϗ ωρος ιοτε ανιμυ· ϗ Δαρεια βασιληϙ εδαμα υπηκυσαν." (Herod. Lib. 3.--248.) The Baron de St Croix fuppofes Herodotus to have been only acquainted with the Indians near Bactria, and the people of Carmania and Gedrofia, with a few other nations.

w " Αλεξανδρϙ γαρ ο μαλιςα τυτ' ανακαλυψας." Strabo. Lib. 15.--1021.

x " Συναποφαινεται δε πως ϗ Μεγασθενης τω λογω τυτω, κελευων απιςειν ταις αρχαιαις περι Ινδων ιςοριαις."

no foreign army, thofe of Bacchus and Hercules excepted, had ever reached this country before this period, and the Indians confirmed by their own evidence, according to Maximus Tyrius,[y] the Greek traveller's relation.—Alexander removed the veil, with which this part of the world had been till his time covered: Seleucus, one of his fucceffors, pufhed ftill farther his difcoveries and arrived at the Ganges.[z] It was referved for later ages to acquire more extended notions of this part of the globe, but they are ftill more limited and imperfect than they might be wifhed to be. Our moft authentic accounts are thofe, which relate to the countries, that have been ravaged by fire and fword, and deluged from avarice with feas of blood. Yet the religion of the mild and inoffenfive natives condemns to exceffive tortures in another world the favage mortal that hath audacioufly attempted the life of any of his brethren,[a] and it hath been their misfortune to inhabit a country,

3 C

αις· ὅτι γαρ παρ' Ινδων εξω ςαληναι ποτε ςρατιαν, ὅτ' επελθειν εξωθεν ὁ κρατησαι, πλην την μις' Ἡρακλιος, ὁ Διονυσε, ὁ της νυν μετα Μακεδονων." (Strabo. Lib. 15.--1007.) "'Ουτω ων ὁ Μεγασθενης λεγει, ὅτι Ινδυς επιςρατευται εδαιμοσιν ανθρωποισιν, ὅτι Ινδοισιν αλλυς ανθρωπυς." Arrian. Hift. Ind. C. 5.--558.

[y] "Αλεξανδρος δε εκεινος, Περσαις ελων, ὁ Βαβυλωνος γην, αβατον εσαν τεως ςρατια ξενη, ὡς Ινδοι ελεγον, πλην γε Διονυσω ὁ Αλεξανδρω." (Max. Tyrius. Diſſert. 38.--399. 8vo Cantab. 1703.) The Baron de St. Croix refers his readers, for this paſſage, to the 18th Diſſertation and 85th Page of this Edition.

[z] Plin. Hift. Nat. Lib. 6. C. 17. Tom. 1.--684.

[a] "Ceux qui les armes à la main auront tué un autre homme, feront eux-memes broyès dans l' enfer (le Patalene c' eſt à dire l' Abyme) et on les fera paſſer par des trous auſſi petits que celui d' une aiguille." (Ezour-Vedam. Lib. 3. C. 3.) "Ceux, qui font mal aux hommes et qui tuent les betes, feront jetés dans un lieu particulier, pour y fouffrir des torments horribles." Bagavadam. Lib. 6.--106.

try, in which nature hath been prodigal of her choicest gifts, only to expose it without ceasing as a prey to other nations!

Strabo, though he acknowledges the advantages that the science of geography has derived from the Macedonian conquests, very justly censures the multitude of absurd stories in which the marvellous had usurped the place of truth. "India," says he, "is at a very remote distance, and few of us have seen it. They who have visited it, have seen only a small part of it, and have described it principally from what they heard. The little they personally learnt was picked up in the hurry of their military expeditions, and yet they have published these accounts with the same confidence, as if they had examined the most authentic memorials with attention."[b] The Greek geographer accuses also these writers with contradicting each other,[c] with exaggerating, and relating notorious falsities,[d] and he allows only Patroclus and Eratosthenes to have compiled their works from documents, whose fidelity was not to be suspected. A voluminous mass of fables might easily be collected from Onesicritus, Clitarchus, Megasthenes and Daimachus, and the two latter authors, in Strabo's opinion, deserve no sort of credit.

[b] "Καὶ γὰρ ἀπωτάτω ἐστί· καὶ οὐ πολλοὶ τῶν ἡμετέρων κατωπτεύσαν αὐτήν. οἱ δὲ καὶ ἰδόντες, μέρη τινὰ εἶδον· τὰ δὲ πλείω λέγουσιν ἐξ ἀκοῆς· καὶ ἃ εἶδον δὲ, ἐν παρόδῳ στρατιωτικῇ καὶ δρόμῳ κατέμαθον· διόπερ οὐδὲ τὰ αὐτὰ περὶ τῶν αὐτῶν ἐξαγγέλλουσι· καὶ ταῦτα συγγράψαντες, ὡς ἂν πεφροντισμένως ἐξητασμένα." Strabo, Lib. 15.--1006.

[c] "Ἀλλ' ἕκαστος ἑκάστῳ τἀναντία λέγει πολλάκις." Strabo. Lib. 15.--1006.

[d] "Οἱ περὶ τῆς Ἰνδικῆς γράψαντες, ὡς ἐπὶ τὸ πολὺ ψευδόλογοι γεγόνασι." Strabo. Lib. 2.--121.

dit.[e] "They have even told of men with immense ears,[f] without mouths and noses, with only one eye, long distorted thighs, and the fingers and toes in a reversed position. They have renewed Homer's fable of the pigmies three feet high, and their wars with the cranes, and accounts are also given of ants that dig up gold, satyrs with unnatural heads,[g] and serpents which swallow both deer and oxen with their horns."[h] The judicious geographer observes, that he had

[e] "Διαφερόντως δ' απιςείν αξιον Δηιμαχω τε κ̃ Μεγασθενει· ήτοι γαρ ειςιν οι τας ενωτοκοιτας κ̃ αςομας, κ̃ αρρινας ιςορύντες, μονοφθαλμας τε, κ̃ μακροσκιλεις, κ̃ οπισθοδακτυλας· ενεκκινισαν δε κ̃ την Όμερικην των Πυγμαίων γερανομαχιαν, τρισπιθαμας ειπόντες· Ουτοι δε κ̃ τας χρυσωρυχας μυρμηκας, κ̃ Πανας σφηνοκεφαλας, οφεις τε κ̃ βας κ̃ ελαφας συν κέρασι καταπινοντες." (Strabo. Lib. 2.--121.) The Baron de St. Croix observes that Caufabon durst not change the "ενεκκινισαν" into "ανακκινισαν," though he wished to make the alteration, but that Monsieur de Brequigny meant to have restored the reading, on the authority of a manuscript in the French king's library. There is not perhaps any Greek author, that hath stood in greater need of emendation than Strabo. A new edition of this Greek geographer has been long in the Clarendon Press, from the hands of a gentleman, (the late Thomas Falconer Esq. of Chester) who was, in every respect, fully qualified for the learned and laborious office. His extensive reading and erudition were only equalled by the virtues of the heart, and without any compliment whatever to his memory, his death was one of those misfortunes, of which it may literally be said "Fuit hoc luctuosum suis, acerbum Patriæ, grave bonis omnibus." Cicero de Orat. Lib. 3. Sect. 2. Tom. 1.--281. 4to 1740.

[f] "Τας ενωτοκοιτας, sleeping in their ears."

[g] "Σφηνοκεφαλας, with heads like wedges." I am desirous of proposing to some future editor of Strabo a trifling alteration in the Text, and of substituting "Κυνοκεφαλας" in the place of "Σφηνοκεφαλας." In many of the old manuscripts, the first letters of words were frequently omitted for the purpose of being afterwards blazoned and illuminated, and a number of errors crept into the text by these means, from the ignorance of transcribers. The mistake of the "ην" for "υν," especially when abbreviated, might easily be made, and the "Πανκυνοκεφαλ☉," will not be a very inaccurate description of the dog-headed baboon, which was a native of that part of the world.

[h] Dr. Shaw, in treating of the great Boa, "Boa constrictor," (Linnæi Syst. Nat. 373.) makes the following observations. "Qui vasta et mirabilia naturæ opera nunquam "Αυτοπται" contemplati

had frequent occasion to animadvert on these tales and fables, in the history of the life of Alexander, but the Prince's historians, having drawn their information from these sources, could not help transmitting to us some of their absurdities. Diodorus Siculus mentions serpents of twenty-four feet [1] in length, and trees of one hundred
dred

plati sunt, ii sane quicquid varie de illis scripserint peregrinatores, caute et dubitanter recipere solent; immo sæpe utpote fabulosum omnino rejiciunt. Inter hæc naturæ magnalia jure numerandi sunt serpentes illi ingentes, qui in nonnullis Indiæ, Africæ, et Americæ regionibus inveniuntur; quique in tantam magnitudinem adolescunt ut quadrupedia etiam majora ingurgitare possint; et longitudine adeo sunt enormi, ut sæpe pedes viginti, viginti-quinque vel etiam triginta superent. Horum temporis progressu multo rarior est conspectus, illosque probabile est regiones olim sane desertas, et nunc excultas, populosque frequentes reliquisse, et in tesqua deserta et remota exulasse. Spectantur tamen aliquando hortos et loca habitaculis suis propiora perreptantes." (Natur. Vivar. Fascic. secund.) It is possible therefore serpents of this extraordinary magnitude might have then existed, and that these Grecian writers, mixing a little truth with much falsehood, may be supposed in the words of Strabo, "Λεγειν δ' αν τινα, κỳ πιθανα, κỳ μνημης αξια, ὡς τε κỳ απιςευτα μη παρ ελθην αυτα." (Lib. 15.--1023.) A more ridiculous account of the ants may be found in the latter part of Strabo, (Lib. 15.--1032.) where Megasthenes reports that they were "Θηριων αλωπεκων ακ ελατίες," not less than foxes.

[1] "Ειχεν ἡ χωρα πολλυς κỳ παρηλλαγμενυς τοις μεγεθεσιν οφεις, οντας εκκαιδεκαπηχεις" (Diod. Sicul. Lib. 17. Tom. 2.--230.) Diodorus Siculus most probably borrowed the idea from Clitarchus, for we learn from Ælian, "Κλειταρχ۞ εν τη περι την Ινδικην φησι γινεσθαι οφιν πηχων εκκαιδεκα." (Ælian. De Nat. Animal. Lib. 17. C. 1. Tom. 2.--918. 4to 1744.) but Valerius Maximus hath given us an instance of a serpent of still more extraordinary dimensions. "Quæ quia usitatam rationem excedentia attigimus, serpentis quoque a T. Livio curiose pariter, ac facunde relata fiat mentio. Is enim ait in Africâ apud Bagradam flumen, tantæ magnitudinis anguem fuisse, ut Attilii Reguli exercitum usu amnis prohiberet: multisque militibus ingenti ore correptis, compluribus caudæ voluminibus elisis, cum telorum jactu perforari nequiret, ad ultimum ballistarum tormentis undique petitam, silicum crebris et ponderosis verberibus procubuisse, omnibusque et cohortibus et legionibus ipsâ Carthagine visam terribiliorem. Atque etiam cruore suo gurgitibus imbutis, corporisque jacentis pestifero afflatu viciná regione pollutá, Romana inde summovisse castra. Dicit etiam beluæ corium CXX pedum, in urbem missum." (Lib. 1. C. 8.--117. 4to L. B. 1726.) The Epitome of the eighteenth Book of Livy, which contained his account

of

dred and five feet in height, whose shade extended to the distance of no less than three plethra.[k] Arrian with a less portion of credulity, when he has occasion to take notice of them, refutes their extravagance, and demonstrates their absurdity.[l]

The manners and customs of the Indians are not described with greater fidelity or truth. Q. Curtius assures us, that these people made

of this serpent, is only extant, but L. Florus, (Lib. 2. C. 2.--232. 8vo L. B. 1744.) Seneca, (Epist. 82.--338. 8vo Amst. 1672.) and Aulus Gellius (Lib. 6. C. 3.--351. 4to L. B. 1706.) have taken notice of it, and Orosius hath left the story at full length. (Hist. Lib. 4. C. 8.--236. 4to L. B. 1767.) Pliny mentions this piece of history, and adds "Pellis ejus maxillæque usque ad bellum Numantinum duravere Romæ in templo. Faciunt his fidem in Italiâ appellatæ Boæ: in tantam amplitudinem exeuntes, ut Divo Claudio principe, occisæ in Vaticano solidus in alvo spectatus sit infans." Hist. Nat. Lib. 8. C. 14. Tom. 2.--153.

[k] "Δενδρων γαρ εχει γενη διαλλατίοντα, ᾗ το μεν ὑψ⊙ εχοντα πηχων εβδομηκοντα, το δε παχ⊙ μογις ὑπο τετίαρων ανδρων περιλαμβανομενα, τριων δε πλεθρων σκιαν ποιεντα." (Diod. Sicul. Lib. 17. Tom. 2.--230.) This is undoubtedly a fabulous narrative, but a part of it may have been founded on substantial facts. Mr. Marsden gives the following description of the Banyan tree, termed by the Portuguese, Arbor de Raiis, and by the Malays, Iawee Iawee. "It possesses the uncommon property of dropping roots or fibres from certain parts of its boughs, which when they touch the earth, become new stems, and go on increasing to such an extent, that some have measured in circumference of the branches, upwards of a thousand feet, and have been said to shelter a troop of Horse." In a note he adds, "The dimensions of a remarkable Banyan or Burr tree near Manjee, twenty miles West of Patna in Bengal. Diameter 363 to 375 feet. Circumference of shadow at noon, 1116 feet; circumference of the stems, in number fifty or sixty, 921 feet." (Marsden's History of Sumatra. 131.) This species of tree appears to be exactly described by the "Των κατακαμπτομενες εχοντων τες κλαδες, ᾗ περι τε μεγεθες· ὡσθ' ὑφ' ἑνι δενδρῳ μεσημβριζειν σκιαζομενες ἱππιας πεντηκοντα" of Aristobulus. Strabo. Lib. 15.--1017.

[l] "Εγω ετε οις τισι νομοις διαχρωνται εν τῃδε τῃ ξυγγραφῃ ανεγραψα, ετι ζωα ει δη τινα ατοπα η χωρα αυτοις εκφερει.------ ουδε τες μυρμηκας, τες τον χρυσον σφισιν εργαζομενες,------ ουδε ότα αλλα εφ' ἡδονῃ μαλλον τι πεποιηται, ἡ ες αφηγησιν των οντων. ὡς ταγε κατ' Ινδες οσα αν ατοπα ψευσανται, ουκ εξελεγχθησομενα προς ουδαμων." Arrian. Exped. Alex. Lib. 5. C. 4.--346, 347.

made great ufe of wine in their entertainments, and that their kings in a ftate of intoxication were carried by their concubines to their beds." But from a conviction that fuch excefles were equally prejudical to the phyfical conftitution of the inhabitants, and fatal to the repofe of fociety, which often fuffered on thefe inflammations of the fanguinary paffions, the legiflators of the Southern regions of the world had wifely prohibited the ufe of all intoxicating liquors," and their laws and ordinances were rigoroufly obferved by all the Indian nations. Strabo relates, that if even any of their kings was put to death in a debauch by his queen, as a recompence for the meritorious deed fhe had the right of marrying his fucceffor.° The Brahmins abftained from wine, and the Hylobian philofophers,ᵖ the firft and moft illuftrious order of the Samaneans were equally abftemious. It was not even permitted to ftop where wine was difpofed of, and a breach of the prohibition was attended with difgrace. ᵠ We learn from Megafthenes, that the Indians never drank any

---

ᵐ "Feminæ epulas parant, ab iifdem vinum miniftratur, cujus omnibus Indis largus eft ufus. Regem mero fomnoque fopitum in cubiculum pellices referunt, patrio carmine noctium invocantes Deos." Q. Curt. Lib. 8. C. 9. Tom. 2.--632, 633.

ⁿ "At reges, et gentes Indiæ permittunt fornicationem, poculum autem inebrians interdicunt: præter regem Camar, qui tam fornicationem quam vinum interdicit." Geog. Nul. 32, 33.

° "Μεθυοντα δε κτεινασα γυνη βασιλεα, γερας εχει συνειναι το εκεινον διαδεξαμενω." Strabo. Lib. 15. --1036.

ᵖ "Υλοβιαι———αφροδισιων χωρις, ᶄ οινε." Strabo. Lib. 15.--1040. See alfo Clement. Alex. Stromat. Lib. 3.--451.

ᵠ "Cela etoit même honteux a un homme du peuple." The Baron de St. Croix cites in fupport of the fentence the "Επονειδιϛον τω μιτρω" of Porphyrius. (De Abftin. Lib. 4.--364. Ed.

de

any wine except in religious duties,' and the Manicheans, who had adopted many Indian customs, considered it, according to St. Ephraim,' "as the gall of the prince of darkness."' Yet it must be allowed, Atheneus tells us, that Alexander proposed at the death of Calanus prizes for those, who drank the most, in compliment to the Indian passion for wine." This writer extracted the anecdote out of the work of Chares, from whom it descended likewise to Ælian,ˣ but Ælian hath added that this species of contention was an Indian custom. Neither the authority however of Q. Curtius, nor that of Chares, can weaken or set aside the evidence, that has been produced, which is confirmed by the relations of modern travellers. The immutability of the Eastern laws and usages, which are exactly what those of their parents were before them, is well known; and neither the lapse of ages, the commerce with neighbouring nations, nor the invasion of foreign armies

de Rhoer. 4ᵗᵒ 1767.) The expression may possibly bear this construction, but the "ingenuis hominibus" of de Rhoer, is in decided opposition to it.

ʳ "Οινον τι γαρ ȣ πινειν, αλλ' εν Συσιαις μονον." Strabo. Lib. 15.--1035.

ˢ "Error Indicus Manetem tenuit." S. Ephr. ex Vers. Asseman. Bibl. Orient. Tom. 1.--112.

ᵗ "Vinum putare fel principum tenebrarum." St. August. de Morib. Manich. Lib. 2. C. 44.

ʷ "Δια την φιλοινιαν των Ινδων." Athenæus. Lib. 10.--437.

ˣ "Χαριζομεν⊙ δε τοις Ινδοις, κȷ τι επιχωριον αυτων αγωνισμα εις τιμην τȣ Καλανȣ συγκατηρι9μησι τοις αθλοις τοις προειρημενοις· Οινοπυσιας γȣν αγωνιαν προυθηκε." Ælian. Var. Hist. Lib. 2. C. 41. Tom. 1.--172. 4ᵗᵒ 1731.

armies have had any influence on them. They are at this day what they were in the most distant periods. Their aversion to all inebriating liquors still continues, and the miserable and slighted Cast of the Parins [y] is the only one, that has been addicted to them. Without recurring to the testimony of numerous writers, the respectable authority of the Ezour-Vedam will be sufficient to appeal to. We read in this ancient commentary on the Vedam, that Bramah and Vichnou followed by a long train of Brahmins, went to visit Chib, (the Lingam) on the mountain of Keilassan. They found him in the midst of his revels, and in the indecent gratification of his sensual passions. The Brahmins on this disgraceful spectacle loaded him with curses, and Chib on a recovery from his debauchery died of despair.[z] This fable, though refuted by Chumantou in the following chapter, proves notwithstanding the horror, which the Indians had of such excesses, as well as their sentiments respecting the manners of Bollodekan or those of the Baudists, which the Eastern philosopher, who is a speaker in the Ezour-Vedam, hath given us. Their king acknowledges no Deity whatever. " His manners correspond with his religious system, and are barbarous to a degree of horror. A human skull serves him for a cup, and one of his great pleasures is to be carried on

---

[y] Lettres. Edifiantes. Tom. 15.--282. The Baron de St. Croix admits however that a commerce with the Europeans appears to have corrupted the other Casts, and Mr. Hodges was a witness to a scene of native debauchery, where the European vices had not then been propagated. See Travels in India. 93. 4to 1793.

[z] Ezour-Vedam. Lib. 6. C. 4.

on a bed which has ferved for the dying.ᵃ Chumantou adds as the laſt trait of infamy, "that his common drink is an intoxicating liquor."ᵇ

In the defcription of the luxury of the Oriental courts, and their refpectful manner of treating the Indian monarchs, Q. Curtius hath been ſtrictly accurate, but in the divifion of their time he is not equally correct. "Their monthsᶜ contained but fifteen days, notwithſtanding which, their years are complete. They compute their time by the courfe of the moon, but not as moſt people do, when that planet fills its orb; but when it begins to hollow itfelf into horns. This is the caufe that they, who reckon after this manner, have them much ſhorter than other people."ᵈ—The Indians have certainly for more than feventeen hundred years, and ſince the time of Salivaganam, employed the Solar year,ᵉ and it is very

3 D probable

ᵃ "Ces ufages repondent aſſez bien a fon fyſtem de religion, et ont quelque chofe de barbare, qui fait horreur. Le crane d'un homme lui fert de coupe, il met fon plaifir a fe faire porter fur un lit, qui a fervi à un mourant." Ezour-Vedam. Lib. 6. C. 4.

ᵇ "Sa boiſſon ordinaire eſt une liqueur enivrante." Ezour-Vedam. Lib. 7. C. 2. See alfo Lib. 2. C. 2.

ᶜ "Menfes in quinos denos defcripferunt dies. Anni pleni fpatia fervant. Lunæ curfu notant tempora, non ut plerique, quum orbem fidus implevit, fed quum fe curvare cœpit in cornuâ. Et idcirco breviores habent menfes, qui fpatium eorum ad hunc lunæ modum dirigunt." Q. Curt. Lib. 8. C. 9. Tom. 2.--633, 634.

ᵈ Digby's Q. Curtius. Vol. 2.--96.

ᵉ Ezour-Vedam. Lib. 2. C. 3.—Bayer. Regn. Bact. 164——199.—Leon. Euler, de Indorum anno folari aſtronomico ad calcem, Hiſt. Regn. Bact. 201,—&c. &c.

probable the fyſtem was in uſe in the days of Alexander. This people divide and ſubdivide their time almoſt to infinity. From Poromanou[f] to Ananden there is the immenſe and aſtoniſhing period of one hundred and forty millions of years![g] Twelve months compoſe the Indian year, and each of theſe twelve months is again divided by the new and full moon.[h] Q. Curtius may poſſibly have been led into his error by this diviſion, which at the ſame time proves the antiquity of this mode of calculation.

Arrian hath preſerved in his fragment of Indian hiſtory ſome valuable relics of geography, and indeed there are few of the moderns, whoſe notions reſpecting the interior part of India are ſo correct. "This little work," ſays Monſieur d'Anville, "affords us more information reſpecting the courſe of the rivers of this country than many modern notions."[i] This able geographer does the hiſtorian alſo juſtice, on the ſubject of his detail of Alexander's marches in India, and he frankly avows that he is the author "entitled to the greateſt credit."[k] Throwing a glance over the fourth chapter of his Indian hiſtory, we may perceive at once Arrian's accuracy and preciſion

[f] Bagavadam. Lib. 3.--44.—Ezour-Vedam. Lib. 3. C. 4.

[g] Extr. du Diragala-Sakkarum dans l'Hiſt. du Chriſtian. des Indes. Tom. 2.--287.

[h] Ezour-Vedam. Lib. 2. C. 4.

[i] "Cet opuſcule nous apprend bien des circonſtances plus propres, que les notions actuelles à inſtruire de ce que deviennent les rivieres de cette region entre elles." Geograph. Ancien. Tom. 2.--340.

[k] "Le plus accredité qui ſoit à conſulter à ce ſujet." Geograph. Ancien. Tom. 2.--334.

precision relating to the Ganges, the rivers that open into it, and the neighbouring nations. It is with concern, we muſt obſerve, that the ſame accuracy and preciſion are unfortunately wanting, when he mentions the Indus and the rivers which empty their waters into it.

Strabo, diſtinguiſhed alike for his critical abilities and geographical knowledge, hath left us a deſcription of India, that is well adapted to explain the country through which Alexander paſſed with his army. With great judgment he hath adopted the opinions that appeared to be moſt probable, he connects a conciſe account of the expedition of the Macedonian troops with his geographical information, and including an abridged hiſtory of the manners, the cuſtoms and philoſophy of the Indians, he hath moulded the whole into a form, from which his readers may receive both entertainment and improvement. On a compariſon of Ptolemy with this able writer, with Pliny whoſe brevity ſometimes renders him obſcure, and whoſe geographical terms are ſometimes faulty, and in ſhort with the hiſtorians of the life of Alexander, it is impoſſible to reconcile him with theſe different authors, or to draw any juſt idea of the courſe of the rivers of India, or the actual ſituation of places. The Bydaſpes or Hydaſpes, according to Ptolemy, receives ſucceſſively two rivers, the Sandabilis and Adrius or Rhuadis, and afterwards empties itſelf into the Zadradus, which after an union on the right with the Bibaſis, (without doubt the Hyphaſes or Hyphaſis) after a ſhort paſſage opens into

the Indus.¹ Monfieur d'Anville judicioufly obferves, "that it is not the diverfity of fome names with which we are diffatisfied in this defcription, but the erroneous manner in which thefe rivers are faid to flow."ᵐ Alexander's marches, as related by Strabo and Arrian, furnifh us with more certain information, and their defcriptions are not inapplicable to the real fituation of the country.

The Conqueror of Afia began his march at Alexandria, the modern Candahar, paffed the Cophena and the Choes and afterwards the Indus, the prefent Sinde,ⁿ and reduced Taxila. After his conqueft, he quitted Taxila and entered into the country now called Pen-jab, which in the Perfian tongue fignifies five rivers, and croffed the Hydafpes. The banks of this river were celebrated for the defeat of Porus, and the Conqueror then advanced to the Acefines, and afterwards to the Hydroates or Heraotes, and at laft to the Hyphafis, as it is termed by Arrian, or the Hypafis of Pliny and Q. Curtius, and Hypanis of Strabo and Diodorus Siculus. It would be at prefent difficult to afcertain thefe rivers,

---

¹ Ptolem. Lib. 7. C. 1.--170.

ᵐ "Ce n' eft pas tant la diverfite de quelques noms qui deplait dans cette expofition, que le defaut dans la maniere de faire courir ces rivieres les unes par rapport aux autres." Eclairciffement fur la Carte de l' Inde. 36.

ⁿ "Indus incolis Sindus appellatur, (Plin. Hift. Nat. Lib. 6. C. 20. Tom. 1,--688.) which is not widely different, the Baron de St. Croix obferves, from the Send of the Oriental geographers, and the Chindou of the Ezour-Vedam.

rivers,[o] but it is probable that by the Hydaspes we are to understand the Shantrow, by the Acesines the Ravei or the river that passes by Lahour, by the Hydraotes the Biah, and by the Hyphases the Caul.[p] In the country of the Choes the difficulty increases. Monsieur d'Anville's opinion, on the whole seems the only one admissible. "We see" says he, "that the Choes being undoubtedly the river Cow, the Cophus, which we previously met with, must be the river (Mehram-Hir) which has its source near Candahar.[q]

The Choes is called by Strabo the Choaspes,[r] but it appears to be an error, and the Choes, which is the name given to this river by Arrian,[s] and confirmed with a slight alteration by the Coa of Ptolemy,[t] carries the appearance of authenticity. The name of the Choaspes indeed might occasion the mistake, and also the confusion

---

[o] "Ces fleuves ont reçu tant de noms particuliers des modernes qui en ont parlé, qu'on a presentiment de la peine à les discerner les uns des autres, et même la plupart de ces noms sont confondus." Thevenot. Tom. 5.--180.

[p] The Baron de St. Croix here adopts the opinion of Monsieur d'Anville. Major Rennel supposes the Hydaspes to be the Behut or Chelum, the Acesines the Icnaub or Chunaub, the Hydroates the Rauvee, and the Hyphasis the Settlege or Suttuluz. The reasons for his opinion may be seen in his valuable Memoir of a Map of Hindostan.

[q] "On voit que Choes etant indubitablement la riviere nommée Cow, le Cophes qui se recontre auparavant doit etre la riviere (Mehram-Hir) qui sort des environs de Candahar." Geograph. Ancienne. Tom. 2.--340.

[r] Strabo. Lib. 15.--1021.

[⁋] "Παρα τον Χοην καλυμενον ποταμον." Arrian. Exped. Alex. Lib. 4. C. 23.--316.

[t] Ptolem. Lib. 7. C. 1.--169.

sion of the Choes with the Choaspes of Susa. Dionysius the geographer has fallen into the error, when he tells us, that the Choaspes rolling along its Indian waters washes the environs of Susa.[w] Eustathius, his commentator, in his explanation of this geographer has added to the error, and pretends that by the Indian waters Dionysius intended to intimate, that the Choaspes, which flowed near Susa, was a branch of the Indus.[x] It might rather have been imagined that the poet, taking Aristotle for his guide, who speaks only of the Susian Choaspes, though he supposes it to rise in the Paropamisus,[y] prolongs the course of this river from the extremities of India as far as Susa, and only intended by the expression of its Indian waters, to point out its source in India. This mode of treating of the situation of different rivers and countries was not indeed without example amongst the Greeks, who have overturned the geography of the universe. Strabo relates that Diotimus, one of the chiefs of an Athenian deputation, had passed up the Cydnus from Cilicia to the Choaspes, which conducted him to Susa.[z] It has been the fate of this river to be the subject of many

such

[w] "―――――――――――Χοασπις
Ἑλκων Ἰνδον ὑδωρ, παρα τε ρειων χθονα Σουσων."
Dionys. Perieg. V. 1074, 1075.

[x] "Χοασπις Ἰνδον μεν ὑδωρ, ἑλκων, ὡς εκ του Ἰνδου σχιζομενου ποταμου, παραρρεων δε και τα Σουσα."
Eustath. Comm. ad Dionys. Perieg. V. 1075.--132. 4to 1577.

[y] "Meteor. Lib. 1. C. 13. Aristot. Opera. Tom. 1.--768.

[z] "Διοτιμον δε τον Στρομβιχου, πρεσβειας Ἀθηναιων ἀφηγουμενον, δια του Κυδνου αναπλευσαι εκ της Κιλικιας επι τον Χοασπιν ποταμον, ὁς παρα τα Σουσα ρει, και αφικισθαι τεσσαρακοσταιον εις Σουσα." Strabo. Lib. 1.--81.

OF ALEXANDER THE GREAT. 391

such errors, and Monsieur de l'Isle is not warranted in his idea of the Choes falling into the Indus and running in a direction, which cannot possibly agree with the actual position of places. The pretended Choaspes, as Strabo assures us, discharges itself into the Cophena,[a] and the march of the Macedonian army, as described by Arrian, fully authenticates the opinion.

At the conflux of the Choes and Cophena we find, according to Monsieur d'Anville, the fabulous city of Nysa, which he fancies to be the Nagara of Ptolemy, and the Nagar of the Turkish geographer, who places this city, from the thirty-two degrees and a half of Latitude which he assigns to it, East of Candahar, and five days journey from Kabal.[b] Monsieur d'Anville appears to have fixed the position of Nysa, from the mountain Merou, which he imagines to be near it, in the thirty-third degree of Latitude. The historians of Alexander's life and actions have spoken of the proximity of the mountain Merou,[c] but instead of authorizing their evidence, it proves their ignorance and errors. The mountain Meru or Merou, which is pretended to have been the Meros of the Greeks, is highly celebrated amongst the Indians. The Bagavadam, one of their eighteen Pouranams or Canonical books, mentions

---

[a] "Και τον Χοασπην, ὃς εἰς τον Κωφην ἐμβαλλει ποταμον." Strabo. Lib. 15.--1021.

[b] Eclaircissement de la Carte de l'Inde. 21, 22.

[c] "Και το ορ᾽ το προς τη πολει, ὅτε εν τησιν ὑπωρειησιν ωκισαι ἡ Νυσσα, Μηρ᾽ κληζιται." (Arrian. Hist. Ind. C. 1.--550.) Situ est sub radicibus montis, quem Merou incolæ appellant." Q. Curt. Lib. 8. C. 10. Tom. 2.--636, 637.

ons it in the following terms. "In the middle of the world there is a great island called Iambam or Iambon, of one hundred thousand Yoſſineys both in length and breadth. A Yoſſiney is a distance of four hours' travelling. In the midſt of this island is the mountain Merou, which is a hundred thouſand Yoſſineys in height, ten thouſand deep, and thirty-two thouſand wide. To the North of this mountain there are two other mountains, one called Nilavarnam, and the other Velleyvarnam, which form a chain from Eaſt to Weſt as far as the ſalt ocean.⁴ The details into which the author

---

⁴ "Il y a au milieu du monde la grande iſle, nommée Iambam ou Iambon, qui a de longueur cent mille Yôſſineis et autant de largeur. Un Yôſſinei eſt une marche de quatre heures en chemin. Au milieu de cette iſle eſt la montagne Merou, haute de cent mille Yôſſineis, profonde de dix mille et large de trente-deux mille. Au nord de cette montagne, il y a deux autres montagnes: l'une nommée Nilavarnam, et l'autre Velleyvarnam, qui font une chaine de l'eſt à l'Oueſt juſqu' a la mer ſalée." (Bagavadam. Livr. 5.-93. A manuſcript in the library of Monſieur de Bertin.) The Baron de St. Croix hath introduced in a note the following curious deſcription of the mountain Merou and its environs, from the Bagavadam, which was originally written in the Sanſcreet language, and reduced into French by Maridas Pouli, the principal interpreter at Pondicherry, who dedicated it to Monſieur de Bertin the French Miniſter and Secretary of State. "A l'eſt de Merou, il exiſte une autre montagne nommée Mandaram; au Sud celle nommée Souvariſvam, à l'Oueſt une autre nommée Coumoudam; et au Nord celle de Sroungam. Ces quatre montagnes ſont dans une poſition ſi exacte, qu'à les voir il paroîtroit qu'on y avoit placé de grandes colonnes pour y conſtruire une voûte. Leurs elevations ſont à dix milles yôſſineis. Il y a quatre arbres aux ſommets de ces quatre montagnes, leſquels ſe nomment Soûdam, Cadapam, Alam, et Nâval, qui portent des fruits et des fleurs dans tous les temps, dont les rameaux paroiſſent avoir mille yôſſineys d'etendue.

Dans le Merou, il y a quatre etangs, etendus chacun à cent yôſſineys en quarré; un rempli de lait, l'autre de beurre, le troiſieme de taïr (lait caillé) et le dernier de ſuc de canne.

Les quatre montagnes ont chacune un jardin de delices; ces jardins ſont nommés Nandam, Saytradam, Raypraſſidam et Sarvalôca-paütram. Celui qui mange le fruit de Soûdam (mangue) de la montagne de Mandoram, acquiert l'immortalité. Le jus de ces fruits courant comme un ruiſſeau,

thor of this work enters refpecting the mountain Merou, are undoubtedly full of fables and puerile tales, and there is no poffibility of afcertaining from fuch trafh its real pofition. The Indian writer adds, "the great mountain Merou is lighted by the fun during fix whole months: in the fix others there is continual night."[e] Soon after we are told, that "one part of the chariot of the fun refts on the mountain Merou, and the reft of it is fufpended by the air."[f]

---

ruiffeau, forme un fleuve et eft nommé Roffòdoram (courant de jus). Le jus des fruits de Naval, qui eft fur la montagne Souvarifvam, produifant de même un ruiffeau nommé Jambou, a donné fon nom à l'île Jambou qu'il arrofe.

Les deux autres arbres produifent de même deux autres rivieres, qui arrofent le pays d'Havroudam.

A l'Eft, et à l'Oueft de même de Merou, il y a deux montagnes nommées Gedâ-Coûdam et Pariatram, qui forment une chaîne en longueur de 18,000 yôffineys, du Nord au Sud. Les Dieux frequentent ces montagnes où ils prennent leurs divertiffemens.

Au fommet de Merou, il y a une grande Ville de dix mille yôffineys en quarré. Cette Ville fe nommé Brahmapatnam et eft toute eclatante d'or. A l'entour de cette Ville, il y a huit autres Villes gouvernees par les Dieux des huit points Cardinaux de l'Univers. Un ruiffeau nommé Brahmânda-Cadam, fortant du haut du Merou, arrofe la Ville de Brahma, fort par les quatre portes de cette Ville, et forme quatre fleuves nommés Sadalam, Sadaffou, Patram, et Alagucy. Un de ces fleuves s'elevant en l'air, lave les pieds de Vifnou. L'autre, qui fort du côté du Sud, arrofe le pays de Nichetam, Yemacoudam, Ymoffalam, et fe jette enfuite dans le pays de Baradam. C'eft ce fleuve que Sivan prit fur fa tête, et delà il a eté nommé Ganga-Taren ou Siven, (celui qui porte fur fa tête Ganga.") Bagavadam. Livr. 5.

[e] "La grande montagne Merou eft eclairee par le foleil pendant fix mois entiers; une nuit continuelle regne les fix autres." Bagavadam. Livr. 5.--100.

[f] "Le chariot du foleil eft appuyé d'un bout contre le mont Merou, et le refte eft foutenu par l'air." (Bagavadam. Livr. 5.--102.) Sonnerat adds "Il n'a qu'une roue; fept chevaux verds le trainent; le Dien Avounin eft le conducteur. Les vagaguilliers au nombre de foixante mille fuivent le foleil dans fes douzes loges, en l'adorant et pfalmodiant differens airs à fa louange." Voyages aux Indes Orientales et à la Chine." Tom. 1.--122. A Work of authenticity and value.

The Ezour-Vedam, an ancient commentary of the Vedam, written in the Sanfcreet language and tranflated by a Brahmin of Benares, fixes the fituation of the mountain Merou, at the fource of the Ganges, which rifes in this mountain. The defcription of it in this Indian book, which fuppofes it to be in the centre of the world and of an immenfe height,[g] agrees however even ftill lefs with the pofition which a modern geographer hath allotted to it. Bayer obferves, that in the Indian geography entitled Puwana-Saccaram, the mountain Merou is defcribed in a very fabulous manner,[h] and perhaps its exiftence has no other foundation than Indian imagination. In a work of Fo or Foe, an ancient Indian legiflator, which has been tranflated into the Chinefe language, the extafies of a Samanian philofopher are compared to the immobility of the mountain

---

[g] "Au milieu de la terre, eft la plus grande de toutes les montagnes, qui s' appelle Merou. C' eft-là qu'eft fitué le pays appelé Zomboudipo, qui eft le pays de l' Inde : au Midi et au Couchant de la montagne de Merou, font fitués differens pays. En voici les noms, Zombou, Pelokio; Koucho, Chako, Krohonro, Pourkoro, Chalmouli. Tous ces pays, ou toutes ces îles, font egalement habites. Il y a plufieurs fleuves fur la terre. Les principaux font Brommora, Bodra, Ganga ou le Gange: ces trois fleuves prennent leur fource dans le mont Merou, et vont fe decharger dans la mer. Le premier coule au Nord et le Gange au Midi. Il traverfe à fon embouchure et inonde quantité de bois. J' ai dit que le Zomboudipo ou l' Inde etoit fitué au Midi de la montagne. &c. &c." (Zend-Avefta. Livr. 1. C. 3.) "Au milieu de la terre eft une montagne d' une hauteur prodigieufe à qui on a donné le nom de Merou. Aux quatre côtés de celle-ci s' elevent quatre autres montagnes ; favoir, les montagnes Ketouman, Mallioban, Mandaro, Chuparchodo. Il y a pareillement fur ces quatre montagnes quatre arbres d' une grandeur prodigieufe; favoir, les arbres Ambro, Kodanbo, Zombou, Niogrodo. Au pied de la montagne Mandaro coule un fleuve qui, recevant dans fes eaux les fleuves qui tombent de l' ambre Zombou, en contracte l' odeur. Tout le pays qu' arrofe ce fleuve eft appelé Zomboudipo ; voilà d' où il a tiré fon nom." Zend-Avefta. Livr. 1. C. 6.

[h] "Fabulofiffime defcribitur." Hift. Regn. Bact. 4.

mountain Siami, which is the Merou or Smerou[i] under contemplation.

To give some credit to the travels of Bacchus, the Greeks supposed that all the monuments, which they met with, were so many vestiges of the progress of this Deity. Stephanus Byzantinus reckons no less than ten cities of the name of Nysa, some in Lybia, some in Ægypt, others in Greece, Thrace and mount Caucasus, and the fourth in the list is that in India.[k] Hesychius, on the contrary, pretends that Nysa was a general term applied to many mountains in different parts of the world,[l] and he mentions no less than fifteen under this denomination. Aristodemus, in his first book of Theban inscriptions, speaking of the expedition of Bacchus into India, takes notice only of the mountain of Nysa, and

---

[i] Histoire des Huns, par Monsieur de Guignes. Tom. 1. P. 2.--233.

[k] "Etienne de Byfance compte jusqu' a dix villes de Nysa————la septieme est celle de l' Inde." This is a gross typographical error, and I have rectified it. "Τεταρτη ει Ινδοις." (Stephan. Byzant. 594. Fol. L. B. 1694.) The sentence however includes another of greater magnitude, and the Baron de St. Croix hath confounded in a very extraordinary manner the cities, which bore the name of "Ναξια," with those termed "Νυσσα" or "Νυσα," whose etymology and derivation were very different. The latter might have a fabulous relation to Dionysius or Bacchus: the former were founded probably on the site of some local victories, and Arrian tells us the Nicæa in India, which Stephanus Byzantinus mentions, was built in memory of the defeat of Porus. "Και την μεν, Νικαιαν, της Νικης της κατ' Ινδων επωνυμον ωνομασι." Arrian. Exped. Alex. Lib. 5. C. 19.--379.

[l] "Νυσα κ̃ Νυσηιον Ορ&. υ καθ' ἑνα τοπον· ἐςι γαρ Αραβιας, Αιθιοπιας, Αιγυπτυ, Βαβυλων&, Ερυθρας, Θετ]αλιας, Κιλικιας, Ινδικης, Λιβυης, Λυδιας, Μακεδονιας, Ναξυ περι το Παγχαιον, τοπ&. Συριας." Hesychius. Tom. 2.--694. Ed. Alberti. 1764.

and Clitarchus confines himself to it in the history of Alexander.[m] Pliny speaks of the mountain of Nysa[n] and of a city with the name,[o] and it appears by a passage of Aristotle,[p] that the Greek writers amused themselves with sketching out descriptions of this mountain. Without any attempt at a decision whether Nysa was a city or a mountain, its existence in India is as problematical as even the expedition of Bacchus, of which the Ancients imagined it to be a proof.[q] Arbitrary etymologies can scarcely be allowed to be sufficient to demonstrate the identity of any of the modern cities with the ancient Nysa, and even from the number which have equal pretensions to the honour, it would certainly be multiplied in such a manner as to discredit their general claim to the antiquity.

[m] "Καὶ Κλείταρχος ἐν ταῖς περὶ Ἀλεξάνδρου ἱστορίαις· προσίστορων ὅτι καὶ Νυσα ὄρος ἐστὶ ἐν Ἰνδικῇ." Scholia. ad Apoll. Rhod. V. 907. Lib. 2.

[n] "In Indiæ vero Nysa monte." Plin. Hist. Nat. Lib. 8. C. 39. Tom. 2.--201.

[o] "Nec non et Nysam urbem plerique Indiæ adscribunt, montemque Merum, Libero patri sacrum." Plin. Hist. Nat. Lib. 6. C. 21. Tom. 1.--691.

[p] De Mundo. C. 1. Aristot. Opera. Tom. 1.--846.

[q] "Εστι δε τις Θνητος ευρρειτην παρα Γαγγην
Χωρος τιμηεις τε καὶ ἱερος, ὃν ποτε Βακχος
Θυμαινων επατησεν."
Dionys. Perieg. 1153----1155.

"Τον δε χωρον ον ὁ Διονυσος Θυμαινων επατησεν, Θνητον καὶ τιμηεντα καλει, καὶ ἱερον· λεγων ὅτι ὁ τοιουτος τοπος Νυσσαια ὁδος ικληθη. ἥτις περι τον Γαγγην εστιν, απο της Αρραβικης Νυσσης κληθεισα, αφ' ἧς καὶ αὐτος ὁ Διονυσος κληθηναι δοκει· Νυσσα δε, κατα τον γεωγραφον, πολις εν Ινδια, κτισμα Διονυσου, καὶ ορθως αυτοθι Μερος." Eustath. ad Dionys. Perieg. 4to Stephan. 1577.—See also Apollodorus. Lib. 3. C. 5.—Philostrat. Vit. Apollod. Tyan. Lib. 2. C. 9.—Q. Curt. Lib. 8. C. 10.—Arrian. Exped. Alex. Lib. 5. C. 2.

antiquity. Abulfeda mentions many cities termed Nyfapaur in Perfia, Bactriana and the Khorafan, and two with the name of Nafa,' which differs little from Nyfa, one in Perfia and the other in the Kerman. Far from connecting the etymology of Nyfapour with Dionyfius or Bacchus, fome learned men have underftood the word to be derived from the name of fome of the Eaftern princes, as in the inftance of Sapor, a king of Perfia.' It feems, in fhort, that we have no more reafon to mark the precife fituation of Nyfa or the mountain Meros in our modern maps, than that of the celebrated ifland of Panchaia of Euemerus. We may be however fatisfied that the fables, which have been interwoven in the defcription of mount Meros, originated from the fuperftitious veneration, that many people and particularly the Eaftern nations, entertained for fome celebrated mountains. Porra in the kingdom of Arrakan, and Pecha in China, the Isje in Japan, Olaimi in the country of the Apalachites, and a multitude of others acquired a great reputation, and from thence followed the fpecies of religious veneration with which they were afterwards regarded. The exiftence of thefe mountains, admitting even the accounts, that have been circulated concerning them, to have been in general fabulous, is neverthelefs certain, though we may not be able, to afcertain their true pofition and that of the mountain Merou in particular.

Alexander

' "Nafa quoque eft urbs in Perfide, et altera ejufdem nominis in Karman." Abulfeda, Vers. cit.

' Golius in Affer. 188.—Schultens, Ind. Geograph. ad Calcem Vitæ. Salad. Bohadini Nyfabour.

Alexander after the conqueſt of the whole country on this fide of the Indus, paſſed that river, and arrived at Taxila, and then marched in a direct line to the Hydaſpes. The ſituation of Taxila ought therefore to be South of the actual junction of the Tchenau with the Indus. On the ſuppoſition of its being ſituated on the conflux of theſe two rivers, the Macedonian army in their march to attack Porus muſt have previouſly paſſed the Tchenau, which by no means agrees with the itinerary of Alexander. This Prince having received, as we learn from Arrian a reinforcement of five thouſand Indians under the command of Taxilus, directed his march towards the Hydaſpes and encamped upon its banks.' Strabo informs us that Taxila, a powerful city and governed by excellent laws, was between the Indus and the Ganges," but he certainly would not have expreſſed himſelf in this manner, if it had been ſituated at the conflux of the Tchenau and the Indus. Theſe obſervations appear to juſtify the hiſtorians of Alexander's life and actions, though Monſieur d'Anville accuſes them with having miſtaken the Tchenau for the Indus, and from this error with having multiplied the latter river. "From the courſe of Alexander's expedition," ſays the learned geographer, "we may ſuppoſe the Tchenau to be the river, that he paſſed under the name of the Indus, for inſtead of four rivers, we meet with five undoubtedly

---

' Arrian. Exped. Alex. Lib. 5. C. 8.--357.

" "Μεταξυ δε τυ Ινδυ, κȷ τυ 'Υδασπυ, Ταξιλα ιϛι πολις μιγαλη κȷ ευνομωτατη." Strabo. Lib. 15. --1022.

doubtedly in the courſe of his expedition."[x] On the contrary there are only four. Alexander marches from Taxila, reaches the Hydaſpes, which he paſſes, and he afterwards croſſes the Aceſines, Hydraotes and Hyphaſis.[y] The Macedonian monarch, agreeable to Strabo, having learnt that the rivers of India formed junctions with each other, directed his march below theſe junctions, to avoid the inconveniency of croſſing the rivers ſo very frequently, and the embarraſſment from his want of boats.[z] When he paſſed therefore the Hydaſpes, he muſt have left the Tchenau to the left.——It might be difficult at preſent to determine what was the Tchenau,[a] as the Ancients have not left us any very clear notions of it, though it ſeems likely to be the Tutape or Toutape, that Arrian ſpeaks of as a conſiderable river, which can only agree with the Tchenau, though he ſuppoſes it to empty itſelf into the Aceſines,[b] whoſe courſe is extended, againſt all probability, to the South of Taxila. Arrian places alſo Peucela at a little diſtance from

---

[x] "La ſuite de l'expedition d'Alexandre veut que le Tſhenau ſoit la riviere qu'il traverſa ſous le nom d'Indus; car au lieu de quatre fleuves à reconnoitre dans la ſuite de cette expedition, comme on verra ci-apres, il y en auroit indubitablement cinque." Eclairciſſement ſur la Carte de l'Inde. 34.

[y] Arrian. Exped. Alex. Lib. 6. C. 14.---437.

[z] Strabo. Lib. 15.---1021.

[a] The Tchenau is one of the moſt rapid rivers of Penjab. See Thevenot. Tom. 5.---174, 175.---Voyage de Bernier. Tom. 2.---258, 259.

[b] "Καὶ Τυταπῷ δε μεγας ποταμῷ ις τον Ακισινην εκδιδοι." Arrian. Hiſt. Ind. C. 4.---556.

from the Indus,[c] a position, which cannot be reconciled even by Monsieur d'Anville[d] to the Tchenau: Peucela is really situated on the Indus, which we meet with immediately after the Cophina.[e] Q. Curtius neither possesses the accuracy nor precision, that distinguish Arrian's geographical details, and whilst he is obscure when he speaks of the different people of India and its rivers that throw themselves into the Indus, he is apt to contradict the historical part of his work. This Latin historian assures us without reserve, that the Acesines augments the waters of the Ganges, which receives it near its embouchure. "The[f] Acesines swells it: the Ganges intercepts this river a little before it discharges itself into the sea; at their first meeting they dash furiously against each other, for the Ganges is very rough where it receives it, and the Acesines is too violent to give way to the other's resisting streams."[g] We are soon afterwards informed that the Acesines becomes confounded

---

[c] "Και αλλη πολις Πευκελα, ετι μεγαλη ᾗ αυτη, ε μακραν τε Ινδε." Arrian. Hist. Ind. C. 1.--550.

[d] Eclaircissement sur la Carte de la I' Inde. 33, 34.

[e] "Μετα μεν εν τον Κωφην ὁ Ινδ☉ ρει." Strabo. Lib. 15.--1022.

[f] "Acesines eum auget. Ganges decursurum in mare intercipit: magnoque motu amnis uterque colliditur: quippe Ganges asperum os influenti objicit; nec repercussæ aquæ cedunt." (Q. Curt. Lib. 8. C. 9. Tom. 2.--623.) We learn from Arrian that the Acesines discharges itself into the Indus. "Ὁ δε Ακεσινης εν Μαλλοις ξυμβαλλει τω Ινδω." (Hist. Ind. C. 4.--556.) And Pliny adds his authority to Arrian. "Indus————undeviginti recipit amnes. Sed clarissimos, Hydaspem ————Cantabram————Acesinem et Hyphasin." Hist. Nat. Lib. 6. C. 20. Tom. 1.--688.

[g] Digby's Q. Curtius. Vol. 2.--92, 93.

founded with the Hydaspes [h] when they join, and the Macedonian fleet suffered exceedingly where these two rivers met,[i] but he is again mistaken, for the Acesines, called erroneously the Tanais [k] by some authors, loses itself in the Indus.[l] Justin is guilty of an error equally extravagant, when he supposes Alexander to descend by the Acesines to the Ocean.[m] The anonymous author of Ravenner[n] hath copied this error, though Justin indeed seems to retract it in the following chapter, where he mentions the arrival of the Macedonian Conqueror at the Ocean, and adds that he happily reached the mouths of the Indus.[o]

3 F   Monsieur

---

[h] "Hydaspes amnis Acesini committitur." (Q. Curt. Lib. 9. C. 4. Tom. 2,--691.) "Acesini Hydaspi confunditur." Q. Curt. Lib. 9. C. 4. Tom. 2.--694.

[i] "Iterque meant navigia, in tenuem alveum cogitur. Itaque quum crebri fluctus se inveherent, et navium hinc proras, hinc latera pulsarent; subducere nautæ cæperunt. Sed ministeria eorum hinc metu, hinc præapida celeritate fluminis occupantur. In oculis duo majora omnium navigia submersa sunt; leviora quum et ipsa nequirent regi, in ripam tamen innoxia expulsa sunt." Q. Curt. Lib. 9. C. 4. Tom. 2.--694, 695.

[k] See Steph. Byzant.

[l] Arrian is particularly circumstantial. "Αλλα ὁ ʽΥδασπης μενες τον Ακεσινην εμβαλλει· εμβαλων δε, το παν ὑδωρ, Ακεσινης παρερχεται καλεμενον· Αυτις δε ὁ Ακεσινης ετ᾽ ξιμβαλλει τω ʽΥδραντη, κ̑ παραλαβων τυτον, ετι Ακεσινης εςι. Και τον ʽΥρανιν ιαι τυτω ὁ Ακεσινης παραλαβων, τω αυτω δη ονοματι ες τον Ινδον εμβαλλει· ξυμβαλων δε, ξυγχωρει δη τω Ινδω." Exped. Alex. Lib. 6. C. 14.--437.

[m] "Alexander ad Acesinem amnem pergit: per hunc in Oceanum devehitur." Justin. Lib. 12. C. 9.--327.

[n] Lib. 2. C. 3.

[o] "Secundo æstu ostio fluminis Indi invehitur." Justin. Lib. 12. C. 10.--331.

Monsieur d' Isle, instead of conducting the Hyphasis, which is the most Eastern river of Penjab, into the Acesines, supposes it to flow into the Indus, and extends its course as far as Patalene, but he has not explained his reasons for deviating so widely from all the historians who have described this river.[p] Notwithstanding the obligations we are under to Monsieur d' Isle for his labours, which have been so very useful to a knowledge of the globe, his map of Alexander's empire is undoubtedly imperfect, and the conquests of that monarch are very inaccurately stated. Arrian, the ablest and best informed guide that could have been consulted on the subject, appears to have been entirely neglected. Monsieur d' Anville hath kept him constantly in view, and hath profited from the luminous manner in which the Greek historian hath treated of this part of the world, which was ravaged by the Conqueror of the East. After having reduced the elevation of Latitude, given to Cachemir by the Oriental calculations,[q] and having by these means allowed a greater extent to the marches of the Macedonian army, Monsieur d'Anville imagines he is able to assert, that Alexander reached Cachemir, though he allows, "that in the details of Alexander's marches, we see nothing that distinguishes the actual situation of this country."[r] But it seems an
indispensable

---

[p] Eclaircissement sur la Carte de l' Inde.

[q] Eclaircissement sur la Carte de l' Inde. 27, 28.

[r] "Quoique dans le detail des marches de ce Prince, on ne voit rien qui ressemble à ce qui distingue ce pays par sa situation." Geographe Ancienne, 338. Eclaircissement sur la Carte de l' Inde, 34.

indispensable rule, in a comparison of ancient and modern opinions on such subjects, and an endeavour to conciliate them, that some regard should invariably be had to the inferences, which may be naturally drawn from the situations of the places in dispute. Cachemir supplies us with decisive ones.—Shut up by the stupendous mountains, which separate India from Thibet and Great Tartary, it is impossible to penetrate into it on any side, except by a painful and laborious ascent in the face of immense rocks.[s] Abulfeda relates, that Oguzkhan was stopped a whole year at the entrance of these mountains,[t] which admitted only three passages, attended with such almost insurmountable obstructions,[w] that they had guaranteed the country against the incursions of many conquerors.[x] If Alexander had penetrated into it, is it to be supposed that his historians would have been silent on his success, and taken no notice of such an important conquest?—Monsieur d'Anville acknowledges there is not any thing in Alexander's itinerary,

---

[s] Notes on Abulgazi. 52.

[t] Hist. Gen. des Tatars par Abulgazi-Khan. 53.

[w] Sherefeddin. Hist. de Timur-bec. Livr. 4. C. 31. "Il n'y a que trois passages tres etroits pour pouvoir passer dans ce pays; on appelle ces passages Derbend. Celui de Khorassan est tres difficile et etroit, les bêtes chargées n'y peuvent pas passer; on est obligé de faire transporter les marchandises sur le dos des hommes qu'on loue pour cet effet; ce qu'ils font avec beaucoup de peine: le passage des Indes est de meme qui celui du Khorassan. Celui de Thibet est à la verité un peu moins difficile que les autres; mais comme à la distance de quelque journees ce terrein n'est couverte que d'Herbes venimeuses, cela est cause que la cavalarie ni les Caravannes ne peuvent pas y passer; c'est pourquoi ce passage n'est guere praticable." Geograph. Turc. 404, 405.

[x] Geograph. Turc. 404.

from which we even may fuppofe it, but "he is unwilling to believe, that a knowledge of this country, fo celebrated in India for its beauties was concealed from the Ancients."[y] The fame reafons would induce us to believe that China was alfo known to them. "Any fimilitude in the name," adds Monfieur d'Anville, "is an argument for the probability."[z] But do we find any ftriking refemblance to juftify the obfervation between the Cafpira of the Ancients and Cachemir, or rather the Kafchmir of the Orientals, ftill called in fome places, Kichimir? Though the firft fyllable indeed has fome refemblance in found, no certainty arifes from it that the two words were intended to exprefs the fame, and the proof, which the learned geographer draws from the pofition of Cafpira, the capital of the country with its name, which Ptolemy places in the centre of India,[a] is equally fallacious.

The Macedonians, on their arrival at the mouths of the Indus, firft became acquainted with the tides, and looked on the flux and reflux of the Ocean with wonder and aftonifhment.[b] A modern writer,

[y] "Que la connoiffance de cette contrée, fi celebre dans l' Inde par fes agrements, ait eté cachée à l' antiquité." Geograph. Ancienne. Tom. 2.--338.

[z] "Un grand rapport de denomination eft un moyen de convenance." Geograph. Ancienne. Tom. 2.--338.

[a] Ptolem. Lib. 7. C. 1.--171.

[b] "Ενταυθα ὁρμισαντων, τω παθημα επιγιγνεται της μεγαλης θαλασσης ἡ αμπωτις· ὡςε επι ξηρα απελιφθησαν αυτοις ἁι νηες. Και τουτο ου το προτερον εγνωκοσι τοις απ' Αλεξανδρου, εκπληξιν μεν κỳ αυτο ου σμικραν

writer, diftinguifhed both for his ingenuity and paradoxes, hath criticifed this relation of Alexander's hiftorians, and remarks that the Macedonian troops could not have been furprifed at the phænomenon, as they had already been fpectators of it in their paffage on the coaft of Ægypt. But the Macedonian troops did not then fee the Red fea, and could only have learnt from information, what they afterwards witneffed on a view of the Ocean in the greateft magnificence, as the higheft known tides are thofe of the gulph of Sinde at the mouths of the Indus, where the fea retires with uncommon rapidity, and leaves a great tract of fand uncovered and dry.[c] This effect therefore of the flux and reflux of the Ocean naturally aftonifhed the Macedonians, and hath been properly obferved by their hiftorians. It was not then fo very trifling as Le Clerc hath imagined[d] in his criticifm on Q. Curtius. But the Latin hiftorian is often cenfured by him, frequently without tafte and with injuftice, and conftantly with keennefs and feverity.

Alexander began his march from the mouths of the Indus, to return to Babylon through the country to the Weft of this river. Plutarch informs us, that after having paffed through the country of the Orites and Gedrofia, the Conqueror of the Eaft employed

feven

σμικραν παρισχε· πολυ δι δη ιτι μειζονα, απο τι διελθοσης της ωρας προσηει τε το ιδως, κ̃ τα σκαφη μετιωριζοντο." (Arrian. Exped. Alex. Lib. 6. C. 19.--445. 446.) Q. Curtius hath launched as ufual into a luxuriant defcription. Lib. 9. C. 9. Tom. 2.--730----736.

[c] Varenius. Geograph. C. 14. Propos. 14.

[d] "Huc etiam accedit, quod æftus in mari Indico exiguus fit, nec tantos tumultus creare poffit."
Judicium de Curtio. 453.

seven days in crossing Carmania, and then arrived at the capital of Gedrosia. This must be an error of the transcriber, and we should read Carmania with Dacier, which is a more natural correction than one suggested by Moses of Chorene,[e] and agrees with the accounts of the other historians, and Arrian[f] and Strabo[g] in particular. The text of Plutarch will then only present the extraordinary transposition of Gedrosia to the West of Carmania.

Of the NAVIGATION of NEARCHUS.

The expedition of Nearchus forms a period of some consideration in the history of the navigation of the Ancients, and has a claim to particular investigation.——Nearchus was the son of Adrotimus, a native of Crete,[h] and one of the ablest of the Macedonian officers. Before Alexander's accession to the throne, Nearchus and the young Prince had been intimately connected, and Philip had even ordered Nearchus into exile for his attachment

---

[e] "Εκ της Γεδροσιας." Not. in Plutarch.

[f] "Arrian. Exped. Alex. Lib. 6. C. 22.--452.

[g] Strabo. Lib. 15.--1051——1053.

[h] Arrian. Hist. Ind. C. 18.--587.

ment to his Son, at which he took offence. Alexander confided to him the command of his fleet, which was to pass from the mouths of the Indus to the Euphrates, and the choice which he made, was highly pleasing to all who were to have a share in the expedition.[i] Amongst the adventurers there were Phœnicians, Cypriots, people from the Hellespont, and Ionians, and they saw with satisfaction Nearchus at the head of the enterprise, of which he hath given a circumstantial relation in his journal; Arrian hath preserved it. Pliny after mentioning that the journal of Nearchus and Onesicritus neither supplied him with the names nor distances of places,[k] attempts to give us an abridged itinerary, with the names of places and their distances reduced into Roman miles, but it hath not any resemblance with that which Arrian describes. The difference is too remarkable to suppose it to be owing to the ignorance of transcribers.

From what Pliny hath told us, it evidently appears that he had not read either the journal of Nearchus or that of Onesicritus, and in all likelihood he had simply consulted the production of Juba, which was only a compilation from Onesicritus. A comparison of it with the journals of Nearchus will at once prove the difference

---

[i] Arrian. Hist. Ind. C. 20.--591.

[k] "Indicare convenit, quæ prodit Onesicritus, classe Alexandri circumvectus in Mediterranea Persidis ex India, narrata proxime a Juba: dein eam navigationem, quæ ex his annis comperta servatur hodie. Onesicriti et Nearchi navigatio nec nomina habet mansionum, nec spatia." Plin. Hist. Nat. Lib. 6. C. 23. Tom. 1.--700.

difference of the two works. Organa is the single word, which hath not suffered alteration, and been varied by Onesicritus or Juba: the foundation of a city, whose name is not known and that of Xilonopolis, of which Onesicritus speaks, are suppressed by Nearchus.

Pliny confounds the situation of many countries: the Orites are placed before the Arbians,[1] and immediately after Carmania. But the Arbians were in fact situated to the West of the Indus, and had the Orites on their borders, who had Gedrosia to the West, bounded by the vast deserts of Carmania. Onesicritus, from a jealousy of Nearchus, endeavoured to appropriate to himself the discoveries of this Admiral, and made a point of contradicting him. To this source may be traced the variance in his relations, which have been inconsiderately adopted both by Juba and by Pliny.

Strabo, according to Monsieur Huet, " treats the works of Nearchus and Onesicritus as fictions, though he admits, that some truth is blended with their fables."[m] Undoubtedly the Greek geographer classes Nearchus with those writers, that have circulated falsities respecting India, but he was not the principal object of the observation, and the censure was more particularly applicable

---

[1] "Oritas ab Indis Arbis fluvius disterminat." Plin. Hist. Nat. Lib. 7. C. 2. Tom. 2.--14.

[m] "Strabon traite ces ouvrages de fiction; quoique il ne nie point qu' ils soient meles de quelque verité." Hist. du Commerce et de la Navigation des Anciens. 349.

cable to Megasthenes and Daimachus.ⁿ When he speaks more circumstantially of the journal of Nearchus, it is without any reflection on the authenticity of the work, and some exaggerations of the facts and hyperbolical expressions were principally criticised. These are the common foibles of travellers in general, who sometimes suffer severely in their expeditions, and are often accustomed to magnify objects, from their fears and apprehensions, beyond the just proportion of the real dangers, which they were exposed to.º The learned Huet in another part, of his work, does however justice to Nearchus and his journal, when he assures us the memoirs of his expedition were both "useful in commerce and in war.ᵖ

Dodwell, in his dissertation on the journal of Nearchus by Arrian, observes that Pliny might have borrowed what he relates, respecting the navigation of Nearchus and Onesicritus, from those authors as well as from Juba's extract out of the work of Onesicritus,

---

n "Διαφεροντως δ' απιςειν αξιον Δημαχω τε κ̔ Μεγασ̱θενη." (Strabo. Lib. 2.--121.) Yet he had before expressed more than doubts of the writers in general on India, and Nearchus comes in for a share of the censure. "Απαντες μεν τοινυν οἱ περι της Ινδικης γραψαντες, ὡς επι το πολυ ψευδολογοι γεγονασι, καθ' ὑπερβολην δε Δημαχ☉· τα δε δευτερα λεγει Μεγασθενης, Ονησικριτ☉ τε κ̔ Νεαρχ☉, κ̔ αλλοι τοιυτοι παραψελλιζοντες ηδυ." Strabo. Lib. 2.--121.

o "Ou la crainte plutôt que le péril grossît les objects, et qui par cette raison doivent selon Strabon mériter notre indulgence." I find no traces of the indulgence, which Strabo is supposed to bespeak for these writers. "Εικ☉ μεν ων προς ὑπερβολην ηδολεσχηκεναι πολλα τυς πλευσαντες· ὁμως δ' εν ειρηκασι παραδηλυντες ἁμα κ̔ το παρασαν αυτοις παθ☉, διοτι προσδοκια μαλλον η κινδυν☉ υπηρχε τοις αληθεσι." Strabo. Lib. 15.--1055.

p "Utiles pour la guerre et le commerce." Hist. du Comm. et de la Navig. des Anciens, 53.

tus,[1] but his criticism on the authority of the journal of Nearchus preserved by Arrian appears to be bold as well as exceptionable. It may be proper to examine the evidence that he produces and to comment on it.

I. Neither the city of Arbis, the rivers Nabrus, Hytanis, nor in short the port of Argenus or Argenis, mentioned by Onesicritus, are to be found in Arrian, who hath added the distances that he specifies, from the extract of Pliny.

If however, Onesicritus, or rather Juba hath corrupted the names of places and hath even interwoven some suspicious circumstances, the journal of Nearchus is not impeachable on account of their imperfections or mistakes. The truth amidst contradictory assertions is easily discoverable on the examination of other evidence, and all the works of the cotemporary authors having perished, the present situation of places and the affinity between their ancient and modern names are what must be resorted to. Monsieur d'Anville hath incontestably proved the result is in favour of Nearchus. If the distances in Arrian do not correspond

---

[1] "Dodwel observe judicieusement que Pline n'a tiré tout ce qu' il rapporte de la navigation de Nearque et d'Onesicrite que de l' extrait que Juba avoit fait de l' ouvrage de ce dernier." Dodwell appears to think very differently. "Erant enim sane, præterea ea quæ retulerat ex Nearcho et Onesicrito Juba, et aliæ quoque separatæ utriusque auctoris editiones, etiam ætate Plinii. Hoc inde colligo, quod in auctorum catalogis, e quibus libros operis sui singulos collegit Plinius, occurrit, præter Jubam, seorsim mentio tam Nearchi quam etiam Onesicriti. Quod sane non fuisset necesse, si, quæ de utroque habet Plinius, ea omnia ex solo hausisset Juba." De Arrian. Nearcho apud Geograph. Vet. Script. Græc. Min. Vol. 1,--132. 8vo Oxon. 1698.

correspond with those in Pliny, they certainly were not taken from the Roman Naturalist.

II. It is universally allowed that Nearchus and Onesicritus marked their tract by the number of days, which were afterwards reduced into stadia: Juba again reduced them into miles in conformity to the Roman measure.—They gave the relation this semblance of exactness to impose upon the world. Dodwell strengthens the opinion by the authority of Marcian of Heraclea. "Many authors have written in haste with the intention of imposing on their readers, and affected to relate the names of places in nations that are totally unknown, and to ascertain their distance from each other in stadia, but Antiphanes of Bergœa hath surpassed them all in imposture. Those, on the contrary, who acquired a real knowledge of places and the dimensions of the different seas with the ports and cities and their respective distances have composed particular descriptive journals, and appear to have compiled them with fidelity." ————Nearchus is not mentioned in this passage of Marcian, but the concluding sentence may be properly applied to him, and he may be truly classed with the geographers, whose accuracy is taken notice of.

III.

---

* " Οι δε της περιπλυς προχεισεως γραψαντες, κ̃ της επιτυγχανοντας παιθειν εθελοντας τοπων τε προσηγοριας κ̃ σαδιων αριθμον διεξιοντες, κ̃ ταυτα επιχωριων η εθνων βαρβαρων, ων ειτε τας προσηγοριας απιαν δυναιτο αν τις, αυτον μοι δοκεσι τον Βεργαιον Αντιφανη νενικηκεναι τω ψευδει· οσοι μεν γαρ μερικας τινας εποιησατο περιπλων διηγησεις· ων κ̃ τα χωρια σαφως εγνωσκον, κ̃ την αναμετρησιν της θαλαττης εκ ηγνο-

III. The journal of Nearchus was unknown to Agatharcides and Eratosthenes, who had the immense library of Alexandria before their eyes. This work ought therefore to be considered as fictitious.'———If even this negative argument hath any force, it remains to be asked from whence this information is derived. Are we peremptorily to decide at once from the short extract of Agatharcides on the Erythrean sea, which Photius hath left us, and what remains of his Asiatic history ' preserved by Athenæus, or from a few mutilated fragments of Eratosthenes, that these authors had never heard of the Periplus of Nearchus?

IV. In the ages immediately after Alexander, the Indus was believed to join the Nile;" if therefore the journal of Nearchus had then existed, this error could not have been adopted. ˣ———Under the same mode of reasoning, it may be insisted, that the works of Herodotus, Aristotle and Diodorus Siculus are suppositions, as we learn from them, that the Caspian sea has no communication with the neighbouring seas, which though erroneous was an opinion,

---

ων, ᾗ πολεις ᾗ λιμνας, ᾗ τα διαςηματα τυτων καταμαϑοντες· ὑτοι δοκυσιν η παντοπασιν πλεισα μετα της υποχομενης αληϑειας εγγεγραφυκι." Marciani Heracleotæ Periplus. 63. Apud Geograph. Vet. Script. Minor. Tom. 1.

' Dodwell de Arriani Nearcho. Geograph. Vet. Script. Min. Tom. 1. Differt. 6. Sect. 7.

' Photii Biblioth. 1322. See also 546, 547.

ʷ The Baron de St. Croix remarks that Arrian borrowed what he says of the Nile, in the sixth chapter of his Indian History, from Megasthenes, and that the journal of Nearchus only commences at the twenty-first chapter, and from this circumstance the argument cannot possibly apply.

ˣ Dodwell de Arriani Nearcho. Geograph. Vet. Script. Min. Tom. 1. Differt. 8.

opinion, adopted in later times.—Truth creeps flowly forward into approbation and efteem, whilft even errors fupported by ancient prejudices and fometimes by vanity, preferve their influence for years.

V. The Periplus of Nearchus was probably fabricated under the reigns of the laft Ptolemies, as Antiphanes of Bergæum, Antonius Diogenes, and Euemerus of Meffina, publifhed about this period many fabulous relations.ʳ

Such an argument has little ftrength, and it may be difficult to point out any relation whatever between the Periplus of Nearchus and the facred hiftory of Euemerus.

From a want of evidence, Arrian is overwhelmed with injurious epithets, and the Jefuit Harduin hath treated him with as little civility.ˢ Yet their joint efforts cannot depreciate the authenticity and merit of a work, which carries internally the powerful impreffion of fidelity, and proves in every circumftance the accuracy of its author. There is a minute exactnefs, which is a fort of decifive depofition in favour of authentic journals, that is not to be found in the romantic and fictitious tales of imaginary adventures. The Periplus of Nearchus may be tried

---

ʳ Dodwell de Arriani Nearcho. Geograph. Vet. Script. Græc. Min. Differt. 6.--139, 140.

ˢ "Hominis mirare in mendaciis confingendis audaciam." Not. in Plin. Hift. Nat. Tom. 1.

tried by this criterion, and the whole of it, from the departure of the Macedonian fleet when it quitted the island of Sangada to its arrival at the mouth of the river Arabis or Arabius, is so very circumstantial as to leave its authenticity unquestionable.

"When the wind was abated, they again put to sea, and having sailed about sixty stadia further, came to a sandy coast, before which was a certain desolate island named Domas; which, by its situation, formed a haven, but as the water upon the coast was all brackish, they travelled about twenty stadia up a level country, where they found water sweet and pleasant; and sailing all the next day, in the evening they came to a country called Saranga, about three hundred stadia from their former station, where they went on shore, and found good water, about eight stadia from their landing-place. Thence, they renewed their voyage and arrived at Sacala, a country wholly uninhabited; whence, they passed between two rocks, so near each other, that the blades of their oars touched them on both sides at once. When they had sailed three hundred stadia, they came to Morontobara, where is a large, spacious, safe and commodious haven; but the entrance into it is narrow and rocky: this the natives called the Women's Haven, from a certain woman, who first reigned in that place. Having passed the rocks with some difficulty, they came into the open sea again, and continuing their voyage left a certain island on their left hand, which is so near joining to the main land, that the channel, which separates them, seems to have been cut through.

That

That day they sailed about seventy stadia. The shore, all along the Continent, was full of thick woods, and the island opposite thereto, was also woody. About break of day they departed thence, and passed through the above-mentioned channel, by the help of the Tide, and after a course of one hundred and twenty stadia, arrived at the mouth of the river Arabius, where they found a large and safe harbour, but no fresh water, because the Tide flows a great way up the river, and makes it brackish; wherefore, passing about forty stadia up the river, they came to a lake, the water of which being sweet, they took what they wanted, and returned. The island, opposite to this haven, is high land, and uncultivated, but round it are vast quantities of oysters, and all kinds of fish, which makes it to be frequented by fishermen. Thus far the country of the Arabii extends itself, being the last part of India, that way, for the Oritæ inhabit the other side of the river."[a]

Nearchus describes with the same minuteness his navigation from the mouths of the Indus to that of the Euphrates where his voyage ended. If he did not enter into the same details respecting the coast of Susia, the modern Khosistan, it arose from the difficulty of approaching the land with safety on account of the shoals and shallows.[b] Pietro della Valle tells us that he sailed at some distance from this track, and found a shoal with four fathom water,

---

[a] Rooke's Arrian. Vol. 2. C. 22.--245.

[b] "Τὴν χώρην τε γὰρ τεναγώδεα τε εἶναι τὴν πολλὴν, καὶ ῥηχίησιν ἐπὶ μέγα ἐς τὸν πόντον ἰσχύσαν καὶ ταύτην σφαλερὴν ἐγκαθορμίζεσθαι πελαγίοισιν, ὧν σφίσι τὴν κομιδὴν τὸ πολὺ γίνεσθαι." Arrian. Hist. Indic. C. 41.--631.

ter, which stretched to a considerable extent: the Persians term this part of the Persian gulph Meidan, and the land is so low that it is not visible but at a very little distance. ᶜ On the plan of Monsieur d' Anville, and with the advantage of his researches, a great resemblance is perceptible between the ancient description of the different places mentioned in the journal of Nearchus, and their present appearances. This able geographer hath proved to demonstration the accuracy of Nearchus from a comparison of all the Oriental and European memoirs that treat of the several places, which the Macedonian fleet touched at, when they ranged along the coasts of Carmania, Persia, and Susia. Monsieur d' Anville's memoirs on the Persian gulph will not admit of being analysed: and his opinion of the journal of Nearchus shall be only cited. "Circumstances, which apply to the precise situation of places, and the resemblance of ancient names with those, that still subsist, and are not to be elsewhere met with, do not admit of a suspicion of fraud or fiction, and there are few ancient geographical memoirs, which will so well stand the test of a comparison with even the real knowledge of them."ᵈ

Yet it would be in vain to dissemble that Nearchus hath intermingled some fables in his journal. Amidst their number, the stories

ᶜ Memoire de Monsieur d' Anville. Acad. des Inscriptions. Tom. 30.--168.

ᵈ "L' application des circonstances qu' il renferme au local actuel, le rapport que des denominations de lieux qui ne se rencontrent point ailleurs, ont avec celles qui subsistent, ne souffrent aucun soupçon de supposition; et il y a peu d' autres memoires geographiques de l' antiquite, qui

ries of men, who cut up fifh and wood with their nails; 'who built and covered their houfes with the larger bones of whales, and employed the lefs in the formation of their domeftic utenfils, ' and alfo that of the ifland of Nofala, inhabited by one of the Nereids, ᵍ are to the laft degree exceptionable. Thefe fables, however, ought not to affect the work itfelf, and fhould be confidered rather as poetical and imaginary epifodes, correfponding with the Grecian tafte, which was always more partial to the charms of fictitious fcenery, than the chafter compofitions of rigid truth.

The Macedonian fleet failed, according to Arrian, on the twentieth day of the month Boedromion, in the eleventh year of Alexander's reign, when Cephifodorus was Archon at Athens, ʰ whofe magiftracy is notwithftanding fixed by Diodorus Siculus, Dionyfius of Halicarnaffus, and by moft of the chronologifts in the year after Alexander's death. It feems then a miftake, and Arrian ought to have related this voyage under the Archonfhip of Anticles,

qui foutiennent mieux la comparifon avec une connoiffance pofitive du local." Recherches Geograph. fur le Golfe Perfique. Acad. des Infcript. Tom. 30.--133.

ᵉ "Τοις γαρ δη ονυξιν οσα σιδηρω διαχρασθαι ελεγοντο, κ̓ τυς ιχθυας τυτοισι παρασχιζοντες κατεργαζισθαι. κ̓ των ξυλων οσα μαλακωτερα." Arrian. Hift. Ind. C. 24.--600.

ᶠ "Χρησθαι δε τοισιν ανθρωποισιν ες τα οικια· ειναι δη τα μεν εν τησι πλευρησιν αυτων οςεα, δοκυς τοισιν οικημασιν οσα μεγαλα· τα δε μικροτερα, ςρωτηρας." Arrian. Hift. Ind. C. 30.--612.

ᵍ "L' habitation des Nereides." "Οικησαι την νησον ταυτην μιαν των Νηρηιδων." Arrian. Hift. Ind. C. 31.--613.

ʰ Arrian. Hift. Ind. C. 21.--592.

cles, the fourth year of the one hundred and thirteenth Olympiad, and three hundred and twenty-five years before Christ, which will be the eleventh year of Alexander's reign. Corsini hath given a very satisfactory solution of this difficulty, and supposes Cephisodorus to have succeeded Anticles, who might have died, or been displaced during his year of office,[i] and the necessity of this correction is evident from the manuscripts in the late French King's library, which concur in the expression of Cephisodorus.—It is also an established fact, that Nearchus finished his naval expedition before the death of Alexander.

Pliny informs us that Nearchus was employed seven months in his expedition, and was three months at sea.[k] Many reasons may be conceived to have occasioned the length of time taken up in this voyage. The construction of the vessels of the Ancients, which were in general small, and of much less dimensions than those of our days, rendered them incapable of weathering any heavy seas or violent gales, and as they had fewer sails, they consequently made less way.[l] They rarely also ventured out of the sight of land, but coasted regularly, and this mode of navigation

must

[i] Corsini. Fast. Attic. Dissert. 9. Tom. 2.--30, 31. Tom. 4.--52.

[k] "Alexandrum invenerunt septimo mense, postquam digressus ab iis fuerat Patulis, tertio navigationis. Sic Alexandri classis navigavit." Plin. Hist. Nat. Lib. 6. C. 23. Tom. 1.--703.

[l] We learn from Marcianus of Heraclea it was a received opinion, that a vessel might run seven hundred and sometimes even nine hundred stadia in a day, with a favourable wind, though others did not exceed five hundred. "Ὡμολογημενον γαρ τυθ' ὁτι ἑπτακοσιυς ωξιοδρομυσα ναυς δια μι-

ας

muſt have been very tedious. The Macedonian fleet, it muſt be recollected likewiſe, had to paſs through unknown ſeas, and without proper pilots they could not venture to purſue their track in the night and in the dark. Theſe were great impediments, and the progreſs of the voyage was retarded by the contrary winds, which they had to encounter in their paſſage.

Monteſquieu ſuppoſes that the Macedonian fleet had to ſtruggle with the Monſoons, and that it ſailed in July, [m] a ſeaſon when no European veſſel in our days would quit a port in India on a return to Europe. This great writer appears, however, to be miſtaken. Nearchus only ſailed in September, which anſwers to the Boedromion of the Attic year, and agreeable to Pliny's calculation, he completed his voyage early in the month Munychion, which is our April. During this time it is certain that the ſtorms, which attend the Monſoon are not felt on this ſide cape Commo-

rin,

ας αυτη της ημερας, ευροι τις αν κ̀ ενακοσιας διαδραμησαν ναυν εκ της των κατασκευασαντ[Θ]- τιχνης το τα- χ[Θ]- προσλαβουσαν, κ̀ ετεραν μολις πεντακοσιας δεκνυσασαν, δια την εναντιαν της τιχνης αιτιαν." Mars. Heracl. Peripl. apud Geog. Veter. Script. Græc. Min. Tom. 1.--67.) The Baron de St. Croix taking the ſtadium at one hundred Toiſes reckons a veſſel of the Ancients might with a favourable wind have made a paſſage from twenty-three marine leagues and a fraction to thirty in a day, and with a contrary wind, computes it at ſixteen.

[m] "La flotte d' Alexandre mit ſept mois pour aller de Patale a Suze. Elle partit dans le mois de Juillet, c'eſt à dire, dans un temps ou aujourdhui aucun navire n' oſe ſe mettre en mer pour revenir des Indes. Entre l'une et l'autre mouçon, il y a un intervalle de temps pendant lequel les vents varient; et où un vent de hord, ſe melant avec les vents ordinaires, cauſe, ſurtout auprès de côtes, d' horribles tempetes. Ce la dure les mois de Juin et Juillet, et d'Aout. La flotte d' Alexandre, partant de Patale au mois de Juillet, eſſuya bien des tempêtes, et le voyage fut long, parcequ' elle navigea dans un mouçon contraire." Monteſquieu, de l' Eſprit des Loix. Lib. 21, C. 9. Tom. 1.--490, 491.

rin, and are confined to the months of May, June, July, and August.

The evidence of Arrian is very peremptory on the departure of the fleet. "As soon therefore as the Etesian or anniversary winds ceased, (which on these coasts blow from the sea towards the land the whole summer, and thereby render navigation impracticable during that time) they begun their voyage on the twentieth day of the month Boedromion, the eleventh year of Alexander's reign according to the Macedonian and Asiatic computation, when Cephisodorus was Archon of Athens." [a]

But perhaps it may be objected, that if the Monsoon was not contrary, no other winds could have in such a manner retarded their course. On the coasts, however, of Guzarat and in general on all those of India upon this side the mountains of Gate, the winds blow almost constantly out of a Southerly quarter from September to March, and from the coasts of Africa towards India, they regularly decline towards the West in proportion as Asia is approached. [b] The winds were therefore very foul for the Macedonian fleet, whose course lay from East to West, and it is a known principle that the velocity of the air, is increased like a current of water, when its channel is narrowed. Nearchus, from this

---

[a] Rooke's Arrian, Vol. 2.--243. "Ὡς δὰ τὰ Ετησια πνευματα εκοιμηθη (ἀ δη τε θερι☉. την ὡρην πασαν κατιχει εκ τε πελαγε☉. επιπνιοντα επι την γην, κ̣ ταυτη αποροντον πλει ποιοντα) τοτε δη ὡρμηντο, επι αρχοντ☉. Αθηνησι Κηφισοδορε, εικαδι τε Βοηδρομιων☉. μην☉., καθοτι Αθηναιοι αγεσιν· ὡς δε Μακιδονες τε κ̣ Ασιανοι ηγον, το ινδικατον βασιλευοντ☉. Αλιξανδρε." Arrian. Hist. Ind. C. 21.--592.

[b] Varen. Geog. C. 21. Propos. 3. See also Dr. Halley. Essay. Philosoph. Transact. 1735.

this last circumstance, on his arrival at the mouth of the Persian gulph, must have found great difficulty, and been much distressed in doubling cape Bendis, now known under the name of Jask. His track must have then been between the North and West,[p] and the East and South-East winds must have carried him at a great rate towards the land. Onesicritus here wished to terminate the voyage, but the courage and good conduct of Nearchus surmounted every difficulty and danger. Having repaired his fleet on the banks of the river Anamis,[q] at some distance on this side the Island Ogyris now Ormus, he continued his course, notwithstanding the contrary and unfavourable winds to which he was exposed, and put into the river Sitaco,[r] the modern Sita-Rhegian, where he employed twenty-one days in caulking and refitting his squadron.

When the winds shift in these seas from North to South and the collateral points, there are many days, and sometimes months of continual calm and tempests, and it was from these causes that Nearchus was detained. This officer having mentioned in his journal some storm or other, Arrian most probably confounded this accidental gale from the South with the contrary Monsoon or Etesian winds. The currents produced by the West and South-West winds, which set directly against the Macedonian fleet,

[p] "Ενθενδε δε ωσαυτως ηκιτι προς ηλιυ δυομενυ επλεον· αλλα το μεταξυ δυσιος τε ηλιυ και της αρκτυ ετω μαλλον τι αι πρωραι αυτοισιν επειχον." Arrian. Hist. Ind. C. 32.--614.

[q] Arrian. Hist. Ind. C. 33.--616.

[r] ——————— C. 38.--627.

fleet, were not therefore the least of the impediments that Nearchus had to combat.

The Jesuit Petau [1] dates the navigation of Nearchus in the magistracy of Chremes, three hundred and twenty-seven years before Christ, and in the year when Porus was defeated. But the authority of Diodorus Siculus, which the learned chronologist followed too implicitly, hath led him into some mistakes. The Greek historian compresses into the Archonship of Chremes [t] a croud of events, which could not possibly have happened in such a short space of time, and he also mentions two other Archons, Anticles, and Sosicles, before the year of Alexander's death. Corsini [w] judiciously observes that the name of Sosicles should be effaced, or considered as the name of an Archon substituted in the same year for Anticles, and the conjecture seems in some measure authorized by the text itself as well as Diodorus Siculus, who brings the magistracy of Anticles and also that of Sosicles under the Consulship of Lucius Cornelius and Quintus Popilius.—[x] Diodorus Siculus does not mention any remarkable event during the magistracy of these two Archons, and seems to have referred them all to that of Chremes, in which he fixes the defeat of Porus, that was previous to this Archon, and ought to be dated in the magistracy of Hegemon, whose name in all probability might have been found

[1] Doctrin. Temp. Livr. 13.--597, 598.
[t] Diod. Sicul. Lib. 17. Tom. 2.--229——246.
[w] Corsini. Fast. Attic. Dissert. 9. Tom. 2.--31——33. Tom. 4.--49.
[x] Diod. Sicul. Lib. 17. Tom. 2.--248.—Corsini. Fast. Attic. Tom. 2. Dissert. 22, 23.

found in the part of the seventeenth book of this historian which is wanting.—The series of later events, and the formal evidence of Arrian leave little doubt of this period.

Hegemon undoubtedly preceded Chremes in the Attic annals, and the navigation of Nearchus ought then to be reckoned in the last year of Alexander's reign, under the Archonship of Anticles or rather Cephisodorus his substitute, and this Archonship included both the events marked by Diodorus Siculus in the magistracy of Soficles, and a part of those in that of Chremes. It appears also that the Greek historian enumerated under Soficles some events, such as the defeat of the Coffæans,[y] and the entry of Alexander[z] into Babylon, which could only have happened in the first eleven months of the year in which Alexander died, when Hegesias was Archon. Diodorus Siculus hath in this manner overturned the entire chronology of the last years of this Prince's reign, and descending to objects of inferior magnitude, his mistake, as to the time of the navigation of Nearchus, hath been occasioned by his erroneous arrangement of the events which preceded it.

[y] Diod. Sicul. Lib. 17. Tom. 2.--248.—Usserii Annal. 206, 207.
[z] ——— Lib. 17. Tom. 2.--248.

THE END.

www.ingramcontent.com/pod-product-compliance
Lightning Source LLC
Chambersburg PA
CBHW020537300426
44111CB00008B/709